NO SLAM DANCING
NO STAGE DIVING
NO SPIKES

To Alan -

Remember the fun we had!

xoxo.
Amy

No Slam Dancing No Stage Diving No Spikes

An Oral History of the Legendary
City Gardens

Amy Yates Wuelfing
Steven DiLodovico

DiWulf Publishing
Morrisville, PA

First published in in 2014
by DiWulf Publishing
527 Barclay Avenue
Morrisville, PA 19067
www.noslamdancing.com

Hardcover: ISBN 978-0-9913447-1-0
Paperback: ISBN 978-0-9913447-0-3
Ebook: ISBN 978-0-9913447-3-4

Library of Congress Cataloging-in-Publication Data
Available upon request

Book design and production by STUDIO 31
www.studio31.com

Printed in the United States of America [MG]

Contents

Photo inserts are placed following pages 176 and 272.

DEDICATIONS

Amy:

To my mother Virginia, who always encouraged me to be my own person, and to my husband Howard for all his support.

Steven:

Dedicated to the most important person in my life: RoShawn Thais DiLodovico, and to my nephew and godson, Lucas James DiLodovico. The music may have saved my life, but you are both responsible for sustaining it.

Also, to the memories of those we lost along the way.

And to Randy Now, the man who created the scene at City Gardens out of nothing....

Randy Now with the infamous sign. Photo courtesy of Ken Salerno.

ACKNOWLEDGEMENTS

From Amy:

I am forever grateful to my coauthor Steven DiLodovico and his wife Shawn for helping me wrap up 15 years of work to get this book done. Without him and his dedication to this project, you would not be reading it. On faith, they turned their lives upside down and moved hundreds of miles with their cats to be a part of this. You guys mean the world to me.

When I began trying to piece this book together, Mark Sceurman, the publisher of The Aquarian, graciously let me spend two solid days going through their archives. I paged through every issue of the magazine from 1979 to 1995 looking for City Gardens advertisements to construct the gig calendar. Without Marc's assistance, I never would have been able to put it all together.

Thanks to Rick Moody and Stephen Elliott for their encouragement. Rick was the person who suggested taking the Butthole Surfers piece to Stephen at theRumpus.net. Stephen publishing that piece set off a chain of events, including meeting Steve Tozzi, director of *Riot on the Dance Floor*. Thank you to Ken Salerno, Ron Gregorio, and all the other photographers for letting us include their photos.

Thank you to Henry Rollins, the first big name who agreed to be interviewed, and to Jon Stewart for making time to chat about his bartending days.

To Maureen Weber, who transcribed countless interviews, and Eric Baker, who gave invaluable editing advice. It wouldn't be nearly as good without you!

Special thanks to Rich O'Brien and Carl Humenik for always being willing to talk on a moment's notice. You guys rule. And thank you to Jason Miller and Joy Lesley for working their magick.

ACKNOWLEDGEMENTS

From Steven:

My sincerest thanks go to the following:

The DiLodovico family.

The entire Gavin family.

Mark Barlam and family.

Vinnie, Len, Marianne, and the entire Luviner family.

Jim Houser and family.

Bill "The Moshing Fetus" Martusky, who took me to City Gardens the very first time.

Jamie Davis for all his generous help in putting this book together.

Brian McCullough, Dan Heacock, Bill Raymond, John Staples, Larry "Creeping Flesh" Blythe (R.I.P.) and "Manic" Chris (R.I.P.), Lorrie Phillips, Linda and Heidi, Jim "The Ripper" Fusco, Tim "Knobhead" Ryan, and the whole WDNR family.

Anne Spina for all the rides to shows and all the fun times we had (I'm sorry I smashed your mom's car!).

The Tri-State Crew

The "Riot" Crew: Steve Tozzi, Ken Salerno, and Pete Tabbot.

Yan and the Enemy Soil family.

Bruce Boyd for the awesome merch.

Linda DiLodovico, who was the first person to ever give me the music.

And, to my "other wife," Amy Yates Wuelfing (and her husband Howard): It is difficult to sum up my gratitude in just one line, so I will simply say, *thank you for everything*.

Thanks to anyone who helped facilitate an interview for this project, or passed along a number, or made an introduction on my behalf. Without such help this project would never have happened. Thanks to all who gave to the Kickstarter campaign that got this off the ground. And special thanks to the people who took the time to sit and listen to my inane questions, especially those who sat for multiple interviews.

And to every band, artist, and song that ever inspired me: Thank you.

Foreword

Mickey Ween (Ween, guitarist)

My obsession with rock and roll began when I was around 13 or 14 years old, and, like a typical teenager, I thought I was the only person in the world who understood its dangerous energy. By 1984 I had given up on playing sports and riding BMX bikes and spent all my time seeking out the coolest records and meeting the hippest people, whether they were DJs, record store clerks, or people who had fanzines or their own bands. And, of course, going to each and every show in the tri-state area. The only problem was my age. I was 14, which meant that, for a couple of years, I had to rely on older people to drive me around or sneak me into bars. I'm certain I was a pest—no doubt an understatement—but there were few shows I didn't see or bands I didn't try to interview for my fanzine.

I spent every day after school hanging at Key Records, a record store in my hometown of New Hope, PA, and most of my nights were spent listening to WTSR, the small radio station at Trenton State College, which was just across the river in New Jersey. Soon I started spending my nights hanging out at the station. I would get rides to and from WTSR from anyone I could con. The most popular DJ at the station was "Randy Now," who was also the promoter at City Gardens, Trenton's most popular—and, to me, the only—live music venue.

Randy used his radio show to promote upcoming concerts at City Gardens, and he would often invite the bands to the station for interviews. His radio show was called "The Other Side." It was the only place I wanted to be on Wednesday nights, and, to his credit, Randy was very tolerant about letting an annoying 14-year-old kid hang around the station, especially since I was always asking so many questions. Some of the bands he interviewed included the Replacements, Nash the Slash, and the Dickies.

The mid-80s, despite what you see on VH1, was an amazing time for underground music. You had labels like SST Records, which signed

9

Hüsker Dü, Black Flag, the Meat Puppets, the Minutemen, the Bad Brains, and too many other bands to mention. Twin/Tone records out of Minneapolis had the Replacements, Randy's favorite band. The Dead Kennedys were still at the top of the punk-rock food chain, and punk music in general was at its peak, in my opinion. There was shit happening everywhere… shows every weekend in firehouses, Elks Club halls, VFWs, people's basements, and, most consistently, at City Gardens. Between the popularity of his radio show and the bands he booked at the club, Randy Now was, in essence, a one-man music scene. Any band that came through Trenton during the '80s played at City Gardens, and Randy booked the show.

The place was almost mythical to me, though, at 14, I had yet to see a concert there. My parents wouldn't allow me to go to the club without adult supervision, and there was no way I wanted to be seen in a club with them. Since they didn't mind me hanging out at the radio station, I started lying to them and going to City Gardens when they thought I was at WTSR.

My first City Gardens show was in 1985, when I saw the Minutemen. They had just released *Double Nickels on the Dime*, and another DJ from the radio station drove me to the club. There were maybe 30 people there. Randy introduced me to the band, and they were the most down-to-earth, nicest dudes you'd ever wanna meet. I did an interview with [singer] D. Boon and [bassist] Mike Watt for my fanzine, and I got their autographs. Their concert was amazing, and I was blown away by the lifestyle of these guys. They drove around the country in a van and got to do this every night. It seemed too good to be true. It sounds corny, but that night altered my life forever. I don't think I missed a show at City Gardens for the next seven years. Shortly after that show I started my own band, and we went on to play City Gardens somewhere between 75 and 100 times.

Any chance my parents had of stopping me from becoming one of the "night people" was now hopelessly lost. This place was Mecca to me. If you have ever seen a flier for City Gardens, you get a pretty good idea of what the place was like in the '80s. In one calendar month, the club might host the Circle Jerks, the Replacements, the Residents, Venom, D.O.A., the Descendents, the Pogues, the Meatmen, and the Ramones.

Looking back, it is unbelievable how many great bands came through that place.

Like most legendary punk clubs of that time, City Gardens wasn't a very nice place. The truth is, Trenton was really awful. I was born there and lived my whole life in the area, so I know what I'm talking about. It's a strange market for touring bands too; not quite New York and not quite Philly. Also, the club was on Calhoun Street in one of the worst neighborhoods in Trenton. My father used to use Calhoun Street as a punch line, like, "We'll see how tough that asshole really is. Go drop his ass off in the middle of Calhoun Street on a Friday night."

The club itself was basically a cement box with a gravel parking lot in the middle of the ghetto. There certainly weren't any "gardens" around it. Even if you wanted to trash the place, there wasn't anything to break. The toilets were always overflowing, the walls were painted black, and there was no furniture to speak of. Of course, none of that mattered; I don't think anyone went there for the ambience.

Within no time I was working the soda bar at the club for the all-ages shows. Then Randy hired me to do lights. Eventually I started dee-jaying at the shows. All of this was in exchange for free admission, which was fine by me. Ween's first show there was on May 3, 1987, when we opened for the Butthole Surfers, one of the greatest live bands of all time, and one of my favorite bands ever. We eventually opened for damn near everyone—the Ramones, Fugazi, Killing Joke, 7 Seconds, Mojo Nixon… the list goes on. At one point we were playing there almost twice a month. We were like the "standby" local band if there was a cancellation. As it turns out, we were the last band to headline at the club in December of 1994.

By that time we had released four albums and were recording for Elektra Records, and the spirit of DIY independent music had drastically changed. In the mid '80s, though, most of the shows still cost between $5 and $10 at the door, and it was a big deal if they had to charge more.

Randy Now had a thankless job. He did EVERYTHING himself with no office or staff, a true concert promoter. He booked the bands, printed the fliers, hyped the shows on the radio, dealt with the owners of the club, and, more often than not, let the bands sleep at his house. He was also on the hook if attendance was poor or some rich kid from the suburbs cracked his head open while stage diving. I remember one night Randy and I had to leave in the middle of an Agnostic Front show to take a kid to the emergency room. A skinhead had pulled out a hammer in the mosh pit and whacked this poor guy in the head. His parents, of course, sued the club.

A lot of the regular touring bands that came through went on to much bigger things, like R.E.M, Green Day, the Red Hot Chili Peppers, the Beastie Boys, Public Enemy, and Nirvana. Much like New York's CBGB, playing at City Gardens was a rite of passage for bands. I have enough memories from the place to fill my own book, but, suffice to say, it was Ween's home club. It was the classroom where I learned about promoting a concert and being in a band, and about how to act in that environment.

Through Randy Now and City Gardens, a lot of the mysteries of rock and roll were revealed to me. Sometimes it was ugly—touring bands with dope problems needing to cop, or prima donna lead singers refusing to go onstage until sound problems were resolved—whatever. It was still a privilege to be a small part of a place so special, a place that was unique to a specific era in music. I made a lot of lasting friendships there and, most importantly, saw a LOT of incredible music.

INTRODUCTION:

How Did It Come to This?

What follows is an oral history not only of City Gardens, but of independent music from 1980–1994. Before the internet, cell phones, email, and social media, those who fell outside the mainstream, or those who were just looking for something different, had to work hard to find other like-minded people. The scene at City Gardens was the result of trial-and-error; there was no blueprint for building an indie music scene. No Google groups to set up, Facebook pages to "like," or Kickstarter campaigns. But once the misfits, rejects, oddballs, and non-conformists found a place to go, it became home. A home located at 1701 Calhoun Street, in the heart of Trenton, New Jersey.

The club meant different things to different people, depending on when you went and who you went to see. Hardcore kids saw it differently from the 90¢ Dance Night regulars, who saw it differently from the punk rockers and the rude boys and girls. City Gardens—as a club—did not discriminate. It did not cater to one audience; in fact, it is the club's inclusiveness that made the greatest impact on people. The bands weren't just punk rock. They were hardcore, metal, rock & roll, new wave, goth, hip hop, ska, reggae, dance, industrial, and pop, too. Comedians, performance artists, and spoken-word poets also crossed its stage. City Gardens challenged the people who went there to try something new, hear something different, meet new people, and have original experiences.

This history is (mostly) chronological and told through the bands that played City Gardens, the people who worked there, and the audience. The authors have made every attempt to capture "the City Gardens experience," but we're sure that many moments and events have been overlooked. Some readers may be upset that a certain band isn't referenced, or that specific person isn't represented, or the best show ever isn't even mentioned! Sorry about that—we tried!

One of the most infamous shows at City Gardens was performed by the Butthole Surfers. Accounts of what went on vary, but people who were there—or claim to have been there—still talk about it to this day.

May 3, 1987:
The Day the Butthole Surfers Came to Town

Randy Now (City Gardens promoter): This Butthole Surfers show is one of those shows that 5,000 people claim to have been at, but only 500 tickets were sold.

I loved the band, I really did. The Buttholes played three shows for me before this one. The first was an all-ages show at a little place called New York South. The second time I booked them was at City Gardens with The Replacements. That weird bill happened because the Buttholes pretty much lived on the road. They would call up and ask for a gig, and then you wouldn't hear from them again until the day of the show. You just had to believe they would show up. The Replacements wanted to play the same day, and we hadn't heard back from the Buttholes, so I thought, *why not just book The Replacements too?* We left them both on the advertising. I'm not sure who opened for who. I guess the Replacements opened.

Gibby Haynes (Butthole Surfers, lead singer): My strongest memory of City Gardens is arriving to play a show on one of our first tours. We didn't confirm the gig in advance, so, when we got to the club, the marquee out front said, "Tonight: The Replacements." I thought it was ironic that we got replaced by The Replacements.

Randy Now: The third time was a great show. They were getting more popular and the audience loved them. They had three or four encores, and the crowd couldn't get enough.

Tony Rettman (City Gardens regular): I was really young. My older brother Don used to take me to shows, but the Butthole Surfers' music was totally over my head. It just sounded like a jet landing… forever. A blur of noise. I remember one show where they had swear words written all over their bodies, including "shit" and "fuck" on their faces. And it wasn't something they did just for the show, because they drove up and were hanging out the whole night before they played with cuss words all over their faces. And I thought, *that's pretty badass.*

Tim Hinely (City Gardens regular): It's hard to describe exactly what a Butthole Surfers gig was like. When kids these days tell me how wild

The Butthole Surfers set the night on fire.

or crazy their favorite band is, like Slipknot or Marilyn Manson, I utter three words to them: The Butthole Surfers. For starters, they were total freaks. Drummer King Koffey and his "sister" Theresa played the double drums like they were from another planet; the bassist Jeff had a backwards Mohawk and looked like he was having trouble staying awake; and guitarist Paul Leary was cross-eyed on purpose; and last, but certainly not least, was seven-foot-tall singer Gibby Haynes. No shirt, gut hanging out, long greasy hair, yelling at everyone. The guy was fucking scary.

Mickey Ween (Ween, guitarist): That was the band we would sit around and listen to when we were getting high. You get these pictures in your head: "What are the guys who make this shit really like?!" It was so insane. And then you find out the truth… and they're even worse, even more insane, than you imagined.

Tim Hinely: Some of the bands that played the club were really polarizing. A skinhead band would play and the skinheads would be into it, but no one else would be, or a non-skinhead band would play and the skinheads would flip them off. But when the Buttholes played, *everyone* was into it. The skater kids, the hardcores, the skinheads, the punk geeks… everyone was into it. There was so much insanity that all genres were put aside.

Randy Now: They were pretty big at this point and starting to break through. They had just released "Hurdy Gurdy Man," which got airplay on MTV, and they had a lot of their own sound and light equipment.

They had a projection screen showing films with nude scenes and Ohio State Trooper accident films and stuff like that.

Gibby Haynes: Those were real 16mm films. To find them I had to do research at the University of Texas, looking in reference books and tracking things down. Back then you had to be pretty imaginative to get those kinds of films. The people who had penis-reconstruction films were very sensitive about distribution. You had to call up and pretend you were a doctor. We would have stuff mailed to our house outside of town that was addressed to The Pathology Wing, at So-and-So Hospital, Dr. Gibson Haynes.

Tim Hinely: Right before this show, they played at The Court Tavern in New Brunswick, NJ, and it was a wild affair to be sure. The band that played prior to them, The Serial Killers, had thrown cans of dog food out into the crowd, so it was smeared all over the floor and made everything slippery. The place was packed to the gills, steaming hot, and there was dog food all over the place. I haven't even mentioned the naked lady dancer—with a beard, who had not bathed in a year—the smoke machine, strobe lights, and the films playing behind them of gory car crashes from the 1960s.

Gibby Haynes: I was in charge of the show. I thought, if I couldn't really sing, then I might as well put on a show. So at first it was smoke and strobes. And then it was *lots* of smoke and *lots* of strobes. Completely fill the club with smoke until you couldn't see your hand in front of your face, with a pulsing, bright-as-shit light that would make you vomit and convulse. We would make effigies from newspaper and then tear them up in the strobe light, which was cool because it looked like you were tearing a human apart. We would dress up the dummies the same way we were dressed, and then jump behind an amp, throw out the dummy, and rip it up.

Randy Now: The show was booked, and I kept hearing from all across the country that they brought a nude dancer onstage. When they showed up that day I asked Gibby to not have the girl dancing nude, because it was an all-ages show and there would be kids in attendance. And he said, "Okay." Which really meant, "Fuck you."

Mickey Ween: There were four bands. We were first, then Cleft Palate, and then a punk-rock accordion player named Malcolm Tent. There were three bands with no drums opening for a band with two drummers. I had seen Buttholes before, and they were my favorite band at the time, but Aaron [a.k.a. Gene Ween] hadn't seen them yet. It was our first real club gig, and it was total luck that we were opening for our favorite band. We watched them do a soundcheck and it all seemed pretty normal, just a regular band setup. Aaron was like, "What's the big deal?" because I had told him all these stories about the mayhem at their shows. But when they went onstage, it was a whole different thing.

Randy Now: The dancer takes her top off the very first song, but it was hard to see her because she was behind the two drummers and the film projections were reflecting off the drums. But she was topless, and I knew when Tut [the owner of City Gardens] saw her, he was going to go berserk, because it was his ass on the line if some little kid goes home and tells mommy there was a naked lady on stage. It was a huge crowd, too.

Mickey Ween: Her name was Tah-Da: The Shit Lady. Like, "Ta-Da!" She had taken a vow of silence and didn't talk.

Gibby Haynes: That was the first tour with Kathleen as our dancer. Usually, she was totally naked. She was from Atlanta and part of the crazy Atlanta music scene. Lady Claire, RuPaul, and Frank Floyd Felicia... that whole group from Atlanta. We used to play a club there with a little bitty stage, and we saw a band with two women. Kathleen played drums and Cabbage danced, but we got them mixed up. When our drummer, Theresa, quit, we wanted another girl drummer, but we were so loaded we got it backwards. We said, *let's get Cabbage*, thinking she was the drummer. And she sucked. Really bad. When Theresa [Nervosa, drummer] came back, Kathleen became our dancer, though she was actually the drummer we wanted but didn't get.

Tom Hinely: Guys started elbowing each other, and some of the punks were yelling lewd stuff at her, not that she noticed. Parents were screaming at Randy... parents who took their kids to the show and were maybe going to hang out in the back but were now freaking out. There was the naked woman onstage, and then Paul Leary, the guitarist from the

Buttholes, pulled his pants down and started flipping his dick around. I remember turning around and seeing some moms and dads totally losing it.

Tony Rettman: I was 12 years old, and I see this topless woman on stage, so I'm like, "Wow! Boobs!" It was the first time I saw naked boobs in person that didn't belong to a family member. And the band looked green, but I didn't know if they painted themselves or if they just had scurvy. I remember Gibby saying all this weird stuff like, "Don't you hate it when your dad walks in and you have a wine bottle up your ass?"

Mark Pesetsky (City Gardens security): I was onstage acting as general security. When the crowd first saw the naked woman, they went crazy, but then it wore off and became old hat. After that they focused on the band.

Tim Hinely: Something seemed a bit weirder about this gig… I mean, all was going smashingly. They played "Cherub," "BBQ Pope," "The Shah Sleeps in Lee Harvey's Grave," and, of course, their hit single, "Lady Sniff." Complete with all the farting noises one can stand.

Mickey Ween: They dropped pieces of confetti that had cockroaches on them. Little white pieces of paper the size of a matchbook with a cockroach picture on each side. I don't know where they got this shit, but they had bags and bags of it. I remember playing at City Gardens six months later, and this confetti was still falling out of the lighting trusses. Up to a year later you would walk around the stage and find these little pieces of paper with cockroaches on them leftover from the Buttholes show.

Gibby Haynes: That stuff hung around. Three years ago, I coughed one up.

Randy Now: I knew Tut was going to go crazy when he saw this whole thing, so I kept him distracted in the back counting bottles of Jack Daniels or something. Their set was almost finished when he comes out, sees what's going on, and tells me to go up on the stage and tell the dancer she has to put her top on. I'm up there doing hand signals and waving, but they ignored me. Of course, Tut wouldn't get involved himself. He's just standing in the back yelling at me to do something. We had this big on/off breaker switch that fed the power to the stage. It was gigantic. It looked like something out of a Frankenstein movie from the '30s it was so huge. He's yelling, "Pull the plug! Pull the plug!" So we pulled it.

Tony Rettman: Gibby set his arm on fire and was waving it at people. I was too young to be scared. I didn't know enough to know that things like that aren't supposed to happen.

Tim Hinely: Everyone realized the plug got pulled and were pissed. People were yelling, "Bouncers suck!"

Mickey Ween: And that set off a whole series of events. The lights came on and the PA went out, and the whole place was filled with smoke, either from a smoke machine or Gibby's burning arm. When the house lights went on, you could see everyone for the first time. The two drummers kept going, Gibby had the bullhorn, and it turned into this tribal hell. That's what was so great about seeing the Buttholes. It was like you were in Hell, especially if you're on drugs.

Randy Now: After we pulled the plug, they kept on playing and starting pouring rubbing alcohol onto the drum cymbals, setting it on fire and then hitting them so that the fire flew all over the place.

Mickey Ween: I was watching them from the dressing-room window, which was up over the stage. And they started doing the thing with the cymbal, pouring rubbing alcohol into it and letting it burn with a low, blue flame… until he hit it and the flames would shoot up. The flames were hitting the ceiling and then going horizontal, creeping along the roof. I don't know if it actually caught on fire or was just smoldering, but it was clear it was all about to go up.

Mark Pesetsky: I see fire flying everywhere. Meanwhile the insulation from the ceiling is hanging down, and I'm thinking, *that's going to catch on fire any minute.* So I started grabbing their beer and throwing it on the cymbals to douse the fire.

Randy Now: Fire was a sore subject to begin with, because before that we'd had Wendy O. Williams from The Plasmatics. She had a little cherry picker that she would use to go out over the crowd, and she set the ceiling on fire. A bouncer had to grab a fire extinguisher and put it out. Bands always wanted to do stuff with fire.

Mickey Ween: A security guard came onstage, and Gibby threw the alcohol on him. The dude just started backing away since it was clear that Gibby probably would set him on fire. And now, knowing Gibby like I do, it was definitely within the realm of possibility.

Mark Pesetsky: Gibby just gave me that psycho look with the Charles Manson eyes. He grabs a bottle of the rubbing alcohol, throws it on me, and then starts walking toward me with a lighter. At that point, John, the other bouncer, jumps offstage. It was every man for himself.

Gibby Haynes: Oh yeah, I do remember that. I mean, I've lit kids' heads on fire and they were smiling! They were happy about it. If I was on fire, they figured they were safe too. When I say light their head on fire, I don't engulf their head in flames. If you cover your hand in alcohol and light it on fire, for a quick moment you can touch the top of someone's head and leave a handprint of flame on top of their head. And it's really cool to look at. And people don't even realize that their head's been lit on fire, that's how benign it is.

Mark Pesetsky: We turned around and went back to the stage, and we were both ready to hit him. I went up to Gibby and tapped him on the shoulder, and he turns around and sticks his hand out to shake my hand. So I shook his hand. But when they were loading out, I stole his guitar tuner.

Gibby Haynes: Alcohol burns at such a really low temperature. You can dump it on your hand and go "one-thousand one, one-thousand two, one-thousand three, whoa!!!" and that's how long you have before you feel it. Gas, you want to put it out quicker, and it's a lot harder to put out. The first time I ever lit my hand on fire, I used lighter fluid and the flame would not go out. You have to deprive it 100% of oxygen before it will relinquish its fiery grip, and it's a bitch. It's a bummer to put it out once it gets going. I learned all this through trial and error.

Randy Now: The insulation caught on fire—or at least it seemed like it was going to—and that's when Tut ran on stage with the fire extinguisher. He didn't say anything. He just walked up there like he was the maintenance man and putting out fires was part of his job. With me, he was panicking, cursing, and yelling, but when he ran up on stage he was calm. Meanwhile, the band had no reaction. They were laughing. It was so surreal that maybe they didn't realize a battle was going on. There was a battle happening on that stage, and it was The Bouncers vs. Gibby.

Gibby Haynes: We tried to create chaos, but it was never mean-spirited. It was never exploitative in nature. I would never play nasty pranks on people. There was no real philosophy behind it.

Mickey Ween: I remember seeing Tut in the middle of all of it. The band was a really intimidating band to look at, and they're not pussies. I know guys in bands who are all artsy-fartsy, playing tough music, but they are not tough people. Paul and Gibby, though, are pretty athletic. They aren't people you'd want to fight. And I always assumed those guys were on LSD. Gibby's one of the smartest people I've ever met. He can talk about anything, but you wouldn't want to mess with him.

Randy Now: At one point I was up onstage, grabbing Gibby and shaking him. I also grabbed a towel and tried to put it on the dancer, but she ripped it off.

Mickey Ween: The drummers kept playing, Gibby is screaming into the megaphone, the staff opened the doors to kick people out, and that was it. The show was officially over. And it got scary when the audience realized the show was over. They started breaking stuff.

Randy Now: The soundman was trying to protect our equipment because we had no idea what was going on. But someone managed to steal that big 24-channel cable that I had just bought! I'm still pissed about it. How did they roll up a 100-foot cable and take it without anyone seeing? But the soundman is up there acting like nothing else is going on. He's putting the mics into boxes. The fire didn't bother him and the fire extinguisher didn't bother him, and he was acting like nothing bizarre was going on. He was oblivious.

Tim Hinely: Everyone was milling around, yelling at the band, yelling at the bouncers, yelling at Randy. Finally, Randy came over the intercom and said, "Okay guys, it's time to go." And then people started leaving.

Mickey Ween: When the crowd got kicked out, they started taking rocks from the parking lot and throwing them. I remember someone throwing shit onto the cars and kicking out the headlights and grills of the cars parked along the front of the club. And that, to me, is what made it a certified riot. It was like, *what the hell is going to happen here?* I think Randy's car got targeted.

Randy Now: Some of the people went out and started smashing cars. They were really charged up. We finally cleared the audience out, but the band *refused* to leave. We had to call the police to get them of the building. I told the cops, "This band refuses to leave the building." The cops showed up and said, "Look, you guys gotta leave."

Gibby Haynes: Was there police involvement? That's because we wanted to get paid. We didn't get paid! I want it known that's why we didn't leave. I remember talking to really absurdly dressed state police. Dudes who looked like they were wearing English riding pants.

Bart Mix (City Gardens bartender): When the police came in, they walked up to the bar and started looking at bands for upcoming shows. One of them goes, "What the hell is an Electric Love Muffin?!" They were angry over the name of a band.

Randy Now: When they agreed to leave, I paid Gibby the other 50% I owed them from the guarantee. I said, "You need to sign this before I give you the money." I counted it out and held it in my hand and refused to give it over until he signed the receipt. Honestly, there was such a large crowd there, they probably could have gotten bonus money, but I wasn't about to give them that. And now I'm glad, especially since they stole the cable! But I paid them their whole guarantee, which was $2,500.

After that, we could never book them again. We told their booking agent what happened: they started a riot onstage and tried to set a security guard on fire. I'm not sure if I told him about the naked woman. Their agent reamed me out and called me a bunch of dirty names. Somehow, when the story got back to him, I was to blame.

Tony Rettmen: When I look back on it, it was fucked up on so many levels. What was I doing in the middle of Trenton? Why was I seeing a naked woman? Why was I hearing this music? I was 12!

Mickey Ween: Sometimes I think people don't believe me when I tell them what our first gig was like. I was never concerned for my safety. It's still the best show I've ever seen, to this day.

PART ONE

WELCOME TO TRENTON, NEW JERSEY

CHAPTER 1

No America Without Trenton

The Trenton of today isn't as grim as the Trenton of the 1980s. While still holding the gritty edge and scars of its storied past, today's Trenton is showing signs of renewal. As a city, it has a lot to offer: 40 minutes from Philadelphia, 60 minutes from New York City by train, dirt-cheap rents, and a few clubs that are open to booking just about anything. Young people—some might say, "hipsters"—have started moving in throughout the city and are credited with giving Trenton a small infusion of artistry and distinction. Driving up Calhoun Street is still off-putting to the average suburbanite, but to any former City Gardens regular, it looks better than it once did. The abandoned Magic Marker factory is gone, replaced with modern low-income housing. The notorious housing project that sat opposite the club is boarded up and slated for demolition. It, too, has become the subject of folklore, much like the infamous Trenton train station, where it is said that Sid and Nancy were sometimes spotting sleeping. Even with this small rebirth, Trenton has no shortage of blight, boarded-up houses, pawn shops, and liquor stores lining its streets. There are still dark corners and a thick history that is equal parts truth and exaggeration.

Dave Hart (Trenton historian): There would be no America without Trenton. In fact, the world as we know it wouldn't exist without the events that took place in Trenton during the Revolutionary War. And City Gardens was right there on Calhoun Street, in the shadow of the reservoir and a short distance from the Battle Monument, which is the historic hilltop overlooking the city of Trenton where Alexander Hamilton placed his cannon during the first Battle of Trenton.

When it comes to the Revolutionary War, many people fail to realize how desperate the continental cause was on Christmas night in 1776. The Continental Army had dwindled to the point that it was just farmers and a few militiamen. They weren't really an army at all. Meanwhile, they were up against the greatest empire in the world. The Continental Army had been fighting for about a year and a half, and, for the previous six months, they had been meeting with defeat after defeat, running backward from New York to a location across the river from Trenton, in Morrisville, Pennsylvania.

Most of the fighters were volunteers, and they were anxious to get back home to their families and to their crops. Their conscription was up January 1, 1777, and they were gone if they didn't get a victory. There had already been rumors of fighters leaving the ranks. So the battle on Christmas Day, 1776 may have seemed like a stroke of brilliance, but it was really borne out of desperation for George Washington.

During this battle, a ragged American army defeated a small garrison of Hessians, though the whole story of the Hessians being drunk and having partied the night before is malarkey. It really was a remarkable tactic by Washington, because nobody expected an army in such bad condition, and in such horrible weather, to cross the river and attack. That event really rallied the troops, showed that Washington could win, and proved that he was a man of exemplary caliber, strength, and courage who could lead his men to victory when it seemed impossible. He was also able to guarantee them a couple extra dollars in their pockets if they stayed on after January 1st by putting up his own money in the hope that the Continental Congress would pay him back.

Few people know that after Christmas, there was a *second* Battle of Trenton, and this Battle of Trenton was even more important than the first. The Hessians had been kicked out of Trenton, but the Americans went right back across the river to Pennsylvania for fear that the British would come down from New Brunswick, New Jersey, and corner them in Trenton… and that's exactly what they attempted. Within a week, British Lieutenant General Edward Cornwallis had marched down through Princeton, but the Americans had returned to Trenton with more supplies. Washington's army was not big, perhaps 1,500 soldiers against 6,000 British regulars. This battle was the last hope for the American cause, the last hope for the revolution, and the Americans were stuck between 6,000 British regulars and the Delaware River. What separated the two armies at this point was a single bridge over the Assunpink Creek.

As the story goes: Night is falling, and Colonel Hand and some riflemen from Pennsylvania employ guerilla tactics, shooting at the British regulars marching down the Old Post Road—which is now route 206—trying to delay this army from getting to Trenton so Washington and his generals can figure out what the heck they are going to do. They don't have time to get back across the river to Pennsylvania. By the end of the day, the British army appears at the Assunpink Bridge dressed in bright red, and pinned on the other side is this motley crew of 1,400 Continentals desperate to get out of there. Cornwallis tried three times to cross that bridge, and it was like cherry picking for the Americans. It was a bloody mess, because Washington had the higher ground looking over the bridge and was able to set up his riflemen so that every time the British tried to cross, they found themselves in a crossfire.

So, after three attempts, night had finally fallen, and Cornwallis said, *you know what? This is it. He's not going anywhere. I'm going to "bag the fox" in the morning. I'll just wait him out.*

When dawn came the next day and Cornwallis marched unchallenged across the Assunpink Bridge, Washington's army was gone. The American general made an unprecedented rear maneuver down to Princeton and caught some British regulars by surprise. The Continental Army almost lost the battle because the Americans didn't expect to find such a large force there, having come upon them by accident. General Hugh Mercer was killed, and it looked like a sure victory for the British, but Washington rode his horse up and down the line to rally his men, and they defeated those British soldiers in the field.

In ten crucial days, there were *two* victories at Trenton which, had events gone differently, could have wiped out the entire Continental Army and the American revolutionary cause.

So how important is Trenton? It's important enough that, when George Washington was elected the first President of the United States, he demanded to come through Trenton on his way from Mount Vernon to New York City, which was the first seat of government for the U.S. It had a special importance for George Washington, as it should for all Americans. When I say there would be no America without Trenton, it is 100% true.

But it is also true that Trenton, like most industrial areas, experienced a decline in urban life as people moved to the suburbs after World War II. Trenton reached its zenith between the Civil War and World War I, when the population was close to double its current size of about 70,000. It was a remarkable place during the industrial era, with products such as wire rope from Roebling, Mercer automobile, tires, porcelain, soda crackers, and let's not forget pork roll. You name it, and it was being made here in Trenton.

Virginia Yates (Trenton area resident): Trenton in the 1950s was a busy place with lots of stores, restaurants, and hotels. Everyone went there to shop because that's where all the fancy department stores were, like Dunham's and Nevius-Voorhees. There were also high-end women's clothing shops like Arnold Constable. Outside of Trenton, to shop in places like that, you would have to go to Philadelphia or New York. I think one thing that led to Trenton's decline was Levittown in Pennsylvania. In the 1950s, shopping centers opened up around Levittown, so people didn't have to go Trenton to shop anymore.

Dave Hart: Trenton was already in a gradual decline, but the line in the sand was 1968. From that point, the move to the suburbs accelerated.

Richard Behrens (author): Trenton experienced a lot of violence before Martin Luther King, Jr.'s assassination. They closed Trenton High several times, and kids were roaming around in gangs attacking people, including a guy who was pulled from his car and beaten. Everyone knew the city was a powder keg waiting to explode.

When Dr. King was killed on April 4, 1968, violent protests erupted all over the country, but they didn't close Trenton High until the morning of April 9. The high school principal thought there was going to be serious trouble if they didn't cancel classes, so he let the students go at 9:30 in the morning, and that's when everything started happening. All the frustration and rage exploded. Kids went downtown and starting smashing store windows. They were grabbing handfuls of diamond rings out of jewelry stores and looting the other shops.

The furniture stores got hit hard. People were running down the street with chairs and sofas hoisted over their heads. Most of these rioters were angry young people, but then what Trenton Mayor Carmen Armenti described as a "criminal element" started getting involved, and that's when the initial wave of scattered violence escalated into a full-scale riot.

The police took a real beating that night. Their riot sticks were old and too short, so they had to be closer to their targets to be effective, which put them in more danger. Some of their guns had been issued in the 1920s and wouldn't fire. One patrolman was thrown to the ground by a gang who kicked him and then ran him over with a truck. Some rioters got a hold of golf clubs and balls and were aiming drives right at the police. The cops had to do some of their own looting to get welding masks and catcher's helmets to protect themselves from the golf balls. When some rioters began tossing bricks down from the roof of a supermarket, the cops brought out a Browning automatic rifle and started firing. It's amazing no one was killed that way.

Then the rioters started setting fire to the looted stores. The firemen had a real struggle to get the fires under control, because rioters were throwing rocks and bricks at them. The area around the Battle Monument was a war zone, which is ironic given its history in the American Revolution. It took the police six hours to get the riots contained, and by then damage and theft was massive. The downtown shopping district had been a thriving community befitting the dignity of a state capital, but on that one day more than two hundred businesses were destroyed. Trenton was badly scarred for decades after that.

Only one person was killed during the riots, Harlan Bruce Joseph, a 19-year old Lincoln University student who was home from school. The college had closed out of respect for Dr. King. The police officer who shot him claimed that he thought Joseph was a looter and was aiming at his legs, but the rioters around him jostled him as he fired, causing him to shoot Joseph in the back, piercing his heart. There was confusion about whether the officer was telling the truth, and then it was learned that Joseph had been a divinity student at Lincoln, President of the Human Relations Council at Trenton High, and a member of the Mayor's Youth Council who was studying to be a minister like his grandfather. It seemed unlikely to most people that he had been looting, but, rather, that he was actually out in the streets trying to stop the violence. His death stirred even more outrage, since many believed an innocent black man had been shot by a white cop.

After a few more days of violence, peace was restored, but for months there was racial unrest. The downtown area was devastated, and hundreds of businesses folded. Insurance companies started to arbitrarily cancel coverage for businesses in Trenton, and there were old statutes on the books that allowed for victims of mob action to hold local municipalities liable for damages. In the absence of insurance coverage, the municipal treasuries were in danger of being emptied.

Dave Hart: After the business exodus, Mayor Arthur Holland, along with some of the state people, decided to replace these businesses. Since Trenton is the capital city of New Jersey, they thought it would be nice if all the state offices were located in Trenton. After all, the State House is here, so why not the other agencies? It was a grand idea, but to bring people here, they had to use up prime property for office buildings and parking lots. They also had to put in a highway so that the people who worked in those agencies but lived outside of Trenton could commute in and out.

That was not what Mayor Holland had in mind. He was hoping to use Trenton's work force to staff these state agencies, but it didn't happen that way. Once they built that highway, Route 29, they cut off most of the city from the river and changed a river town into something else. It's not a pedestrian city anymore. It's a ghost town after 6 p.m., because the employees don't have a reason to stick around after work.

Nikki Nailbomb (Trenton-based musician): Trenton rent is cheap as fuck, and it's so awesome here. And I mean awesome, but not in the conventional way. We're turning this place into a plant-covered, colorful, compost pile, gardening, musical place. The laws aren't strict about certain things, and it's the first time in history where we can take this place over as our own. So exciting. We're turning Trenton into Portland. All the muthafuckas who doubt me are the kind of people who thought the world was flat.

CHAPTER 2

It begins... 1979–1982

City Gardens opened sometime in 1978 or 1979... no one is exactly sure of the precise date. Like most historical events, it began without much herald and no one really thought to document its earliest days. Numerous local bands played the club in 1979 and early 1980; however, finding out exactly who played when (especially before August 1980) has proven impossible.

Before discovering City Gardens, Randy "Now" Ellis had been spinning records at various clubs in New Jersey and finding little acceptance for the type of music he wanted to play. But he was a man with conviction, and he wouldn't quit until he found an audience.

1979

Top Ten Songs in 1979:

1. My Sharona, The Knack

2. Bad Girls, Donna Summer

3. Le Freak, Chic

4. Da Ya Think I'm Sexy?, Rod Stewart

5. Reunited, Peaches and Herb

6. I Will Survive, Gloria Gaynor

7. Hot Stuff, Donna Summer

8. Y.M.C.A., Village People

9. Ring My Bell, Anita Ward

10. Sad Eyes, Robert John

Randy Now (City Gardens DJ/promoter): In 1979, I was deejaying new wave music anyplace that would have me, but all anyone wanted to hear back then was ZZ Top. I vividly remember playing *Planet Claire* by the B-52's at one place and getting thrown out. At Central House in New Egypt, NJ, I would play the Talking Heads, Ramones, and Blondie, and one night they simply said, "Get out! You're not the DJ we want. We want to hear *Crazy Little Thing Called Love* by Queen!" I got spit on, beat up, and even punched in the face for playing this music.

Jello Biafra (Dead Kennedys): A lot of times, bars preferred cover bands, maybe who could play '50s songs, or Beatles and Beach Boys songs, or that dumb Bill Clinton and Tipper Gore Don't-Stop-Thinking-About-Tomorrow type music. We were up against that.

Tom Christ (City Gardens regular): I was 18, but most of my friends were still 17, so we were always looking for places that would serve underage drinkers... which wasn't too hard back then. A friend told me, "There's this DJ over at Central House who plays that punk-rock shit you're into." So I went out there, and I couldn't believe it... it was true! Randy was playing all this amazing stuff, and we became friends instantly. Everyone I knew was into Skynyrd and Pink Floyd. Through Randy I met other people, and it became a scene. A small scene, maybe 8 or 12 people at first, but it was a scene.

Gregg Delso (City Gardens regular): If you were into what other people thought was "weird music," pretty much your only options were Philly and New York. There was no other choice, because there was nothing in between the two cities. So we would follow Randy around to find the alternatives to "It's Raining Men" and that kind of thing.

Randy Now: To understand the beginning of City Gardens, you have to go back to the '50s, when [City Gardens owner] Frank "Tut" Nalbone's father was a landlord. Nalbone is a big name in Trenton, and his father had a club in the '50s that was pretty famous, as well as other properties.

City Gardens was on Calhoun Street, which used to be called Route 1 before they built highway Route 1 with the toll bridge in 1952. The building that became City Gardens was a car dealership with a huge neon sign on it that said "US 1 Motors" and a giant flashing arrow. You could see it for miles and miles; in fact, I could see it from the roof of my house in Bordentown. Afterward, when it became the club, he had to have the sign dismantled because pieces kept falling off, and he was afraid someone was going to get hit by a chunk.

Virginia Yates (Trenton area resident): That building has been there a long time. In the 1940s, before it was a car dealership, it was a grocery store called Giant Tiger.

Randy Now: The building was also a warehouse, and for a while it was an African-American club called Chocolate City, like the Parliament song, and they had a big mural on the wall of the album cover. Kurtis Blow played there once before he got really popular. Frank—or "Tut" as he was known—had just graduated from NYU and opened up a fireplace-insert store that wasn't doing much business. His family had the building and a liquor license, so they opened King Tut's City Gardens. This all happened before I met him. Whenever I saw a new club, I would try to get a gig there. I cold-called Frank and told him, "I'm a DJ and play new wave music," and he said, "New what?"

Tom Christ: One day Randy told us, "I'm going to start deejaying at City Gardens," and we all started going there. I had never been in Tren-

ton before, but I thought the place had a lot of potential. I was used to going to New York and Philly, and the best places back then were always in crappy neighborhoods, so I wasn't put off by the location.

Randy Now: Frank's nickname was King Tut. That's what they called him when he played pool, which he was really good at. In fact, he was a pool shark. The name City Gardens came from Frank's dad, who owned the building, and I'm not sure where he got that. So it was King Tut's City Gardens, although we later dropped the King Tut part.

Johnny Pompadour (City Gardens regular/musician): A few years before there was a place called the Rum Runner in Trenton, where some of us would go to hear blues. It was a bad neighborhood, but Calhoun Street was even more legendary as a bad neighborhood.

One of the bands I played with at City Gardens in the early days was called Dash Weaver. One night after a show, we went out to put the drums in the car at 2 a.m. and discovered it had been stolen. That was devastating to us, but not uncommon. People routinely got mugged or hurt, or their car was missing or their stuff was missing, because that was the environment. But we were proactive that night! We jumped in the guitar player's car and drove around until we found the car thief driving up Calhoun Street. He was some kind of a druggie with hemorrhoids or something, because he had all these diapers in the car. The drummer didn't really want the car back after that.

Anthony Pelluso (City Gardens bartender): I was the first bartender they hired. The first weekend Randy deejayed there, I went to the club. I'm sitting at the bar, chatting with Tut's wife Patti, who was the bartender that night. She asked me if I ever bartended. I told her no, and she said, "Do you know what's in a rum and coke?" I guessed, "Rum and coke?" and she said, "Okay, you're hired! Now get back here behind the bar and wait on people." And that was it.

Joe Knotts (City Gardens regular): I had followed popular music very closely since I was young kid, but it fell apart in the '70s. Bands like the Eagles were popular and were what people wanted to hear, but I felt music had left. I had a glam phase, but overall, music was in the doldrums. I'd read about Iggy Pop and the Ramones in *Creem* magazine, but I had a hard time hearing the music, which seems so strange now… having a hard time hearing the music of bands you knew existed.

In July 1977, I was driving through Philadelphia. There were only three stations you could listen to at that time, and one was WMMR. The DJ suddenly says, "I'm going to play the biggest song in England right now. The band is the Sex Pistols and here it is." He put the song on, and I had to pull over to the side of the road. I'm thinking, "Holy shit! This is amazing!" It electrified me. The song came to an end, the DJ waited a beat, and then he said, "You will never hear me play that again. That was the worst thing I have ever heard." I turned that station off and never listened to it again. But it made me realize that there was a whole other universe out there. I discovered college radio stations that played what I needed to hear. Every hour they would give a rundown of local shows in the area, and I kept hearing City Gardens mentioned as the venue. I thought, *I have to find this place.*

Mike Watt (Minutemen/fIREHOSE bassist): It was hard, especially with rock and roll clubs, because rock-and-rollers hated punk more than the "squares johns." Square johns didn't know what the fuck you were, period. Whereas rock-and-rollers thought punk was some perverted, wrong music. So you ended up playing a lot of VFW halls and non-rock and roll venues… gay discos, ethnic halls, community centers. It's really surprising now that you have people—younger people who can really play—with huge respect for the old punk scene. Whereas in the old days, people who thought that they could play really hated punk rockers, because we were just starting out, and being provocative and obnoxious, and we didn't play "real" music.

Randy Now: The crowds were young. My first day, I was 24, but my brother was 17 and would come with his girlfriend who was a year younger still. The thing that helped us was the lower drinking age; in New Jersey it was 18, but Pennsylvania was 21, and we were a half a mile from the border. Times were different then. We could drink a 12-pack of beer and drive, and no one would bother you. Worst case scenario, if you got pulled over, the cop would take the beer away from you and give it to his own kids. Clubs would card people at the door, but if you had any kind of fake ID they would let you in. The laws were so loose then, no one cared if underage people came in and drank.

Larry Kirwan (Black 47/Major Thinkers): To me, it was better when you had 18-year-olds drinking in that environment. Now they are drinking too much, and it's outside of that environment. They aren't around older, experienced adults who are into the same music and can teach them by example how to drink and act in a club.

Greg Frey (The Groceries): The drinking back then made a huge difference. It was college-age music, but college kids aren't 21 until they're seniors. Back then you marketed to colleges and college radio, got college gigs, and got kids out to the club.

Randy Now: I found a home at City Gardens. And Tut, the club's owner, and I got along really well.

Russ Smith (City Gardens regular): The tag line of the original promos said, "King Tut's City Gardens ... Central New Jersey's ONLY New Wave Club ... Just blocks from the Old Korvette's Plaza."

Tom Christ: Tut gave me a job working the door and cleaning up. I used to have business cards that said "Tom the Doorman." But the club itself back then was a little scary.

Randy Now: With the original layout of City Gardens, when you walked in the front door, to your right was the "big" room where the main stage ended up, and to the left was a much smaller room with a tiny stage that was left over from Chocolate City. In the beginning, we only used the small back room.

Tom Christ: We would be in the back room because the front room was full of junk. It was pitch black with no lighting, and way out in the distance from the bar was a little light above the men's room. The big room just sat there, unused.

Johnny Pompadour: They were only using a small part of the building, and I'd ask the owner, "Why don't you use the whole place?" He'd explain that it would be too expensive to heat the whole building and hire enough staff to cover it.

Randy Now: The original DJ booth was on the small stage in the back, so I would DJ onstage. Things were so rickety that every time somebody slammed the freaking door, the record would skip. I would scream at everyone who slammed the door. We tried to rig it up so the turntables hung from cables, but nothing worked. The records were always skipping. When New Order played the first time, [bassist] Peter Hook came through and slammed and the door. I didn't realize it was him and I screamed, "*Don't slam the fucking door!*" And there was no heat in the building when we started. Tut was in the wood-burning stove business, so the backroom was heated by a big wood-burning stove… until a guy fell on it and burned his hands.

Tom Christ: Toward the beginning, a notorious motorcycle gang started coming and hanging out at the club. Why would bikers come to a punk rock club? Well, it was in Trenton, it was close to their clubhouse, and maybe they thought they could sell some speed. They made no bones about being outlaws, even the girls. They would beat up other girls in the bathroom and steal their pocketbooks. And they weren't even sneaky about it; they would do it right in front of you.

Randy Now: The men were tough and women were even tougher. They had one black guy in their group and his name was—I'm not making this up—"Nigger." It was stitched on his jacket.

Tom Christ: We had a rent-a-cop by then, Old Man Jack, and he wanted to give me a piece [gun] to protect myself. I wore a leather motorcycle jacket, but I didn't ride and I caught all kinds of hell for it. One day Nigger told me to stop wearing the jacket.

Jim Nevius (Neighbors & Allies): Wherever we went, it seemed like the bikers would come, and they showed up at City Gardens. They would sit there and no one would get near them, so they'd have this buffer zone around them. They would sit there and watch, never clapping or anything. We're like, *what do these guys want?* So we dedicated a song to them.

We had a gig at a place on Long Island opening for Steppenwolf. We got there and the entire place was filled with bikers. To the rafters. Bikers and their "chicks" as we would call them. After playing our first couple of songs, the crowd has figured out, *this isn't Steppenwolf!* Then they figured out, *this is a punk band!* And then they figure, *if this is a punk band, let's throw bottles at them!* We're standing up there and it's like a machine gun of bottles flying past my head. I looked back and said, *guys, cut out the middle of the set*, because we had to play 20 minutes to get paid.

Randy Now: Attendance was dropping because women were afraid to go to the club. It was getting bad. And then one day, the bikers stopped coming around. I think Tut's father had some kind of connections and he told them to go someplace else.

Joe Knotts: I could never figure out how City Gardens made any money. I thought it was a money-laundering operation.

Tom Christ: Once the DJ nights started getting more popular, we realized we could probably have cool bands too.

Randy Now: Tut would book blues and local bands, like Joe Zook and Ernie White. But to see really cool bands, even local ones, you'd have to go to Philly or New York City. One band, Neighbors & Allies, were very popular and from the area, but they had never played locally. They skipped New Jersey altogether because there was literally no place to play.

I was deejaying on Sundays, and we were up to about 150 people. I said, "Hey, there's this band called The Shades that plays over at [competing club] Brother's." I considered Brother's the competition because they wouldn't let me deejay there, and they played disco music. So, we brought The Shades in to play Thursday nights, and attendance started climbing. Henry, the owner of Brother's, got pissed off. He wouldn't even let me in the door anymore. Finally, The Shades stopped playing Brother's altogether.

George Messina (The Shades): We played cover songs, but they weren't your regular cover songs. We played the The Kinks, The Move, Roxy Music; it was out of the ordinary, not Top 40 stuff.

Jim Nevius (Neighbors & Allies): City Gardens was a great place to play. We could play to a younger crowd and pack that place out. The only thing I didn't like about City Gardens was the dressing room. You had to walk through the crowd to get to the dressing room, which is okay; it's not like you want to be Mr. Rock Star. But when you get done playing and you're all sweaty, you have to walk 50 yards through the crowd. All the glamour washes away. All you want to do is go backstage, shut the door, and take a breath. I noticed some of the bigger bands bagged that whole idea and went right to their tour bus when they were done.

Jack DiStefano (The Shades): Randy would come see us play, and he wanted to get this club going. It was right up our alley, so we jumped at the chance. It started out with no heat and no air conditioning; 5000 degrees in the summer, 10 in the winter. We were in this little area between Philly and New York, and no bands would play around Trenton. We were it! So we had a pretty good following. We played once a week for almost a year and half, and we were the house band during the week. We had been playing Brothers, which was a small, confined place… 230 people maximum. We would get 600 people a night at City Gardens, all packed in and sweaty with this tiny stage. We were so young and arrogant. We assumed our crowd would follow us to City Gardens. And they did.

George Messina: It ended up being the place to be. It was the only place in the area to hear that type of music. Every other club was The Eagles, Van Halen, or that type of thing.

Russ Smith: It was so obvious which cars were going to City Gardens. When you got gas at the stations near the club, there would be a steady stream of people pulling in and asking directions. The station attendants started telling people they never heard of the place because they were getting annoyed at all the punks bothering them and not buying gas.

Jeffrey Lubbers (City Gardens regular): Actually, the first act Randy ever booked in his life was when we were in high school. There was DJ on Saturday nights on WPRB in Princeton, NJ named Bob Baker, and his show was called *The Other Side*. It was kind of risqué for that time. Randy called the radio station and got to know the guy, and Randy said, "I'm going to book this for our high school." The act was four people onstage, kind of like Firesign Theater, but more off color. At intermission, the principle of the school got up on stage and announced, "That's it, show's over" and pulled the plug. It was a big controversy. So Bob Baker went back on the radio and made fun of Bordentown, telling Elsie the Cow jokes and calling us a little farm town. But Randy always had a knack for booking shows, starting controversy, and causing an uproar.

Randy Now: It was too dirty for that time, though now it would be nothing. And that guy Bob Baker? He is now Howard Stern's doctor, and he's a ventriloquist.

Jeffrey Lubbers: Other bars weren't like City Gardens. You either had to dress a certain way or drive a certain car. At City Gardens, everyone was equal, and it didn't matter who you were.

Randy Now: The cool thing about City Gardens was that you could have been an executive, you could have been in sneakers, you could have been an early punk rocker or an early new waver, or a hippie. You could be whoever you were, and it didn't matter.

Joe Knotts: Very rarely did I go to clubs in Philly. I saw Killing Joke once in Philly and thought the crowd was pretentious. I was used to the family setting that had established itself at the Garden. It was a causal place, and you didn't get dressed up to go there. I would show up no matter who was playing. Sometimes I didn't even know who was playing, I would just go, and I was rarely disappointed.

1980

Top Ten Songs of 1980:

1. Call Me, Blondie
2. Another Brick in the Wall, Pink Floyd
3. Magic, Olivia Newton-John
4. Rock With You, Michael Jackson
5. Do That to Me One More Time, The Captain and Tennille
6. Crazy Little Thing Called Love, Queen
7. Coming Up, Paul McCartney
8. Funkytown, Lipps, Inc.
9. It's Still Rock and Roll to Me, Billy Joel
10. The Rose, Bette Midler

Major Thinkers (from Ireland) — November 7, 1980

Larry Kirwan (Black 47/Major Thinkers): You really had to hustle to get gigs. You would form a band and rehearse and write songs and then have no place to play. And no manager or agent is going to take you on because you're unknown.

Randy Now: It was especially hard for original bands playing original songs. I learned about a lot of bands through [DJ subscription service] *Rockpool.* With the Major Thinkers, their single "Back in the '80s" was popular, and since I wanted to book them for a show, I actually had to write them a letter. This was before the internet or email or cell phones… You had to write a real letter and send it through the post office. Like, "Hi. My name is Randy and I have a club…"

Larry Kirwan: There was a very small scene in New York then. You look back and think it must have been a lot of people, but it wasn't. Just a few clubs, and bands would be associated with the club they played most often. We were thrilled to be playing outside New York City. Since I'm not from this country, I guess I never had the same impression about New Jersey that most New Yorkers had. We thought Jersey was really big musically, that people from Jersey were really into music, so we were always thrilled to perform. A lot of bands would complain, "Jersey this, Jersey that..." But to us, it was like, "Wow! We're going to Trenton! That's the capital of New Jersey!"

Randy Now: I drilled that song "Back in the '80s" into people's heads.

Larry Kirwan: Randy takes a lot of joy in music. That enthusiasm went out of a lot of clubs as they became more corporate. That was the good thing about the New Wave/Punk scene: When you went to a new place, the fans would come and check you out just to see what you were about.

We used to play in New York at a place called the Bells of Hell, and the first location of CBGB was across the street from Bells, down in a basement. A lot of people didn't realize CBGB moved from its original location. Hilly [the owner of CBGB] used to come across the street and drink in the Bells of Hell, yet he told us we couldn't play CBGB because we played at Bells. But then when he moved the club to the Bowery, we began to play Mondays and Tuesdays. He had these two huge Egyptian dogs that would lie on the floor in front of you. And it was us, the dogs, the bartender, and maybe one or two drunks. And then he ended up banning me from CBGB for being too demonic! I got out a ceremonial dagger and did a magickal ritual onstage, and he wasn't too happy about it.

As the club grew in popularity, Randy Now and Frank "Tut" Nalbone decided to branch out from booking local bands to national and international acts. The first non-local band to play City Gardens was England's 999.

999 — November 27, 1980 (Thanksgiving Day)

Randy Now: I owe nearly everything that City Gardens became to Ian Copeland and Ruth Polsky. The first national act I booked was 999, and the only reason I got them was they were booked to play the Wednesday before Thanksgiving at Hitsville, a club in Passaic, NJ that unexpectedly closed down. I heard this through the grapevine, so I found out their agent was Ian from FBI. Ian was Miles Copeland's brother, and Miles managed The Police and IRS Records. Their other brother was Stewart Copeland, the drummer for The Police. Since 999 was our first big non-local band, we set up a makeshift, temporary stage in the front room just for them, so they could have more room.

Sim Cain (Rollins Band/Regressive Aid/ GONE): 999 toured like crazy and used to play there all the time. But I remember the first time they played, the bass player was doing this manic sideways pogo and kept falling off the stage. It wasn't deep enough, and he kept eating shit. Eventually one of their road crew planted himself just off the stage on the floor to keep the guy from flying off the edge.

Randy Now: The show went well, the band was happy, and Ian Copeland was happy. The next day he started offering all kinds of acts. Ian was a great guy. At his office at 1776 Broadway, the elevator doors would open up to an entire floor filled with pinball machines and posters of The Police, and a lonely receptionist sitting at a small desk. That lonely girl turned out to be [actress] Courtney Cox. But Ian would visit City Gardens frequently. He loved the club, the layout, the sound system, and the promoter.

John Lennon was killed on December 8, 1980.

Randy Now: That Monday night, December 7th, I was deejaying at what would become Zadar's for a fashion show. I played until 2 a.m., drove home 40 minutes, went right to bed, and got up to deliver mail at 7 o'clock. With no computers or cell phones, I had no idea about anything that had happened. I got to the post office and one of my co-workers told me John Lennon had been shot. I didn't believe it. But then I saw a newspaper with the headline that he had been murdered. He was my favorite Beatle, and I had met him just five years before. The first thing I did on my break from delivering mail was call my girlfriend. I was so depressed. It was a rotten day to be a mailman on the street.

I had just received a 12" single for "Just Like Starting Over," which I never would have played. This was also the very beginning of VHS video, and the record store Rock Dreams came into the club with a big old, 200-pound, 25-inch RCA TV that took two people to carry, set it up on the stage with a VCR, and played John Lennon tapes so everyone could spend time together. I still can't believe it, even after all these years.

Hooters—December 12, 1980

Eric Bazilian (Hooters): We did our very first show ever in June or July of 1980. City Gardens was a godsend. It was the first thing in the area that looked like a real New York rock club. It was funky... down and dirty. It was real.

We were playing five nights a week in Levittown, PA. Back then we would play four sets a night. One shot before the first set, two shots before the second set, three shots before the third set... you get the idea. Our fans were following us everywhere. We had a really eclectic audience at that point, because we were still doing the ska and reggae thing, so we had Jamaicans coming out to see us all the time. It was great. Life happens though, and we eventually morphed into the rock band that I guess we were meant to be, but that reggae thing was fun. Redneck bikers were standing next to dreadlocked Rastas, and everybody got along just fine. But crossing the river and going into Trenton brought us a whole different audience, along with our regular fans. It was like dropping dye into a pond and seeing it spread out.

Anthony Pelluso: The Hooters were pompous asses. Something about Philadelphia bands... they thought they were too good. But the Hooters always brought in a crowd.

David Uosikkinen (Hooters): It was probably my favorite place to play. I loved it. The room had a special vibe, and there weren't many places like that. I did a lot of partying at that time and raised some hell in that place. I loved the smell, too. It was funky and I dug it. It's still the vision I have in my head when I think of slamming, sweaty rock clubs: City Gardens.

Neighbors & Allies — December 27, 1980

Jim Nevius (Neighbors & Allies): The first shows we did at CBGB were with the Bloodless Pharaohs, which was Brian Setzer's band before the Stray Cats. We didn't do that well on that first outing. But me and some guys in the band had been working as roadies for Richard Hell. It was fun. We convinced Richard to let us play with him at CBGB if we roadied for free, and he took the deal. So we played with him for three nights, and on the second night we really had it together. We rocked the house. On Friday night somebody comes up to us and says, "David Bowie is in the house." We're like, "That's cool. He must be here to see Richard." And they're like, "No, he is here to see you and he wants to meet you." We found out that members of Blondie had been there the night before, and we had created a buzz. That was how it started for us. That's what it was like then.

1981

Top Ten Songs of 1981:

1. Bette Davis Eyes, Kim Carnes

2. Endless Love, Diana Ross and Lionel Richie

3. Lady, Kenny Rogers

4. (Just Like) Starting Over, John Lennon

5. Jessie's Girl, Rick Springfield

6. Celebration, Kool and the Gang

7. Kiss On My List, Daryl Hall & John Oates

8. I Love a Rainy Night, Eddie Rabbitt

9. 9 to 5, Dolly Parton

10. Keep On Loving You, REO Speedwagon

On January 1st, 1981 the legal drinking age in New Jersey was raised from 18 to 19, but that was still lower than Pennsylvania's 21. A "grandfather" clause allowed people who were of drinking age before the law changed to continue to drink legally, even if they weren't 19. City Gardens was located less than two miles from the border of Pennsylvania, so the club could still rely on kids from the neighboring state to make the drive up Calhoun Street.

Neighbors & Allies—January 17, 1981

Jim Nevius (Neighbors & Allies): There was a little tavern called Duffy's near City Gardens, and the guy who owned it tried to make it a date-type place. His drinks were so strong and so sweet that you would drink one and be on the floor. One night we were getting ready to play City Gardens, but we couldn't find our guitar player Freddy. So we figured he has to be at Duffy's and sent someone over to get him. Well, he had drunk three of these things and was three sheets to the wind, or maybe even five sheets. We got him back to the club, propped him up against an amp with his guitar, and told him, "Just lean back and play guitar, and we'll take care of the vocals." I remember looking over, thinking, *is he okay? Is he going to stay there? Is he going to stay upright?*

Bauhaus—March 13, 1981

Randy Now: I charged $4 for the show and argued with Tut's father about it. He thought we needed to charge more, because we would need 500 to break even. But when we got over 500 people, he was like, "Hey, congratulations!"

Trish Barry (City Gardens regular): Lead singer Peter Murphy could stretch from the ceiling to the floor in that back room. He hung from the ceiling and was practically naked. He was also so skinny he looked like he had a hole in his stomach. It was very eerie, with great lighting.

Peter Murphy (Bauhaus, vocalist): I wouldn't have anything significant to say [about City Gardens]. We were setting fires in Manhattan and surrounding bits at that time. And the Trenton gig to us was not so outstanding, being new to the USA. I only remember ripping out the foam tiles of the stage ceiling.

Randy Now: Bands were always hanging from the ceiling and ripping shit out of it back then. I couldn't stop it.

Neighbors & Allies—March 28, 1981

Jim Nevius (Neighbors & Allies): One of the last gigs we played before breaking up was at City Gardens. Chrysalis Records had asked me to take John Waite's place in the Babies, so my head was getting really big. Another band member, Scott, had gone to L.A. to join Our Daughter's Wedding. In the end, we lost the vision. We went through the motions but really wanted out.

We did a tour outside of the area and what stalled us, I think, was getting signed too quickly. We got hooked up with Richard Gottehrer, who wanted to keep us in New York to get us a deal. It would have been a stepping stone for us, since he had worked with Robert Gordon and Blondie. Everyone looked at Neighbors & Allies and saw dollar signs. But not touring really thwarted our ability to build an audience outside of the area. By this time, the band was getting on two years old, and all these outside factors weighed on us from every side. We were all being pulled away to do other things. We were supposed to open up for the Clash at Bonds in New York City. I was reluctant to do it, but now I wish we had done that show. When you're young you have all these opportunities coming at you left and right. We opened for a lot of big acts, but we didn't see it as fabulous.

[Sire President] Seymour Stein offered us a deal, but Richard Gottehrer had worked with him before and wouldn't sign with him. We got offered a deal at RCA, but we didn't take it. Why? Because David Bowie told us, "Don't sign with RCA." We let opportunities pass us by, and we didn't get good advice. Labels were reluctant to spend a lot of money to develop bands for two reasons. One, punk was still a little scary. They saw it as violent and anarchist, which it really wasn't. That was an element, but there was also a lot of humor in it and a lot of intelligence. One of the biggest problems was that the record industry was going through its first big recession. They were coming off the massive success of *Frampton Comes Alive* and *Saturday Night Fever*, but then everything tanked. There was a lot of pressure to write a hit, but if you listen to a song that we did called "Say So," and then David Bowie's "Fashion…" They were too darn similar. I'm just saying.

New Math — April 16, 1981

Randy Now: We had a pool table in the back room, and the DJ booth used to be right above the ladies' room. That night, I'm up there and hear a bunch of screaming. I thought it was two girls fighting. But then it got too intense for even a fight. I looked downstairs and told the bouncer that two girls were fighting and screaming in the ladies' room. It turns out that a guy had escaped from the Trenton Psychiatric Hospital that day and was pouring battery acid on barstools. Just before I went up into the DJ booth, people were coming up to me and telling me that their asses were burning, like, "My ass is hot!" After that, the guy grabs a pool cue from the pool table and began beating a woman in the ladies' room with it. He was beating her over the head, so she put her hands up to protect herself, and he broke her hands. The pool table was gone after that, and that was our first lawsuit.

LOCAL/REGION

Woman beaten at night club

Former inmate wields pool cue in city attack

By DAVE PALOMBI
Staff Writer

A 19-year-old Pennington woman remained in guarded condition last night at Mercer Medical Center after being beaten over the

Kevin Patrick (New Math/Jet Black Berries): I think it happened when we were playing. From the stage, we could see to the back toward the bathrooms, and I remember a big commotion. It disrupted the night. There was a lot of blood, and the atmosphere was very somber. People were paranoid, upset, and freaked out. I think that was the first date of the tour.

As for City Gardens, everybody played there. Bands put their stake in the dirt, and playing there established you as a band at the level you wanted to be at. It was like the 930 in D.C. or Danceteria in New York. It was weird, because it wasn't in a town that was big or hip or anything, but it was a place that every band performed. It was always a nice environment, and they were very generous to the bands.

Johnny Pompadour: City Gardens was an incredibly dangerous place, but we were young and not too bright, so we went anyway. The first night I was there, I went with some college girls, and when we left one of the girls said, "Oh, I recognized quite a few people there." She was a Psych major at Trenton State. I said, "What, some other students?" And she said, "No. I work at the psych ward and I recognized a lot of patients." That is what made the early days of City Gardens unique, because you had some real lunatics going there. There was one guy who would roller skate around the dance floor. You were leaving your sane environment to go there.

Anthony Pelluso: You could be whoever or whatever you wanted to be. There was another New Jersey club at that time in Cherry Hill called Emerald City that had bands too. We went there to see some shows, and it was fancy with big lights and everything—and they had punk bands. But I thought, *this doesn't fit.* The music didn't fit the club. Soon, a lot of bands started bypassing that place and coming to City Gardens. That's when we started making a name for ourselves.

Randy Now: In the beginning, when I played "Rock Lobster" and it got to the part where the lyrics go, *down, down, down...* everyone would get down on the floor and do the worm. We thought nothing of it. We'd pogo and jump up and down like idiots. City Gardens was the one place you could go and do something like that and not get your ass kicked.

Dead Kennedys /The Sic F*cks—April 18, 1981

The Dead Kennedys show was the first performance in "the big room" with the big stage that most people remember.

Jeffrey Lubbers: We worked all day trying to get the stage and the front room ready in time. We were still building the stage the day of the concert. The front room was a mess, just crap lying around, junk everywhere, and we had to scramble to try and get everything ready. The stage was already partially built, because we planned on moving bands to the front room anyway, but we knew there was no way we could have the Dead Kennedys in the back. I guess we were dragging our feet getting it all ready, but we were working right up until the band showed up.

Anthony Pelluso: That whole thing was ridiculous. We weren't quite sure how many people were going to show up. We figured it would be busy, that we'd get a good crowd, but it ended up being total chaos. It was a great atmosphere to be around... something that was so new and so much cooler than anything any of us had ever experienced.

Jello Biafra (Dead Kennedys): Compared to clubs in New York and other big cities, City Gardens was just a big old warehouse… a barn painted black inside. It was punk and rock-and-roller proof.

Tom Christ: I worked at City Gardens until the first Dead Kennedys show. Before the show, they sent all this really cool promo stuff—posters and whatnot— so I stole it. Tut caught me, took all the stuff back, and fired me. I kept hanging out at the club, though. There were no hard feelings.

Jello Biafra: In those days, it wasn't all split up into the booking agent, the manager, and the tour manager. Usually, if a band had a manager, the manager was booking the shows on the road via phone booths at gas stations, because cell phones weren't invented yet, nor was the internet or email. The manager booked the shows and did the accounting and traveled as the tour manager with the band. The manager, agent, tour manager, den mother, you name it. It was all that.

Randy Now: All the power to the front room was going through a little piece of wire the size of a spaghetti noodle. Tut's uncle, Sam, did the electrical work. He took these two pieces of wire, tied them together, and, *voilà!* it was lights and sound. We had over 1,000 people come for the show, and it was the first time we had to turn some away.

We had to give the band a $2,500 guarantee, which was unheard of then, and we could only charge $6 a ticket. The band wouldn't let us charge more. To get the show, I kept in touch with them and sold them on the fact that this was *the* place to play. People came from far and wide to see them, because it was the only date outside of New York and Washington D.C. The Sic Fucks were the opening act and they had this mystique about them because they were Tish and Snooky from [legendary punk-rock store] Manic Panic.

Jello Biafra: I'd never seen so many Trans Ams at a Dead Kennedys show as I saw in the parking lot of City Gardens. We noticed that every single time, which told us a little bit about the demographic we were dealing with.

Sim Cain (Regressive Aid/Rollins Band): It was an unbelievable show and so exciting to be at. It was before slam dancing became really violent, when it was more like rough-housing with your buddies. We invented the term "regression" at that show. We wanted to start a band so that we could get people to do the same thing we saw the crowd do that night.

Joan Jett—May 30, 1981

Kenny Laguna (producer/songwriting partner of Joan Jett): Joan had a real strange ascension when she came here from California and started playing all the East Coast clubs. Nobody went to those shows at first. We'd get, like, 17 people. But within a few months they were closing streets around her gigs. I remember the City Gardens shows always being crazy sell-outs for Joan. It was a great spot to stop on the way from, say, Washington DC on up to New York. We would play Philadelphia and then play City Gardens and work our way around. When we moved Joan out to the Northeast it was great because she could play 20 different cities and still go back home. City Gardens was a key spot on the way back. It was part of the network of clubs that enabled acts to succeed then.

Nancy Petriello Barile (Philadelphia promoter): That girl always put on a good show. She put her complete heart and soul into it, and she probably still does to this day. She was a touring goddess. The show was pretty crowded, but I wouldn't say it was packed. "I Love Rock -N- Roll" hadn't really broken yet. Joan Jett was important to me. I loved the Runaways, and here she was, a chick playing hard rock, and I loved it.

Vanessa Solack (City Gardens regular): I was probably in 11th grade, and only 16 years old, when I won tickets from Randy Now's radio show to see Joan Jett. They asked for my name, and I said, "Should I give you the name on my fake ID or should I give you my real name?" They said to give the name that was on my fake ID, and that's how I got in. I walked in, and it was as if the walls opened up and went, [angelic singing] "LAAAAA, you're home." I didn't fit in the "normal" space, like high school, but when I walked in to City Gardens… Everybody had different things going on, but it was a common place that everybody went to and could be themselves and not have to worry about anything.

Lydia Lunch 1313—June 18, 1981

Randy Now: 1313 were the guys from the Weirdos. Lydia Lunch and her band didn't have their own equipment so they had to borrow my brother's band's equipment, since my brother's band was the opening act. And you remember in *Spinal Tap* when they turn it up to 11? They turned it up to 11, and my brother was worried they were going to blow the amps. He's yelling at me, "Go up there and tell them to turn it down!" And I'm like, "I can't. They're playing!" They were a real pain in the ass to deal with.

The Cramps—June 26, 1981

Randy Now: The first time they played the club, the leather jacket that Poison Ivy wears on their first album cover got stolen. Tut felt so bad that he gave her $200 to replace it, even though we lost money on the show.

Henry Hose (City Gardens regular): Every show the Cramps did was freakin' awesome. [Cramps' lead singer] Lux Interior always had these real low-cut leather pants, and the one question everyone had was, "HOW DO THOSE PANTS STAY ON?!" At one point during the show he was down at the edge of the stage singing, and some girl came up and popped a Quaalude in his mouth. He said, "I work hard for THIS?" He looked at it and put it in his pocket. We would always try to grab his pants and pull them down because they were only one tug away…

On January 10, 2001, Cramps guitarist Bryan Gregory died of complications following a heart attack at the age of 46. Lux Interior died of aortic dissection on February 4, 2009 at age 62.

Black Flag/Sadistic Exploits—July 8, 1981

Randy Now: Dez Cadena was the vocalist at that time, having replaced Keith Morris. I remember the show being really, really loud. On the way home, I was playing my car stereo and my brother was fooling with equalizer buttons. We were pushing the buttons all around and laughing because our hearing was so damaged that, no matter what we did, it all sounded the same.

Nancy Petriello Barile: City Gardens had this crazy reputation at the time. I remember somebody telling me, "Be really careful there since you're a girl. One time, this biker gang kidnapped some girl and tattooed her." Here I am, this suburban Catholic school girl, and I remember being very apprehensive about going to a punk rock show at City Gardens because it did have a little bit of a rep. But seeing Black Flag there was amazing. A really great show. I liked the toughness they brought to the stage. They were a pretty physical band. It was a very physical dance floor, too.

Brian Lathrop (Sadistic Exploits): Pretty much my entire City Gardens experience was limited to that one show opening for Black Flag. We were pretty excited about it. They, I guess, were too cool for school because we were some small, little Philly hardcore group, and they weren't too big on socializing in the dressing room. We did our set and everything went fine. Then, during their set, I was out in the pit and slipped on a little puddle of beer. Somebody with steel tips on his boots ended up teeing off on my skull and gave me a hairline fracture. I basically saw nothing but white and was out of it for a little bit. We didn't ride in an ambulance but, somehow, I was carted off to the hospital.

Nancy Petriello Barile: That was the first time I'd ever seen Black Flag. They had a huge reputation at the time. The scene was small then. We talked to each other across the country, so we knew when a band was coming that we had to see. Black Flag was always mentioned as a band you had to see! I think the guys in Autistic Behavior were the ones that said, "You have to see Black Flag." Not long after that, maybe a week or two, we saw them at the Starlight Ballroom in Philadelphia, and it was one of those crazy-big riot shows. We were lucky to get out alive.

S.O.A. had played, and this was when Henry [Rollins] was still singing for S.O.A. A lot of Washington DC kids came up. Starlight Ballroom was in Kensington, and the Kensington kids hated having punk rock in their neighborhood. The Kensington kids did not distinguish between Philly kids and DC kids. And the DC kids didn't distinguish between us and the Kensington kids, so it was this giant melee. I got hit in the head and ended up with two black eyes.

Brian Lathrop: I was so out of it, but I vaguely remember Greg and Chuck from Black Flag cracking up after they found out what happened. I guess my fractured skull was funny. I don't really hold it against them. There is something kind of cool about it. That was the night I fractured my skull opening for Black Flag.

Psychedelic Furs—July 10, 1981

Randy Now: Me and Richard Butler peed on the same tree together after drinking in my car in Princeton. I had picked them up at the airport and took them to Princeton for a radio interview, and we were drinking it the car. You were allowed to drink and drive back then. It was literally legal to drink and drive.

Del Byzanteens—July 11, 1981

Jim Jarmusch (The Del-Byzanteens): At that time, everyone in New York had a band. The idea was that you didn't have to be a virtuoso musician to have a band. The spirit was more important than having technical expertise, and that influenced a lot of filmmakers.

Grandmothers of Invention—July 17, 1981

Randy Now: The Grandmothers of Invention were a great story. They only played three, maybe two, shows in the U.S. It was the Mothers of Invention without Frank Zappa, Ruth, and Ian but with everybody else from the *Uncle Meat* album. Someone called me out of the blue to ask if I wanted to do it. It was tough for me to sell it because it had nothing to do with the City Gardens music scene. They didn't want that much money, so it wasn't that risky, but there were so many people on stage, and they played for hours and hours and hours. It was a long night. I couldn't tell you what songs they played, but that was a real rare thing. It was a totally different crowd from the usuals, so I guess it was just word of-mouth amongst Zappa freaks.

Randy Now Clone Contest—July 22, 1981

Randy Now: We would do that a lot...have look-a-like contests. But instead of being of famous people, it would of club regulars. We had one for Tom the Doorman too. For my look-a-like contest, a lot of people wore post-office uniforms with pillows on their stomachs.

Trish Barry: I was Randy's girlfriend and one of the judges at the contest. The guy who won? He looked exactly like Randy.

Romeo Void—July 24, 1981

Randy Now: Getting them was a big coup, since they were just getting ready to break with "Never Say Never." I booked the show in May for $1,000, which was high at that time. By the time they played in July, 800 people came out, which is amazing for a Wednesday night in Trenton, NJ. I took them to WPRB, and they were drinking beer in my car. I had to pull over on Washington Street so Debra Iyall could go piss behind a tree.

Henry Hose (City Gardens regular): Debra Iyall was a big girl and the crowd was not kind to her. But she took it and put on a great show.

Anthony Pelluso (City Gardens bartender): The awning at the front of City Gardens ended up on the cover of Romeo Void's album *Benefactor.* It's bottom row, second from left.

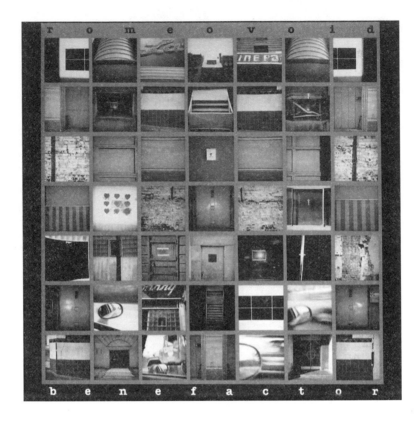

Toots & the Maytals — July 25, 1981

Randy Now: Next to the club was a soccer field, and then a public swim-ming pool, and about a block away was a little chicken joint. Three wings for $2.99 or something like that. I'll never forget driving up to the club during the day and seeing [Toots frontman] Freddie Hibbert walking down the street eating a chicken wing. He was like royalty in Jamaica, and here he is walking down Calhoun Street eating chicken.

There's a big Jamaican community in Trenton, and I knew a guy who owned a Jamaican curio store. We would make up posters and fli-ers for the store, and he would sell tickets for the show. There was also a Jamaican cop on the Trenton vice squad, and he would get the word out, so we would let him in for free. Another guy would cater the shows for the Jamaican bands, and they loved him... until he went to jail for years following a huge coke bust. When I was deejaying at the club, I would mix in reggae so people would know the songs and come to the gig.

Timi Dreadlock (Timi Dread & The Dubwarriors): City Gardens gave my band opportunities to open up for some major recording artists from Jamaica. Those shows in Trenton were really outstanding for us because it afforded us the luxury of meeting and greeting with a lot of those major artists, not only the vocalists but also the musicians, and I really appreciated that association… that honor to open as a local artist for major artists, particularly those coming out of Jamaica.

On July 29, 1981, City Gardens was shut down by the City of Trenton.

Randy Now: At the Toots show, a reporter from the *Trenton Times* named Bonnie Rodden showed up—I remember the name because it sounds like Johnny Rotten—and she went to the city and complained the building was unsafe. The city came in and did a surprise inspection. All the shows we did were powered through an electrical wire that we sort of tied together from the front to the back. A ten-thousand watt PA and with a 1,000 people in the club, and it's all going through this little tiny wire. Like speaker wire you have on your stereo. No conduit or anything. We were also supposed to have so many toilets per hundred people, but the capacity was never figured out. We used to put 1,300 people in there. She complained, the inspectors came in, and the club was shut down… just like that. I had Nash the Slash scheduled and I ended up booking him into the Hamilton Bowling alley. He was not happy about it, but what could I do? When I talked to him on the telephone, I said, "Look, at least we got you a gig." And he's like, "Yeah, in a fucking bowling alley!" We got the word out and about 100 people showed up.

Trenton inspectors shut City Gardens

Popular night spot cited for building, fire and electrical code violations

By BONNY RODDEN
Staff Writer

After an inquiry by The Trenton Times

inspector, said the police were given an order to shut the building down and to make sure it remained closed.

certificate of occupancy.

A written order from city officials said the building was closed "for the welfare and safety

To get the club open again, we had to work like crazy to put more bathrooms in, the exit signs had to be illuminated, and we had to upgrade the electrical system. It became the safest building in Trenton, but the city went out of its way to make an example of us.

Tom Christ: When the club was shut down, those were desperate times. We had no place to go! People went to other area clubs, but no one could wait for City Gardens to reopen.

Randy Now: I had a ton of great shows booked that got cancelled. It totally sucked.

Trish Barry (City Gardens regular): We all pitched in. We painted the bathrooms and everything. Tut told us that, because we worked at the club fixing it up for no pay, we would all have free entry for life. That lasted about one night.

Anthony Pelluso: The ladies' room was really disgusting, but the men's room was... something else. Something. Else. No doors on the stalls. Very prison-like. It had tremendous graffiti, but it always smelled like urine. It was brutal. I worked behind the bar in the back of the club. That was my excuse for using the ladies' room. It was right there.

Amy Yates Wuelfing: The men's room was right next to the stage, to the left. And if you were on that side of the stage—especially if it was hot—you could totally smell it. I think it was second only to CBGB in terms of sheer disgustingness. I always made sure to stand on the other side of the club from the men's room. It was that bad.

Bart Mix (City Gardens bartender): My biggest concern was that I'm kind of short, and some of the urinals were kind of high. I did not want my junk touching those urinals, so I had to stand back and try to arc it in. It was disgusting. Some guys used to actually go in the sink.

T.S.O.L./Autistic Behavior—November 7 1981

Craig Surgent (Autistic Behavior bassist): That show was great fun. We played two nights with T.S.O.L. The gig at City Gardens was fantastic because they still had [Adolescents guitarist] Frank Agnew playing extra guitar with them.

Nancy Petriello Barile: That show was incredible. At that time, hardcore had started to take off, and it was really macho. [T.S.O.L. vocalist] Jack Grisham came out in a skirt! He had the makeup on and everything. But he could sing, and he is an incredible frontman. I fell in love with T.S.O.L. then, and I am still a fan now. That performance showed Jack's whole attitude about everything… he didn't give a crap. He did what he wanted to do, and I loved that. I embraced that. To him, there were no rules for hardcore music or for anything else. People had certain ideas then about what hardcore should be, and he didn't care. I liked the music a lot, and it was more melodic than some of the other bands. There was a lot of energy, and it sort of had a surf-vibe feel to it. They were great.

Craig Surgent: We liked their record a lot. *Dance with Me* was the first one we'd heard, and then we went back to their first EP, and that's really the core of what I liked about them. T.S.O.L. had the same management as the Dead Kennedys, and I think that's how we ended up getting the gig with them. We got along with the dudes, too. T.S.O.L. stayed at the house for a while, and it was a lot of fun.

Jack Grisham (T.S.O.L. vocalist): [Adolescents guitarist] Frank Agnew was playing with us on this tour, and this was our first time back east. Before this, we were in Salt Lake City, and I shot off a fire extinguisher on stage. It wasn't like a wet fire extinguisher. It was a dry, chemical fire extinguisher. Now, I don't know if you've ever been hit in the face with that, but it's like breathing in fucking sawdust. So, we were in this place in Salt Lake City, a tight little club, and Lena Lovich was there. It was a weird show. We walked onstage, fucking around, and I grabbed the fire extinguisher and opened it up full-blast, shooting Frank Agnew right in the face. He went right down. It had knocked him out. Then I turned the other way and kept firing. But pretty soon I'm like, *fuck, I can't BREATHE!* No one in the place could breathe! The band's mad at me, there's fucking fire extinguisher shit all over the place, and everyone is pissed.

After that, we went to City Gardens, which was our first time. Right when we got there, we were upstairs in that kind-of dressing room, and one of our guys shot me with a fire extinguisher. I picked it up and threw it down the stairs at the other guys, and then we all started fist-fighting in the fucking lobby! That was it. It was like, *we're the idiots from California.* Nobody knew anything about us, and hardly anybody showed up that night.

Craig Surgent: There's a story where someone from T.S.O.L. or their entourage, perhaps Jack, sprayed the inside of a TV black.

Randy Now: We were a little scared of T.S.O.L. No, I take that back… we were deathly afraid of them! We were new to hosting bands from out of the local area. We had no security, except for a 70-year-old uniformed rent-a-cop named Jack, who didn't do shit. The only thing Jack ever did was to drive at midnight on Saturday nights to Kramer's Bagels, a bagel place in what had become one of the worst areas of the city.

Jack Grisham: We're basically beating our own asses in the middle of this empty fucking club. We hadn't even fucking played! All the other bands were staring at us like, *look at these guys!* We already had the reputation for being assholes, and we're not even fighting people on the street… we're just beating up our own asses. But, it was cool. I loved the club. It had a great stage. There's still a video from the show, shot with an 8mm camera. The guys from Autistic Behavior have it. The show was all right, I guess. But after all that it was kind of bizarre.

Randy Now: The guys in the band were wrestling around, probably drunk, definitely smelly. They probably hadn't showered or rested properly for days on end. T.S.O.L. fought, got up, brushed themselves off, and played a killer show—drunk. Even though it was the early days of the club, [City Gardens owner] Tut and I were 25-27 years old. T.S.O.L. were 18, straight out of wherever the hell they were from in California. We became good friends, and they were always welcomed back year after year, tour after tour. I always remember each T.S.O.L. show like D.O.A. shows: Great, but no one would show up.

New Order—November 21, 1981
(afternoon show)

And later that evening...

Chandra Dimension and Tom Verlaine
November 21, 1981

Randy Now: This was the weekend the club reopened. Tut refused to cancel Tom Verlaine, who he already had scheduled, but said New Order could play in the afternoon if they wanted. To my surprise, they said yes. Because it was an afternoon show, I had to call in sick to the Post Office.

Joe Knotts: It was at an odd time, 1 o'clock in the afternoon. It was rainy and warm, and nobody was there. I couldn't believe it. I thought it would be packed. They didn't play on the stage, either. They played on the dance floor, in a circle in the middle of a crowd.

Randy Now: That was the first time we started getting calls from places like Baltimore and Schenectady asking how to get to the club. We got at least 300 people to come out, which is amazing for a show in the middle of the afternoon.

Anthony Pelluso: It was really strange being there for a show in the middle of the afternoon. Everything was frightening to look at in the daylight. At night, it didn't look too bad. You'd pull up and think, *this is where I'm supposed to be.* But during the day? Not so much. And we're like, *who the hell is going to drink at a show in the middle of the afternoon?* That day it seemed more like a job, really.

Peter Hook (New Order bassist): I remember Trenton very well actually.

Randy Now: Peter said that Trenton reminded him of Birmingham.

Peter Hook: That's not a compliment. But the band had played in every red-light district in England. Me and [New Order drummer] Stephen got picked up by the police for the [British] Ripper murders because we were considered suspects. So these [types of] neighborhoods didn't bother us.

Regressive Aid — December 23, 1981

Sim Cain (Regressive Aid drummer): We started in the spring of 1981, and I had only been to City Gardens two or three times before we began playing there. And then we did a gig opening for a progressive rock band that was friends with Randy. I was impressed with the drummer and asked him after the show how old he was. He told me he was 30, and I said, "Wow." Then he got really defensive and said, "How old are you? 52?!" I said, "No, I'm 18." Then he promptly turned around and ratted me out to Randy for being underage. So after that, I had to bring fake ID in order to play there, which was pretty funny because it was clearly a license I borrowed from some guy. It was just a formality for me to show it to him and for him to look at it. Randy would say, "Okay, but only drink Coca-Cola when you're here!" That lasted about six months.

I was going to high school with [Regressive Aid bassist] Andrew Weiss. He was playing guitar at the time, but we recruited him to play bass in the high school jazz band, and that's how we got to know each other. We would either skip school or go directly after school to Andrew's basement and play for hours. Andrew knew [Regressive Aid guitarist] Billy Tucker through his older brother, and we all started hanging out. We were at a Dead Kennedys show, and it was absolute hysteria. It was at that show that the three of us decided to start a band so that we could play some parties and pick up chicks.

Keene Hepburn (City Gardens soundman): Billy [Tucker] was a couple years older than me in high school, and eventually I started taking guitar lessons from him. One summer, I bought a mixer and started doing sound for a local band. Billy saw that and asked me to be the soundman for Regressive Aid. I did all equipment and sound for them. I hauled everything in my van. I was with them until they began recording the unfinished last album. The first time I walked into City Gardens, I think [New Order's] "Blue Monday" was playing, they had the disco balls going, and I thought it was great. From that point out, it was our hangout. If we weren't gigging, we were there.

Sim Cain: When we started playing, Philadelphia had this kind of club syndicate, so it was difficult to get in the door. You had to play the smaller clubs before you could play the larger ones. Jersey was little clubs all over the place with young promoters who simply wanted to put on shows, and then New York was CBGB, Danceteria, and places like that. We worked really hard at the time. We really had tunnel vision and were dedicated to getting the band happening. We would rehearse every single day of the week. We started our own label and were booking our shows. We were tireless.

Keene Hepburn: They would play for hours and hours, for weeks and months on end. They really had chemistry. When they were playing well, it was magical to see. They were all so versatile. They would play anything.

Sim Cain: I knew Randy from going to the club. Nobody else was doing what he was doing. He was determined to get a Trenton scene off the ground. I owe a lot to him, because Randy is the one who let Andrew know that Black Flag was looking for a bass player in 1985. Andrew sent [Black Flag guitarist] Greg Ginn material, and then Greg contacted Andrew to see if Andrew and I were interested in starting a band. And that band was Gone. None of that would have happened if not for Randy. In our generation, we had such a healthy subculture and were very consolidated, and it seemed like it was something completely separate from… *adults.* Maybe it was the age we were.

Banging on oil drums was a large part of the Regressive Aid sound.

Keene Hepburn: The oil cans were pillaged from a place right near my house, a furnace place down the street. I think those barrels held some kind of industrial absorbency material.

Sim Cain: We would go to some industrial yard in Pennington and load up on these empty oil drums. We would nick as many as possible. Basically, we would fill the van with our gear and then cram as many oil drums as we could in the leftover space. And then we would leave the drums at various clubs, since they were fairly disposable, and they were a distinctive blue and yellow. After a while, we would see them popping up all over clubs in New Jersey, New York, and Connecticut, being used as trash cans or sitting out back. We littered the east coast with our oil drums.

We had so much energy for stupid shit then. We were so incredibly, pathetically serious about what we were doing. Regressive Aid took priority over everything else in our lives. If you didn't make it your first priority, you were letting the other members of the band down. We were over the top. And the irony is the side projects—the splinter groups we did—got a better response and more offers to play.

Amy Yates Wuelfing (author): Regressive Aid, when they played live, had an intensity that I think some people might have found threatening. It was very in-your-face.

Sim Cain: We would deliberately try to make people uncomfortable. In the early days, we would single people out in the audience and stare at them until they were uncomfortable. Or, if people weren't dancing, they were likely to be kicked or spat on by someone. We were kind of militant about it. All dancers were allowed up front, and if you were going to just stand there, then you had to get behind the dancers. Chuck Brown, the D.C. go-go artist, has a live recording where he keeps imploring the audience, "Gentlemen—please! Ladies up front!" Over and over again, "Ladies up front!" That's what I'm talking about.

1982

Top Ten Songs of 1982:

1. Physical, Olivia Newton-John

2. Eye of the Tiger, Survivor

3. I Love Rock N Roll, Joan Jett and The Blackhearts

4. Ebony and Ivory, Paul McCartney and Stevie Wonder

5. Centerfold, The J. Geils Band

6. Don't You Want Me, The Human League

7. Jack & Diane, John Cougar

8. Hurts So Good, John Cougar

9. Abracadabra, Steve Miller Band

10. Hard to Say I'm Sorry, Chicago

Gang of Four/Regressive Aid—January 1, 1982

Amy Yates Wuelfing (author): The night before this show, Gang of Four played a New Year's Eve gig at the East Side Club in Philadelphia. The problem was that the club had its electricity cut off due to non-payment. The show that night was sold out, it was New Year's Eve, and it was going to be packed. A huge money maker. The people working there ended up jerry-rigging something in which they basically stole electricity from the tenants living in the apartments above the club to power the whole place. I remember seeing all these orange extension cords going down the back of the building, and they're like "Yeah, we've got this all worked out. No problem." Things like that happened at clubs all the time.

Snakefinger/Ministry—May 1, 1982

Al Jourgensen (Ministry): Ministry was supposed to be the headliner for this show. I'd met Snakefinger in San Francisco when we were rehearsing down the hall from The Residents. Now, we had already sold out the show at City Gardens, but he showed up at the last minute because some other gig he had got canceled, for whatever reason. He showed up, joined our bill—which we had already sold out—and wanted to be the headliner! His knickers were in a twist, man! He was saying, "No, I'm headlining!" We didn't care, so we let him headline the show that night.

Henny Youngman—May 30, 1982

Randy Now: This show didn't do too well. I had to pick him up at his apartment in New York City in my '81 Datsun v210, which was a tiny piece-of-crap car. He was really big, and when he got in, the car sank about six inches. Meanwhile, I'm so excited to be meeting Henny Youngman. It was a life-long dream for God's sake. So I'm driving kinda fast to get to the tunnel, making all kinds of turns, and he was saying, "Sloooowlyyyy, slooooowlyyyy." I asked him to tell me a dirty joke and he told me a couple.

I took him to a well-known restaurant in Trenton called Greco's, which is gone now. They took photos and it was in the paper the next day. But when we got there, the first thing he did was find a phone booth and call his wife to let her know he was okay and say "I love you." So sweet. On the way back home, Henny took us to the Carnegie Deli to get something to eat, and Kal Rudman was there. Kal Rudman, known as "the man with the golden ears," had an uncanny ability to pick which songs were going to be Top-40 hits. He has his own trade newspaper for the music industry and was very well respected. But Henny yells, "Kal! Get over here!" And Kal comes running over, "Hello Mr. Youngman, how you doing?"

Black Flag—June 7, 1982

Henry Rollins (Black Flag/Rollins Band): June 7th, 1982 was the first time I set foot in City Gardens. In the book *Get In The Van*, there is a photo of us playing there. I had been hospitalized the night before, after a show in Baltimore, because I'd cut my hand punching a mirrored wall out while onstage.

Back then we had to crash on floors or sleep in the van. We were always, always, without exception, cool to anyone who let us stay at their place. We wouldn't necessarily run out and buy a new bottle of shampoo, but we wouldn't steal or trash anything. No one in Black Flag was ever like that. We were more like the earnest, starving musicians grateful for a shower and floor space. We did nothing but be helpful, and I was always the first to wash the dishes. We were all kinda like that. We would come back to some of these people's house every year, sometimes two times in a year. If you notice, my mother is thanked on all the early SST records, because all those bands crashed at my mom's… Saccharine Trust, Minutemen, Meat Puppets, Black Flag. It wouldn't even be a Black Flag tour, and the bands would come through and call Iris. My mom would go down, see the band play, and then lead them back to the condo, and they'd all sleep and do their laundry. They all thanked her and were cool to her. You found that a lot in those days. Any mom who ever met us liked us, because we were always really polite.

The Dickies — June 30, 1982

Randy Now: The guys in The Dickies went to high school with [Quiet Riot frontman] Kevin DuBrow, and they used to make fun of him. Leonard from The Dickies would wear a wig and say, *Hi, I'm Kevin DuBrow from Quiet Riot.* When Leonard recorded a station ID for WTSR, we all sang in the background, *Come on, feel my socks.*

Gang of Four — July 10, 1982

Randy Now: The band didn't know they were going to play in front of a 1,000 people that night. They thought that they were going to be rehearsing for an upcoming tour and that this was supposed to help them get used to playing on a big stage. They were really caught off guard by the whole thing, but they played a great show.

Ministry — July 17, 1982

Randy Now: This was before *With Sympathy* came out… before they signed with Arista even. I got their first 12" single called "I'm Falling" from [DJ subscription service] Rockpool. I found my copy of it recently and saw that I had written "Patty" on it, and a phone number. That must have been Patty Jourgensen, his wife, who was also his manager.

Al Jourgensen (Ministry): This was before the *With Sympathy* nightmare started. We had a nickname for Randy: Goofy Grape, after the Kool-Aid character from the '60s. We called him that because he always had a big old smile on his face, even as the owner of the club was yelling at him. He had to deal with so many egos in so many bands. Randy was in over his head, man. But he would just grin and bear it.

City Gardens was like CBGB West. In the middle of Bumfuck, Nowhere, this club springs out of the woods. City Gardens was like a mirage. You come out of the woods in Jersey, and all of the sudden there's these lights and this big parking lot, and everyone played there. If you were anyone, you played there. You'd drive through woods and forest, and then Goofy Grape would be there to greet us.

In New York, we played the Peppermint Lounge and some other club, so we had to be there a week. We lived at the Iroquois Hotel, seven of us in one room, because it was cheap and the only thing we could afford. For food, we would go over to Times Square where this movie theater would throw out their stale popcorn. We would take 50-pound bags of popcorn back to the hotel to eat for the whole week. This was not glamorous, trust me. You must tell people this! It's not glamorous, sharing a hotel room with seven people... seven stinky people in a van, playing shithole clubs. City Gardens was a haven for us. We always sold it out. Other places, 50 scraggly looking people would show up, and we'd be in the van eating stale popcorn.

City Gardens was a complete fire hazard. I got electrocuted there. I never got shocked so bad. I went up, plugged in my guitar, went to the mic to sing, touched it with my lips, and got thrown back six feet. I passed out and they were deciding whether to call the paramedics, and then I woke up and yelled at Randy.

In 1977, I had a band called Slayer in Colorado, where I went to college. It was originally Reign Slayer, but I made them drop the Reign. We would play three sets a night, mostly covers, Aerosmith and the like. You would barely be able to get away with a couple of original songs without people throwing stuff at you. Like, beer and fruit or whatever. And bands had to be brave, because we didn't know if clubs were going to pay us! We'd show up, and it would be touch and go, and we'd hope that they would pay us so we could get the hell out of there. But Randy always hooked us up.

Dead Kennedys/Flipper/AOD/Autistic Behavior—
July 18, 1982

Nancy Petriello Barile: I just never got the whole Flipper aesthetic. I think I was supposed to like them... I appreciated what they did, and I respected what they did, but it just didn't appeal to me as much as some of the other bands that had come through.

Craig Surgent (Autistic Behavior bassist): Playing with the Dead Kennedys there... it was like fabled times. I was very young—I guess I was 17— and playing on a stage was something I never thought I'd do. I remember seeing Jello Biafra out in the audience, watching us. We actually played with them the very next night in Kensington in Philadelphia, at the Starlight Ballroom. And it was the second time within a year that we had played the Starlight and witnessed a riot. The Kensington locals were not happy about any bands playing there.

Dave Schwartzman (Adrenalin O.D.): The first show I can remember playing there was opening for the Dead Kennedys in 1982. I actually have a soundboard cassette recording of the show. I remember most of the crowd hanging in the back, and we were coaxing them to the stage area to watch us. Once we started playing it filled up quick. At the time that was one of the most crowded shows we had played.

Jello Biafra: Playing with Adrenalin OD was a very different experience. The audience had changed, and the music had gotten more extreme.

Dave Schwartzman: Randy, back in the day, was not very local-punk band friendly. He had an ongoing rivalry with a New Jersey scenester-musician-writer named Paul Decolator. If Paul came to one of our shows, Randy would get pissed off. I was still a high-school kid back then, and sometimes Randy would come across as an angry camp counselor. I personally got along with Randy, but I was the straight edger in A.O.D. and never had to argue with him about the free beer we were promised. As time went on, we all mellowed. Randy also had that annoying habit of talking over the PA from the sound booth while we played. Hey Randy, did we ever go out on your mail route and hand out priority letters? I think not!

Jello Biafra: Adrenalin OD was an interesting reaction to the same kind of moronic behavior of the herd that now gets kind of glorified and satirized at the same time in programs like *Jersey Shore*. Some of the bands were so extreme right-wing politically and racist they make the Tea Party look like nice people. There was U.S. Chaos with their *We Got the Weapons* release. Of course, Dave Scott of Adrenalin OD said, "Yo, watch out for Stormtroopers of Death and their anti-immigration bigot anthem, "Speak English or Die." I mean, people are just loving that here." That's what A.O.D. was up against. The Circle Jerks satire skewered the more absurd way people behaved in L.A., and Adrenalin OD did the same for New Jersey. It does not mean every single person in New Jersey is stupid or moronic, far from it. But there is that element, and, of course, some of them went to City Gardens shows.

Bruce Wingate (Adrenalin O.D.): It took us a while to work through our initial mutual distrust. In the beginning, the relationship between hardcore and the typical NJ "rock" venue was adversarial. To us, [City Gardens and other clubs that size] represented everything punk was diametrically opposed to. To them, we were those assholes with shaved heads that trashed their bathrooms and called their stage lights "Pink Floyd shit." The camp counselor comparison is pretty apt. Randy was forever rounding up rag-tag groups of incorrigible punks and hoping against all odds that they could beat the kids from fat camp.

Jello Biafra: So imagine [the audience's] reaction during the jazzier, "We Got a Bigger Problem Now" version of "California Uber Alles." I had a chance to talk and talk and talk if I wanted to, so I thought; "Aha! These are still the people with the Trans Ams. I am going to go off on Bruce Springsteen." So I made fun of Bruuuuuce Springsteen and his fans, for what seemed like 15 or 20 minutes; maybe it was only five, I don't know. The crowd was getting more and more riled up, more and more annoyed, and even if I was just distancing myself from a mainstream artist to them, I was insulting their very New Jersey soul, which is what I was trying to get people to get away from. They were throwing everything they could find at me, but on we went. We played the song, and then they wanted another song.

Nancy Petriello Barile: [Philly punk promoter] Chuck Meehan decided we were going to stage dive together. We were sitting on the side of the stage during the Dead Kennedys and Chuck was like, "Nancy, we're gonna do a double stage dive together." And I'm like, "Cool." But I didn't realize he meant right that second! So before I had the time to set up and get ready, he grabbed me and we ran across the stage—and that stage was high! I jumped and landed head first, and I ended up with two black eyes. Again! This was after two black eyes at the gig at the Starlight. I was working for a law firm in Philly at the time, so after the second round of black eyes, the lawyers were calling me in to their offices and asking if my boyfriend is abusing me! How could I possibly explain to them stage diving and riots and hardcore? They just totally did not get it.

Bruce Wingate: I remember Jello catching us doing impressions of him and calling us "trout butts."

Flock of Seagulls — July 28, 1982

Anthony Pelluso: I was up on the stage taking pictures and the manager had to escort me off the stage, because the one kid with giant glasses, perhaps the bass player, was facing me and posing for pictures instead of playing to the audience. And then another guy in the band saw what was going on and started turning to face me. Finally the manager was like, "You have to get off the stage. This isn't working."

Nico — August 7, 1982

Randy Now: She asked for all her money up front, before she played. She had stayed at a hotel in Camden the night before and didn't pay her bill. Someone from the club had to go down and pay for the room and then give her a ride to New York so she could score some heroin. The next day, her agent said, "I'm really sorry about that; I was told she was clean."

Billy Idol—August 25, 1982

Henry Hose (City Gardens regular): Billy Idol was staying at a hotel on the corner of Calhoun and State Street that had a rotating restaurant on the roof. The band wanted to bring in a couple of cases of champagne, but Tut wouldn't let them. We hung out with him for a little bit, and we ended up helping them sneak in the champagne. We distracted Tut, and one of the roadies brought in a case of champagne. They took it to the dressing room, and they were partying up there like you cannot believe. Billy Idol was wasted, but he got on stage and put on a great show.

A lot of times when shows were really crowded we couldn't get up to the stage, so Vanessa [Solack, City Gardens regular] would act like she was completely drunk. She would start falling down, or pretend she was going to throw up, and eventually people would move out of her way. She would keep falling, and I'd keep trying to pick her up, and she'd fall, and people would keep moving, and we'd end up right in the center of the stage. And then she'd act normal. Sometimes people would get the bouncer and the bouncer would come over, see it's her, roll their eyes, and walk away.

Russ Smith (City Gardens regular): I had a whole series of tricks to get closer to the stage. The "inch ahead" method is where you adjust your weight but you really move up an inch at a time. The "my friend is over there" method is where you pretend your friend is off to the side and you are trying to get to them. The easiest maneuver, "wait for the drunk," is where you wait for a drunk to push his way up and you follow behind and act like you are being pushed. They get in all the trouble, and once they get up there, they usually leave to get another drink. You take their spot. I got a few bloody lips here and there, pushing my way up, but I never really got hurt.

The day after the City Gardens show, Billy Idol played the East Side Club in Philadelphia, and Regressive Aid opened.

Sim Cain (Regressive Aid/Rollins Band): Mick Jones from the Clash came to the show, and this event was huge in my development. I had been working with a woman named Alison East, a real New York fixture, who died at the age of 24 of Hodgkin's disease. She was kind of a power pop, Joan Jett-type guitar player, and everyone said she was going to be huge. She claimed that Blondie wanted a bunch of her songs for *Parallel Lines* but she told them to fuck off. Not sure I buy it, but it makes for a great story. So Alison had been writing songs with Ellen Foley, who was dating Mick Jones.

Mick came to the show, and I went over to him at the bar. I explained that I had worked with Alison East, who had just passed, so we were commiserating about that. And he kept asking my name, and I was like, "What does it matter?" And he said, "No, really. Tell me your name because I'll remember it." That night, as he was leaving, he walked out with his entourage, his coat over his shoulder, and he stopped and said, "See ya, Sim." And all my friends were like, "Whoa!"

The next day a buddy of mine called and said he had Clash tickets, and he asked me to go. He was like, "You guys are friends now, right?" because his big thing was getting backstage. What we didn't know was, at that time, the Clash would let whoever stayed an hour after the show go backstage. They would do a meet and greet if you hung out long enough. We go back, and it's a cattle call. We filed past them, like, "There's Joe Strummer; there's Paul Simonon," and you could say a few words to each. Mick was at the end, sitting regally, and he seemed a little spaced out. What I noticed was that when someone would give him something to sign, he would stop and look at them for a good ten seconds, really look at them. Then he would sign it and hand it back. I observed this and when I got to him, sure enough he looked up and said, "Hello, Sim." And I said, [mumbles] "Oh man, uh, uh... That's great." He said, "How you doing, man? Alright?" And I was just like, "Uh... great." He looked at his bodyguard who was standing next to him, and the bodyguard motioned for me to move it along.

From that experience I developed this uncanny memory for faces and names. If I was introduced to you, I would remember you, and it became this weird thing. Andrew [Weiss] had this photographic memory for cities, so when we got into a town, he could feel where we needed to go. There was no GPS back then, but he had that part down. And

I was the go-to guy for people we worked with 18 months earlier on tour. You know, like, "The monitor engineer's name is Joe, and he's got a cousin in Detroit." I don't know how I did it, and then one day it was just gone. I couldn't do it anymore. But that experience with Mick was what gave me the ability. Someone would come into the dressing room, "Hey guys! How you doing?!" The person would leave, and the whole band would look at me. And I'd be like, "That was the bass player from the band that opened up for us in Utrecht last year." I wish I could still do it.

Lords of the New Church — September 18, 1982

Henry Hose: I remember two things about [Lords of the New Church frontman] Stiv Bators overall. One, he got beat up in the men's room behind the big stage. He was being really cocky or something, and some guy punched him in the stomach a few times. Two, Stiv took the mic and threw it over that big high beam in front of the stage, and he was swinging back and forth over the audience like Tarzan.

R.E.M. — October 2, 1982

Randy Now: That show had 42 people who paid, and the band's entire rider was a six-pack of beer and four towels. The tickets were $5, and we probably lost money on the show. R.E.M. had been doing a lot of opening slots, but, on this tour, they were just starting to headline.

Deidre Humenik (City Gardens caterer): I remember Michael Stipe sitting in a corner, writing songs. I asked him what he was doing, and he said that he was writing a song, which turned out to be "Perfect Circle."

Peter Buck (R.E.M. guitarist): I was standing in City Garden in Trenton, New Jersey at the back door, and it was getting dark. These kids were playing touch football, the last game before dark came, and for some reason I was so moved I cried for twenty minutes... I told Michael to try and capture that feeling. There's no football in there, no kids, no twilight. But it's all there.

Anthony Pelluso: It was the middle of the week, and not many people showed up. Maybe 50. But there was something about R.E.M. Everyone stood in one spot and didn't move; we were mesmerized. A couple months later, they were playing New York and getting really popular. But that was a night I remember thinking, *this is really something else.* It was right in our backyard, we didn't have to go anywhere... this was OUR CLUB. Not living in a big city and having the club there made you think that it was your place, like your own clubhouse.

Iggy Pop—October 13, 1982

Randy Now: Iggy had a Playboy bunny with him. I guess it was his girlfriend, I don't know. I went up to the dressing room with a bouncer named Big Mike, who was a weightlifter... a muscle guy. I introduced them and explained that Big Mike is going to walk Iggy through the crowd to the stage for the show to begin. Iggy looks him up and down and says, "Oooooo, can I blow you?" And Big Mike is like, *ah, no.* Iggy replies, "Well, what about my girlfriend? Can she blow you?" And Mike said, *Yeah!* So they went into the bathroom, she blew him, and Mike's got a big smile on his face. Iggy watched and jerked off.

Ralph Michal (City Gardens regular): My brother was Big Mike, and he said that Iggy was high that night, running around in his underwear and chasing people around the bar. I never heard that Iggy wanted to blow him, but maybe he cleaned the story up for me.

Gail Gaiser (City Gardens DJ): At the end of the show, Iggy said, "I'd like to fuck each and every one of you!"

Randy Now: He probably tried to!

Public Image Limited—October 29, 1982

Randy Now: PiL were pretty infamous at this point. In 1981, they had played a show in New York at the Ritz, standing behind a screen. The audience got pissed and started a riot. They had also appeared on NBC's

The Tomorrow Show with host Tom Snyder, and that went down in the annals as one of the most contentious interviews ever broadcast.

Before they performed, I talked to [guitarist] Keith Levine and [drummer] Martin Atkins on the bus, and Johnny Lydon was in the background making duck-quacking noises the entire time. We talked about Tom Snyder, and they told me that on the show he looked all calm and smug, but during the commercial breaks he was cursing them out and screaming, "What's the matter with you fucking assholes?!" So after the break they come back and Tom goes, "Where were we?" Johnny says, "I think you were just having a temper tantrum."

My memories of the show are a little hazy, but people were jumping on stage throughout the show, probably stage diving. At one point a girl kissed John on the cheek, and he shouted, "Blasted! She bit me!"

Henry Hose (City Gardens regular): The show was packed. I think Randy and Tut probably oversold it. I don't know where some of these punks came from, because it was like the earth split open and all these street punks came out. The entire club—front to back—was solid people. It was an intimidating crowd, and when the band came on, they opened with "Attack." One minute, we were on one side of the room, the other minute we were thrown across to the opposite side. It was a seething crowd. It was more than just a pit, because you couldn't escape it. A pit you can choose to be in or not, but this…you had no choice. The crowd was so rowdy, and they were getting up on the stage, and security couldn't even get to the stage. John Lydon was taunting the crowd, spitting, really instigating. For the last two or three songs he sang from that side pit off stage. There were so many people onstage that he jumped off. It was probably one of the most intimidating shows I ever attended, but it was awesome.

Bauhaus—November 27, 1982

Vanessa Solack (City Gardens regular): I think one of the best shows there was Bauhaus. We walked in and it was real eerie, because there might have been 14 people at the most in that front room. There was nobody there, and Henry [Hose] and I looked at each other, saying, "Why is there nobody here?" We waited for people to come and nobody came. We were pretty much the only people there. It was a strange, weird, eerie night, and I have to say it was one of the best shows I ever saw.

In December 1982, one of City Gardens' biggest competitors for shows— Emerald City in Cherry Hill—shut down.

Randy Now: I remember getting a phone call that Emerald City had shut down. I started jumping up and down, hooting and hollering I was so happy. Even though I was deejaying there, this meant more shows and bigger bands for City Gardens.

1983–1984

1983

Top Ten Songs in 1983:

1. *Every Breath You Take,* The Police
2. *Billie Jean,* Michael Jackson
3. *Flashdance…What a Feeling,* Irene Cara
4. *Down Under,* Men At Work
5. *Beat It,* Michael Jackson
6. *Total Eclipse of the Heart,* Bonnie Tyler
7. *Maneater,* Daryl Hall and John Oates
8. *Baby, Come to Me,* Patti Austin and James Ingram
9. *Maniac,* Michael Sembello
10. *Sweet Dreams (Are Made of This),* The Eurythmics

On January 1, 1983, City Gardens was dealt a blow when the drinking age in New Jersey was raised to 21.

Bow Wow Wow—February 11, 1983

Anthony Pelluso (City Gardens bartender): I was working the back bar, and [Bow Wow Wow lead singer] Annabella was sitting there with a hoodie on, and the hood was pulled tight on her head. Like most 16-year-olds, she had a scowl on her face, pissed off at the world for no apparent reason, and the drummer was sitting next to her. She was

drinking white Russians, and I'm putting them on her tab. Tut pulls me over and goes, "You know who that is, right?" I'm like, "Yeah, Annabella from Bow Wow Wow." He says, "You know she's underage, don't you?" And I'm like, "Yeah." So he said, "You're serving her drinks!" I say, "What am I supposed to do? Should I stop serving her drinks?" And he goes, "Are they paying for them?" I told him yes, all the drinks are going on a tab, so he said, "Ah, then keep on serving her drinks."

Henry Hose (City Gardens regular): My friend Vanessa and her friend Michele were in the back bar, and Annabella and guitar player Matthew

Ashman were playing pinball. We started talking to them, and my friend was showing her all these rubber bracelets. Annabella said how much she liked them, and my friend said, "I'll give you this one if you give me a kiss." Annabella's like *ok*, so they start kissing. Then Annabella said, "I like that one," and my friend said, "Okay, I'll give you that one if you give me a kiss with tongue." At this point, Matthew Ashman rolls his eyes and walks away. This went back and forth, kisses for jewelry.

When they went on to perform, there were some really rough punks [in the audience], and you could tell Bow Wow Wow was getting nervous. People were getting confrontational with the band, which was more poppy than punk. I think some punks found out that they were working with [former Sex Pistols manager] Malcolm McLaren and weren't happy with what they heard.

Plasmatics—April 2, 1983

Anthony Pelluso: Wendy O. Williams was so pleasant. I brought my little brother that night to be a barback, and we were walking up to the front door at the same time she was. She was in regular clothes with her giant Mohawk, and she opened the door and held it for me and my brother. She was just so sweet, sitting at the bar chatting with us. A couple hours later she's up on stage in her costume, screaming her head off. It was awesome.

Randy Now: That Plasmatics had a reputation of blowing up things and chain-sawing things in half, so before the show, the Trenton police came into the club and went up to the dressing room. The band was up there, calmly eating vegetarian food. The cops went in and looked around. It was like they were expecting trouble.

Russ Smith (City Gardens regular): Wendy O. Williams got arrested twice the previous week for indecent exposure with a shotgun. She didn't go that far at City Gardens, but it was one of the more interesting shows. I had to fight through some of the largest Mohawks and hairdos I ever saw to get close to the stage.

Tracy Parks-Pattik (City Gardens bartender): My aunt had a friend who worked part time as Wendy O. Williams' bouncer. Wendy loved me. I was basically her little plaything when I was a kid.

Anthony Pelluso: She had giant Bunsen burners on either side of the stage. The show is building and building and getting louder and louder. And then it goes into this big crescendo, and these things explode into huge balls of flame. Now, things at City Gardens were done *just enough* to get by. The insulation on the ceiling was exposed, and that's what caught fire. I'm behind the bar and hear all this commotion, and then

I see Randy running with a fire extinguisher over his head through a packed crowd. The place was crowded, and he's knocking people over, yelling, "The ceiling's on fire!"

Randy Now: Wendy had a cherry picker that she used to go out over the audience. After the pyrotechnics went off and the ceiling was catching on fire, a security guy got up on the cherry picker with a fire extinguisher to put it out while the band was still playing.

Russ Smith: I tried to catch a part of a guitar she sawed in half. This short guy dove into the pack just as she threw the guitar into the crowd, and I was sure it hit him in the head. I thought he was dead, but when the pile cleared he came out with the half-guitar.

The Fall—April 30, 1983

Russ Smith: I saw The Fall every time they played. [Lead singer] Mark E. Smith would always leave the stage pissed off, and people say it had something to do with City Gardens. But it happened every time I saw them, no matter the club, until I saw them in London. I realized then that drinking and traveling didn't mix for the guy, and his tours were sometimes scheduled to coincide with court dates from the drunken episodes on the last trip.

New Order—July 9, 1983

Randy Now: Sometimes in the soccer field next to the club they would have carnivals, and those turned into black vs. white. City Gardens kids would have to run from the parking lot to the door of the club because neighborhood kids would throw rocks at them. One time, kids were throwing rocks at punkers and, as the punks got to the door of the club, Tut slammed it on them. He left club patrons out in the parking lot full of rock-throwing teenagers. He was like, "Save the club, and if a few people get hurt, so be it." I couldn't believe he did it.

Amy Yates Wuelfing (author): I was still too young to go to City Gardens, but I knew it existed and that it was like Mecca. I saw a photo of New Order in [British music tabloid] NME, and I was so excited because it was taken across the street from City Gardens. It was like a brush with greatness.

Peter Hook (New Order): Yeah, I remember that photo. [Photographer/Filmmaker] Anton Corbijn was waiting for the car to go back to the airport, and he'd been with us for two days, pissed as a fart the whole time. He just sat there. He was really hung over, and he kept saying to us, "There's something I've forgotten. I've forgotten something, but I can't think of what it is." We said, "We don't know. What could it be?" And then he went, "Oh my God, I'm not taking any pictures!" He had flown over to America for the NME article, forgotten to do the pictures, and was about to get on the plane to go home. He ran across the road and bought two disposable cameras from the garage, came back, and shot us in the fun fair. That was the cover. That guy is either very lucky or very talented. I haven't decided which.

Henry Hose (City Gardens regular): [New Order singer] Bernard Sumner had little white shorts on, and my friend Vanessa kept saying to me, throughout the whole set, "What's with the fucking white shorts?" When the show was over, there was hardly anyone left in the club but Vanessa and me. They were packing up to load out, and Bernard comes up to the edge of the stage. He's leaning over, talking to the stage crew, and Vanessa says, "Oh, those fucking shorts!" She walks up behind him and pulls the shorts down to his ankles. It was hysterical, the look on his face. But he just pulled up his pants and walked away.

Vanessa Solack (City Gardens regular): We always made our way to the front of the stage, and whenever we had urges or whims to do something, we did it. We paid the consequences sometimes, and sometimes we didn't. Back then boxer shorts were the thing, everyone wearing boxer shorts as clothing. It was a no-brainer to yank his shorts down. I remember him being on stage when I did it, but Henry has different recollections than I do with some things. I don't know whether his memory is a little better than mine or my memory is a little better than his, but I remember [Bernard Sumner] being up on stage playing the guitar when I pulled his shorts down.

Amy Yates Wuelfing: Peter Hook always had the reputation of being the spikey member of New Order, the one who was difficult, would speak his mind, and always show up late.

Peter Hook: That is what makes bands great, that type of chemistry. I never looked like the rest of the band, did I? People would tell me I looked like I should have been in Judas Priest, which I took as a compliment, actually.

I must say my life has been pretty surreal. I've had two different actors portray me in movies, and that fits in quite well with everything else that I've been through. [Ed.–The movies are *24 Hour Party People* and *Control.*] *24 Hour Party People*… we weren't very hands-on with that, so that was the weirdest moment. The guy didn't play me very well I don't think, which was kind of odd because he worked with my ex-wife. I thought she would've given him a few pointers, but she mustn't have. But in *Control*, Anton [Corbijn] was adamant that the actors had to act like us, and they were schooled very, very much in being like us. They came to meet us, they came to watch us play, and they watched a lot of videos. That was a bit freaky, because the guy was too much like me. But it's very flattering to be in two films, or three films if you count the Joy Division documentary, and still be alive. Thank God!

And there was a play in Manchester called *New Dawn Fades* where we were portrayed again!

Men Without Hats—July 13, 1983

Karey Maurice Counts (City Gardens regular): I can tell you about a particular show that always stands out in my mind, which is Men Without Hats. MTV had just broke, so I spent my whole entire senior year watching MTV. I didn't go to school or nothing. It was MTV and City Gardens.

I saw the *Safety Dance* video, and it was a big record. The band was booked to play City Gardens, so I had to go see Men Without Hats because I was interested in meeting the little guy, ok? I wanted to meet… I guess I would say the physically challenged person? I want to be politically correct; I don't want to say midget.

[Ed.—They are called "little people."]

Ok, little people. I wanted to meet the little person, see the band, and I wanted to safety dance, because everybody had to safety dance. I'm getting ready for this concert, and someone introduced me to Quaaludes. I got myself some Quaaludes, and I figured I'd get some beer, because I had a little ritual of drinking before I went to shows, even though the drinks were so cheap… you could have $5 in your pocket and be smashed at the end of the night. So, I did the 'ludes, drank some beer, and had no idea what was going to happen to me. I went to the concert with the intention of meeting the little person.

The show starts, and I'm dancing… I'm doing the safety dance and everything. I'm feeling great and wonderful, and half drunk and—actually more than half drunk. I was out-of-my-mind drunk. After the concert, I decided to meet the band. I go outside and get on the tour bus. I walked right on that bus looking for the little guy, and I'm thinking *he's got to be in here somewhere*. He wasn't on stage, wasn't with the band, but he's there, I know it. The bus was so nice, laid out really cool, and I'm amazed while looking for the little guy. One of the band members got up and said, in a very heavy accent, "Excuse me mate, what are you doing?" I said, "I'm looking for…" then he said, "Excuse me, but this is our home away from home. You wouldn't want anybody to come into your home, now would you?" And I said, "Well, no." I sobered up a little bit, but mind you, I'm on Quaaludes. I was thinking he was being logical with me, and he said again, "You wouldn't want anyone to come in your home, would you?" And I thought, "Well no, my home's horrible! I'd never want anybody to come in my home. I don't even want to be there. That's why I'm here!" These two guys get up, and they're like, "Sorry chap, but you've got to go." They grabbed me by my waist, grabbed me by my belt, and threw me onto the ground in front of City Gardens, right into the rocks. I got up, shook it off, looked at them, and said, "I'm sorry." I walked home that night, but I didn't take the shortcut through the landfill because I was too smashed. I walked the long way, and it seemed like forever. I laid on the wall at Bell Telephone on Prospect Street until the sun came up.

Violent Femmes—October 9, 1983

Gordon Gano (Violent Femmes, guitarist): I don't have specific memories of City Gardens other than I enjoyed playing there. On that first tour, there was a fundamental aspect [of touring] I felt comfortable and familiar with. As a kid, every summer, my dad would pack up the family for vacation. There was usually about seven of us in a station wagon with a trailer. We would make a circuit around the whole country; a big loop visiting other members of our family in various places. We were often packed in very tightly, and I was the youngest and littlest in the family. So I was comfortable in small spaces. Being jammed into a vehicle and traveling hundreds of miles a day tapped into my childhood training.

1984

Top Ten Songs in 1984:

1. When Doves Cry, Prince and The Revolution

2. What's Love Got to Do With It, Tina Turner

3. Say Say Say, Paul McCartney and Michael Jackson

4. Footloose, Kenny Loggins

5. Against All Odds (Take a Look At Me Now), Phil Collins

6. Jump, Van Halen

7. Hello, Lionel Richie

8. Owner of a Lonely Heart, Yes

9. Ghostbusters, Ray Parker Jr.

10. Karma Chameleon, Culture Club

The Smiths (Canceled) — January 6, 1984

Randy Now: The drummer, Mike Joyce, had the flu or the mumps or something. Mike later played drums for the Buzzcocks, and when he played the club with them, I told him that I was supposed to have The Smiths, but the drummer got sick. He said, "That was me, and I did get sick."

The Replacements — February 11, 1984

Randy Now: I would announce on the radio, "This band is going to be the next Beatles." Even when they didn't draw too well, I would tell Tut to stick with them. At this first show they had maybe 30 or 40 people. I told Paul [Westerberg, Replacements singer], "There's a guy in town who looks just like you." It was Billy Tucker [from Regressive Aid]. I dragged Tucker upstairs to the dressing room to introduce them, and Paul said, "You're right! He's a good-looking guy!" Paul also corrected me on the pronunciation of Hüsker Dü. He said, "It's not Husk-ker Doo, it's *Hoo-sker* Doo."

Henry Hose (City Gardens regular): The first time the Replacements played City Gardens, there was a problem because [bassist] Tommy Stinson was so young. I remember [Tut's wife] Patty being so pissed off she wasn't going to let them play. In the end, they played, and they all got drunk after the show.

Hüsker Dü — March 25, 1984

Amy Yates Wuelfing: I am not exaggerating when I say that here is another legendary band, and they drew about 30 people to this show.

Grant Hart (Hüsker Dü, drummer/vocalist): It seems to me that by the time we were playing City Gardens, we wouldn't have played there in front of 30 people, would we? I mean, we wouldn't have been hired unless the crowd was a little bigger.

Randy Now: If they drew 60 people to their first show at the club, they were lucky.

Grant Hart: We're looking backwards from this whole eBay, Record Store Day world where people don't know. I mean, a lot of the younger people don't have a clue about real scarcity. The first Hüsker Dü record is worth a lot of money because there weren't that many of them made, not because the record label decided, *oh, we're going to make it for Record Store Day* and intentionally make it scarce.

When we first started touring, we did it in a succession of crappy Dodge vans, and I was the only one in the band who knew how to drive a stick. Meanwhile, my mother drove a stick. But, for example, [Hüsker Dü guitarist] Bob Mould and I took a Mensa test at the same time—just for kicks—and I scored higher. Of course, he's like, "Well, those kind of tests, they're biased towards people who are blah blah blah." It was the same with driving a stick. His brain was so evolved he couldn't figure out how to do it.

I don't want to sound like a broken record about the past 30 years, but certain things were rationalized according to his worldview. I'm really surprised at some of the stuff that [Mould's coauthor] Michael Azerrad let him put in the book [*See a Little Light: The Trail of Rage and Melody*]. It was almost like Azerrad threw up his hands and said, "Go ahead, make a fucking complete ass of yourself." Bob and I are the famous feud, which is like… I don't know? Are there any others currently? Morrissey and Johnny Marr. The Sebadoh dudes, maybe. But whenever I talk to the British press especially, there's so much manipulation. They'll be like, [fake British accent] "Well, before we break into some Hüsker Dü questions, I interviewed Bob when the book came out, and he was saying quite unabashedly how he really intended this book to hurt people." In the end, the only one he hurt was himself, because he looks like a jackass.

For my latest project [2013's *The Argument*], I did quite a bit of thinking when [record label] Domino wanted to print on a poster, "A Must For All Hüsker Dü Fans." Eventually I was like, *sure why not?* I'm not the one who spent the last 30 years denying that that band ever happened.

Minutemen/Krank—July 25, 1984

Mike Watt (Minutemen bassist): When we started going to punk shows, I said to [Minutemen guitarist] D. Boon, "We can do this." I never said that when I went to an arena rock show. Those people seemed like the anointed ones from Mt. Olympus. But punk shows were empowering. The idea of playing outside your town was insane for us. We thought it was just an incredible opportunity and a miracle it was happening. As far as the scene went, a big factor was the fanzines, and when you went out on tour you would actually meet these people. The old days were a lot about people. Touring was pretty much do-it-yourself.

Punk in the U.S. was very small for a long time, until hardcore, and even the beginning of hardcore was small. For a lot of towns Black Flag would be the only punk band that came around. The idea that anybody can start a band, do a fanzine, do a label, put on gigs… I think that's great. Really not about a style of music, hardcore did generate an orthodoxy with its sound, but it's more about going for it and not having a gatekeeper get in the way of you trying to channel your energy and let loose your expression.

On some tours, it was ten of us in one van! Minutemen and Black Flag in one van, pulling shit in a trailer. We got a couple of boards in there to build bunks, and there were layers of people. I was so far up that my nose was only inches from the roof. I couldn't even read because I couldn't get my arms up to look at a book, so I would have to lie there. Also, because of the situation, we couldn't always tour in a logical sequence. Sometimes you would have to double back, depending on the opportunities to play. So there were major hell rides. Sometimes you would have to leave right after playing to make it to the sound check at the next gig. But it was all worth it. Those things were minor compared to not getting to play for people in other towns. It's not just about you bringing your music to other towns, it's about you going to those towns and learning about why all those places were there.

For Black Flag, [guitarist] Greg Ginn was into ham radio, so he knew about people in other towns and thought—tour! Don't keep it in town, take it to other towns. So, that was a whole other experience, and we got into it pretty heavy. Black Flag seemed very industrious and motivated, and I liked that. Those people were from very different backgrounds than us, but they impressed us. This whole idea of taking stuff into your own hands... we never thought it was possible, coming from an arena-rock world. They taught us so much.

It was harder for us to tour than it was for Black Flag, since we all worked and it was tough getting time off. I was a paralegal, I worked at SST, and I was a pot-and-pan boy. Me and D. Boon worked at Jack in the Box for $1.65 an hour. I was a parking-lot man. Even though I got a college degree, I had to take lower-paying econo jobs to be more flexible with my time.

The first couple years we were into punk, we wore regular clothes. We tried the punk clothes that we painted on, and we got so much shit that we went back to high-school clothes. I can't imagine going to high school back then as a punk.

You had a scene that didn't have rules and allowed everybody, and some people aren't that together. I was never into the fighting. But I live in [San Pedro], a harbor town, and there was fighting there way before there was punk. There was time in the '40s when [San] Pedro was the murder capital of the U.S. Most people are longshoremen, and you have a lot of transients. So when there was fighting at gigs, it was not new to me.

We loved every gig we got to play. And D. Boon would say, "Every pad has got something to teach us." I've been doing diaries for the last ten years, but I should have been doing it back then. Maybe then I'd know the lesson of City Gardens. I'm just glad there was a place for us to play, and a scene that was kept alive. Every pad was up against a lot of adversarial conditions, and they were true troopers. It wasn't that popular of a scene, and people had to really love it. And it built in them some self-reliance, more so than if things were easier. There was a lot of individuality. It empowered you to try to be yourself, not a Ken doll or a G.I. Joe doll.

The internet is an extension of fanzine culture. It's a different delivery method, but the ethic is the same: creating parallel universes. I remember in the '70s, with CB radios, people were like that, fake names and stuff. So the mechanics change, but I wonder if the basic way humans operate changes. Other people are sort of doing the same thing you're doing, so you should be allies, but everything is fraught with dangling duality. The Minutemen were notorious for fighting with each other, but it was kind of a vetting. It's just part of the human experience.

Gordon Gano's Mercy Seat—August 11, 1984

Gordon Gano: Playing with Mercy Seat was a whole new experience that even two months—or two weeks—before I never would have imagined. I was used to a certain way of doing things: I write the songs, I sing, I play guitar. But in Mercy Seat, I was the band director and arranger working with traditional gospel songs and other material. It was a huge boost to me as a musician. The Violent Femmes were my first band, so to play with other people was a big thing for me. Maybe because I spend time in small clubs now, I run into more and more people who tell me that they saw the Mercy Seat play and how much they loved it. But even then the reception was very positive. Was I upset that Randy used my name before the band name to draw more people? My name being thrown around [to bring more people to shows] is not a successful strategy, then or now. It doesn't affect things at all. But if people came just because of that, then maybe they were introduced to something new.

Replacements/The Rettmans—September 19, 1984

Deirdre Humenik (City Gardens employee): I made all the food for the bands and overall, they were wonderful to deal with. I had crush on Paul [Westerberg, Replacements vocalist], and he specifically requested my roast beef. Then I find out that he stuffed his pockets with it and threw it from the stage. So he had pockets full of roast beef and gravy... roast beef and gravy I spent all day making.

Randy Now: This is the second time they played, and I was the drummer in The Rettmans, who opened for them. We played a couple of Replacements' songs, and they never had that happen to them before. Before the show, I had Tommy [Stinson, bassist] and Paul down at the radio station for my show playing Match Game. I promised them beer if they did it, but they weren't into it at all. I was doing my shtick on the show and the listeners were digging it and calling in, but they weren't into it. They had no idea what was going on, and still remember Paul saying in a whiny voice, "Can we go now?" with his stupid accent. I had someone drive them back to the club so they could drink beer. It was a Wednesday night, and there weren't even a hundred people there.

This was the first time we charged $10 to see them. Before that it was always $3, and this was one of the drunken shows. $10 was a high-priced ticket. Man, people were pissed off at me, demanding their money back. The audience was yelling, "You Suck!" at the band and booing. Paul came right off the stage after they were done and sat at the bar and ate a couple of hot dogs with me. He's sitting right next to me, people are yelling at me, they want their money back, I'm like, "Tell him! He's sitting right here!" But he was so fucking drunk, it didn't matter.

Billy Kearns (City Gardens regular): I tried to tell my metal friends that the Replacements were the greatest band in the world. They went with me to this show, and it turned out to be a classic drunken mess from them. We were drunk on Fosters oil cans. My friend Tim literally tried to climb over the men's room wall to the stage to mug Paul Westerberg and get his money back.

Rich O'Brien (DJ/City Gardens employee): The thing about the Replacements is that you never knew what you were going to walk into. They could be great, or they could decide to play all covers, doing 30 songs in 45 minutes, everything from old spirituals to "Iron Man." You never knew. But even when they were in their most drunken state, they still had something. Paul still had a stage presence you couldn't deny. He could carry that rock-star persona. Everyone would say, "Tommy wants to be a rock star," and now he's in Guns N' Roses.

Around this time, Randy began doing all-ages shows for the bigger bands that came through town. There would also be a 21-and-up bar show later in the evening. This meant that you could see bands play two complete sets in one evening…but the bands also had to play two sets, which could be tricky.

Randy Now: When we were booking the bands, we had to ask them—or tell them— that they had to do two shows. Some would do both shows for the price of one, but some bands demanded to be paid for two shows. Many bands said *no thanks*. I'll bet more bands would have been willing to do it if they knew the deal, but I have a feeling many booking agents flat-out said *no* without even presenting the offer to the bands for two shows.

Ministry—September 29, 1984
(Two Shows: All Ages and 21+)

Al Jourgensen (Ministry): Doing two sets a night didn't bother me. What bothered me was… poor Randy. That owner dude [Tut] was vicious, and Randy was such a nice guy. But our shows were better at night. We're not a real picnic band, playing picnics during the day. We are pretty much a heroin and pot, nighttime band. The kids might have been more enthusiastic, but the night shows were always better.

Touring has been drudgery since day one. It's not a glamorous lifestyle. Being in the studio is creation, whereas playing live is recreation. Plus you have to be at a certain place at a certain time, and there's no flexibility. I'm not a fan of touring.

Hüsker Dü—October 5, 1984

Amy Yates Wuelfing (author): Hüsker Dü were at this point insanely popular, and this show was packed. While the band was playing, someone in the crowd kept throwing handfuls of ice at the stage, hitting

Bob Mould in particular. A couple times he said, "Please stop throwing ice," but it continued to fly. At the very end of the show, Mould leaned down to shake hands with the ice thrower, and as the guy reached up to grab Bob's hand, Bob yanked it away and called him an asshole. As everyone was leaving the club, I saw the ice thrower, who I happened to know, and asked him what the hell he was thinking. He said, "I thought they liked it! It's hot up on stage." Why would someone like getting pelted with ice? I said, "You didn't hear him when he said 'Stop throwing ice?'" Ice thrower was like, "No. Really? He said that?" We're not talking about the brightest person in the world.

Randy Now: This was the last time they played at the club, during the *New Day Rising* tour. Throughout the song "New Day Rising," drummer Grant Hart kept singing, "Turn up the monitors, turn up the monitors." And some asshole was throwing ice at Bob Mould, which I think he thought was spit. When he came back and played with Sugar, I talked to him about it. I told him we wanted Hüsker Dü back many times after '85, but they never played. He said the ice throwing wasn't the reason. He had forgotten all about it.

Black Flag — October 19, 1984

Henry Rollins: There was that little market, the Fine Fair. I'd always go there almost every time we played. Everyone in that neighborhood was looking pretty beat, but I look pretty beat when I tour. I never had a problem there, as I didn't look like a good target for agro, and I don't look like prey. I probably looked more broke down than they did. I would go in there before soundcheck to get a drink and wait for some of the more long-distance or fervent fans to show up, and then just kick it with them in the afternoon. I never had a problem with the neighborhood at all, but I never really went hiking through it, either.

Violent Femmes — November 14, 1984

Gordon Gano: This was the Hallowed Ground tour and, at the time, there was some negativity toward *Hallowed Ground*, or at least it was mixed. There was somebody, somewhere, who was talking to me about it, and I think they used the word "betrayal." I believe it was all in their head, and that it was too bad for them. But I'm also happy to not cross paths with a person who could feel "betrayed" by an album.

All of those songs had been written and performed live before we recorded the *Hallowed Ground* album. Those songs were even from before the songs on the first album. I believe it was [Femmes' bassist] Brian Richie who thought of it, and in hindsight it was an enormously successful choice, which was to focus on the "rock" numbers for the first album. We were confident we would be able to make a second album, and on that one we would do more folk, gospel, and jazz. To us it wasn't any kind of big change, but if all you knew of us was the first record, the second record would have been a surprise. I've also had people tell me that they didn't like *Hallowed Ground* when it came out, but years later they heard it again and loved it. At the time, they weren't ready for it. As a group, I think it's our favorite album because of the variety.

"Country Death Song" was a challenge to myself. I was in high school and wrote one verse in every class period, so at the end of the school day I had the whole song. I didn't pay close attention to my classes that day, and I don't regret it.

Replacements—December 15 and 16, 1984

Jeff Feuerzeig (City Gardens regular/filmmaker): I remember literally crying the first time I heard "Unsatisfied" by the Replacements. I'm not exaggerating. And just a couple weeks later, when they played City Gardens, I took a small handheld tape recorder with me. To me and my friends, they were the biggest band in the world, but there were maybe 20-25 people there. Before the show, I remember seeing [Replacements' frontman] Paul Westerberg sitting at the bar reading Kafka or Dostoyevski. [Guitarist] Bob Stinson was walking around trying to score drugs, and I had no idea what to tell him. Then we waited for the show, and although they were famous for these wild, drunken shows, that's not what we saw that night. We saw the tightest set you could ever imagine of *Let It Be* and some earlier stuff. They played it straight and they played it for keeps, and I recorded the whole thing on my little cassette. And it was jaw-dropping to see this band at the top of their game, not fucking around like clowns onstage. But they came back a few months later and the place sold out, and it was one of those insane, drunk shows where they could barely get through a whole song. I never got to see them play for keeps ever again.

It was a moment in time where your own obsessions were speaking to a generation your own age, and you felt the tide turning, and then all of a sudden your favorite thing on earth was, like, it. And it didn't feel like that was ever going to happen. It was a zeitgeist moment to me.

We all really believed the SST bumper sticker that said, "Corporate Rock Sucks." These were our favorite bands, and we didn't want them to sell out. We wanted them to stay indie. We really believed it, and I still believe it. Those bands all ended up making shitty records when they went to major labels, and we felt vindicated because of that. They all fucked up what was good. Nobody is really pure… they all sell out.

Anthony Pelluso: The Replacements played two shows, two nights in a row. The first night was a kick-ass show. They screamed through their set and it was amazing. The next night, they're hammered. They'd start a song and then stop. Start another song, then stop. It was crazy, but you never forget it. I'm in my fifties, and I still remember this stuff.

NRBQ with the Ben Vaughn Combo— December 22, 1984

Ben Vaughn: That room could be cavernous if you didn't have a big crowd. There could be a lot of people, but it would look empty. You could have 150 people in there, but it would look empty. We would have 350 people, and it was half full.

We opened for NRBQ right before Christmas. I was big fan and would go up to the Bottom Line in New York to see them. The night we opened for them, they were doing a bunch of Christmas songs. [NRBQ keyboardist] Terry Adams says, "Well, Merry Christmas everybody, because—when you think about it—we're all gonna die anyway. So enjoy it while you can. No one escapes death." Everyone in the crowd looked at each other like, *what the hell?!* Merry Christmas!

Flipper/Scornflakes (Two Shows: All Ages and 21+)— December 29, 1984

Amy Yates Wuelfing (author): At the time, I was interviewing a lot of punk and hardcore bands for the magazine *Hard Times*. Never had a problem, except for the Butthole Surfers, who were tripping balls so hard they could barely talk. Even so, they were still nice about it. Then, I met Flipper. Even among fellow punks, they had a reputation for being a bunch of assholes, and on this night they lived up to it.

Keene Hepburn (City Gardens soundman): I never liked Flipper, and, at that time, it was cool to be into Flipper. They were obviously talentless. They couldn't play their instruments. They were like the Sex Pistols' retarded brothers. They were awful.

Sim Cain (Regressive Aid/Scornflakes drummer): We started Scornflakes because we loved Flipper, so we put together an improvisational, slow punk band. We heard that Flipper was coming to the east coast because they had a bunch of [criminal] court dates, so they decided to turn it into a tour. It just so happened that I knew the booking agent at all three shows in the area, and I called each agent and said that we were opening for Flipper on the other two shows. It worked! We opened for Flipper on all three shows, and over the course of the three shows, they successfully stole most of our backline [equipment] and sold it for drugs.

Keene Hepburn: The first time Scornflakes played with Flipper, I was sick so I wasn't there. They played with Flipper at City Gardens and then CBGB. Sim called me after the City Gardens date and asked me to go back to the club and search for the missing stuff. Some of Sim's drum kit was gone, a guitar pedal board that I built for Billy was gone, and some other stuff. And Flipper stole it. I knew they did. They stole it for drug money.

Sim Cain: A year later they came back to City Gardens and we opened for them again. Someone vandalized their truck, and they tried to steal our amp.

Keene Hepburn: Scornflakes opened for Flipper and they blew them off the stage, because Flipper was awful that night… not that they were good any night. I was in back trying to wrap stuff up, getting my gear packed, when someone came running up to me and said, "You have to help [Scornflakes bassist] Andrew Weiss out." I looked up and saw Andrew and Bruce Loose from Flipper throwing punches. And sure enough, Bruce is trying to steal more of our equipment. I had to pry the equipment out of his hands. It was like they prided themselves on stealing other bands' gear.

Amy Yates Wuelfing: After the show, another woman and I were sent to the dressing room to do the interview we had arranged earlier. The band seemed okay, if not totally drunk, but then something set them off. I believe we asked them, in a joking way, about the alleged equipment stealing. The next thing I know I'm in a shoving match with Bruce from Flipper. He grabbed me by my hair and attempted to push me down a flight of stairs. I punched him in the balls, which had shockingly little effect, but it was enough for him to let me go. My friend and I got out of there, went to car and looked at each other like, *what the hell just happened?*

Sim Cain: In retrospect, it was messy and fun. After that, if they came to City Gardens, on their rider it specifically said that we were not allowed to open for them. And when they did the *Public Flipper Limited* album, the cover graphic has a map of the U.S. and they put Trenton out in the Atlantic Ocean.

Amy Yates Wuelfing: *Hard Times* editor Ron Gregorio saw them at Maxwell's in Hoboken two nights later. They were adamant that they did not try to steal anyone's equipment at City Gardens, but that they had "put it to the side so they wouldn't accidently kick it." The band also had no memory of anything that happened with me and my friend. Surprise, surprise. Even weirder than the fight with Flipper was the lack of commiseration I got from everyone about it. My own mother told me I should have known better then go to a drunk band's dressing room—which was probably true—and the magazine's editor told me to toughen up. There's no whining in punk rock.

PART TWO
THINGS TAKE OFF

CHAPTER 4
Radio, Raconteurs, and Record Stores

Before iTunes, Pandora, and Spotify, hearing new music wasn't easy. Most people relied on the radio, and if you weren't into Top 40, it was college radio. College radio was responsible for launching many artists who later went on to enjoy worldwide, commercial success, but it also gave a home to all the types of music that commercial radio was unaware of or had no intention of playing. Like 'zines and tape trading, college radio was another powerful tool used to connect listeners with the music they were searching for.

Also filling a need were independent record stores, where you could go in and hum a song you had heard, and the clerk would tell you the title and artist. Still, it was easy to get caught up in a wild-goose chase to find a specific song. You could love a band but not be able to hear them simply because you couldn't find their records. Records might be out of print, import only, or distributed regionally. You could hear a song on the radio, fall in love with it, and never hear it again because you didn't catch the name. What follows is a snapshot of those times when music could be elusive and hard to get.

Nancy Petriello Barile (Philadelphia punk promoter): Back then, booking shows was different. You made phone calls. I was lucky enough to work at a law firm, so I could make free phone calls, but I never made so many that they noticed. Another way was to get phone-card numbers. We did a lot by snail mail too. I remember writing letters to people the old-fashioned way. For example, I met [future husband] Al (Barile, from S.S.D.) because of what was written on S.S.D.'s first album: *S.S.D. wants to play your town.* And it had Al's mother's phone number on it. I was booking shows at the time, so I called him to do a show. It turned out we knew a lot of the same people in the scene and ended up talking on the phone for four or five hours, and the rest is history.

It was like an underground railroad of information. You got to know people. Usually somebody would tell you; "Here's how you get in touch with this band." The times necessitated that you had to become superb communicators. You had to make these crazy, expensive, long-distance phone calls, and you wrote letters delivered by the post office. We were bound together by that. At the same time, you created a place for people to stay. And it wasn't as if people stayed at your house because you were a groupie or anything like that. They stayed at your house because that's just what you did. It was like it was a community. A punk rock, hardcore community, and you wanted to see the bands that you loved. It wasn't about the fashion, it wasn't about the guys... it was about the music. I couldn't play an instrument, so I tried to contribute the best way that I could, which was through booking shows and helping out bands.

Andrew Weiss (The Groceries, Regressive Aid, Rollins Band): To have a scene you have to have a club, and City Gardens was the club. You also have to have a radio station. WPRB was one radio station and WTSR was another. They were really accessible. A band could go in there with a tape, and they would play it. You had colleges where people are the right age to be into the music. There were other clubs, but they didn't fit in the scene the way City Gardens did. It also had cachet that the other clubs didn't because of the bigger national acts that played. The club would let local bands open for national acts, and if you were in one of those local bands, it was a good experience. You had a tie-in to the big time. Opening for a national act was stressful, though. Their equipment would be on the back of the stage, and you had about five square inches to move around. Local acts never got a soundcheck, either, so it sounded like hell, but it was still fun.

Amy Yates Wuelfing (author): To have a music scene, you really need clubs, you need radio, and you need record stores. And if you were into music at all, the coolest job you could get was at a record store. Even if it was a cheesy record store in a mall, it was still cool. Your best hope was to trade up from a chain store to a cool indie store, and even better if it was a legendary indie store. I learned the ropes at Wall to Wall Sound in the Oxford Valley Mall, and then moved to Third Street Jazz in Philadelphia. Third Street Jazz was insane. I met Sun Ra there. I lived the dream.

Sim Cain (Regressive Aid/Rollins Band): I was working at the Listening Booth record store in Quakerbridge Mall. At the time, there were three record stores in the mall, all with different names, but they were owned by the same company. Beaky's was the edgy store, Listening Booth was everything, and Wall to Wall was the upscale store that also sold stereo equipment. People would come in and tell us that the Quarterflash record was 50¢ cheaper across the hall, and we would happily tell them to go across the hall and buy it. If you were hip—if you were really cool—you ended up working at one of these records stores and got the appropriate new-wave haircut. And by working there you able to hear a lot of new music and check out all the stuff that came in.

When Andrew Weiss and I worked at the store, we had a Ticketron, which was the predecessor to Ticketmaster. It was the early version of computer hacking in which the people who worked at the store could get into the system and pull up the first ten rows of seats, so we would go to shows simply because we had great seats. Andrew was even more fanatical than I was. We were in high school, and he was going to three or four shows a week, but I couldn't keep up that pace. He spent all his money on shows. We were always going to Philly and New York, chasing Devo all over the East Coast.

Michael Cabnet (record store veteran): The same company, Shulman, owned all three mall record-store chains. The business was wacky from top to bottom, from start to finish. It's still a record store, and that doesn't change in the corporate environment. The people who own record stores are all nuts. All the stores would get visited by the guys from the record companies, like Capital, who would come in and say, "This is gonna be big." CBS would come in and say, "Cyndi Lauper, this is going to be big. You should buy 50,000 units of this." It was all returnable at that point.

Amy Yates Wuelfing: One of the best parts about working in an indie store was you were allowed to be mean to people. At a mall store you were expected to be nice and not make fun of crappy music.

Steven DiLodovico (author): I don't think the importance of record stores can be overemphasized. Record stores and tape traders were the life's blood of the underground. Even before we discovered college radio, there were tape traders. They were the original internet, the pipeline for stuff you couldn't buy in record stores—live bootlegs, demos, etc. The "mom and pop" record stores had no qualms about selling these kinds of bootleg items, and I'd venture to guess that most underground bands did not mind that their music was being traded, as opposed to being sold. Most were happy to know that people were listening, that people were connecting with whatever they were doing.

Record stores, once you were brave enough to endure the scorn heaped upon you by some skinny, malnourished, holier-than-thou counter jockey, were havens for people obsessed with music that no one else knew anything about. You had a few fanzines to guide you, as far as new bands to look for, but the true pleasure was going into a dirty, cramped record shop with a fistful of allowance dollars and wandering for hours through the bins. Sometimes you bought records for no other reason than the cover art. Sometimes you bought records simply because the band's name or the title of the record pulled you in. These places, and even the snotty bastards that worked there, were immeasurably important.

Michael Cabnet: The Record Cellar in Philadelphia was another legendary store. A lot of people worked there, but nobody was actually paid to work there. It was like [the Nick Hornby book] *High Fidelity*. It was more like you were hanging around, so why not work there?

One day we're at the store and we got a call from a guy saying, "Hi, I'm Stevie Ray Vaughn's manager." Yeah, right—click. The guy calls back. "No really, I'm Stevie Ray Vaughn's manager," and we're like, "Stop calling, it's Saturday morning." Then the guy calls back a third time and says, "Listen, I'm really Stevie Ray Vaughn's manager, and to prove it to you, call the Mann Music Center and ask for the green room." So we did and it was really Stevie Ray Vaughn's manager. He's like, "Do you guys have any blues records? Yeah, how many?" I don't know, we said, a couple hundred. He says, "Can you bring them down here?" Me and [store owner] Craig load up his car, drive down, and the manager says, "How much do you want for all of them?" We gave a price, which he paid, no questions asked. Then he asked if we wanted to hang out. Sure! Stevie Ray is there, hanging out, all junkied up, and I got to play his guitar. Why did he want all of the blues records we brought without even looking at them? Why not just buy one or two? Because it was easier to buy them all and go through them later. That's the kind of stuff that went on.

Don Rettman (DJ): I had a radio show on WTSR at Trenton State College. I was probably the only person playing whatever was termed punk rock or new wave, and I think that's before they used the term alternative. Randy called and said he was deejaying at this club in Trenton and invited me down.

Randy Now: I used to call Don during his show. He was the only one playing anything hip, like Adam Ant or Squeeze, which at that time was radical. I told him he should come down to the club and check it out, and we became friends. We went together to see the Ramones at Six Flags Great Adventure [amusement park] in the early '80s. Can you imagine the Ramones at Six Flags? This was way before they played City Gardens. A friend of mine was a fire-eater at the park, and he smuggled us in. He ate fire at the club once too, and he always smelled like gas.

I got a radio show at WTSR through Don Rettman. Ever since I was a kid I wanted my own radio show. I went to William Penn College in Oskaloosa, Iowa for about a week. I was the first one there that semester, having driven out in a 1964 Rambler with no second gear. I brought my records and stereo, and I had the best set-up there. My roommate had deejayed at WFIL in Philadelphia, so he was like a star, but he decided to quit and get a college degree. He got a show at the college right away then took me down to the station and got me a show too. I even said in my high-school yearbook that I wanted to be a DJ.

Jeff Feuerzeig (TV producer): This little kid would come and hang out at my radio show. His nickname was Mickey the Dickey, and he was 12 years old. I was never really sure how he got to the station, but he would hang out and spin records with me. Afterward, I would drop him off at his dad's car lot in Trenton somewhere. Then I started writing for his fanzine called *YUCK!* It wasn't long after that he proudly gave me a cassette of his band Ween. I think the atmosphere and being around all these creative people and realizing that anything is possible helped Mickey launch his band.

Scott Lowe (radio personality): I met Mickey Ween in sixth grade, and we stayed friends throughout high school and did music together. We would play records over the phone to each other. He would get the new Adam Ant single, call me, and play it over the phone. Then I would get the new Waitresses single and do the same thing. Aaron [a.k.a. Gene Ween] came along a couple years later and was really into Zappa and Randy Newman... cool, progressive '60s and '70s stuff. I told Mickey this Aaron guy was pretty cool and that he should talk to him. They wound up forming Ween. In the early days, when they started playing out, I was the tape operator. I would sit on a bench with the tape machine on pause, turning it on and off between songs.

We started hanging out at City Gardens when we were pretty young. I was about 15 and Mickey was probably 13 or 14. Which is funny, because you were supposed to be 18 to enter, but no one ever questioned us. Randy would just wave us in. One of the cool things about City Gardens was that everyone was accessible. I met so many of my heroes. Once Mickey and I were sitting at the bar chatting with these guys for a half an hour, and later we looked toward the backstage area and saw the same guys getting into their Residents costumes.

I got my own show on WTSR when I was 15. It was summertime and they needed people to fill in, since it was supposed to be on the air 24/7. The big game-changer for me and Mickey was a short-lived radio station out of Philadelphia called i92. They had DJs like Lee Paris and people with names like Mohawk and Mel Toxic. To hear a station like that, a big mainstream station, that played Lena Lovich every three hours, and the Damned and Violent Femmes around the clock, was amazing. It only lasted about six months, from February 1983 to July. But it had a huge impact. It gave mainstream exposure to popular alternative artists.

Amy Yates Wuelfing: I remember when i92 first came on and started playing those songs, and people my age were like, "This is insane. This is

DJ Mel Toxic and Deborah Harry

the best thing in the world!" They played cool stuff, and the signal was strong enough that you weren't struggling to keep it tuned in, which was always an issue with college radio at the time. People were so excited. It really seemed like a whole new world.

Mel Toxic (Radio personality): Well, even though everybody was nice at i92, it was really just a straight-up radio station. Before the format switch to *Rock of the '80s*, it was just a Top 40 station, and believe me, the culture, the surroundings, and the environment was just a boring, old cubicle farm. It was not a hip, cool place, let's just say that. The only radio I did prior to i92 was at Drexel University. I knew I could get on that station just by being a student at Drexel. My part-time job would pay for one class per semester. So I said, "Hey, I think I'll take one class every semester at Drexel." I was still going for my degree, but I also had an ulterior motive, which was to be on that radio station.

I don't recall that many people liked me at the station, either as a person or for what I played. Number one, because I wasn't a full-time student. Everybody there was super smart—engineers and all that—and I was just some guy going to business school. I might have been the only one at that radio station at the time who was serious about having a career in radio, since everybody else saw it as a hobby. And they weren't too thrilled that I had a goofy name like Mel Toxic. Although other people had goofy names, they were trying to be hip, but I just tried to be goofy. When the word got out that [the radio format] *Rock of the '80s* was coming to town, I got my tape and brought it to the station. It's funny, but that's exactly what they were looking for... somebody to do a Top 40 delivery of modern rock with some kind of a character.

Michael Cabnet: The big thing in those days was promos, which are records and CDs distributed for free by the record label to promote an upcoming release. Because they weren't sealed, the store couldn't sell them for $9.99, but they were new records nonetheless, so you could sell them as new for $5.99 even with the promo stamp. The labels would make hundreds and hundreds of these, and the guys from the record companies would unload them for cash. Illegally. So, before there was illegal downloading, there were illegal promos, and you still want the promos sticker on it because it was like a badge of honor. I probably still have a Record Celler coffee cup in my kitchen, and it was my idea to put the "Not For Sale" promo label on it.

Steven DiLodovico: Promos! They were the best thing about college radio. Having that one snipped corner, or the hole-punch through the sleeve that marked a record as a promo... that was a badge of honor. It was like having a different version, almost like an import or a picture disc. I had many doubles in my collection: the ones I bought at the store and the promos I got from the station. Same record, same pressing, same songs, and no "real" value at all. But it meant something to have it.

Scott Lowe: Mickey and I used to hang out at a record store called Key Records in New Hope, PA and WTSR. DJ Karen Ray worked there on weekends. She and Randy had a fake on-air rivalry. She was good look-ing, but Randy always said she weighed 300 pounds, and she'd be like, "I don't weight *that* much!" Randy came to the record store one day to visit her, and we met him. We were already calling into his show on a regular basis, so one day we decided to take a ride there. We would go and be part of the audience or his entourage. When he was on the air it always sounded like a party, with lots of people clapping and yelling. For a college radio show at that time, it was really something.

Randy Now: My show had two halves. There was *Noise: The Show*, a title I stole from Tim Sommer at WNYC, and the other half was called *The Other Side*.

Jeff Feuerzeig: Randy had a great show. He thinks that Howard Stern stole his act. I think Randy's delusional, but he did have a great show. I was already a punk rocker, but at the station I was being exposed to all this other music, and hardcore just started around then. Early hardcore was really comedy mixed with speed and nihilism. There were a lot bands with really funny songs, and Randy played a lot of that. The Angry Samoans, Ism, The Dickies, even early Hüsker Dü… they were doing the Gilligan's Island theme song. People didn't take it that seriously. Black Flag's biggest song back then was *TV Party*. It was almost like "jokecore," and that really appealed to me.

Mel Toxic: On college radio, they would go deep into an album and play the most obscure cuts. They rarely played the big hits. Suddenly, in 1982, some of these bands started getting popular and making hits. But everybody still played these deep tracks, the stuff that people weren't familiar with. I decided I was going to play nothing but the hits. I'm going to play the Top 40 version of that stuff, because I thought that's what people want to hear. So I would put together my two-hour show where it was hit after hit, and then I would do a top-five countdown, kind of like Casey Kasem meets punk rock.

Jeff Feuerzeig: I started doing a radio comedy show—part comedy and punk rock like Randy—but I was the kid doing it. *The Jeff F Show: Radio of the Absurd*. It was based on *Theater of the Absurd*, which I assure you I didn't know much about.

Punk rock opened up a whole world to me. In my high school in Jersey, there were only about three of us who were into it. When I got to college, it didn't change; there weren't that many people. But at the radio station and City Gardens, everything seemed realistic.

Michael Cabnet: Indie record stores, the good ones, had connections in England who would buy the stuff when it came out there on Monday and ship it to them. That way, the store could have it on Friday before anybody else in America. This went on for a while, but imports disappeared a couple years later when American copyright holders realized, "Wait a second, you're buying a $15 import and not buying the $9 American version, which is the one I make actual money on!"

Amy Yates Wuelfing: It's strange when you think about it… people were smuggling records into the country like it was contraband, which it was. As a record store owner, you had to have all these underground methods for getting imports, because they legally weren't allowed in the U.S.

Michael Cabnet: I remember working at an indie store called Sound Odyssey and came up with the idea of Midnight Madness. I'm to blame. I stole it from college basketball, with its NCAA rules that say you can't practice before December 1st at 12:01 a.m. So, when a hot title went on sale, I would open the store at midnight to sell it. Can you imagine that now? This was the singular height of the record industry. It was Bon Jovi, ZZ Top, Phil Collins…things that sold tens of millions. It was just one 25-million seller after another. And now if you sell two million copies, you're considered huge.

Amy Yates Wuelfing: Around Christmas 1986, the Bruce Springsteen Live/1975–85 box set came out. We literally opened the doors that morning and had five or six employees standing at the door with cartons of product. We handed it to people as they walked in, and then they would go to the cash register. We couldn't hand them out fast enough.

Michael Cabnet: I drove to the warehouse three times that day, filled up my Chevy Cavalier with more boxes of it. I also bribed the UPS driver to make me the first delivery so we had it first thing, because people were lined up outside the mall. We were selling it before anyone else, and I think, other than the two Tower Records stores, my store sold the most. That was the record industry back then.

Mel Toxic: I always saw myself as a marketer. Kind of like Malcolm McClaren. He saw music as a product that could be sold and marketed, and you need people like that. He figured out Bow Wow Wow, he figured out Adam Ant, he figured out the Sex Pistols. Maybe, if it wasn't for Malcolm McClaren, a lot of that stuff wouldn't exist. You really need somebody to put it all together and package it the proper way.

My idea was to find the biggest hits of these artists, play them over and over again, make them familiar, make them popular, because I thought the stuff was going to be mainstream one day. Back then it wasn't mainstream. It was still considered alternative. They weren't using the term *alternative*, they were just calling it either punk rock or new wave.

Randy Now: I never in my wildest dreams thought that this type of music would go mainstream. I remember when Devo came out and we saw them on their first little tour, after they played *Saturday Night Live*. They were so weird. Who knew they would become so huge?

Mel Toxic: The format of *Rock of the '80s* was a very fast rotation of the biggest hits. To the best of my knowledge, we would play the most popular songs, the A-songs. Devo's *Whip It*, for example. We would play that literally every two and half hours. This guy from Los Angeles, Rick Carroll, knew you had to hammer these big songs over and over, because that gets people familiar with the station, because they've never heard of most of these songs. I learned a lot about programming and the concept of rotating the same things over and over.

i92 was truly one of the first radio stations to take the format called *Rock of the '80s* from K-ROC in Los Angeles, but in the end they couldn't make money with alternative. When they decided, after six months, to change the format, I was so desperate to work in radio that I begged the program director, "Let me stay on the air, let me stay on the air." He gave me overnights. There I was, Mel Toxic, a B-level local celebrity, on the air from something like 2 a.m. until 6 a.m., or some crappy time, and I'm playing R&B. I hated being on the radio playing music that was not something I thought was up and coming.

Jeff Feuerzeig: There was this horrible idea that every radio station around the world at a specific time would play "We Are the World." And every radio station was supposed to participate, so that for that moment you could spin the dial and hear the same song on every single station. This time was, coincidently, during my show. So Mickey Ween was with me, and we're like, "Tune in at noon, we're going to play 'We Are the World.' Don't miss it!" When noon came, we played the Dead Kennedys' "Kill the Poor," with Mickey and I singing along during the chorus, which we thought was hilarious. After the three minutes or so was over, the phone rang. It was a huge, famous DJ from a big station in Philly, calling us and chastising us and telling us we should go back on the air and apologize. He told us we were breaking all the ethical rules of being a broadcaster. I did not apologize, but I did tell the listeners that he called us. And then I was thrown off the air.

Mel Toxic: All of the sudden, a big Top 40 station, WPST, was looking for somebody and, boom, I did overnights from 12 midnight to 6 a.m. for almost two years. I had to drive all the way from Philly to Princeton every night. It was pretty brutal. But it was a great radio station, and it was a Top 40 station that was pretty hip for its music and the format. The station had a massive signal that could be heard in lower Manhattan, as far up as New York and as far down as south Philadelphia, so everybody could hear me, which was pretty cool. Around 1989, some of this modern rock stuff was starting to get big. They finally moved me out of overnights into prime time, around 1991. Jane's Addiction was getting big and Nirvana was starting to come around. This is when Scott Lowe, who was already a DJ at WPST, comes in and says, "Let's do a specialty show focused on all this new music."

Jeff Feuerzeig: When The Beastie Boys' *Cookie Puss* came out, I was going to NYC film school. I had made a short film called *Texas Road*, which ended up being shown at City Gardens before a Ben Vaughn show, since they were in it. One of the stars of the film was Adam Yauch from the Beastie Boys. We knew the Beastie Boys were going to explode... this was before *Licensed to Ill*. So Adam Yauch came out to Marlboro, New Jersey, froze his butt off, and acted in this movie for one day. And then he blew us off and never showed up again, and we had to reshoot all his footage.

It was a rockabilly film, and Adam was to play the lead character called Stain Cottrel. We might not have even developed the film; it was

16mm and would have cost a fortune. But you could make a student film and show it at City Gardens and actually have people watch it. It was a good experience for me, as it encouraged me to go on and make more films.

Steven DiLodovico: I was a pre-teen, college-radio-obsessed "caller." WKDU in Philly played some of the craziest punk and hardcore, but another station, in the small city of Chester, PA, was really my home base. WDNR at Widener University was a mighty five-watt station that could almost be heard by all of Delaware County. I found this insane metal show on Friday nights called *The Darkside* that was hosted by a guy named Dr. Death. He played the heaviest, fastest thrash metal around— early Exodus, Bathory, Sodom, Possessed, Venom, Slayer. My entire musical experience sprang from this tiny little station. Not only was I learning about bands that you could never hear on mainstream radio, I was also learning to branch out into other forms of extreme music. I was still in grade school when I accidently discovered this station. I called every night, several times a night. I got free records and started to hear about shows, but I was way too young to even think about going. I didn't even know what "shows" were. I had only ever heard of "concerts" before.

I was eventually befriended by Dr. Death and started hanging out in the studio. I had full access to their library, and it was a whole new world to me. While it was a cool novelty to be "on the air," I spent far more time in the record library, and it was in this library that I first saw what would become my personal Holy Grail: The Misfits *Walk Among Us*. It was also the first time I ever heard the name "City Gardens." The station managed to strike some kind of promo deal with Randy in which the station would get a certain amount of space on guest lists for shows. These were supposed to be given to listeners as prizes. Well, WDNR had about 17 listeners, and we were all friends, so every week we would just put our own names on these guest lists. That's how I got to City Gardens all the way from the suburbs of Philly. And we went to EVERY show, no matter how shitty the bands were.

Scott Lowe: In 1988, I got a job as a DJ at WPST, a Top 40 station out of Princeton. It was Top 40, but you could slip in a Morrissey record or two. I remember they played "Eardrum Buzz" by Wire. Mel Toxic moved over to PST, and I was really excited about him coming. He and I got together and came up with a show called *Post-Modern PST*. It started out as an hour, but it ended up being a four-hour show that lasted for two years. We played trendy stuff, the type of material that would appeal to a Top 40 audience, but we would slip in hardcore every once in a while. I thought of the show as a stepping stone for people who might like underground stuff. We got a lot of letters of support, but it's interesting how tastes change. We played "Hey Ladies" by the Beastie Boys and got a lot of negative feedback, like, "What's this rap stuff you're playing? What's this Beastie Boys garbage?!" Now Beastie Boys are a modern rock radio staple.

Mel Toxic: Scott was lobbying for something like this for a long time. So every Friday night for three hours, out of all the things I've done in radio, that might have been the best work. The best team, the best concept, the best activity, the best opportunity, everything. It was a great time for music, and we had a monopoly on that music, because nobody else was playing it. It was becoming well-produced mainstream, very poppy, and very hit oriented. The record labels were getting behind it, yet nobody else was playing it. Scott brought along his production and his encyclopedic knowledge of music, and he played the straight man while I played the goofy guy. And we got every rock star that came through, because they would always come in for interviews. If they played Philadelphia or anywhere in the mid-Atlantic, they stopped by PST. We'd get every CD, we'd get every interview, tickets, everything, great prizes to give away. Then we started doing nightclub events because everybody wanted to go out and drink and dance to that kind of music. And here we are out in Princeton, and we're doing jobs and gigs in Philadelphia and in South Jersey.

You can probably tell there's a theme going on here, because I'm real serious about marketing and promotion and trying to kick ass all the time. Sometimes I come head-to-head with somebody who says, "Listen, it's all about the music, let's focus on the music." And I'm like, "Yeah, the music's important, but if you don't package it and market it, then nobody knows about it." You've got to have a little bit of sizzle. You have the steak, but you have to have the sizzle too. Believe me, a lot of people in modern rock found that offensive. Of course, me being me,

I didn't give a shit. I got yelled at a lot because of the Mel Toxic name, which is basically just a marketing term. I never was Mel Toxic; it was a character or a brand. When you come up with a goofy-ass name and say, "Hey everybody, this is Mel Toxic and here's Jane's Addiction!" you get a 15-year-old kid saying, "Hey, that's cool!" They remember that name right away.

All those bands from the past that have legs… they're still being played on rock stations today, but they're no longer called "alternative." In the beginning, alternative radio stations positioned themselves as weird. Advertisers don't want to advertise on weird stations. They want to advertise to young adults 18-34. When you position yourself as the oddball station, it might come off as cool, but it kills the perception in the eyes of the media buyer. So I always thought, *play the music, but stop positioning yourself as the oddball station*, because the media buyer is going to say "Nah, I don't want to put any money toward that format because that format is all spikey-hair kids wearing black leather and chains." That's the perception, even though it was entirely wrong. "Oh, they don't have any money, either." Even so, if you market this stuff the right way, it becomes mainstream, and that's what happened.

Randy Now: Now? I see college radio as dead. College radio won't even exist in the future. It's like the 8-track: a dead medium. I listen to the big college stations around here, and I don't hear anything that is off-the-wall or new or unusual. They don't push the boundaries. At the station where I work, the kids have to play 80% of their show from a pre-designated rack of new stuff, and there are only about 20 CDs in that rack. Then they can play two older songs and maybe one or two things for themselves. It's a tight format on silly college radio. In the old days at WTSR, if I couldn't do my show, there were 50 people waiting to step in and do it for me. Now, if someone calls in sick, it's dead air because no one wants to be bothered. People listen now to Pandora, which picks for you. People let a computer algorithm pick music for them.

Mel Toxic: It's a funny thing about music clubs then and now. The East Side Club in Philadelphia and City Gardens were open seven days a week, whereas now you can't even find a nightclub that's open two or three times a week. So, clubs are sort of out of the picture.

Rich O'Brien (DJ/City Gardens employee): It was an adventure back then. I love it when I deejay now and people come up to me and say, "What's that?" I like introducing new music to people. Back then, going to a record store was a little hit or miss. You'd buy stuff because it looked interesting or it was a word-of-mouth title. When you found stuff you liked, it was more fulfilling. It kills me now when I hear people saying, "Oh, I deejay." And a lot of these people, they aren't really deejaying, they're just acting like a human jukebox. You're not a DJ; you're a guy with an iTunes account and a hard drive full of music. You're not discovering anything or introducing people to new music.

Michael Cabnet: Like everyone else in the music business, chain record stores decided they wanted respect and to go legit. All the stores in the Shulman chain fizzled because they over-expanded and decided to sell washers and dryers. Their slogan became "Trying to do it right for you." They arranged this big early-morning meeting that me and a co-worker crawled into, straight from an all-night drinking session. They announced this whole new management program. Bringing all these trainees in, they were going to open a bunch of new stores. Listen, you have to spend money to make money, but they ventured into an area where they had no expertise.

In 2013, the Princeton Record Exchange celebrated its 33rd anniversary.

Randy Now: The indie record stores that are left are the last front in creating any kind of local scene. If the people who work there do it right, they open things and play them in the store. The other day I was in my store [The Mancave, Bordentown, NJ] and I played Bill Black, and this guy goes crazy. He never heard it before and bought it right then and there. That happens a lot. Record stores introduce new music to people and—even more important—get them to buy the actual product. The whole CD or vinyl, not just one song from iTunes. When I did the Punk Rock Flea Market, I saw 12-year-old kids buying vinyl, and it really surprised me. There *is* a market for it. You need good, knowledgeable people to make it work, though. People who can direct customers to the best releases and make suggestions.

Michael Cabnet: Record stores? They're still relevant today. At least they are to me and a lot of other people.

Amy Yates Wuelfing: Third Street Jazz closed because the guy who founded the store—a bona fide music fan—sold it to a lawyer who thought it would be fun to own a record store. The guy didn't have a clue about music or much else. I think he thought it would be glamorous. He ended up firing me because I asked for a raise. He let the store become a shadow of its former self, ran it into the ground, and then it went out of business. If you don't love music, don't own a record store. Running a true indie record store is not for the faint of heart. The mark-up on product is very low, and so is the profit margin. You have to do it because you love it.

CHAPTER 5

1985–1986

1985

Top Ten Songs in 1985:

1. Careless Whisper, Wham!

2. Like a Virgin, Madonna

3. Wake Me Up Before You Go-Go, Wham!

4. I Want to Know What Love Is, Foreigner

5. I Feel for You, Chaka Khan

6. Out of Touch, Daryl Hall and John Oates

7. Everybody Wants to Rule the World, Tears For Fears

8. Money for Nothing, Dire Straits

9. Crazy for You, Madonna

10. Take On Me, A-Ha

City Gardens gained momentum as it entered the mid '80s, an era many consider to be the club's heyday. It was a perfect confluence of time and circumstance. The end of the '70s saw punk rock morph into a harder, faster art form and become the subgenre "hardcore." Many bands now considered legendary were hitting their creative prime, and City Garden played host to some incredible shows that, with the passing of time and the clarity of perspective, are spoken of in reverent tones.

While commercial radio and MTV largely ignored these genres, those who saw the shows and bought the records knew they were experiencing something extraordinary that comes along once in a lifetime. By 1985, the indie-music

movement was in full swing. Bands that had slogged through the beginning of the decade were now full-on touring machines relying on a tight network of club and 'zine support. These bands had honed their chops to a precision previously thought impossible for this type of music. Meanwhile, the newer generation—kids who had grown up on this DIY ethic—were starting to realize that they could also do these things, both for and by themselves. Every day new bands were springing up, and with them came indie labels, fanzines, and shows booked at any venue available. An already well-established net-work of support grew larger and stronger. And, as always, there were shows.

Minutemen/Sorry/Sic Kidz
(Two Shows: All Ages & 21+)—January 4, 1985

Ron Gregorio (Editor, *Hard Times* magazine): The Minutemen were a great band live. Lots of energy. [Frontman] D. Boon really kept your attention because he was just a great performer.

Amy Yates Wuelfing (author): They played two shows, one for all ages and then a bar show for 21 and up. The all-ages shows were in the early afternoon, and afterward the club would kick everyone out, set up all the equipment again, and then let in the bar crowd. The good thing was, if you loved that band, you could see them twice in one day if you were over 21 or had a fake ID. Ron and I were set to interview the Minutemen that day before the all-ages show, but when we got there, the road manager said that the band had gone "across the street." I had no idea what that meant since across the street was a housing project. He said, "No, they are in the grocery store." The Fine Fair grocery store looked abandoned. In fact, up until that day I thought it was.

Randy Now: It was a weird little place. We'd go over there and get fish and chips for, like, three dollars. It was probably the worst, greasiest stuff in the world, but it was good at the same time. We went in there all the time for random stuff like ketchup. When you're in a place long enough, you get used to the surroundings. Everybody used their parking lot, too. When the club first opened, I would go over there and clean up all the trash in their parking lot after shows.

Mike Watt (Minutemen bassist): We did chow there. Fuck, man… Like sub sandwiches and real big helpings of potato salad. D.'s favorite was macaroni salad. He loved that shit. When I first met him, when we were boys, he loved macaroni salad.

Amy Yates Wuelfing: We go over and, sure enough, D. Boon is standing at the deli counter with a big heaping helping of fried fish in each hand. The fish was in those red and white checkered, cardboard bowls that places usually use for French fries. I thought, "Wait, you're actually going to *eat* that?" But before I could ask, D. said, "I got all of this for $6! This place is awesome!" He carried it back to City Gardens, sat down in the dressing room, and ate it all. During the shows—we stayed for both—D. jumped up and down like crazy person, and me and Ron looked at each other like, *he's going to go through the stage.* You could see the floorboards bending beneath him.

Mike Watt: That stage wasn't the strongest. I remember one time, I think it was in Portland, he went right through the stage and kept playing. He put everything he had into a gig. In some ways, working with Iggy Pop reminds me of D. You play like it might be your last gig. D. Boone always went like that. I wasn't a born entertainer, and it was very scary for me. I got into music to be with my friends. But when you had a guy like D.

next to you, how could you be afraid? He was incredibly inspiring. Our teen years were in the '70s, and all we knew was arena rock. We didn't know about clubs until punk. He became the antithesis to all of the caricatured rock clichés we had lived through. Many times D. would be pulled off the stage by bouncers who thought he was just some guy trying to get up there. It happened to me a few times too, but it happened to him a lot.

I don't know what other people saw in punk, but for me it was this great, weird revenge against all the fucking poofery that we thought held us back from playing gigs. A lot of that was our own fault, but some of it was the culture of the '70s and why punk came about. Punk was the perfect thing for people like me and D. For us it was not a style of music, it was a way of getting to do gigs and write our own songs. Seeing these other cats go for it was infectious. That's why I call it a movement. It wasn't so hierarchal. We were all in it together, trying to find our own way to express ourselves, but still be influenced by each other. From bands in England that we never saw, to guys who were in the boat with you, like Black Flag, Meat Puppets, or Hüsker Dü... we never would have made *Double Nickels on the Dime* if Hüsker hadn't have done *Zen Arcade* about the same time. We all had different sounds. The worst thing we thought you could do was copy your brother, so it's hard to say how we were connected, but I know we were.

Amy Yates Wuelfing: I remember feeling bad because City Gardens was so huge. It was hard to make the place look full. And that day—both shows—it was empty.

Mike Watt: We felt, since we came from working people, you owed the audience something. These people work all week to get the money up to go to the gig, so you can't take them for granted. You gotta give them something. It's hard to define exactly, but they don't want to feel like they've been fucking pissed on, or used and abused. At the same time you want to challenge them and try to trip them out somehow. And, then there are the guys [in the band] who are coming to do this with you... you owe them too. I wouldn't put big value judgments on City Gardens. People called it a shithole. I used to hear a lot of bad things about the sound, the acoustics. A lot bands did great gigs there, but people start nitpicking. But as I see it, every gig you play is an "o" word—opportunity. Not the "b" word, which is "burden."

The Ben Vaughn Combo—April 20, 1985

Ben Vaughn: We headlined at City Gardens and did really, really well. We went out for dinner and came back, and there was a big, long line to get in. I was really happy about that. I went to the front of the line with my soundman, and he says to the door guy, "I'm with the band," and the guy goes, "Cool." So I say, "I'm with the band too." He looks at me and says, "No, you're not." And I'm like, "No, I am. Really." And he says, "No, you're not. The guy in front of you is, but you're definitely not." And I'm like, "No, I am! I am the band. The band's named after me!" He goes, "You don't even look like you're in a band." I'm like, "What does that mean? My jumpsuit's inside!" I had to show him my driver's license to prove who I was, which the sound guy thought was the funniest thing in the world.

Dead Kennedys/Butthole Surfers—April 28, 1985

Jello Biafra: People who take the underground and punk and indie rock scenes for granted today sometimes have no idea what it took to build those scenes. When punk started, it was a very visceral reaction against the sheer stupidity of the '70s. You know, we didn't want adult rock, soft rock, Eagles, *Hotel California*, let alone disco. Punk rock brought back the spirit of rock and roll in a way that shocked the people you wanted to make uncomfortable. It also meant a lot of hostility toward us being able to play anywhere. You know, cranky old bar owners who only wanted to listen to the Grateful Dead and hated the way we looked, and there would be sound men who didn't want anything to do with us because we were playing too loud. There was also the police, so cracking open a national circuit town by town took a lot of work and a lot of guts. I mean, Black Flag did more of that than anybody else to open up the national touring circuit. D.O.A. did a lot and Dead Kennedys were somewhere behind that. But you never knew what was going to happen.

It's amazing in the San Francisco Bay area how hostile older counter-culture people and ex-hippies were toward the punks. They shocked what they called "The Establishment," and we shocked them. Paul Kantner from the Jefferson Airplane went to punk shows, but almost nobody else from that generation would give us the time of day, and some, like Bill Graham, were actively hostile to other venues and other kinds of shows even existing. I guess part of the reason City Gardens survived was the lack of residences around the building. It was kind of a desolate industrial area with a beat-up old warehouse building that, if it wasn't going to be used for something positive like this, it wasn't going to get used at all. I don't know how much Randy was harassed by the powers that be in Trenton, but it couldn't have been that much or he wouldn't have been able to stay open that long. I don't recall there was ever fear that the police were going to storm the doors and start beating people up the way they did in Los Angeles and occasionally in San Francisco.

Ron Gregorio (Editor, *Hard Times* magazine): I interviewed Jello that night, and it got kind of hostile because I asked him a question he didn't like. He was going on about politics, and he was obviously far left, which was one of the reasons I liked his band. I asked him, "What are you doing? You have a lot of political sentiment, so what are you doing to push the movement forward?" He said, "Well, I'm a musician. That's what I do." And I remember saying something really stupid like, "You're out there preaching, so maybe you should be doing more than just playing in a band." It went downhill from there. It didn't get confrontational, but that ended up being first and last conversation I ever had with Jello Biafra, who was my hero at the time.

Carl Humenik (City Gardens security): I used to love the Dead Kennedys. I loved their music, and I loved what they used to say—the political stuff. But at one show, Jello comes over to me—I was working the front door—and said, "You just let that person come in with a camera!" I said, "Yeah, people come in with cameras." He said, "No! No cameras." I said, "Alright, why not?" And he goes off that people will sell that picture and he doesn't get any money out of the deal. I'm thinking, *he sings anti-capitalism songs and now he's saying he's not making money off a 13-year-old girl taking a picture of her idol?* And you know the picture is not going to be great, because it's one of those dollar-store cameras. But I'm like, "Okay, fine. Whatever." So then Jello walks around the club and finds a guy who sold records in the coat-check area, and Jello finds a Dead Kennedys album. He picks it up and snaps it in half. Grabs the next one, snaps it in half. I was like, "What the fuck are you doing?!" He said, "These are bootleg copies!" I said, "Yeah, but they're HIS!" He replied, "I'm not making any money off these bootleg copies." I said, "You're Jello Biafra; you're not supposed to worry about someone making a dollar off of you! If you're really worried about it, go after the person that he bought it from. Do you think he knew he was buying a bootleg copy?" And he's like, "I don't care. He's not selling this bootleg shit of my stuff. I'm not getting any money out of it." I said, "Fuck you!" From that point on I had no respect for him whatsoever.

Amy Yates Wuelfing: That was the night I inadvertently outed Randy to Jello. I let it slip that Randy was a mailman, and therefore a U.S. government employee. I think Jello was probably more taken aback by the fact that someone in punk rock had a real job, since no one else did.

Randy Now: Biafra didn't give me shit about being a mailman, but when he found out, he taunted me jokingly about it. It was also because I owned a brand new Thunderbird and picked him up in it. I told him I was a mailman, and that's how I could afford that car.

Bo Diddley with The Ben Vaughn Combo— May 10, 1985

Ben Vaughn: In addition to opening that night, we were Bo Diddley's back-up band. I had a song—it was one of our big numbers—called, "I'm Not Bo Diddley," and Tut loved that song. He thought it was the funniest thing ever. So, when he got the chance to book Bo Diddley, he put two and two together and BANG! He called me up and said, "Do you want to be Bo Diddley's back-up band? He needs one. You can be the opening act too." I found a guy to play piano, and we got to the club to rehearse with Bo Diddley during the soundcheck. Of course, he didn't show. So I ran down what I thought Bo Diddley was going to play with the band. I said, "I'll be Bo. And you're not allowed to play the Bo Diddley beat." Because I knew that was Bo's thing—you're not allowed to play the Bo Diddley beat—because he got ripped off. I had seen Bo Diddley a couple times before, and he actually argued with a drummer on stage, because the drummer really wanted to do the beat. So I rehearsed the band based on what I had seen Bo put back-up bands through. Bo never showed, and it was time for the club to open. We went on and played our opening set.

Joe Z. (City Gardens soundman): We're all wondering where Bo Diddley was and when he was going to show up. Out of nowhere, this canary yellow Dodge pulled up to the door—smoking, burning oil—and it's Bo and his keyboard player. Bo had his guitar with him, but the keyboard player had nothing.

Ben Vaughn: Bo came in and went up to the dressing room. He came in right as we were playing "I'm Not Bo Diddley." We finish up and Tut comes over and says, "Let's go up and meet Bo." We go up and Bo is totally holding court. He's sitting behind a table like a CEO about to conduct a board meeting. He says, "Sit down, boys." So we sat down, and he goes, "Which one of you is the singer?" And I said, "I am." He says, "Did you write that song that you were singing down there?" I said, "Yes sir, I did." And he goes, [suspiciously] "Ummmm humm." I have another song called "I'm Sorry, But So Is Brenda Lee." He goes, "Did you write that one about Brenda Lee too?" I said yes, and he said, "Did she hear it yet?" I said *no*, he goes, "Ummmm hummm." Deadpan. I couldn't tell what he was thinking.

Then he says, "Let's go." So, we go up onstage and immediately he goes off. He doesn't like the amplifier I brought for him. The place is packed, people are waiting for us to start, and he's complaining about the amplifier. He's like, "I'm not gonna play if I don't have four speakers in my amp." It was a great two speaker amp, but for some reason he wanted four speakers. He didn't care what kind of amp, so long as it had four speakers. I said, "Well, there is no other amp in the building." And he said, "Well, I'm not gonna go on then." I replied, "Alright. But maybe you should have brought your own amp if it was that important to you." And he got really mad at me. Really mad. He finally agreed to play under protest, but he was really mad. He wouldn't look at me for the whole set.

I saw Bo Diddley numerous times, but he really put on a great show that night. He dug in and did one of the best modern Bo Diddley sets I'd seen, since sometimes he could be a little lazy and goof off. But I think because he was so mad at me, he wanted to do a good job. Every time I started to play harmonica, he would wince at me and tell the soundman to take the harmonica out of the mix.

We had our picture taken with him after the set, and I'm all the way at the end because he didn't even want to know me. It was the ultimate Bo Diddley experience. When he was "on" as a performer, there was no one better than Bo Diddley.

Joe Z.: I was out in Santa Fe about a week after Bo played, and I was telling my friend who picked me up at the airport about Bo Diddley. No band, the whole amp fiasco… then, just as I'm wrapping up the story, we pull up to an intersection and I see the same canary yellow Dodge—still smoking—go through the intersection with Bo and his keyboard player.

Hüsker Dü @ New York South — May 11, 1985

New York South was another Jersey venue that Randy Now started booking in addition to City Gardens. It didn't last long.

Mark "Repo" Pesetsky (City Gardens employee): One of the first shows I went to was Hüsker Dü at North York South. I was wearing Guess? jeans. Oh man, those jeans were so fucking appalling. They cost $75 in 1985, and they had a triangle of leather right in the front over the crotch. So I'm standing there in these horrible jeans, and probably a "puffy" shirt, and my friend had a Billy Idol t-shirt on. We were such targets. He looked like Kip Winger, I'm "leather crotch," and this huge guy comes around—full on speed and power—and hits me right in the gut. I go down, I come back up, and go over to the girls I came with and told them what happened. And they're like, "Yeah. Look at you! Look at what you're wearing. You look totally gay!" I knew right then I was out of place. So the next time I went to a show, I made sure I dressed appropriately.

Randy Now: New York South was a kiddie club. They were doing disco stuff. It was just a big, empty space in Florence, New Jersey I rented to do all-ages punk shows.

Amy Yates Wuelfing: It was even more barren than City Gardens. It had cinderblock walls, a little stage, maybe two chairs, and that was it. Zero atmosphere.

Randy Now: The stage was only about a foot off the floor and there was a railing in front of it, the kind you would use for outside steps, and they had it *right* in front of the stage. Kids were always getting crushed up against it. They would be completely bent over. And the stage lights were *right there*, because the ceiling was so low. The lights were always hitting people in the head.

This place was on a main highway, and the New Jersey state troopers were always coming around. Here were these kids with purple hair and Mohawks. I told the owner of the club that we were getting hassled, and the guy says, "Give me $100 for the troopers and they'll leave you alone." I gave him $100 to give to the cops… and it was amazing. They never bothered us again. Meanwhile, kids were drinking in the parking lot, six packs all over the place. It was the times then. No way could you get away with that now.

Ricky Nelson with The Ben Vaughn Combo— May 12, 1985

Ben Vaughn: We opened for Ricky Nelson two days after we played with Bo Diddley. It was our "Rock N' Roll Legends Tour!" Tut went to the Trenton municipal airport to meet Ricky and the band, and Tut actually went onboard to have his picture taken on the plane. Six months later, that plane went down and Ricky Nelson and his entire band died. The word was that they bought the plane from Jerry Lee Lewis which… they should have known. God only knows what went on in that plane when Jerry Lee Lewis owned it.

At the end of Ricky's shows, the band would keep playing while he walked out the door into a waiting car to be whisked away. Like, "Elvis has left the building." It was really something else. When I heard Ricky Nelson died, the first person I called was Tut.

Loudness — May 26, 1985

Rich O'Brien (City Gardens bouncer): I started worked at City Gardens in May 1985. I called Randy's radio show and won a Hüsker Dü poster, which I had to go to the station to pick up. Randy and some other people were there, and they invited me out for pizza. Then he hired me to work as a roadie for the Japanese heavy metal band Loudness or, as they called themselves, "Roudness." As in, "We are Roudness, let's go flucking clazy!" They had an Australian road crew, and there was only one guy— he weighed 400 pounds—who could translate between the two of them. Every time the roadies wanted to know where to put a speaker, they had to go and talk to a guy who looked like Buddha. Buddha after several shots of Jack Daniels.

I got a few scars from working at City Gardens. Most times, everyone was relatively good as far as throwing people out, but it seemed to change when the "alternative" became mainstream. Before that, there was slam dancing, but people were well behaved and looked out for each other. When it became mainstream, like '87 or '88, when bands started to cross over, then these college idiots would be like, "Let's go mosh, man."

The whole scene at City Gardens was something I had to be a part of, and it wasn't just for the money I was being paid to work security. The money was nice, but it was more about being part of something bigger. I've never encountered that anywhere else in my career, and I've been working in bars and clubs for 28 years. It was the atmosphere and excitement of what could happen. In some unconscious way, you knew you were part of something cool. I never really knew it until later, but it was almost like being part of a brotherhood. I'll see someone from those days now, and we'll look at each other and go, "City Gardens!" and start talking like no time had passed. There is nothing like that City Gardens camaraderie.

I hated high school. I was the weird kid. I didn't like anybody, I was strange, I didn't have many friends, and I wasn't part of a clique.

But when I got introduced to City Gardens, I felt like it was a group of people just like me… people who didn't fit in with the Reagan-era youth. We didn't shop at Chess King, we didn't wear Z. Cavaricchis, and we didn't blow our hair out and listen to disco. We liked a lot of strange things. So even though we were all individuals, we became part of a collective weirdness.

You could do things at City Gardens that, if you did it anywhere else, you would be made fun of or picked on, or people would give you a look. The analogy I use is that at City Gardens, someone could go out to the dance floor and set himself on fire, and everyone would just look and go, "Hey, someone set himself on fire," and go back to their conversation. Nothing was wrong with you if you were weird. You always knew there was going to be somebody you could connect with. People shared your beliefs, and fashion and stuff like that didn't matter. People were accepted universally. I think that's why the club seems to have spawned a lot of creative people. It was a real breeding ground.

Lords of the New Church — June 5, 1985

Amy Yates Wuelfing: During the show, Stiv turned his back to the audience and took a pee on the drum riser. I wasn't quite sure I was seeing what I was seeing, but I was right up against the stage and there was no mistaking what was happening. The drummer seemed unfazed, which made me think that this was probably a common occurrence. After the show, I was set to interview Stiv for *Hard Times*. He politely answered my questions, but all he wanted to talk about was [the British TV show] *The Young Ones*. The show was already over in Britain, but MTV was going to start showing it in the U.S. and they were promoting it heavily. I would ask a question about the tour, he would give a short answer and then go back to the *The Young Ones*. He proceeded to tell me the plot, the characters, the actors, which episodes were his favorites, his favorite lines, and on and on. I hadn't seen the show yet, so this meant nothing to me. But now, having seen *The Young Ones*, I understand what he was so excited about.

D.O.A./Corrosion of Conformity/Dicks—June 30, 1985

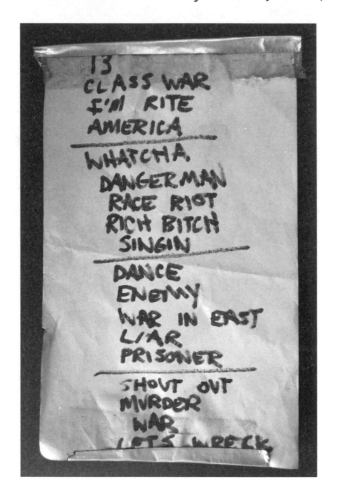

Beastie Boys—July 26, 1985

Mike Diamond (Beastie Boys): We recorded "She's On It" before opening for Madonna on her Virgin tour. It was one of two songs we would perform to the boos and shocked expressions of her audience every night. Thanks are due to her for keeping us on the tour. Because it was our first single on Def Jam as part of their new Columbia Records deal, we got to make a video. Shot on Long Beach, Long Island, it was directed by Rick Rubin's NYU roommate at the time, who was going through the film school. Basically, it was a low-budget, amateurish attempt at a David Lee Roth video, the only difference being that instead of getting hooked up, we got dissed. Aside from getting to spend the night at Rick's parent's house, and meeting his parents, the only high point came when this channel in the New York area called U68 started showing the video. U68 was somewhere between public access and MTV. They would show all kinds of crazy stuff from that time. That gave us a little bit of juice, enabling us to get booked at one of NJ's most infamous clubs, City Gardens. We drove through pouring rain in a rented milk truck, only to arrive at our gig to an audience of, like, five people, not including the members of Washington D.C.'s Junk Yard Band, who opened the show.

Henry Hose (City Gardens regular): We went to the show, and it was getting later and later and later, and the Beastie Boys didn't show up. Most of the people had left and Frank [a.k.a. Tut] was pissed that he had to give people their money back. He had to refund money and was furious. The band finally showed up well after midnight. It was just the three Beastie Boys and Rick Rubin, and I saw Randy having words with them. They grabbed a table from the back of the club and put it up on stage, set up two turntables, and they started doing the show.

Deirdre Humenik (City Gardens employee): They didn't show up until a half hour before closing time, then they jumped on stage and started busting and smashing record albums and throwing them into the crowd.

Gal Gaiser (City Gardens DJ): I was hanging out with [Regressive Aid guitar player] Billy Tucker that night and stood next to him for the whole thing. Rick Rubin was breaking records in half and throwing them into the audience like Frisbees, and he hit Billy Tucker square in the head. And Billy loved it! He thought that it was the best thing that ever happened to him.

Henry Hose: I saw someone—I won't say who—go over to the bar, grab something from behind the bar, and then bolt out the door.

Deirdre Humenik: The crowd chased them off the stage and they jumped into their Mustang convertible and took off. People were booing them and were pissed, and there was a fair amount of people there. People came out and slashed their tires, and they drove away on flat tires.

Henry Hose: They did their show, which I thought was great, and everybody started leaving. This was probably around two in the morning. As I was pulling out the driveway and saw that the Beastie Boys had flat tires on their box truck. "Someone" took an ice pick and picked their tires because they were pissed off about having to give everyone their money back. So they had flat tires, it's two in the morning, and they were stuck in Trenton.

Gal Gaiser: On my radio show the next Monday, Billy Tucker came down and talked about the show. The Beastie Boys only played for about 15 minutes, but I clearly remember Billy saying, "That was the best 15 minutes of music ever."

Beastie Boy "MCA" Adam Yauch died of cancer on May 4, 2012. He was 47 years old.

Descendents/Fright Wig—August 4, 1985

Milo Aukerman (Descendents vocalist): City Gardens was a very distinctive club, and we always looked forward to playing there. If nothing else, any tour we were on, we could always count on having a show there. Places like Philly, every time we would roll through there would be some new club. It would be something pulled together for a short time, and then a month later the club would be gone. There was never like a stable venue in that area except for City Gardens. Even in New York we would play a whole bunch of different places, but City Gardens was always there. I guess that's why people remember it so fondly.

'85 was the first tour we had ever done in the U.S., and it was pretty dicey, in terms of booking shows and keeping cancellations from happening. [Drummer] Bill Stevenson was doing the booking, and he had learned the ropes from Black Flag. Black Flag set the standard for where you would play, what cities were cool, who the booking agents were, what clubs you would be able to play, and so on. We would go out, probably for two months, and try to hit the whole U.S. We were always guaranteed a good booking at City Gardens from Randy. We would tour, go back home and try to regain our sanity, and then we'd go back out.

We were in a tiny little van, doing all the driving ourselves, and usually sleeping on top of all of the amps that were stacked up in the back of the van. We had this platform that we built above the amps that we called "the stack," and that was where we all slept. It was about a foot below the ceiling of the van. You kind of wriggled back into that and tried to get some sleep. I'm kind of a light sleeper, and I would be back in the van, thinking, "I really need to sleep, but I can't sleep because I'm waiting for this van to flip over." You figure if that van flipped over, you're on the bottom, and what's on top of you is several hundred pounds of equipment, which is kind of scary. I would try not to think about it. Between that and the fact that there was no air conditioning. We had one of these old vans with AC in the front, but that AC was not filtering to the back. I would open up the side window to get some air, but that just happened to be right next to the exhaust. So it was this trade-off, like, "I'm dying back here, I need some air," and then you open the window and go, "Okay, now I'm going to die for a different reason. I'm going to die from carbon monoxide poisoning." It was always fun to make that decision: I need some air, but I may die of carbon monoxide poisoning. *I'm just going to take that chance.*

We had another van with a vent on top, and that was better because it wasn't near the exhaust, so you could get some air through that. However, we sheared off that vent when we drove through the Chicago airport one year. We had to duct-tape the hole, and it became a non-functional vent. Those first vans were crazy, little death traps that, luckily, we never died in.

The Replacements/The Rettmans—August 17, 1985

Joe Z. (City Gardens soundman): Randy had this band The Rettmans, and they opened the show. I was in charge of watching the dressing room so nobody went up the stairs and bothered The Replacements. Before The Rettmans played, Randy said, "We're going to do something interesting tonight: we're going to play nothing but Replacements songs." I thought, *well, that's going to be interesting.* The Rettmans go up and play a Replacements song… and then another one. [Replacements frontman] Paul Westerberg comes down from the dressing room, walking real slow, scratching his head, looking at me. He peeked around the stairs and saw them playing, then goes back up. The Rettmans play a few more Replacements songs and then Paul comes down again, but now he's all pissed off. He said to me, "What are those guys doing?" I said, "I don't know; they're playing Replacements songs." He looked at me and said, "What the fuck am I supposed to play?!"

Ken Hinchey (City Gardens regular): Bob [Stinson, Replacements guitarist] was onstage wearing a housecoat, and when he bent over you could see everything hanging and dangling.

Randy Now: He used to wear a diaper a lot too, although he never did that at City Gardens. When they played down south they would wear make-up, just to piss people off.

Ken Hinchey: During the "drunk shows," they would take requests and everyone would yell out songs. Paul Westerberg would yell out, "Give me a band that starts with a k!" Someone would yell, "The Knack!" and they'd play "My Sharona." Most people yelled for Replacements songs or classic rock, but one time I yelled out "Ghostbusters!" Paul looked over at me and chuckled.

Meatmen/76% Uncertain/Detox — September 8, 1985

Rich O'Brien (City Gardens employee): Tesco [Vee, Meatmen vocalist] was talking about the upcoming Slayer show and said, "We're going to do some of our favorite Slayer songs tonight. This one's called "My Uncle Floyd is Satan." But, no really, they're really good. We don't want to piss off our friend Randy, so come out and see them!"

Randy Now: I booked a couple of Meatmen tours trying to get them into markets they hadn't hit before. There was a promoter in Detroit, and the Meatmen either didn't get their guarantee or they drew enough that they should have got some bonus, and the promoter wouldn't give it to them. The band's arguing with the guy, and the guy pulled a gun on [Meatmen guitarist] Lyle Preslar. Lyle calls me at 4 a.m. to complain. What am *I* gonna do about it?

Once we did a small tour in my van, and the van was filthy. Tesco took his finger and wrote "Poop For Sale" in the dirt on the side of my van, and it was there for the entire tour. All we needed was for a cop to stop us, with a bunch of guys in a van, a U-Haul trailer, and "Poop For Sale" on the side.

Tesco is tall—like six foot, seven inches—and he would hide a whoopee cushion under a long coat. We were walking around the hip, trendy part of Providence one time, and whenever he went in a store or a restaurant he'd squeeze the cushion to make this horrible fart noise. Then he'd look around and go, "Pardon me."

On an episode of Pee Wee's Playhouse, there's a segment where Cowboy Curtis is teaching the kids how to pogo, and you see one kid with spiky hair in the background. You can't see it real clear, but he's wearing a "We're the Meatmen and You Suck" t-shirt.

Violent Femmes — September 13, 1985

Ben Vaughn (Ben Vaughn Combo): Going to City Gardens was great for a lot of reasons, but my friendship with [owners] Tut and Patti was a big part of it. Tut got the word out that we were worth seeing.

We couldn't get booked in Philly to save ourselves. We would play on street corners, but the Violent Femmes' manager starting managing us in 1985, and we began opening for them on every New York City gig. By then we were getting booked everywhere *except* Philadelphia. It was really strange. It took a New York booking agent to get us into clubs in the very city where we lived.

Philadelphia is a strange place. I love it, but there is this adversarial and territorial attitude. I have no idea why we couldn't get booked. We had an accordion and an upright bass, so maybe people just weren't ready for us. We would play places like [New York club] Danceteria, opening for crazy punk and industrial bands, and people loved us, but Philly wasn't ready. In Philly, you had blues bars, punk clubs, and new wave dance clubs, and we didn't fit into any of that. Bookers would hear our tape and be like, "What are we supposed to do with this? Why don't you play the Philadelphia Folk Festival?" They just didn't understand that it could work.

I played trombone a little bit, and when the guys in the Violent Femmes found out, they insisted I be in their horn section, "The Horns of Dilemma." When we would finish our set, I would hang around in the wings with my trombone and then they would bring me up. I could hardly play and I barely knew where the notes were. I could play in two keys, F and A, I think. But they thought I was great. They liked the chaos of it.

Gordon Gano (Violent Femmes guitar/vocals): The Horns of Dilemma was a band idea, but I loved it and fully endorsed it. Certain songs were good for improvisation, and we would invite different people on stage, particularly horn players. It was free improvisation, so it wasn't necessary for the people playing to know the song. The idea was to have people who could play really well, and they would add textures and colors into the cacophony. Basically, if someone is a musician, they can make some kind of sound with an instrument, even if they haven't been trained on it. A lot of people played in band in high school and then never picked that instrument again, so this was the chance to play the instrument again. Ornette Coleman and Sun Ra were big influences on the Violent Femmes, so we were drawing on that. The response was always great. A lot of people in the audience had never heard anything like it. Those are still my favorite parts of the show, when we use improvisation. We sort of had it somewhat planned when it would happen, but it could actually happen at any time in any song.

Ben Vaughn: Opening for the Violent Femmes was an interesting gig. Musically it made a lot of sense, but their audience was there to sing along to "Add It Up." That's why they were there, and the Ben Vaughn Combo was delaying the audience's performance. And I know the Femmes had trouble with it too, because the crowd would be restless during other songs, and then go nuts during "Add It Up". But it was really bad for us, the sacrificial opening act. Once that song caught on, and the Femmes caught on, anyone opening for them was in trouble. It always felt like we were getting ready to go into a gladiator arena. It was work.

Gal Gaiser (City Gardens DJ): A lot of bands hated walking through the crowd to get to the stage from the dressing room, especially when it was packed. Well, this show was packed to the rafters, and the Violent Femmes not only walked through the crowd, they did it playing their instruments and singing. People heard a commotion at the back of the club and it was them coming through the crowd, parting it like the Red Sea, playing a song.

Anthony Pelluso (City Gardens bartender): Gordon Gano was an unbelievably nice guy. They always hung out at the bar afterwards and talked to everyone. We loved the Violent Femmes so much, and he was just this regular, skinny guy.

Gordon Gano: I never get tired of playing the songs people want to hear. That joy and response, that interaction with them singing along, and that feeling from the audience is part of the live experience.

Neighbors & Allies — September 14, 1985

Jim Nevius (Neighbors & Allies): We reformed again in 1985. Our other bands had fizzled, so Tim and I got together and said, "Let's do this again." We had Ian MacDonald from Foreigner working with us. It was coming together, but all of our songs sounded like Foreigner. We started getting gigs and climbing back up the ladder. We weren't as raw and edgy, but the songs were better and more rehearsed. We got signed to a development deal at Island Records. I was in another band called World At A Glance, and I had to choose which project I wanted to do. I chose Neighbors & Allies, and then World At A Glance got the deal we should have gotten at Island. Our A&R guy passed away, and everyone sort of lost interest. That was the end of the road for us.

Slayer/Megadeth — September 29, 1985

Deirdre Humenik (City Gardens employee): I didn't want to work the show. I was nervous about the band and the crowd, but they turned out to be the nicest people, and the crowd was the nicest. When I would walk through the crowd carrying stuff, they would clear the way for me, telling people to let me through, getting the door for me. I remember telling Randy that the metal bands who were supposed to be the bad-asses were the nicest ones to work with.

S.O.D.—October 6, 1985

Randy Now: S.O.D. only played about six shows, and this show was before they got really big. We were the only club that had them twice. I was friendly with Scott Ian because he was a fan of Suicidal Tendencies, and I had worked with them. They would come out and open with "Diamonds and Rust," which was two-seconds long, and then go, "Good night everybody!" and walk offstage. The rest of the show was the encore.

Nick Lowe—October 25, 1985

Michael Cabnet (City Gardens regular): Nick Lowe had played City Gardens once before. That time, I was in the men's room taking care of business, and at the urinal next to me was Nick Lowe. I really loved Nick, but I said something like, "Hey…" So the next time Nick Lowe played City Gardens, sure enough, I'm in the men's room, and here comes Nick in the stall next to me. He looks at me and I look at him, and we both start cracking up because we realize that this was a very sad déjà vu moment. But the fact that he remembered me… He was just a cool guy. At that time, the tours weren't sponsored by any corporation. You didn't have "Clear Channel presents…" and "Bud Light presents…" It was a whole different vibe seeing bands live. I still would rather see a live band than anything else, that hasn't changed. To me, that's the test of a great band.

Samhain—October 27, 1985

Eerie Von (Samhain bassist): I don't remember how many people were there. It was a good-sized room, all black, which I thought was cool. We did our regular killer show. The Samhain shows were always cool, and there was always the stage diving and stuff like that. Since we all lived in Jersey, it was easy to get down to City Gardens. It was a good room, it always sounded good, the people were always happy to see us. It was a good place to play and a good place to see a band.

Amy Yates Wuelfing: Knowing how rabid Glenn Danzig fans were, and knowing the crowds he got in New York, I expected this show to be huge. I was shocked at how few people were there. And the few who did turn up weren't very enthusiastic. I actually felt bad for the band that night.

Eerie Von: Glenn [Danzig] used to book all the Misfits and Samhain shows himself. They were usually booked with a small promoter who was typically a friend or a fan, or just some kid who was booking shows so he could get his favorite bands to come through town. It was very informal, like, "Okay, we're playing here. Do you know anyone in the next town over or the next state? Do you have any numbers for any other promoters?' And the promoter would tell you, "Oh yeah, just call this guy. He puts on shows." You would call the next guy and you would try to set up the whole tour like that. That's basically the way it was done. We'd bring t-shirt screens with us [to print shirts] because we knew we'd run out of shirts. There were times when Samhain would have people give us their leather jackets and let us screen print the back. That started with The Misfits. When we'd have a day off, we would buy a bunch of t-shirts, print them right there, and bring them to the next show. We didn't have a merchandizing company. We did it all ourselves.

Gene Loves Jezebel—October 31, 1985 (Halloween)

Deirdre Humenik: It was Halloween, and there were girls and girls and girls, just crying their eyes out. I have never seen anything like it. Of all the bands that played City Gardens, this band had the most girls with the screaming mimis. Screaming, crying, begging, and pleading. It was shocking. I had a girl with a huge Mohawk and cockroaches tattooed on both sides of her head, crying, "Please let me up to their dressing room!"

Dead Kennedys—November 10, 1985

Randy Now: As he was going onstage, Jello Biafra turned to me and said, "Hold my wallet and glasses." And I'm like, "Why?" And Jello says, "You'll see."

Jello Biafra: I couldn't very well tell people not to stage dive, because I liked to stage dive, and I'll do it in the middle of a song to this day. But sometimes the same people would jump off again and again and again and again. It didn't matter if they broke the guitarist's equipment. They were not there for the music, let alone the message. They were there to jump off the stage again and again, and that was as far as it went. I mean, in some cases on the West Coast, people were jumping off with the expressed purpose of picking a target, punching him in the back of the head, and running off like a chicken shit. Or ten people jumped one in the crowd. I thought, wait a minute, these guys are acting like a bunch of Nazis. We love this music and we love hardcore, but we don't want to play for this. People were coming up to me in San Francisco saying, "Are you down with this kind of stuff?" I thought it might be a good time to say something, so I wrote "Nazi Punks Fuck Off." It wasn't aimed at any organized ideological Nazis as much as what I thought was the goonish Nazi behavior. But, of course once the song came out, then real ones came out too, and you never knew what was going to happen at any of our shows.

Keene Hepburn (City Gardens soundman): There was always a palpable fear at Dead Kennedys shows. It was always so packed and so hot. You never knew what was going to happen. Jello seemed to have control of the crowd. He would let them out a bit, then reel them back in. He was good at that, and that energy was always there.

One time, I tried to take a cable from the DJ booth to behind the stage during the show. The place was packed, I'm working my way to the front, and I feel someone shove me into the mosh pit. Every time I tried to get out, this group of skinheads would push me back in, and I'm getting elbows thrown at me. Being in a mosh pit when you don't want to be isn't fun. I'm a normal looking guy, and I probably didn't have the right t-shirt on, and these skinheads would not let me out. A bouncer saw what was happening and yanked me out. Until that, I was thinking I was going to get a Doc Marten in the face, or I was going to have to punch my way out.

Randy Now: That was the only band that I had to pay for their hotel rooms, and I had to buy four hotel rooms because they hated each other so much they wouldn't share.

Jello Biafra: There were organized, white-supremacist skinheads who wanted to beat the living crap out of people. We had to diffuse that from time to time, but that never happened at City Gardens, as far as I know.

Neal Dallmer (City Gardens regular): I remember sitting in the back bar with [Dead Kennedy members] East Bay Ray and Klaus Fluoride. A friend of mine asks the band, out of the blue, "What's a 'pole pot?'" I put my head down. I couldn't believe it. I tried to interject with an answer so that he didn't look too stupid. But the band was actually very nice about it and explained who Pol Pot was, a dictator who ruled Cambodia, killed a lot of people, and so on. It was embarrassing, though.

Motörhead — November 24, 1985
(cancelled day of show)

Randy Now: This show was on a Friday, and that Friday I quit the post office after eight years to go on tour with Suicidal Tendencies. It was a huge gamble to quit a guaranteed government job with benefits. The very first show I did after I quit was Motörhead, and they fucking cancelled the day of the show. They didn't like the sound system. We brought in the biggest sound system possible, but they really just wanted to go to Los Angeles. They brought up every excuse in the book.

When they booked the show, they asked me to put them up at the cheapest and closest place I could. Normally a band as big as Motörhead would be put up at the Red Roof Inn, which was about five miles away. I mean, the club was in the ghetto! There aren't any nice hotels! But they wanted the cheapest place, so I put them in the Trent Motel, which was $25 a night. I guess they got there, saw roaches and all the welfare people living there, and freaked out. I'm losing it... I just fucking quit the post office for this?! What the hell is the matter with me? I got a speaker with a microphone, put it outside on top of Suicidal Tendencies' Winnebago, and told everyone who showed up that the show was cancelled.

Rich O'Brien (City Gardens bouncer): I remember Randy standing on top of the Winnebago telling people they could come in and see Fates Warning play if they wanted to, but if they had anything they wanted to say to Motörhead directly, go to the other side of the building where the road crew was loading the band's stuff.

Randy Now: Before I made the announcement, Motörhead was in a car at the back of the building. I went back and talked to them, just me and the band in the car. I said, "We got a thousand people here who want to see you play." And Lemmy—I couldn't even understand most of what he said—was bent out of shape about the cheap motel. I said, "Hey, your manager said to put you at the cheapest and closest place!" And then he's like, "Your sound system sucks." I told him that his soundman is the one who agreed to this system. But they still refused to play.

Rich O'Brien (City Gardens employee): I remember standing outside the door while Randy was getting yelled at by the road manager, and the word that kept coming up was "inadequate." Like, "The food is inadequate, the sound is inadequate, the accommodations are inadequate." Everything was inadequate.

Deirdre Humenik (City Gardens employee): Bands were never the problem. It was the managers of the bands that were the problem. A case in point was Motörhead, which was one of my worst shows ever. The show didn't actually happen onstage, but it sure happened in my world. I had to cook for 25 or so people. I made a huge spread, and they ate every scrap of food. There was not a morsel left, not a noodle in the pasta salad, not a carrot, nothing. Everything was gone. So the manager goes upstairs to the dressing room to eat, and the food was all gone and he flips out on me, screaming, "You call this fucking food?! You call this food?! We asked for food!!" Typical manager. Screamed at me in front of a lot of people, but by the end of the night he apologized. He told me the band, including Lemmy, said the food was wonderful. But I had attitude, like, "You find all the people who were there when you yelled at me and apologize to me in front of them."

Randy Now: After the band refused to play, I'm out there with the microphone going, "How's everyone out there doing?" and everyone's yelling and shit. I say, "Well, the doors were supposed to open at 8 o'clock, but Motörhead has decided to cancel because they aren't happy with the room, the sound, and the hotel. They're around the corner if you want to go talk to them, but it's out of my hands." And then I tried to sell them on all coming to the Anthrax show the next week. People wanted their money back, and we didn't have that much money on hand! We had to scrape the bottom of the barrel to refund everyone's ticket.

Deirdre Humenik: I think I was the one who had to go and tell people that the show was cancelled. Some people say they were the one, Randy says he was the one. But I remember having to answer to a lot of angry, angry people who had waited so long to see Motörhead.

On December 22, 1985, D. Boon from the Minutemen was killed in a van accident in Arizona. Because he had been sick with a fever, D. Boon was lying down in the rear of the van without a seatbelt when the van ran off the road. He was thrown out the back door of the van and died instantly. He was 27 years old.

1986

Top Ten Songs in 1986:

1. That's What Friends Are For,
Dionne Warwick, Elton John, and Gladys Knight
2. Say You, Say Me, Lionel Richie
3. I Miss You, Klymaxx
4. On My Own, Patti Labelle and Michael McDonald
5. Broken Wings, Mr. Mister
6. How Will I Know, Whitney Houston
7. Party All the Time, Eddie Murphy
8. Burning Heart, Survivor
9. Kyrie, Mr. Mister
10. Addicted to Love, Robert Palmer

Though City Gardens wasn't in the best part of town, it is important to remember that neither Philadelphia nor New York City were the tourist-friendly destinations they are now. Both cities were in the throes of economic depression and not appreciably "safer" than Trenton.

Jeff Terranova (tri-state punk club aficionado): At that stage of our lives, it was all about music. Going to school all week sucked, and all you looked forward to was Friday, Saturday, and Sunday. If you could go to three shows that weekend, that was the best weekend ever. And if you had to drive three hours to City Gardens or two hours to Albany, New York, or 45 minutes to [punk club] Anthrax in Norwalk, CT, that's what you did. Or you hopped on the train to New York to see a show at The Ritz or at CBGB, it was just that youthful energy and that excitement of being a part of something.

Amy Yates Wuelfing: New York City shows were awful. I saw Social Distortion at the Ritz in New York in 1986, and the whole experience sucked. The band didn't go until almost 2 a.m., they charged $5 for water, and the place was disgusting. If City Gardens was bad, this was ten times worse. While the show was great, we missed the last train out of Penn Station, which meant hanging out and getting hassled by the police until the first train of the day, which was around 6 a.m. I got off the train in Trenton and went right to work, wearing the same clothes I wore the night before. The person I went to the show with fell asleep behind the wheel when driving home from the train station that morning and totaled her car.

Jeff Terranova: '85 to '89 was a rough time everywhere, especially in New York City. Walking to CBGB was dangerous. New York at that time was dirty, and rough and tough, and walking through Thompson's Square Park or Washington Square Park was scary. Going to Times Square was scary. Inside CBGB I felt safe. Yeah, there were bigger dudes with boots and braces dancing, and the vibe in the club might have been a little more... I don't want to say violent, because I don't think it was violent, but maybe more aggressive. They were aggressive hardcore shows with a bunch of shirtless skinheads, who may or may not have slept on the street the night before, because a lot of these dudes in NYC were the real deal. They weren't suburban white kids like we were used to. The vibe in City Gardens was definitely different in the same way the vibe at the Anthrax was different.

We would walk through Washington Square Park and, I'm not exaggerating, from one corner to the other, every 15 steps it was, "Yo, yo, smoke, smoke, yo, yo, what you need, what you need, we'll hook you up, we'll hook you up." That's, like, eight people trying to sell me shit or putting shit in my pocket when I'm just walking down the sidewalk. That never happened to me in City Gardens parking lot or inside the venue. At the Ritz in NYC there would be people passed out in the balcony, you'd smell weed all over the venue. People were throwing up in the back corner, and it's like, *what the hell's going on?* People would carry their passed-out friends down the stairs after the show.

One other difference about City Gardens was that Randy seemed older than a lot of the promoters. A lot of times when we were booking our band it would be another hardcore kid. Randy obviously wasn't a hardcore kid.

Residents/Snakefinger—January 12, 1986

Rich O'Brien: Every photo of The Residents showed them wearing eyeball masks to hide their identities. They got one of their eyeball heads stolen at the beginning of the tour, so they started using a giant skull head as a replacement. Onstage it was three eyeballs and a skull. You could tell from the silhouettes of the costumes that two of the Residents were female, which surprised a lot of people.

Randy Now: That was the 13th Anniversary show, and Snakefinger was part of the band. That was a big coup for me as a promoter. I had to work every connection to get them. But I can tell you that there are really only two Residents. The two other people in the band are just sidemen. I insisted on this show being all ages instead of 21 and over, and in retrospect, I should have done 21 and over, because the crowd was 31 and over. Meanwhile, I'm thinking 18-year-olds want to come to this. So we had no alcohol, and everyone was pissed off.

Craig Surgent (Autistic Behavior bassist): I was able to touch one of the eyeballs! I was able to shake Snakefinger's hand. That was a big thrill for me.

Scott Lowe (City Gardens regular): One of the cool things about the club was that everyone was accessible. I met so many of my heroes. Mickey [Ween] and I are sitting at the bar chatting with these guys for a half an hour, and then we looked to the backstage area and we see the guys we were just talking to getting into their Residents costumes.

Joe Jackson—January 18, 1986

Jon Stewart (City Gardens bartender/TV personality): Joe Jackson was my first night as an actual City Gardens bartender. I loved it. I wasn't big on going out, but I loved to watch shows as a bartender more than I did as a spectator. It gave me something to do when I was watching it, instead of standing there with my hands in my pockets pretending I had friends there.

Randy Now: I don't remember Jon Stewart at all. He was pretty quiet I guess.

Anthony Pelluso: When Jon worked there, he was basically the same person you see now on TV—always cracking wise. He was not quiet at all. No way. He was a lot of fun to be around.

Jon Stewart: Deirdre was the hot chick all the guys were in love with.

Deirdre Humenik (City Gardens employee): I had a huge crush on Jon and still get teased about it. He was sarcastic, funny, cynical… he always made me laugh.

Jon Stewart: Did I learn any life lessons from bartending? It's not that important to clean the bathroom. Nobody's paying attention. People will mark up any wall space you give them. And when the band needs beer, the band needs beer.

Milo Aukerman (Descendents, vocalist): The nice thing is that City Gardens was host to a lot of mainstream artists or mainstream musicians as well. I remember having a day off and being in the environs, realizing, "Oh, well there's probably something going on at City Gardens." Sure enough, Joe Jackson was playing, and I said, "Okay, we'll go see Joe Jackson." It wasn't our style of music, but it was a chance to go and be in the audience at City Gardens and see the stage from a different perspective. They were bringing in a lot of national and international acts. That allowed me to reflect on our band's success and say, "We can fill City Gardens. That's pretty cool." I always felt good about that.

Descendents/Dead Milkmen — January 26, 1986

Milo Aukerman (Descendents, vocalist): When we first started playing, the crowds were tiny. It grew, but when I say that, it grew incrementally. By the time we took our long '87 hiatus, we were playing to 500 people, which is still a lot better than playing to 50 or 10. The biggest crowds were in major cities, so in '87 maybe we could hit 500 in New York. But when you're in the middle of the country, you're playing to the same 30 kids, so it took a while for punk rock to permeate. People look back at those early years, and I look back at them, and I feel like they were great salad days. For me it was a magical time, but not because we were the best thing since sliced bread or the most popular band. We weren't very popular, but I enjoyed it, and it didn't matter to me the size of the crowds we were playing to. If we could get people thinking and rock someone's heart, that was the main thing. But there is this perception that we were huge back then, and we definitely weren't. It was pre-Green Day, so mall punk didn't exist. The people showing up at shows may have only been 30 people, but they were really committed. They were really hardcore, die-hard kids. And a place like City Gardens, where you could get a few hundred kids to show up, those were the die-hard kids. It had its positives and negatives. The positives being we felt like these kids were committed and they weren't just going to a "punk rock show." They were coming to see *us*.

We had this great show in Lincoln, Nebraska, which I wrote "Hürtin' Crüe" about. We get there, no one's there, the doors open, and still no one's there. We come to the realization that the opening band, a heavy metal cover band, is going on stage and the room is empty. We decide that we'll be their audience. We watched them play and cheered them on, and we keep thinking maybe people will show up, but no one ever showed up. When we go on, the heavy metal band was our audience. That was the way things worked. It was very sweet because we were supporting each other's loser-dom. Of course, they yelled out for "Free Bird" during our set. True story.

Replacements/Ben Vaughn Combo—February 2, 1986

Ben Vaughn: It was an all-ages show on a Sunday, which meant it started early and there was no booze. I think all the booze had to be locked up. It was snowing and freezing cold outside, and everything was covered in ice. The Replacements showed up, and when they found out there was no booze... I never saw people look more scared than those guys. They were absolutely frightened that they were going to have to play a gig with no booze. They were like, "Where's the nearest bar?" I said, "There's one really bad one down the street." They walked down there, down Calhoun Street through Trenton. They didn't even have jackets on. They're like, "We're going," and they left. Someone comes up to me and says, "Did you let those guys go?!" and I'm like, "I'm not their road manager." The person was all panicked, saying "They might not come back!" I said, "That's not my problem! But I think I know where they are." They made it back and were appropriately disheveled, and they started off with Paul Westerberg on drums, which is not a good idea. He stayed on drums for the first half hour of the set, and I remember thinking, "Man, these guys suck." And then we opened for them a couple nights later someplace else and they were phenomenal! The greatest thing I'd ever seen.

Randy Now: This was after *Tim*, their first release on a major label. All the shows prior had dismal turnouts, but this was the first that was well attended. And, of course, this is the last show they played for City Gardens because they got too big. This was the first show I charged $10 for. I got such shit from people who thought they sucked. Paul Westerberg was in the back bar after the show begging for a free hot dog—probably from Jon Stewart—and people are yelling at me for their money back.

Jackie Zahn (radio DJ): I went to the show with another DJ, Bill Rude, and we were Replacements fanatics. Before the show, we somehow we ended up talking to [Replacements guitarist] Bob Stinson, and the three of us decided to go look for a bar or someplace to get a six-pack. So the three of us walked around the neighborhood and talked. There was a shopping cart involved at one point… was Bob in it? I don't know, but I do know that we walked around the neighborhood and that we were outside, drinking.

Rich O'Brien: This show was before we had the 21-and-up lounge in the back. If you put on an all-ages show you couldn't have alcohol. It was an all-or-nothing thing. So, this was a no-alcohol show, and even the band couldn't drink. I guess Bob Stinson couldn't take it and was nowhere to be found when it was time for them to go on stage. I have a tape of the show, and you can hear Paul Westerberg say, "We're looking for a guy named Bob! A big old fat guy. If you see him, tell him to come up on stage."

Jackie Zahn: Bob was with me and Bill. We were standing outside City Gardens drinking, and I heard music. I heard the band playing, and I turned to Bob and said, "You know, that sounds a lot like the Replacements." He laughed and said, "That can't be. I'm in the band." So we all had a bit of a laugh. A couple minutes later I said, "Listen, that really sounds like your band," and he was like, "No, I don't think so." Then, suddenly, their road manager, or somebody, comes storming over to us, screaming at Bob, "Get in there!" He called him a bunch of names. "Where have you been? Everybody's looking for you! Get on stage!" Bob was like, "Oh, okay."

Rich O'Brien: On the tape, you hear Bob finally get on stage while they were playing "I Will Dare."

Jackie Zahn: Bob, Bill, and I walk in, and we had to walk through the crowd. We didn't walk backstage or anything. Everybody was looking at us. We got up to the stage, [Bob goes up], and Paul Westerberg *spit on him.*

Rich O'Brien: I can still picture Bob climbing up on stage and Paul saying, "You're fired!" He spit on him. It wasn't long after that that Bob got kicked out of the band.

Jackie Zahn: That look that Paul Westerberg gave him was …. I felt like shit. I was like, *this isn't my fault,* but I felt like it was my fault. But it wasn't my fault, because I told him twice! Twice I said I thought his band was playing and that he should be in there.

Rich O'Brien: The thing about that show was that they weren't drunk. By then, the "drunk" shows were legendary, and people were pissed that they were sober and only played their own songs. They didn't do covers anymore.

Jackie Zahn: After it was over, Bill [Rude], Bob, and I got into Bill's car. I don't know where we went, but I don't think we got very far. At one point Bill turned to me as he's driving and said, "Oh my God, Bob Stinson is in my car." But one thing I will not forget is that I said to him, "That sounds like The Replacements," and he said, "It can't be."

Bob Stinson was not in the band much longer. Later that year, he left the Replacements. Whether he left voluntarily or was kicked out is still a point of contention. Bob Stinson died of organ failure related to long-term drug abuse on February 18, 1995. He was 35 years old.

The Fall/Volcano Suns—March 2, 1986

Jeff Weigand (Volcano Suns bassist): That Fall show was where [Fall frontman] Mark E. Smith and I became friends. We did a tour with them, and I believe this show was about three days in. Funny enough, over the years whenever I would run into Smith, he would always bring up that City Gardens show. I'm not sure why. I think either the place or Trenton itself must have horrified him...something about it definitely got to him. That was our first van tour and probably the only enjoyable tour I did. I loved playing outside of Boston, as everyone there was into roots dork bands and awful stuff. The Boston scene sucked, but I hated touring. Just endless driving and bullshit, though the shows could be fun. By the end [of my run with the band] we pretty much had to play mostly outside of Boston, since we had been banned from [Boston clubs] The Rat, The Paradise, and the rest.

City Gardens itself didn't really impress me as either good or bad; it was just a venue. Trenton was fairly interesting. After one of those shows we stayed in a motel downtown, one of those double-decker things built in the '50s that looked like the place where Martin Luther King was shot, with the long walking balconies. I got up in the morning and went outside, and there was quite a scene going on in the parking lot. It reminded me of having just woken up and walked out into the exercise yard of the local prison or something. Lots of guys down there looked like they set the fashion standard for white, wife-beater tank tops. A bunch of groundbreakers. And I thought, "Thanks Trenton!"

Fear/Mentors—March 16, 1986

Carl Humenik (City Gardens security): Fear was the first band that came up to me afterwards and were like, "We love to have you up there [working security]. We saw you singing every single song and having a great time." I would get up on stage, and I knew everyone was jealous that I was standing right next to the band, singing along with them. And that was a band that wouldn't care if I punched someone.

Neal Dallmer (City Gardens regular): Some kid had recently gotten a broken arm, so Randy was holding the security guys to the "no slamming" rule. There was a real lockdown on that stuff, but there was no way you could stop it. The crowd was like a herd of cattle, and you could see them getting ready to go at it hard and strong. Everybody was waiting. Fear came out and played a few songs, then during "Let's Have A War," I looked at Repo—who wasn't working security that night— and he looked at me, and we went for it. And from there on out it was mayhem. It was gorgeous, just absolutely beautiful. Repo and I were going at it along with everyone else, and the security guys rush in, grab Repo, and toss him out. Even though they knew us, and Repo was a bouncer there, no one was doing anyone any favors.

Mark "Repo" Pesetsky: Yeah, even though I worked there, I got thrown out. Neal and I talked about it. We knew we were going to get thrown out. I didn't work a lot of shows during that time, because I didn't like throwing people out just for mixing it up.

Neal Dallmer: Repo was my ride, so I had to leave too. And there was mayhem in the parking lot.

Don Rettman (City Gardens DJ): I remember driving [Mentors' lead singer] El Duce around. I was stopped behind a cop, and he's like, "Hey, is that *a pig* up there?!" I sat there, like, *Oh God, no.*

Randy Now: Say what you want about The Mentors and El Duce, but of all the bands I worked and toured with, El Duce was the only guy who would call me up and say, "Just wanted to call and let you know we made it home okay, and thanks for everything!" The only one!

Sadly, one tragic night El Duce did not make it home okay. In the mid-nineties, after the death of Nirvana frontman Kurt Cobain, El Duce began making the claim that Cobain's wife, Courtney Love, had offered him money to kill Cobain. El Duce told his story to The Jerry Springer Show, The National

Enquirer, and in the documentary "Kurt & Courtney." On April 19, 1997, El Duce's body was discovered on railroad tracks in Riverside, CA. He had either fallen asleep on the tracks while walking home from a bar or stumbled in front of it. Some believe he was pushed to his death in an effort to silence him.

Venom/Black Flag—April 2, 1986

Jamie Davis (City Gardens Regular): That was my first show at City Gardens, and it was weird. I got a ride over with my parents. It was only five minutes from where I grew up. I know people who used to walk there from our town. I know a dude who walked there a bunch of times with a big Mohawk, right through Trenton. And Trenton was a little different back then. The world was a little different back then. To be

honest, we didn't know that much about Black Flag. We really went to see Venom.

Henry Rollins: Gimme an S! Gimme an A! Until I spelled out "Satan." Oh, yeah I did that. We put pentagrams on our palms, a la Richard Ramirez, and terrorized the members of Venom who were slouching around near their dressing rooms. We were just kinda being in the way. They chose the upstairs dressing room. We were lounging around, and they were being polite going, "Excuse me," and we would hold up our hands and go, "Hail Satan!" Our roadie, Joe Cole, blocked their way as they were making a hasty exit after their set. They ran out of there. Joe lurched in front of them, almost falling on them, and did his "Hail Satan!" It was a great night.

Jonathan LeVine (City Gardens regular): I think the craziest show I ever saw was Black Flag playing with Overkill and Venom. All I remember about that show was the singer from Venom was a tall, skinny dude, and he was walking around with cherry-red Doc Martens that went up to his knees. I remember thinking, "This is a weird fucking show."

Jamie Davis: I remember Henry Rollins making fun of Venom. When Black Flag came on, Henry came out in his little shorts and he had big pentagrams drawn on his hands. He kept saying, "Satan! Satan!"

Eerie Von (Samhain/Danzig bassist): I had gone down to City Gardens before with Glenn [Danzig] to see Black Flag. I didn't have a driver's license at the time, so they wouldn't let me in. I'm friends with Henry Rollins, and I got Glenn Danzig into the show, but they still wouldn't let me in! So I sat in the car for the whole show. Glenn drove, and he's gonna hang out after the show and everything, and I'm sitting in the car. There's a picture of Glenn and Henry floating around somewhere from that gig.

Jamie Davis: Black Flag was cool. But it was later Black Flag. I guarantee you if it had been early Black Flag, it would have been a lot better.

Henry Rollins: It was a 45-minute set. The deal was either we had a night off or we could open for Venom… and City Gardens would rent our PA and pay us as the opening band. So, we said, "Yeah, we'll play." We loaded in, Overkill played, then us, then Venom.

Jamie Davis: They seemed to throw Overkill on all the metal bills. Overkill was Overkill. They were still good back then. That was the *Feel the Fire* days.

Henry Rollins: We made a little money, but the best part was getting to see Venom and walking away with that board tape, the original of which is sitting right on my shelf.

Eerie Von: I was really pissed I couldn't get in to see the show and hang out. That would have been nice.

Henry Rollins: The between-song raps are the stuff of legend. We gave a copy of the tape to Thurston Moore from Sonic Youth who made a 7-inch single of all the between-song-raps, and it is beyond belief, it is so cool.

Venom reportedly laughed off Rollins' comments, saying, "Henry didn't have the balls to speak to us back then. He hid backstage, but now he mouths off behind our backs. His band was useless, and that's why he writes books now. He even got the date of the show wrong. Go write some more books, and we'll keep making music."

On April 3, 1986, City Gardens ads triumphed: The Restaurant is Open!

Randy Now: Tut bought a hot dog roller machine, the kind you see at 7-11, and set it up by the door. He bought a meat slicer, too, and made sandwiches. By buying that, he made the club into a "restaurant," and thereafter we could have all-ages shows and serve alcohol.

Bart Mix (City Gardens bartender): I sold sandwiches for a couple days. Tut bought a meat slicer and wanted to use it. I almost cut my finger off. No one wanted to buy a deli sandwich from that place!

Randy Now: We called the hot dogs "Tut Dogs." On the punkcards I sent out, I wrote, "City Gardens: Home of the Tut Dog."

Rich O'Brien: Tut Dogs sustained many a bouncer after a long show. We would eat all the unsold, completely overdone hot dogs at the end of the night.

Randy Now: It was all ages in the front of the stage and 21 and up in the bar, and we would card people to get back there to drink.

Amy Yates Wuelfing: There were two problems with this arrangement. First, you couldn't take your drink with you when you went to the front to watch the band. So unless you were content to stand a football field away and watch the show from the back, you would have to suck your drink down when you heard the band start to play, or throw it away. And then you were basically done drinking for the night. Second, if you really liked a band, and the show was going to be crowded, you had a choice. You could either go up front and grab a good spot and not drink, or say *screw it*, and go drink with your friends in the back until the band came on. That takes us back to problem one.

Rich O'Brien: There was one person at the entrance to the back room checking IDs and one person watching the bar crowd. It was fairly obvious when someone was trying to sneak a beer out. If you've been a bouncer for long time, it's easy to spot people when they're about to do something stupid. There are so many tells. Once the band started, you would look around and see a guy over in the corner, hunched over and moving his arms around in his crotch area, and you know, *this guy's putting a beer in his pants.* If he was cool about it, you would just tell them to go back to the bar. But if he's all, "*what, what, what?*" you would grab his pants and shake the beer so it spilled all over his over his crotch. A lot of guys would walk out of the bar looking like they shot porn star-quality loads with soaking wet crotches.

Carl Humenik (City Gardens security): Frank [a.k.a. Tut] told us that, if someone gives us a hard time, knock the drink out of his hand. I would do that, and it would end in a fight with someone getting thrown out. It was an awkward time.

Rich O'Brien: The other problem was that the entrance to the dressing room was in the bar, so you'd have underage kids hovering around the dressing room to see the band. The kids would be right next to the bar, which was only separated from the all-ages section by velvet rope. It was always a bit of a mess back there.

Bart Mix: It would be 100 degrees in there, and Tut started charging kids 25 cents for a cup of water. Tut was notoriously cheap. The soundman went up to him one night and asked for a can a soda, but Tut wouldn't give it to him. So the sound guy slammed a handful of change down on the bar and said, "Tut, you're the cheapest person I know!" Tut goes, "Yes, I am." He never did anything for the patrons who came there, like give-aways or contests. He was pennywise and pound foolish that way. They had people who came all the time and spent a lot of money on shows, and I thought that we should slide them a drink once in a while to make them feel special. I got fired for that.

Ministry/Faith No More—April 4, 1986

Randy Now (promoter): Faith No More was a new band, and this is back when they still had original lead singer Chuck Mosley, before Mike Patton. I loved them. *We Care A Lot* had just come out, and I really wanted to give them a break, so I gave them a slot opening for Ministry in front of 700 people. This would be a whole lot of people in New Jersey watching a band from San Francisco no one had ever heard of.

Chuck Mosley (Faith No More, lead singer): I remember that night pretty clearly.

Al Jourgensen (Ministry, lead singer): I encountered problems by doing *With Sympathy*. The band had been going for a while and then [Arista president] Clive Davis made us—MADE US—sell out. He appointed backup singers and engineers, producers, and everything. It was this big spectacle. We had to go record in London and Boston. It made us complete sellouts. It was horrible. It was horrific. Before that and after that we were doing our own stuff, and I think it stands the test of time. But for that brief period, it was a nightmare.

Rich O'Brien (City Gardens security): This was before Ministry's *Land of Rape and Honey*, and they were best known for songs like "Every Day is Halloween." There were a lot of synthesizers onstage, and Faith No More didn't have much room. I think Faith No More's drums weren't even on the drum riser; they were in front of it.

Amy Yates Wuelfing: Ministry had so much stuff on stage that Faith No More had very little room to play. The band had maybe five feet to move around.

Randy Now: Ministry had a brand-new $50,000 piece of equipment on stage, an Emulator, which was given to them for signing with Sire. That's $50,000 back in 1986. Imagine what that translates to now.

Al Jourgensen: But that's why Faith No More happened. We were playing this pop music then, on Clive Davis's instruction. We were like Milli Vanilli. Faith No More wanted no part of that, and good for them! Even though they destroyed my $50,000 synthesizer…

Rich O'Brien: This was when the club had all-ages shows and there was no alcohol. My job for the night was to control the door that all the bands used to load in, so I could see what everyone was doing. Before Faith No More played, they hung in their van, which was parked right outside the door. I hung back there with them for a while, and they were definitely drinking… not out of control, but drinking.

Chuck Mosley: I might have had one or two shots, and maybe a beer, but that's not enough to get me drunk. I am clumsy by nature. I could have be completely sober and still be falling all over the place. I've been accused of being intoxicated a lot, and I'm not saying I never have been, but I remember that show pretty clearly. I had a couple of beers at the most that night. I probably sound stoned to you right now, right? I haven't even smoked any weed today. This is just how I am. People have always been accusing me of being intoxicated when I wasn't.

Rich O'Brien: Right before they went on stage, I remember Chuck guzzling a beer, just chugging it down. And it looked to me like he might have been drunk, but if I had to perform in front of 500 people I'd be drinking too.

Mike Judge (vocals, Judge): Not that we had a bunch of gear, but we never would take up three quarters of the stage with our gear and everybody who opens for us can only use the remaining part. We would never do that.

Chuck Mosley: Ministry had all this gear set up on the stage already. They literally had their monitors right by my feet and the mic stand. The whole stage was congested. I am an uncoordinated klutz. I have home movies of when I was a little kid, and I'd be falling down, tripping over myself, and bumping my head all the time. I was accident prone. So I was doing what I normally did when we played, jumping around and stuff.

Mike Judge: That night Ministry had a truckload of shit, and Faith No More had to play in a broom closet pretty much. I don't know if they were really knocking into shit or if they were trying to establish that they needed a little bit more room to play for the rest of the tour or what.

Amy Yates Wuelfing: At first they were bumping into Ministry's equipment, but it looked innocent enough, like it was happening because Chuck was really animated onstage and had so little room. But then it started to seem more deliberate.

Chuck Mosley: Ministry had some computer thing set up as part of their act, and I did everything I could to avoid it. I probably did come pretty close. But I didn't smash anything. I didn't destroy anything, and I didn't break anything. I didn't even kick it. The one thing I might have done was spill some beer or water on something that was at my feet, and that would be the extent of it.

Rich O'Brien: I think there was friction between Ministry's road crew and Faith No More to begin with. Then Chuck was jumping around onstage like crazy, which is what they were known for, and at one point he bumped into someone else in the band. They fell backward and knocked over a beer, and the beer spilled all over one of the keyboard set-ups.

Al Jourgensen: It was actually a Fairlight synthesizer. We weren't sure how it was going to last on tour, and it certainly didn't last with Faith No More spilling beer on it. Either way, good for them.

Gal Gaiser (City Gardens DJ): I was deejaying that night between bands, and, from what I could see, they had beer on stage and were spilling it all over. It was like, "I'm not knocking this beer over, I'm intentionally ruining equipment by spilling liquid into it." That seemed to be the straw that broke the camel's back. Randy comes running up to the DJ booth and says, "Gal, get on the microphone and tell them to get off the stage!" Oh, really? How do you throw someone offstage from the DJ booth 100 feet away? I got on the PA and said, "Um… guys? Can you guys get off the stage? Please?" It didn't work. They didn't get off the stage. But it did seem to inspire more chaos.

Rich O'Brien: Chuck was the main offender, which I blame on the alcohol, but Ministry's sound guys were being a little prissy if you ask me.

Randy Now: Ministry's road manager Sean Duffy and I both agreed, along with Al Jorgensen from Ministry, to get them the hell out of there.

Al Jourgensen: I got no problem with Faith No More. I thought they were kinda cool and they were, because they tortured us and we tortured them back.

Chuck Mosley: At the time Faith No More was pretty in-your-face, and we were proud and competitive with other bands. I know we came in that night with every intention of blowing Ministry away, and I am pretty sure we were doing that, as far as excitement and aggression goes.

Gal Gaiser: Randy then came back to the DJ booth and grabbed the microphone.

Amy Yates Wuelfing: Randy got on the PA and calmly said, "Guys, you're fucking up. You're fucking up up there. Get off the stage or we're throwing you off."

Rich O'Brien: Within five minutes of Randy saying that, Chuck drank a beer and threw it up in the air, straight up. It landed in the crowd and smashed all over the dance floor.

Chuck Mosley: I definitely wasn't throwing beer bottles at the audience. I've never done that, ever. Now, I've deflected plenty of beer bottles thrown at me, but I never threw any at the crowd at a show. I've never tried to hurt anybody. I've been hit in the head by flying bottles myself plenty of times. It's not fun.

Randy Now: One thousand percent, bottles came off the stage. Chuck was always blamed for it.

Rich O'Brien: And that's when everything went nuts. About a minute later, the music just stops and there's a whole crowd up on stage.

Amy Yates Wuelfing: I was about halfway back and saw a huge bouncer or security person pick Chuck up by the waistband of his pants—he didn't have a shirt on—and toss him like a paper airplane. The crowd wasn't sure what to make of it. Is this a comedy routine? Is this really happening? Everyone looked at each other like, "What the... ?"

Chuck Mosley: Right out of the blue, maybe during our third song, they kicked us right off the stage. The security guys came up and started throwing all our gear out the door and told us we had to get out of there. So we packed up our stuff and went back to the hotel.

Rich O'Brien: There was City Gardens security there, but also Ministry's road crew, and they went up on stage, grabbed them, and threw them out the door. They all spilled out into the parking lot, and that's when I went out there. Since I had been hanging out with the band earlier, I tried to step in and make peace, but it wasn't happening. People started bringing the band's equipment out to them, but at one point they let some of the band members go in, the reasonable ones, and load out their equipment. Chuck didn't go back in, and at one point the other members of the band isolated Chuck from everybody else.

Chuck Mosley: We didn't want to stick around, since we had no reason to. We might have hung outside for a little while, but we pretty much left after they threw us out.

Rich O'Brien: Faith No More weren't a big band at the time. "We Care A Lot" didn't become a big song until a year later because they revamped it. At the very end of the night, I bought a t-shirt and an album from them. I actually thought they were great.

Al Jourgensen: We got the Fairlight fixed after that night. We took it to some computer geek in Pennsylvania, and we kept on going. That's actually how I met Trent Reznor. I accidentally spilled beer on my four-track machine during a Revolting Cocks tour in Cleveland and broke it, and we couldn't get fixed in time for the show. The people at the club said they knew this local kid who had the exact same four-track. We brought him over and rented the gear from him, and then we said, "We're taking this." Trent said, "No, you're not taking this. You already destroyed one and you're not going to destroy mine." So he came on the road with us. Trent Reznor from Nine Inch Nails was Revolting Cocks' roadie. We used to throw firecrackers in his bunk and call him Techno Kid. We used to torture that poor bastard.

Randy Now: About three days later after that show, I was at Niagara Falls, in the tunnels under millions of gallons of rushing water. It was so loud I couldn't hear a thing. I was at the very end of the tunnel, leaning on the railing, wearing the raincoat that they make you wear, and I turned around. There was [Faith No More guitarist] Jim Martin. It was all 6 foot, 4 inches of him and his goofy red-framed glasses, standing right in front of me. Behind him were another 20 or so people. All I could think was, "Shit, man. They're all behind me in this tunnel and they recognize me for sure. They'll keep me trapped down here until no one else is around, pick me up, and throw me over the railing into Niagara Falls to my death!" But they didn't. They just gave me dirty looks.

Rich O'Brien: One funny thing was Randy yelling, "You'll never play here again!" A year later they opened for the Red Hot Chili Peppers.

Chuck Mosley: When I went back to City Gardens after I joined the Bad Brains - and you can ask Randy about this - the first thing he did was apologize to me for that night. He explained that it was either Ministry or their manager that ordered security to kick us off the stage. He said that Ministry didn't like us.

Randy Now: Well, I don't remember apologizing when he came with Bad Brains, but maybe I did try to show him that everything was in the past.

Chuck Mosley: Randy explained that that night in particular the band or the manager told the guys to get us off the stage, that they just did not like us, period. Stuff gets so blown out of proportion over the years. I've read stuff about myself on the internet that's ridiculous. I've read that I supposedly pulled a gun in Heathrow Airport one time. I've read all kinds of stuff that I've done that I have never done. It's always stuff that makes me look very cool in the eyes of the fans, but it's also made it very hard for me to work. In reality, I'm a calm family man.

Black Flag/Gone/Scorn Flakes—April 20, 1986

Sim Cain (Regressive Aid/Gone/Rollins Band): Regressive Aid broke up in 1983 or '84. We were making the second record and we were really hard on each other. We were young and harshly critical of each other. We hadn't really developed our [communication] skills yet. We were really driven—we rehearsed every day—and every spare moment was spent on the band.

The second record was very ambitious. This was the pre-sampling era, so we were recording pneumatic tools and wood chippers and making tape loops. It was a really involved process and it took a long time. The idea was that one side of the record would be rock stuff, and the other side would be more electronic stuff, with programmed drums and layers of noise. The pressure created a falling out and Billy [Tucker] had enough. We went our separate ways for a while.

Around 1985, Black Flag contacted Randy Now and told him that they were looking for a new bass player, since Kira Roessler had split. Randy told Andrew [Weiss], and Andrew sent [Black Flag guitarist] Greg Ginn a letter. Andrew told Greg that he was interested and would be on the next plane out. The short story is that Andrew didn't get the gig as Flag's bass player, but Greg did tell Andrew that he was interested in starting a side project with the two of us. He said that wanted to continue the Regressive Aid sound. I'm sure he'd disagree with that now, in retrospect. But what he wanted was an instrumental guitar trio. Mind you, the way Billy [Tucker] played and the way Greg plays is radically different. Andrew called me and explained that Greg wanted to start a band with us, and he said, "If you don't say yes, I'll kill you." That turned into Gone.

In December of 1985, I flew to Los Angeles and started rehearsing with Ginn, and he had a similar work ethic. We also drove up to San Francisco to see the Grateful Dead—I bullshit you not. This was shocking to me. I realized that whatever preconceived notions I had about Black Flag were wrong. Black Flag never espoused any straight-edge philosophy, and a lot of marijuana and hallucinogens went down [on tour], but there was very little alcohol.

And basically, to be on a Black Flag tour [as an opening band], you were there as a roadie. Black Flag had a massive amount of equipment because they wanted to be a self-contained unit, so that no outside influences could mess with the show. We were hauling a lot of gear, and the fact that we got to play was a bonus. After I joined that tour, I lost 15 pounds, and we were all strapping young men. Everybody was looking good! I figured out that Gone played over 600 sets in 10 months in 1986. It was insane. I had open wounds on my hands.

Greg Ginn (Black Flag/Gone guitarist): We just really like playing. If you're not playing, what are you doing? Sitting around waiting to play. So why not just play?

Sim Cain: We would play at least three times a day. We would load in this stadium-sized PA, no matter what sized club we were playing. Then Gone would jump back in the van and go to play a record store or a street corner or whatever, and then go back to the venue and play the opening set. Greg would get a one-set rest while Painted Willie played and then play again with Black Flag. If it was a two show night, he would up playing six or seven sets.

Greg Ginn: Playing that much didn't bother me at all. I like playing. It's what I do.

Sim Cain: Once I got out on the road with some of these bands, I realized that City Gardens was one of the country's best clubs to both play at and see music. It was in the top five in the country on that level. People in New York City were well aware of City Gardens. But City Gardens was also where I saw the most severe audience-to-band conflict. Ween had the ability to fill the room, as an opening act mind you, with people who hated them. I saw them opening for Fugazi and people despised them. There was something unique about that era in music. It was pre-internet, and it felt like a generational subculture. We held bands like Metallica and Public Enemy in the same light, because at that time they had no radio play or exposure but they sold millions because of word-of-mouth. Information would pass via touring bands from club-to-club. I don't know if that happens now.

Lords of the New Church—May 3, 1986

Jon Stewart: MTV was just coming around and VJ Martha Quinn came to the show. And, listen, every suburban boy's dream at the time was Martha Quinn. I remember her sitting at the bar, cute as a pixie, and I thought, "Stiv Bators and Lords of the New Church… Wow, how hard-core that she's here for a show like that." And then I went upstairs to the dressing room—it was the night Stiv vomited onstage—and the two of them were making out. I thought, "Okay, now I can't watch MTV anymore *or* listen to Stiv Bators. Great." I lost two things in one night.

Stiv Bators died on June 2, 1990 after being hit by a taxi in Paris. He refused treatment and died in his sleep of a concussion. He was 40 years old.

Descendents/Dag Nasty/ Volcano Suns/Agent Orange/ Squirrel Bait—July 27, 1986

Rich O'Brien: Dag Nasty cancelled because they wanted to play last. And for a lot of the audience, I think this was their first "punk" show. At least that's how they acted.

Dave Smalley (Dag Nasty, vocalist): That sounds like a good show. I think what happened is that I quit in the beginning of July. The big tour was going to be that summer, but then I quit. I remember one of my regrets was missing that tour. I think that was Dag's first tour with Pete Cortner singing. I remember hearing that Pete caught some grief because the album had just come out and all these people were like, "We really like this record." But then the audience got somebody else singing! That's not a diss on Pete; it's just one of those things. I think he was having a bit of a hard time with it at first because some people were not particularly kind.

Jim Norton (City Gardens stage manager/security): I started to show up to the club early. If doors were open at six o'clock, I would get there an hour or two earlier to help the bands load in. I did it because it was punk rock, and who doesn't want to hang out with Dag Nasty? Since you'd get thrown out for stagediving, what would people do? Well, you wait until the encore and then you go nuts. Now, bouncers are stupid, but they're not that stupid. They're not so stupid that they don't see it coming. I have to say I always hoped that a band wouldn't take an encore, that they would say, "Encores are for wussies, so we're not doing it!" But they always did it. The Descendents did it, and by the end of their encore I was carting people out three at a time. I grabbed two kids in each arm and scooped them around with a third kid in the middle, pushing all four of us to the door. I did that a couple of times. Now, that says a lot about the generally friendly nature of the City Gardens patron, when you consider it. It was like, "Okay, I'm getting thrown out. It's just part of the game." For us it was like, "Yeah, I'm doing my job. I'm the bouncer and I'm throwing you out because you know you did something you weren't supposed to do. But if the three of you did not want to be thrown out…" I'm not that big of a guy. You did not all have to be thrown out.

That was, to me, the hallmark of my time there, at least from a security perspective: a very friendly, collegial vibe. This week I can throw someone out for diving, and next week I see him and shake his hand. Now, that may not have been everybody's take on it, but it was mine. To this day, years and years later, I'll run into people who'll say, "Hey, you're that guy from City Gardens. Dude, you totally threw me out for stagediving!" And I'll be like, "Well, was I nice about it?" They always say, "Oh yeah, totally. It was cool."

Jeff Weigand (Volcano Suns bassist): I really have no idea why they put us on the bill. I think sometimes the promoter would be a big fan and would want to see us, so he would add us to the line-up. That show was pretty intense. It was a big crowd of skinheads and hardcore guys up front, with lots of repressed homosexuality and groupthink... It was that whole "safety in numbers" thing I hated about hardcore. Anything slightly different that wasn't loved by the group couldn't be seen for what it was. Most of those hardcore kids were as bad as their parents in terms of the herd and wanting to be accepted and loved for their mediocrity. They looked different from their dull folks, but they were pretty much running at the same boring, unthinking level. I used to love shows like this with that us-against-them thing going on, which was much more interesting than a love fest. We usually played a lot better in terms of the aggression that was inherent to our music and attitude.

The thing about the hardcore crowd is you have to attack and do it in a way that they don't quite know what to do. It was like facing down a herd of wildebeests who might stampede you. When you walk right up to one of the lead wildebeests and smack him in the nose, they back down as a group, stunned into dumb retreat. That was pretty much that show. We didn't want to be liked by such morons to be honest, and the last thing we wanted were followers.

I never saw myself as a long-term musician. It wasn't something I wanted to do forever and it always sickens me to see folks still hanging around trying to squeeze out a few more drops from a long dead and decayed mop. I could mention names but won't, since they are easy enough to see. To us, the band was a chance to fuck around with the order of things in rock music—a Dada project—and we knew if we carved out anything original, which I think we did, we wouldn't be accepted. We pretty much disdained acceptance. Fuck that. Rock music, then and now, is a sleazy business. I have more respect for the porn industry. At least they present themselves as they are: a bunch of sleazeballs. When it was time to move on, call it a day, the timing seemed right. The band was talking to major labels and I thought, "Time to get out or you will become one of these people." I quit and moved to Europe to work on my Ph.D.

X—August 1, 1986

Henry Hose (City Gardens regular): Billy Zoom had just left the band, and Dave Alvin was touring with them playing guitar. [X bassist] John Doe, I have to say, is one of the nicest people I've ever met in my life... so humble, down-to-earth, and friendly. Exene [Cervenka, singer] and I got along pretty well, talking about books and stuff, and she gave me this book called *Pissing in the Snow and other Ozark Folktales.* She had finished it and gave it to me. Dave Alvin sat there the whole night in the dressing room with these reflective sunglasses on. I kept talking to him about guitars and he wasn't responding. I said, "Are you awake?" And he's like, "Yeah yeah, I'm listening, I'm listening." Exene was waiting for a guy she was dating and it ended up being [actor] Viggo Mortensen. He was coming down from New York on a motorcycle, and as soon as he got there, Exene just glowed. You could tell she was in love with him, and as soon as the show was over they were in each other's arms the rest of the night. We helped Viggo get his motorcycle on the back of the equipment truck.

Bruce Markoff (City Gardens regular): I was working at City Gardens from time to time, and this was one of the busy shows. A ton of people were calling who had never been to the place before. This is before cell phones, so people were calling from pay phones. This woman calls and she's like, "I don't even know where I'm at. I'm in Trenton, and I don't know where I am." She was freaked out. I said, "Well, what's around you? Is there a gas station? Is there a bar, can you see anything?" She's like, "I'm by this big warehouse building" and she starts to describe the outside of City Gardens. [Bouncers] Carl and Rich are listening to my side of the conversation, and the three of us are looking at each other, like… Carl looks out the front door toward that phone booth that was at the end of the building, shaking his head. I said to the caller, "When you look at the building, is there a guy there hanging out the front door waving to you?" And she's like, "Oh my God."

GBH/Cro Mags/7 Seconds—August 10, 1986

Harley Flanagan (Cro Mags): To be honest, I hadn't heard too much [about City Gardens], because I really didn't know anything outside of the city. I remember the first time we played City Gardens. It was I guess '86 with GBH, which was our first real U.S. tour. We did half the tour with them and then Agnostic Front picked up the second half of the tour. It was a great show. That club in particular stands out in my memory because there weren't many places to play in New Jersey back then. I mean, there weren't too many places to play anywhere. There were only a few venues in each city that had hardcore or punk-rock gigs, and that was one of the few places that had a "scene." It was kinda run down and beat up, which made it the proper type of venue for our shows. It wasn't CBGB, but it had a similar vibe as far as it was definitely underground.

JFA/ BL'AST—August 31, 1986

Jim Norton (City Gardens stage manager): The next week I showed up, and it was supposed to be JFA, BL'AST, and somebody else. JFA had booked themselves a CBGB matinee in the afternoon, and then they went skating and never made it to City Gardens. BL'AST played, and they had a real low-end kind of sludge sound. Like a Black Flag sludge that was so strong and such a heavy, heavy sound that it was actually putting me to sleep on the side of the stage. There's an innate reaction babies have called a "shut-down reflex" which, when stuff is really loud, they go to sleep. And that's what it was. I was 17 years old, sitting on the side of the stage, and the sludge coming out of BL'AST's amps was so heavy that I started to fall asleep.

Dickies/Mojo Nixon/Ed Gein's Car/ Electric Love Muffin — September 21, 1986

Ken Hinchey (City Gardens regular): The Dickies had a penis puppet named Stuart, which they used during the song *If Stuart Could Talk*. In the middle of the song, Leonard [Graves Phillips, Dickies vocalist] would get the puppet out and have it sing, "See me, Feel me, Touch me, Heal me," from that Who song. Before the Dickies played this show, they were hanging out at the bar and were upset because Stuart had been stolen in New York the night before. Leonard was showing me this sad little muppet, made out of pantyhose and stuffed with toilet paper, and said, "This is what I have to use tonight." He was really pissed off about it.

Leonard Graves Phillips (The Dickies vocals): In those days, we went through a lot of Stuarts. People would just mess with him and steal him. The Stuart I use now I've been using for about ten years and he's in good shape.

Randy Now: I road managed The Dickies, and they used to take that Stuart puppet and smash it, step on it, and I would have to fix it. When it got stolen, we had to make one from scratch.

We put together a replacement puppet, and it was pretty sick looking.

Leonard Graves Phillips: The song *If Stuart Could Talk* is an homage to The Who. I've always had kind of a love-hate thing with The Who and Pete Townshend always had this juvenile fascination with boyhood and manhood. As it turns out from reading his autobiography, he is really fascinated with his manhood.But the song is a tip-of-the-hat to them. My point is, the song was written about a talking penis, so it's only logical that we have one on stage.

Ken Hinchey: During the show, it gets to that, "See me, Feel me..." part, and he takes out the homemade puppet and starts using it, and you could tell Leonard was not into it. After a couple seconds he threw down the puppet, unzipped his pants, pulled them down, and whipped out "the real Stuart." It was out there for a long time, and the spotlight was right on it.

Leonard Graves Phillips: What?! Where does this stuff come from?! That didn't happen. A complete rumor. Someone is confusing me with Jim Morrison. Who told this story, a he or she? A he? Then it definitely did not happen. But we got a couple of guitars stolen from City Gardens, for what that's worth. It was after the set, and these kids just grabbed a couple guitars and ran out the door.

Ken Hinchey: I interviewed Leonard once for an article and he talked about being a Satan worshipper. He was totally serious. I asked him, "Aren't you afraid of going to hell?" And he said, "Who says hell is bad? You know who says that? The other side… That's what they want you to think. The only reason we think hell is bad is because we're not getting Satan's perspective on it." I asked him if [Dickies' guitarist] Stan Lee was a Satan worshipper too, and Leonard goes, "No. He's just a Jew."

Leonard Graves Phillips: I said I was a Satanist? No, but here's my Satan story. [Dickies' guitarist] Stan Lee and I got on a plane once with a human skull that I had purchased from [the now-closed New York store] Maxilla & Mandible. I don't have her anymore, but I called her Moronie, as in [the Ritchie Valens song] *Bony Moronie,* and I got a little story as to her origin. I wasn't going to pack her of course, so I took her on the plane with me in a box. She was on my lap and I had Stan on one side of me, and a really nice born-again Christian lady on the other side. She had that kind of happy, desperate joy that nervous people have in general, let alone born-again Christians. She tried to make conversation and she said, "Oh, what are you reading?" And I had some nineteenth century satanic, Joris-Karl Huysmans book, *Là-Bas,* and Stan kept saying, "Tell her what you got in the box." I'm like, "Stop it. I'm trying to be nice."

As it happened, that was the most turbulent air flight I have ever been on. We're flying and there's a little bump and you get some nervous laughter around the cabin. Then there's this big dip, and you hear a collective groan. The woman next to me said, "Oh, I fly all the time, it's really nothing." And then we hit another one, a huge air pocket, and cups and stuff flew everywhere, and she started freaking out. Then Stan started waxing philosophical, "We're on this thing and it's hundreds of tons, and it shouldn't even be in the air, they don't know what keeps it up. We shouldn't even be here!"

It was one of those existential moments where I'm in the air, I got freaking-out, born-again lady on one side, Stan on the other, a human skull on my lap, and I'm thinking, "This plane is going to go down in a fiery ball and there is going to be one more head in the rubble than was on the flight manifest." That's my satanic story.

Circle Jerks/Agnostic Front — September 27, 1986

Jim Norton: After the shows, Randy used to go either to Denny's in Bordentown or to a truck stop called The Iron Skillet. There'd be maybe four or five people who went. I remember one night being at some restaurant, and I think it was just me and him, after a Circle Jerks show. The Circle Jerks drew about 650 people or something like that. I said, naively, "Well, 650 people at ten dollars or twelve dollars, I guess you had a pretty good night." And he broke it all down for me. What each of the bands got paid, what he paid to the club… you know, a lot of people thought he owned the club. He didn't. He paid rent for each show. Then you've got each of the bands. You've got security, the sound guy, the lighting guy, the DJ, the posters and the punkcards, and the advertising, and the insurance. I'm like, "Wait a minute. This guy, who I not long ago thought was the ultimate parasite gorging on the fertile flesh of the punk rock community, walked out of the show with something like $500 for all of his hassles and hard work." I realized very quickly he was not a multimillionaire. He was not living in a huge castle someplace. Not doing shows, not at this scale.

fIREHOSE — November 23, 1986

Mike Watt (fIREHOSE bassist, former Minutemen bassist): It was very difficult without D. Boon. But I had guitarist Edward [Crawford] helping me. He was very enthusiastic. First tour with Sonic Youth… they helped me. But it was rough. I didn't think that people wanted to see me play without D. Boon. My pop once told me, "Don't think. Do." And that's what I did. I got back in the saddle.

Fishbone — November 29, 1986

Rich O'Brien: I was working at a liquor store [at the time]. Randy called me because on their liquor rider—it must have been some sort of joke—they wrote that they needed two gallons of Mad Dog 20/20 and assorted flavors of Boone's Farm wine. This is the first time they played at City Gardens, and they weren't well received. Toward the end, for their encore, they were making fun of the crowd because people weren't jumping up and down and going crazy the way the band was used to. But after that, people went crazy whenever they played.

7 Seconds/AOD — November 30, 1986

Bruce Wingate (Adrenaline OD): I remember this show clearly because it was the largest crowd of people I ever puked in front of. We had played in Philly the night before and had to be in Trenton by noon, since it was an all-ages matinee. We had been up all night drinking beer with our buddies in Flag of Democracy. Right before we left Philly, I bought a forty-ouncer for the ride, on the theory that maintaining my buzz would keep a hangover at bay. When we got to City Gardens, I kept up a slow and steady intake all afternoon until it was our turn to play. The place was packed with kids, we went over well, and I still felt okay. The last song of our set was a cover of "Down in Flames" by the Dead Boys. It was my job to scream the three lines right before the song ended. As soon as I did, I felt all the color leave my face and my vision started flickering like a strobe light. I hit the last chord, took off my guitar, leaned over my amp, and puked my guts out. Then I managed to compose myself enough to walk across the stage, where I leaned over the side and promptly puked on a drum set belonging to our friends in the band Dirge.

Slayer — December 5, 1986

Jamie Davis (City Gardens regular): We got there super-early. Slayer had their bus parked there and, for some reason, they put their laundry basket out. My friend stole their laundry basket! We thought it was super-cool that we had Slayer's laundry basket! That show was great, and we taped it with an old tape recorder, but you couldn't hear anything. The guy who had the recorder stood right next to one of the speakers the whole show. The show was nuts. They came back around later, but [Slayer drummer] Dave Lombardo had left by then.

Jim Norton (City Gardens stage manager/security): I threw a punch at one guy in the four or five years that I worked at City Gardens, and that was a guy at Slayer show who punched me directly in the face. I went over and said, "Hey dude, you need to chill out." It was two metalhead guys who were standing in the pit punching each other in the face. They were matching each other punch for punch, and they were fine with it. It wasn't a fight; it was two guys punching each other in the face for fun. My first reaction was, "These two guys are punching each other in the face for fun, what are you gonna' do with that?" They weren't breaking the rules and no one was complaining. It was one of those things you knew was going to get out of hand. I went over and put my hand on this guy's shoulders and stopped him. I was motioning to him, because no one was going to be able to hear me in the pit of a Slayer show. I was like, "Calm down, calm down," and the guy looks at me and punches me in the face. It wasn't like he cleaned my clock, but he did punch me in the face. I had been about as cool as one could be in that situation, up to that point. I didn't throw either one of them out, and I was asking them nicely to stop. But after he hit me, that's when I was like, "You gotta' go." I punched him in the face right back and dragged him by the lapels of his jeans jacket to the door, and out he went. That was the one punch I ever threw. It wasn't outside. It wasn't around the corner with six other bouncers. Dude landed a lame punch on me; I landed a lame punch on him back. I didn't clean his clock either. He fought the whole way to the door.

Red Hot Chili Peppers/TSOL—December 7, 1986

Henry Hose (City Gardens regular): TSOL and the Red Hot Chili Peppers did this tour together, and they were alternating the headlining spot because they were equally as popular at the time. They're all really fun guys. We were hanging out in the dressing room with them, and all the Red Hot Chili Peppers wanted to do was play poker. When it was time for the Red Hot Chili Peppers to go on, we couldn't get them to stop playing cards. Finally they went out to play their set, and when they got back to the dressing room, they played cards again. I asked one of the guys in TSOL, "What's the deal?" He answered, "I don't know what their deal is. All they want to do is play cards." And really, it was the whole night. It got to be 2 a.m., and we said, "Do you guys want to party with us?" They're like, "No, we're going to go to the room and play cards."

The drummer from TSOL had these really big spikes on his hair, and we asked him, "How do you do that? How do you keep it up like that?" He said, "I use Jell-O." He spiked his hair with Jell-O. After that, we all started using Jell-O to make really hard spikes with our hair.

CHAPTER 6

Hey Ho, Let's Go… Again!
The Ramones in Trenton

The Ramones hold the distinctive position in City Gardens history as the band that headlined the most—22 shows. The New York City–based group was a touring machine and, given their proximity to Trenton, it is no wonder they played City Gardens so often. Ramones shows were always an event, and just about everyone who ever went to City Gardens saw them in some form, at some point.

Tax Assessment Photos of 1701 Calhoun Street from 1956.
Note neon sign that could be seen for miles.
(Photos courtesy of the Trenton Free Public Library.)

Hard Times

VOL. I... No. 3   HARD TIMES, OCTOBER 84   Cheaper than a comic book!

50¢

RAMONES   Ten years already ?!

MEATMEN

" WE'RE GOING TO INCORPORATE OUR
NAME IN CASE ANYONE SUES US."

Hard Times cover with Glenn Danzig and Henry Rollins.
Not pictured: Eerie Von waiting in the car.

*City Gardens
caterer Deirdre
Humenik and
Angelo from
Fishbone.*

BELOW: *Ministry's
Al Jourgensen.*

Harley Flanagan of the Cro-Mags.

Age of Quarrel-era Cro-Mags at City Gardens.

Token Entry's
Tim Chunks.

Roger Miret of Agnostic Front.

The gun show's in town! Dee Dee Ramone, locked and loaded.

Gabba Gabba Hey! It's the Ramones.

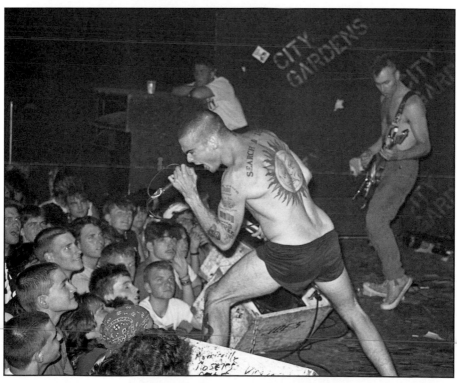

Henry Rollins moves the crowd.

Local NJHC band Vision.

City Gardens' security Big Ed with Vision's Peter Tabbot and City Gardens owner Frank "Tut" Nalbone.

*Keith Morris of the Circle Jerks doesn't let a little injury stop him.
From April 26, 1987.*

Keith Morris and promoter Randy Now survey the stage.

The Bad Brain's H.R. sails on during one hot night at City Gardens.

The Mighty, Mighty Bosstones' Dickie Barrett expresses his displeasure with City Gardens' bouncer Carl Humenik.

ABOVE: *Judge, the quiet after the video shoot storm.*

Promoter Randy Now works to keep the peace.

Spur-of-the-moment Descendents reunion on October 24, 1993.

RAMONES AT CITY GARDENS

December 26, 1981

April 13, 1985

November 27, 1985

June 7, 1986

July 11, 1986

October 10, 1986

January 3, 1987

August 29, 1987, with Elvis Ramone on drums

January 1, 1988, with Adrenaline OD

April 22, 1988, with Prong

August 5, 1988, with The Dickies

Oct 14 & 15, 1988 (two shows back-to-back)

April 14, 1989

February 23, 1990, with The Fiendz

October 7, 1990

May 29, 1991

October 4, 1991, with Ween

April 12, 1992, with Blitzspeer

April 17, 1993, with Outcrowd

October 3, 1993

November 20, 1993, with Bouncing Souls

Monte A. Melnick (Ramones tour manager/author *On The Road With The Ramones*): They weren't just a simple, three-chord, go-up-and-play, dumb band. They thought out a lot of the details. While the production looked really simple, people don't realize that behind the band was a very large crew whose job was making sure everything ran like a well-oiled machine. It was not seen by the audience. The band was much better because of the lighting, the sound, and stage crew. We tried to never reveal what was going on behind the scenes. All you got was the show.

Randy Now: They were the first band to have a tractor trailer full of equipment, and we weren't ready for it. I probably had one guy to help them unload it all, and we needed ten. We were disorganized and running way late, so we had to delay opening the doors. When we did finally open, we had everyone go in the back room so the band could soundcheck. That's also the show were I learned you must have towels for bands—very important. The band is all sweaty and they're up there yelling, "Where's the towels?" Of course I didn't have any, and they're like, "Didn't you read the rider?" I was confused. *What's a rider?* I had no idea. Before that, I would get riders in the mail but never even look at them. I just tossed them aside.

Monte A. Melnick: One funny thing we asked for on the rider was Yoohoo. Yoo-hoo is a non-fat chocolate drink that has vitamins and minerals in it. For some reason, that's one of the things Johnny Ramone added to the rider from the beginning. Johnny probably did it because Yogi Berra used to do Yoo-hoo commercials. Yogi would say, "Me He for Yoo-hoo." A fan made Johnny a Yoo-hoo shirt with Johnny playing guitar in front of a Yoo-hoo bottle. It was one of his favorite shirts. Hell, I got addicted to the stuff. In the beginning it was a local thing in our area, so I'd talk to some promoter in Idaho, and he'd say, "What the hell is Yoo-hoo?" I was flexible.

Deirdre Humenik (City Gardens employee): The Ramones were wonderful. All they ever wanted was pizza and Pepsi. One show, I was carrying two cases of beer and ice to the stage and it was very heavy. I was trying to walk through the crowd and usually people would get out of my way. An older guy turns around and says, "I've been waiting 13 years to see this band, and you're not getting past me." I said, "Thirteen years is a really long time when they play everywhere, all the time. And if they don't get this beer, they aren't playing tonight." So he punched me in the chest and got tossed out. He waited 13 years only to get thrown out for being an asshole.

Randy Now: When I lived in Pennsylvania I had to drive down Calhoun Street and over the Calhoun Street Bridge to get home. I remember after a Ramones show having thousands of dollars in cash on me at two or three in the morning, thinking, "What am I doing?"

Monte A. Melnick: We played so many places, so many clubs. The guys learned early enough to carry their own PA so they'd have consistency in sound at every show. In a lot of ways, City Gardens was a local gig for us. It was only 70 miles from New York, so it was easy enough for us to drive there and back. No overnight expenses and all that. It also hit the markets around Philadelphia. The crowd was always great and the guys liked it. You know, City Gardens wasn't the ritziest place in the world, but Randy did a great job taking care of all the things on the rider. A lot of clubs, you had to fight for stuff, and we didn't really ask for a huge amount. Randy set things up the way we wanted it and made us feel comfortable. That's why we came back so many times... Randy would do anything we wanted. He took care of the crews. He took care of the load-in and load-out. He made sure people were there. Some clubs would say; "Don't worry, there's some people coming to help you load in." But then they'd disappear at the end of the night, and my crew would get pissed off because there was nobody there to help them. The thing is, we lived on the road. If we liked a place and knew we were going to make money there, why would we trash the place? Trash the place and not be able to come back and make money? It didn't make sense. The whole rock and roll story about bands trashing hotel rooms and stuff... great if you're Led Zeppelin and you have a billion dollars. We caused some damage in the early days, but the band learned the hard way after having to pay the bills: Don't trash the hotel rooms or the club.

Dave Franklin (Vision): In 1989, when *Ramones Mania* came out, they were booked for two nights at City Gardens. Randy called us up and said, "Hey, do you want to open up for The Ramones? It's gonna be just you and The Ramones." I was like, "What? Are you kidding me? YEAH!" So we ended up opening for The Ramones in 1989, my first year out of high school. I tell people that and they're floored by it. Now, especially after some [Ramones members] have unfortunately passed away, they are recognized as one of the most legendary bands ever. That one night, it was just us and them.

Of course, the show was completely sold out and the range of people went from 15-year-old kids to 40- and 50-year-olds. The Ramones drew all kinds of people. We had brought 100 Vision 7-inch singles with us to sell that night. We played our set and then boom—all of them were gone. I'm a 19-year-old kid walking through the crowd, and I've got 30-year-old dudes saying, "That was awesome! Great set!" and stuff like that. I thought *this is crazy!* Sharing the stage with The Ramones was the best part.

When we were doing our soundcheck, something funny happened. Our drummer played double-bass, meaning he physically kicked two bass drums at the same time. The Ramones brought their whole sound system… everything, the whole nine yards. All their equipment was already set up on stage when we got there. We're setting up the drums out front, and their stage manager comes out and asks if we were the opening band. We told him *yes*, and he says, "Oh no, you guys got double bass drums? That's a no-no." We're like, "What do you mean?" He explained that there wasn't going to be any room on stage for it with all The Ramones stuff up there, so we had to go up and rearrange everything. You know that little room above the stage at City Gardens? It was a little area where the bands would sit and then come up on stage. Our drummer, Matt, had to set his drums up right at the edge of the stage by that room, because it was the only place he could fit his whole kit. With all The Ramones' gear, there wasn't even room enough for us to move. I had maybe this four-foot span between two monitors, and I kind of went back and forth, back and forth, and that was it. While we were doing our soundcheck, The Ramones came in, saw us do soundcheck, and then left. And that was it—that was all the contact we had with them! Even so, on that night it was just us and The Ramones.

Bruce Wingate (Adrenalin OD): There were three risers set up on stage for The Ramones to stand on during their show. Their road manager goon warned us before we went on that not only were we not allowed to stand on them, but if we even put one foot on them, they'd cut our set short. So of course we immediately mentioned this fact to the audience and while we were playing, we each took turns dramatically lifting a foot as if to step onto the risers. If it were any other band in the world, we would have went for it, but if The Ramones needed to be two feet higher then us, we weren't gonna step on shit.

Ken Hinchey (City Gardens regular): Of the 20 shows I saw The Ramones play, I only ever saw Joey acknowledge the opening band once. That was the Dickies.

Leonard Graves Phillips (The Dickies vocalist): That's a nice distinction. But I don't remember opening for The Ramones at City Gardens.

Jim Norton (City Gardens stage manager): You know what happened every time The Ramones played City Gardens? Somebody in the opening band stepped on the lightbox. *Every* time. I played in a band called the Shock Mommies. We were really into being funny, but then we'd mix it up with this super-serious, dry, political stuff that was just awful. Our stage banter was much more interesting than the music, the music was really there to clear the way for a round or two of joke telling.

One night, we played with The Ramones and experienced what it was like to play with *The Ramones*. The Ramones would come in, set their stuff up, and use up a good 70% of the stage. They took all the space they wanted, which was fine because they were The Ramones. You didn't really begrudge them anything—until you were in the opening band and you had to set your stuff up alongside theirs. They brought their own monitors, which were twice as many and twice as big as what the house had, and that ate up all your front-of-stage space. They had these big, honking, side-fill [monitors] which ate up the sides of the stage. They had Johnny Ramones's three Marshall Stacks and Dee Dee's three stacks, and that ate up the whole back of the stage. They had their own drum riser. You had very little space to set up, but you were opening for The Ramones! You knew that it was a trade-off, and you always knew going in that this was the deal. You knew it was going to be sold out. You knew there was going to be a minimum of 700 people watching you. They might hate you, but they were watching you.

You would be told by one of the roadies not to stand on the lightbox. Now, the easy way for The Ramones' crew to have handled this would have been to, you know, put something on top of the lightbox. Perhaps put a case lid on top of it, so if you stepped on it you would slip and fall and die. But, being The Ramones' crew, they decided to take the path of most resistance. Every night they would set up the lightbox, leave it exactly how they wanted it, and police it during all the opening bands' sets. So now you've just created a situation where somebody in The Ramones' crew has to be "the cop."

Admittedly, these were pretty cool and effective stage effects. When you think of all the low-budget effects people have used before, a box that shoots light up into your crotch is pretty fucking cool. Naturally, our guitar player Mark Saxton, who was a total character—a complete piece of work—gets up on one of the boxes and does this one-legged jig he was prone to do. What happens when you get up on the lightbox is not nearly as bad as you think it is. What happens is all the lights go out—that's it. Then you get off the box and the lights come back on. The penalty really did not match the crime. I just picture those poor bastards, every night, browbeating these opening bands rather than finding a solution that would solve the problem. And then the punishment was that if you did it they were going to turn the lights out. I still have no idea why we didn't spend the whole show on those damn boxes.

Jeff Feuerzeig (TV producer): I got to interview Joey Ramone in 1986, and it was a big deal that I scored this interview for WTSR. I went backstage, and all The Ramones were lurking about but not talking to each other. I talked to Joey for ten minutes or so. It was a Jewish holiday and I knew he was Jewish, and I'm Jewish, and I made some stupid Yom Kippur joke. It was not appreciated.

Ken Hinchey: I went up to the dressing room once to get the Ramones to record radio IDs for my radio show. Joey was super friendly and really nice. In front of me was a girl who gave him a stuffed rabbit with a box of Sucrets. She was like, "Joey, I heard you had a sore throat and wanted to give you this." She walked away and Joey looked at me and said, "I got a bunny!" Everyone was hanging out and the mood was upbeat. But at a later show, I went to talk to them and Joey was totally different. He wasn't rude… he was practically asleep. He was leaning over a table and grabbed my tape recorder and put it under his hair. I couldn't even see his face. The atmosphere in the dressing room had changed.

Monte A. Melnick: One of the biggest celebrities to ever hang with the band was none other than The Boss, Mr. Bruce Springsteen. We were playing the Fast Lane in Asbury Park in 1978 and, as soon as I put the band onstage, I wander over to the back bar and see Bruce Springsteen sitting there by himself, watching. I figured I'd give him about three or four songs and then he'd be gone, as you had to have an acquired taste for the band, but he stayed for the whole show and loved them. At the end of the night he was still at the bar, so I walked over to him and asked if he wanted to come back and meet the band. I brought him back and Joey said, "Hey, why don't you write a song for us," which he did.

Stephen Brown (City Gardens regular): I dove off the amplifier stack at a Ramones show, and I think I broke some guy's collarbone because my boot came right down on him. Randy had me thrown out of City Gardens that night because I climbed the stack, but I snuck back in the side door. Willie Nelson let me in. Willie Nelson was that biker dude who was also a bouncer. I'm sneaking around, keeping a low profile, and Randy doesn't see me. Everything's going great. Right up until the black bouncer saw me, and he was like, "Hey, I gotta talk to you for a second." I was cool with him, so I went up to him. He takes me right the fuck up to Randy! Randy loses his mind. "That's it! You're banned for life!" I said, "Wait, you already banned me for life. You can't ban me for two lifetimes!" He said, "That's it, Brown—two lifetimes! You're outta here!" I was banned for two lifetimes. What the fuck?

Alex Franklin (City Gardens regular): Ramones. Everybody talks about hardcore nowadays and how the dancing is so violent and malicious. Let me tell you something—there was *never* anything like a Ramones show. They would play a Friday and a Saturday. Sometimes they would be booked for an entire weekend. They would come by at least twice a year; maybe even three times. It's funny to me how legendary The Ramones have become, because they were not cool back then, especially in the mid '80s. People thought they were sell-outs for being on a major label. Especially the real hardcore crowd. There was a time when people thought The Ramones were soft and kind of corny. I always loved The Ramones, but a lot of people thought I was a dork for liking them. They thought I wasn't a real punk! It was the same with the Sex Pistols. People said you weren't a "real" punk if you liked the Sex Pistols. Can you imagine?

Ramones shows were always insane. They would be so big and so packed that there were three mosh pits going at one time. When The

Ramones played, everybody went crazy. There was nowhere to stand that wasn't pandemonium. People would be jumping off the bleachers or off the bar. It was so packed that the sweat was pouring off in waves. You would sweat so much that your sneakers were soaked, and when you went outside there would be steam coming off your body.

The worst pit injury I ever received was at a Ramones show sometime in '89. I was standing to the right of the stage by the side door, next to the bleachers, and I was trying to watch them play. Suddenly this elbow hits me directly in the eye. I got hit so fucking hard that it broke the orbital bone, broke my cheek, and broke my nose. In one shot. My face looked like I had gone six rounds with Mike Tyson. The membrane that separates your eye from the rest of your face was broken, too. I was sick at the time, so when I blew my nose, the whole side of my face filled with air. I looked like the Toxic Avenger! It was horrible. My mom got so pissed at me that I wasn't allowed to go to any shows for a month, and at City Gardens there were at least three good shows a week!

Stephen Brown: Randy did some messed up stuff like taking bands from two different ways of thinking and putting them on a show together, and he would expect a fight *not* to start. Except for The Ramones. The Ramones were a band that everybody kind of liked, so you weren't going there for a fistfight. At least not that night.

Steven DiLodovico (author): The first time I saw The Ramones was '87 or '88 and, at that time, the punk rock "elite" had deemed it uncool to like The Ramones. Their records had always been really important to me, but I had never seen them live. Bands in the punk scene have a very short shelf-life and, by this point, The Ramones were already "old." I honestly wasn't expecting much from a bunch of old guys, but they completely blew me away! They were like a machine on stage. It was amazing.

Tim Chunks (Token Entry, vocalist): I worked as a stage manager at City Gardens in 1991 and it was awesome. I was living in New Brunswick with the Bouncing Souls, and we went to City Gardens one night. After having played there so many times with Token Entry, I had built a friendship with Randy. He was always a great, great promoter. He did his job really well. He got the word out that bands were playing, and he got kids to come to the shows. That's what bands wanted. There's nothing worse than showing up to a place, especially a club the size of City Gardens, and finding out that the promoter hasn't promoted your show and that a place that can hold almost 1200 people has only 200 in it. So I was at the club one night, and Randy asked me if I wanted to stage manage. I had no job at the time, so I was like, "Certainly. I totally want to stage manage." I remember when The Ramones played they brought in a full semi, or maybe even two semis' worth of gear. It was insane. I couldn't believe they brought so much stuff, but it was The Ramones.

In 1987, Clem Burke from Blondie played drums for the band as Elvis Ramone. He only did two shows, one of which was at City Gardens.

Ken Hinchey: I saw the Ramones about 20 times, and most of those shows were at City Gardens. The band had the show down to a science, so there wasn't a lot of variation. But I remember the Clem show, and it seemed like he couldn't keep up with them, which is strange because he's a great drummer. I think he literally joined the band the day before the show and didn't have a chance to rehearse. At the time I thought he couldn't keep up, but I think he just didn't know the songs. No disrespect to Clem, but he didn't fit in at all.

Monte A. Melnick: The Elvis Ramone show was at City Gardens. It was his second and last show! The thing was with The Ramones...you know their songs were so fast and tight... any tiny, little thing... the guys would... well, Johnny noticed things and was kind of tough about it. Clem's a great drummer, but he didn't have enough time to work into the group. He was thrown into the fray. He did a good job. Within the group, they noticed. They were uncomfortable with him and then [Ramones drummer] Marky came back. Clem went on to better things.

Clem Burke a.k.a. Elvis Ramone (Blondie, drummer): I was offered the drum slot for The Ramones when Tommy [Ramone] was leaving. I had a sit-down with [Ramones manager] Gary Kurfirst at his office at that time and said, "I'm in the middle of the Blondie thing." The second time I got offered the gig was when I came off the road with the Eurythmics in 1987. Richie [Ramone] had just split and they had shows coming up. I said I'd fill in. As I started to get into it, I was thinking, "Yeah, this could be really cool." I told Gary I would not do it on a permanent basis... just until they found someone else. Gary said it would be easy, but I knew better than that. I knew The Ramones weren't easy. Tommy was a big influence on me when I was watching him play at CBGB. The songs weren't that easy to play, and Tommy definitely had the knack for it. It had a lot to do with the fact that he wasn't a drummer. Playing drums wasn't his life. He was just trying to be a part of the band, make it work, and lay down the beat.

Monte A. Melnick: Clem was a good friend and a great drummer. He came up in the scene with us and loved the band. He wanted to be a Ramone right from the beginning. He got his leather jacket and we tried him out. But he only did two gigs, and just wasn't right. It wasn't his fault. He was a different style of drummer.

Clem Burke: All their songs are like tongue twisters, so a cymbal crash in the wrong place was disastrous. They were very fanatical about it. My style is more related to jazz, I kind of get in the moment more. I'm more influenced by Keith Moon or Elvin Jones. I don't necessarily believe in playing the same thing at the same time each time. In a live performance, that can get extremely boring. I don't know if I could do that continuously without any improvisation or variation on the theme. But that's what made them what they were.

I was probably a better player than they had been used to, and I don't know if they could actually keep up with me, to tell you the truth. Dee Dee was great, but he didn't play the bass with precision. He was performing when he was onstage, which I can understand, 'cause that's kind of how I feel when I'm onstage. Johnny was into things being exact. That's his vision, his concept.

Monte A. Melnick: Clem didn't really fit in. He would come with his Platinum American Express card, cologne, and Armani suits and then trot out in his leather jacket and go onstage.

Clem Burke: We did a couple of disastrous gigs and that was it... I got the feeling that Johnny wasn't very happy about how it went.

Jim Norton: We would have problems at Ramones shows when people showed up because they had heard City Gardens was a "punk club" and The Ramones, of course, were a punk band. They would come to "get their punk on" as it were. It would be some guy shoving another guy's girlfriend because he thought shoving a girl was acceptable at a punk show. He'd end up getting his face pounded in by her boyfriend and his two friends. They thought it was okay to pound his face into a piece of hamburger meat because that's what punkers do. Those were sort of constant things at Ramones shows. Some guy would walk away with a gigantic egg on the side of his head because someone else thought it was really "punk" to punch him.

Rich O'Brien (DJ/City Gardens bouncer): This is the only time I remember the cops coming, because usually you would call and they wouldn't show up. But this one time, another security guy, Ronny, and I tackled a guy in the back bar after he pulled out a gun, and somehow the gun got knocked behind the bar. The clincher? The guy with the gun was an off-duty Trenton cop who started a fight with somebody. I still remember running back there and diving on him, and guy's yelling at me, "You're under arrest!" I said, "What the hell are you talking about?" The main guy from the Trenton police force had to come out and do an investigation. He grabbed the off-duty cop by the hair and threw him into a patrol car. The investigating cop told us he was sorry and left. That was the last I ever heard of it.

Rowan Bishop (The Outcrowd): We dragged our asses down to Trenton to see The Ramones. It was really hot and, on our way into the club, we saw some guys hanging out by the entrance. I look like I'm gonna join Motörhead, with my long hair and my Black Sabbath t-shirt. One of these guys says, "Hey remember when we beat up that fat hippie the other day?" Really loud. I walked past without even looking at them, head down, arm out, middle finger up. The funny thing is, *they* didn't look like they belonged there. They looked like generic Jersey guys. Guys you would never expect to see at a punk show.

We came out after the show and the same guys were *still* out there. I don't think they ever went in. I walked past them and they started again with, "Hey you fat hippie… Yeah, we're talking to you!" Of course I gave them the finger again. Then I feel something go sailing past my head. It was a big bottle. It missed me and hit the back of the head of some guy who was walking in front of me. He was a young kid, maybe 17 or 18, a little guy. The bottle shattered on the back of his head, and he turned around with a "What the fuck?" look on his face. The guys who threw the bottle start walking over to him and then ten other guys just appear out of the bushes, like they had been waiting all night. They all pounced on the dude. Ten guys were wailing on him, and the poor kid's girlfriend was trying to protect him. There was a huge crowd of people coming out of the club, and everybody was taken off guard. Next thing you know, the Trenton police show up, and there were a lot of them. They got there really fast, which never happened. There were blue lights everywhere. As soon as we saw the cops we ran to the car and got the fuck out of there. About a month later in the [music tabloid] *East Coast Rocker*, there was a cover article on skinhead violence with one of those headlines like, *Skinheads… Out of Control?* that were so popular at the time. They had the famous picture of the skinheads running full force in the Wall of Death. That was one of the last times Dee Dee played with them.

Ken Hinchey (City Gardens regular): I was a huge Ramones fan, and in 1989 I had a chance to interview Dee Dee Ramone when he was promoting his rap album. I didn't care what it was for. It was an excuse to meet one of the Ramones. The day before the interview was scheduled to happen, Dee Dee's publicist contacted the magazine's editor and said, "Don't bother going up for the interview because Dee Dee's missing." That whole thing—they couldn't find Dee Dee for a couple days—was supposed to be off the record, but it's such a good story. It's what you want to hear about the Ramones! It adds to the mystique.

When the interview finally did happen, the photographer and I went to Dee Dee's apartment in New York City, and his girlfriend was there with him. I guess he was friendly, but every question I asked got a yes-or-no answer, and I couldn't get him into a conversation. I've seen other interviews, and I think that's just how he was… he didn't have much to say. I had read in a 'zine that the Ramones did a song with Dusty Springfield called *1-2-3-4*. I asked him about it, and he looked at me and said, "How do you know about that?" I let it drop.

His rap album was getting panned, but during the interview he played me some stuff that has never been released and was much better. It sampled Duke Ellington and was much more hip that what he had put out, which sounded like a novelty record. It was horrible. While they were setting up to do the photo-shoot, I saw his acoustic guitar in the corner and I asked him if I could check it out, and he said sure. So I picked it up and started playing "Blitzkrieg Bop." He looked at me, like, "Oh, brother..."

When the photographer started taking the photos, he said, "Let me pose with my gun!" He grabbed the gun, and then he said, "Let me get the clip." He put the clip in, so the gun was live! As he's putting the clip in, his girlfriend is yelling, "No, Dee Dee, no!" It was an odd experience.

Jerry Jones (The Fiendz vocalist): That show in 1990, opening for the Ramones... we were scared to death. It was the scariest thing, but the most exciting thing. When we started our band, we loved the Ramones but we never dreamed that we would have the chance to open for them. Back then, the audience would throw things at the opening band and just yell, "Ramones!" through the whole set. We were terrified to get up there, it felt like suicide. But by that show, we had already played there a bunch of times and had a following. When Randy announced us, the crowd was like, "Yeahhhhhhhhhhh!!" And we were like, "What, they want us?! They like us?!" We had an amazing show and we sold an unbelievable amount of merch. At the end of the night, I said to Randy, "I didn't even get a chance to talk to the Ramones." And he said, "Jerry, they aren't going to talk to you. They don't even talk to each other!"

Monte A. Melnick: Being that we were so close to home, you know, coming from New York, we didn't have to worry about getting... *anything* for some of the band members. Dee Dee had his own spot in New York, and it was only an hour away. It got crazy when we went overseas. I would call the promoter to tell him that when we got off the plane, he had to have this.... you know, *supply,* whatever you want to call it, for Dee Dee. But an hour from New York? He was able to bring his own.

Johnny Ramone: As Dee Dee got more serious, the problem got worse. Early on, he was straight for the shows, but then he would show up hung over on pills or drunk. In the beginning, we were all straight all the time, at least when we played the show. But even when he got really bad, Dee Dee would always play. He would never cancel. Dee Dee was on the road with hepatitis and could still play fine.

Stephen Brown: The only asshole I ever met in the back bar was Dee Dee Ramone. He was a dickhead. He didn't want to talk to nobody.

Ken Hinchey: During the interview I asked him if he was going to leave the Ramones, since he had this solo thing out, and he said, "No, I'm not leaving." Not a month later I see Kurt Loder on MTV Music News saying that Dee Dee was leaving because being in the band was a threat to his sobriety.

Rich O'Brien: A few weeks before he died, Dee Dee was in Philly for the premiere of the film *Bikini Bandits*, and I was working at a club down the street from the premiere after-party. I'm outside and I see this motley crew of people walking down the street—and two of them were Dee Dee Ramone and Corey Feldman. All I could think was, "You both look old."

Monte A. Melnick: The only difficult thing about City Gardens was getting the band to the stage, because we had to go through the crowd all the way from the back of the building to the front. Everyone liked to touch the band on the way up, and sometimes it got a little crazy. But Randy took care of that. He always had plenty of security. In fact, he got extra security for those nights.

Jim Norton: The other thing about The Ramones was the dressing room. The security protocol for The Ramones was like this: The Ramones would show up right before doors opened and they might—might—hop up on stage for a quick soundcheck. And by "quick," I mean ten minutes at the most. They would go up to the dressing room and they would stay there most of the night. Then, when it was time to perform, we would assemble five or six security guys at the foot of the stairs by the dressing room. We'd assemble another seven or eight guys at the single door that was to the right of the stage between the soundboard and the stage. It was one of the doors you got thrown out of when you were stagediving. You'd have one or two guys outside those doors as well. The Ramones would come down the stairs, and we would walk to the back bar room and go through the set of double doors to the outside, go around the building to the single door near the stage, and bang on that door a few times. The door would open and security would basically form two cordons and walk through with the band. Sometimes a person would specifically be walking between the band members, so you didn't have all four band members in one shot. You would spread it out a little bit.

The prestige gig for the security guys was to guard Joey Ramone. Of course, he's *Joey Ramone*. I am proud to say that on more than one occasion I was Joey Ramone's personal bodyguard for a whole 15 feet. But there was one time in particular that stands out. I was walking behind Joey Ramone, holding my left arm out to move the crowd and protect him, and he reached out his left arm to shake hands or high-five somebody, and he put his arm back down, but he put it over top of my arm. There was a bit of a crush, and his left arm pushed my left arm further into his body. Now I am behind Joey Ramone and I am spooning Joey Ramone while standing behind him. My arm is around his belly and it's getting pushed in by the crowd. Let me tell you something creepy: his gut was so loose and gelatinous that it is not much of an exaggeration for me to say that I felt his spine. My arm just kept going. It was like his entire body was hollow and he had no organs. It was the strangest god-damned thing I ever felt.

Ken Hinchey: The Ramones didn't have set lists, because it was always the same and they had it memorized. When a new record came out, they would take out a few older songs and replace them with some new ones, but that was it. It didn't change. They always started with "Durango 95," then "Teenage Lobotomy," followed by "Psycho Therapy" into "Blitzkrieg Bop." One time I saw Joey Ramone had a piece of paper with him, and I'm like, "Are they changing the set list?!" I went up to the stage to see what was written on it, and it said, "City Gardens, Trenton, NJ." That's what he needed to know. Not what songs to play, but where he was.

Randy Now: The Ramones told me that City Gardens was the hottest club they played. In all the years, and all the places they played, City Gardens was it. It would get so hot that Johnny would take off his leather jacket.

Amy Yates Wuelfing: In addition to being hot and swampy, the place would be so packed that everyone spilled beer on you. But you couldn't get mad if someone spilled beer on you, because it wasn't their fault. I have a vivid memory of standing by the stage at a Ramones show, my shoes so soaked with beer that they squished when I walked, and I could see wind coming off the speakers. It was so loud, it made wind.

Randy Now: The Ramones played so loud that they once tripped a circuit breaker and we lost power. They actually had to play quieter to keep the sound from going out.

Johnny Ramone: At the first show with the Marshalls I deafened everyone because I didn't know you only need a half stack for a club that size.

George Tabb (Ramones' road crew): On John's side of the stage they had one Marshall so John could hear himself, and one bass cab. On Dee Dee's side was one Ampeg bass cabinet so he could hear himself, and one Marshall to hear Johnny. Then you had all these other Marshalls with nothing coming out. They were decoys.

Scott Foster (1124 Records): No matter how early we got there, the line was always wrapped around the building ten times. You had to stand out there and wait forever.

Monte A. Melnick: I couldn't have written my book [*On The Road With The Ramones*] with the stuff about Joey's obsessive compulsive disorder while he was still alive. It was rough what he went through. He overcame that and did what he had to do onstage. Back then, we didn't know what it was—even he didn't know what it was, for years. We just thought he was out of his mind. It was unbelievable. Nobody knew what the heck was going on.

Tracy Parks-Pattik (City Gardens employee): Back then, it wasn't like hanging out with rock stars or anything. We were all part of the same scene. I'm pretty tall for a girl, and I remember standing next to Joey Ramone one night and only coming up to his chest. I had to look up at him. We were just hanging out, shooting the shit. He didn't really talk much. When you look at it in this day and age, I have a 20-year old kid who's long past the age of idolizing people, but he likes The Ramones.

For him, to hear about his mom growing up and hanging out with these people is pretty weird. Nobody believes him when he tells them about it.

Monte A. Melnick: When they were onstage and doing The Ramones thing, it was what they lived for. They knew that they had a good thing going. By the end they couldn't stomach each other, but they'd get up there and play a show and you'd never know. That's The Ramones magic. That's why they tolerated each other, because being in The Ramones was a special thing, and when you get onstage in front of an audience like that, there's nothing like it. That's why a lot of people take drugs when they are off the stage, because they want to replace that high. You can't get a drug as good as that.

Jeff Stress Davis (City Gardens regular): I went to City Gardens so often there are times where it almost became routine. I'm almost embarrassed to admit this, but I saw The Ramones several times and never even paid attention while they were playing because I was hanging out with friends and stuff. It was so common for us to see these great bands over and over again, that it almost became like background music.

Henry Hose (City Gardens regular): The Ramones played City Gardens so many times, and it seemed like they were always playing somewhere in the tri-state area. We had a running joke... If we can't find anything to do this weekend, we can always go see the Ramones—because you know they're playing somewhere.

Bruce Markoff (City Gardens regular): I probably saw the Ramones 12 or 15 times, and one of my regrets is not seeing them more. If I had the offer to take a year off my life to see them again, I'd say yeah, I'll go for a year. Back then, I took them for granted because I saw them so many times. There were times when they were playing the club, and me and [bouncers] Rich and Carl would be at the front door, laughing and naming the song they were going to play next. I look back at most of my life and say, *what a jackass I was*, but I was so naïve and stupid and jaded... Christ they're not even alive now, let alone playing. It's embarrassing to think back. And you know, there are probably a million people on the planet who would kill to see just one of those shows I saw, and there I was, rolling my eyes at them.

Joseph Kuzemka (Trenton Punk Rock Flea Market): One thing I'll never let myself live down is that the first punk record I ever bought when I was 12 years old was The Ramones self-titled record. They've been probably one of my favorite bands ever since then, and I never saw them. In the span that I was going to City Gardens, they probably played 10 or 12 times, and I always said, "Well, I'll see them next time." I was into the straight-edge scene at the time, and if there was a straight edge show the same night, I'd go to that. I said, "I'm going to see The Ramones next time they come, because they're always going to be playing City Gardens." I actually showed up at a Ramones show once, and I met up with some friends outside, and they said they were going to TGI Friday's to get some food and then go back and see the Ramones. I went, and we didn't make it back in time. That was my last opportunity to see the Ramones. One of my all-time favorite bands played 22 times within three miles of my house, and I never saw them. I'll never forgive myself for it. Any time I know someone who says that they saw The Ramones X amount of times, I want to kick myself. It's difficult to think about a band that I adored so much, that played so close to my home, and I never made the time to see them.

Joey Ramone died of lymphoma on April 15, 2001. He was 49.

Dee Dee Ramone died from a heroin overdose on June 5, 2002. He was 50.

Johnny Ramone died from prostate cancer on September 15, 2004. He was 55.

PART THREE
COME AS YOU ARE

CHAPTER 7

Every Thursday...
It's 90-Cent Dance Night

For many people, their entire City Gardens experience was 90¢ Dance Night. Later it became 95¢, and then 99¢, but most remember 90¢. Enormously popular, 90¢ Dance Night was the cash cow that kept City Gardens afloat and served to underwrite the live-music aspect of the club. In addition, while there were a couple of other clubs in the area—Brothers, and the Granada— only City Gardens offered universal acceptance. The non-judgmental, "anything goes" atmosphere of dance night made it a place where everyone was welcome. Gay, straight, black, white, preppy, jock, punk, whatever... as long as you didn't bother anyone, whatever you were was perfectly acceptable, as was dancing by yourself. And by "dancing," we mean full-on interpretive dance. It was an entire dance floor packed with people who danced like no one was watching.

Jon Stewart (TV host/City Gardens bartender): There was no place [like City Gardens], nothing else. If there were another place in the area, we all would have gone there. Do you really think we would have gone to Calhoun Street?

The first time I ever went to City Gardens was for 90-cent Dance Night. I went there a lot by myself... that's what a loser I was. It was one of the few places where you could dance by yourself. You could wear a broach and no one would say anything. It was the '80s. We all dressed like Molly Ringwald and we didn't know why. Even the guys.

Gal Gaiser (City Gardens DJ): A lot of people didn't understand the concept of dancing by yourself at a club.

Randy Now: Thursday-night dance night was Tut's idea. In the beginning, The Shades played every Thursday, until they broke up. We were already doing a lot of dance nights during the week to keep the place open and make money. When we launched Thursday nights, we also had Sunday-night dances, which were really popular. And then I started doing a '60s music night on Monday. Back then, I was doing what Little Steven is doing on his show now, totally mixing things up. I went from Devo's "Mongoloid" into Johnny Rivers'"Memphis Tennessee," or James Brown coming out of The Pretenders. It was a mix of new things and old standards. But for some reason, 90¢ Dance Night on Thursday took off like nothing else. My pay was based on attendance, but I usually got about $100 or $150 a night, even if there were 700 people there. I spent the money on more records.

Ron Kernast (City Gardens regular): When I first started going to dance nights in 1980 or '81, the front room wasn't open yet. It was all in the back. There were maybe a couple dozen people, and the DJ booth literally looked like a phone booth. I went by myself because I didn't know anyone else into that kind of music. And after the first night, that was it. I was addicted.

Carlos Santos (City Gardens DJ): I graduated in 1980 from UMass and, at the time, I was dating a woman who was heading to Princeton to pursue graduate work. She said, "You're unemployed, so why don't you come down with me? I can pack my stuff in your car." I packed my boxes of records into this little Volkswagen Beetle, shoved all of her stuff in too, and then a few personal things of mine. We managed to get down to Princeton with this car, which at one point broke down on the New Jersey Turnpike. It was so jam-packed full of stuff, I could barely see. I didn't have a place to live in Princeton and didn't have any money, so I stayed illegally with my friend in her dorm for about six months.

Trenton Times *article from July 1992 about City Gardens shedding its "punk" image and setting the tone of "Anything Goes." The band Regressive Aid is misidentified as "Recessive Aide."*

Rich O'Brien (City Gardens employee): The allure of 90¢ Dance Night was that it was dirt cheap. It was 90¢ to get in and 90¢ for a draft beer. You could go there with $10, get in, drink seven beers and leave a $2 tip. And even at 90¢, the bar was probably still making 50¢ a beer. Everyone who was different could go there, be themselves, and not worry. No one would give you a hard time or try to pick a fight with you.

The reason City Gardens still comes to my mind at least a dozen times a week is the fact that you could go there any night of the week and be entertained. It wasn't the same boring, cookie-cutter stuff night after night. You could go on a Wednesday and see reggae, or go for dance music on Thursday. Friday night could be a big band like the Ramones or Violent Femmes, and Sundays was hardcore. I have never seen it duplicated in any of the bars or clubs I've worked in since, and I have worked in a lot of places. Nothing comes close.

Deirdre Humenik (City Gardens employee): The door was 90¢, drinks were 90¢. To break a dollar, you needed a dime. There were dimes all over the place. Dimes everywhere. Dimes, dimes, dimes.

Carlos Santos: Thursday night was basically a night where you could let off steam and then cruise through Friday, whether it was Friday classes or work. It was the perfect night to go out for a lot of people, but it needed to be local, and it needed to be some place where they could leave early if they wanted to, with no pressure. Go hang out, have some fun, and have a few drinks.

Ron Kernast: My parents sent me to calisthenics and dance classes when I was a kid, and I took up German dance since it's part of my culture. At City Gardens, you were free to express yourself that way. You could roll around on the floor and it didn't matter. If people looked at me strange, who gave a shit? There were some people who came to dances nights just to watch the crazy dancing.

Karey Maurice Counts (City Gardens regular): City Gardens was very close to my neighborhood and, basically, was my world for a good ten years of my life. I discovered the place through the [daily newspaper] *Trentonian*. City Gardens would advertise in the entertainment section. The club was located on the other side of the Ewing landfill from my neighborhood, so it was within walking distance, but to get there I had to travel across the landfill, which was a pretty interesting. They had junkyard dogs, and the first night I went to the club I had to run through the landfill, chased by dogs, and I fell and ripped my jeans. So the first time I walked in, I looked kind of shabby and it was pretty much—I won't say an all-white venue—but there weren't many blacks who went there. So when I got to the door with ripped jeans, looking a little tattered, I fit right in. I was a little bit standoffish, basically getting the feel of the place, but I felt comfortable. No one threatened me. There were a few people dancing, skanking around. I was like, *this is it*, this is home. I never wanted to be "home" in my real house, so it was a place for me to go every week.

Vanessa Solack (City Gardens regular): I was a bad girl there. If someone was leaning on the bar, I would come up behind them, grab their ankles, and give an upward motion. They would go right over the bar. That was kind of my signature move. I got in a lot of trouble and, at one point, had to pay $75 to get into 90¢ Dance Night. If I was good, at the end of the night, I got my money back. If I wasn't, they kept my $75. That's how much trouble I got into there. Within a month, if no incidents occurred, it would be $50 to get in, like I was on probation. Each month it went down until I got to the regular price. What incident led up to that probationary period? My girlfriend beat up one of the bouncers. She was more than able to beat up pretty much any guy in the bar, and she did. That was the straw that broke the camel's back. And I think it was more that the bouncer was embarrassed he got beat up by a girl than anything else.

Jon Stewart: If you went there and you drank and danced long enough, they assumed you worked there. I was out of school and bartending at another joint up on Route 1, and I used to go to City Gardens a lot. Eventually, I started working there. We were all bar friends. We spent more time around that bar than anyplace else. The other bar I worked at, Franklin Tavern, was more of a "bar." City Gardens offered the chance to be yourself, whereas the Tavern offered the chance to buy an "Ayatollah Assahola" t-shirt and yell at the news on TV. City Gardens was a blast. Tut and Patti put together a great family atmosphere.

Gal Gaiser: I used to deejay Saturday dance nights at City Gardens if there wasn't a band, but it wasn't nearly as crowded as Thursday. I could play whole album sides until people started to show up. I would go over and talk to Jon Stewart, and all he ever wanted to hear was the Psychedelic Furs. A while later, I went to see Gilbert Gottfried at a local comedy club, and the opening act was Jon Stewart. I couldn't believe it. I had no idea he did comedy. I saw him before he went on and said, "What are you doing here?" He said, "Opening for Gilbert Gottfried. What are *you* doing here?" I said, "I guess I'm watching you open for Gilbert Gottfried!"

Doug Reinke (dance night regular): I came to the New Jersey area from Middle America. I always knew I was different on some level, but I really didn't know what my options were. I think what impacted me the most about City Gardens was the gray scale of alternative choices; it wasn't just black or white. You weren't gay or straight, or you weren't a punk or a preppie. There was hardcore, there was gay, there was straight, there was new wave... there were all these different elements that intermixed. I mean, there were certain nights I would not go to City Gardens because I'd probably get killed. At some shows you would see all the guys with shaved heads punching each other in the face. But there was an element of that crowd that would show up to dance night, and then there was an element of the dance night people who would go to those shows, so there was a crossover. It blended into this culture that I found really interesting.

Rob Reid (Dance night regular): Back in the early '80s, you didn't know what was acceptable and not acceptable. Growing up in suburbia, you were afraid of anything taboo. I partially credit City Gardens with who I am today. Where I grew up in Levittown, Pennsylvania, you didn't venture too far outside Levittown, Pennsylvania. At City Gardens, you met people who were different. I was allowed to be who I was. I wasn't out [of the closet] when I first started going there, but it absolutely made it easy to come out. Like, who am I kidding? I'm gay! I never officially "came out." It was more like I stopped pretending to be somebody else.

Amy Yates Wuelfing: I had been to dance nights at new wave clubs in Philly, and it was unnerving. Everyone was dressed to the nines, the hair, the make-up, the whole thing. The dancing was very much about show… people were performing in the hopes of impressing everyone. It was all about going to see and be seen, and I hated it.

Carlos Santos: I got the chance to deejay Thursday nights because Randy got an offer from a club called Zadar in New Hope, PA. Randy approached Tut, told him what was happening, and to make a long story short, the two of them had a big argument. A big falling out. Randy walked out and asked me to come to Zadar with him. I've always been of the opinion that you should stick to what you have, because you could go to something that turns out to be worse. I stayed at City Gardens and said, "Best of luck, hope it all works out. But I'm hanging around here."

Randy Now: I went to Zadar because that guy promised me the world. He actually told me that I could live there too, in apartments near the club. But it all fell apart the first night. The first night Zadar was open, I had booked the Waitresses. The band broke up that very day, and no one ever called to tell me! So, here were are, new club, grand opening, no one called, and the band didn't show up. We had to give everyone their money back. I booked a few more shows there—Dead Kennedys, Circle Jerks—but it fell apart.

I think that guy is in jail now for dealing cocaine.

Carlos Santos: Tut didn't have any DJs to do Thursdays, so he brought in outside radio DJs Mel Toxic and Lee Paris. They did a night or two, but they didn't have an understanding of what the crowd wanted to hear, because it wasn't their gig. They were focused on the more popular new-wavy stuff, not the alternative new wave stuff and post-punk music that the club had built its reputation on. People got pissed. They threw drinks at them and booed them. At least that's how I heard it.

Randy Now: The first Thursday night I was gone, Tut had Lee Paris and Mel Toxic come in, and I heard that they got booed. It made me kinda proud, actually. Here I am, getting replaced by two pretty famous local DJs, and the crowd didn't like them as much as me!

Carlos Santos: Whatever happened, people complained to Tut, so I asked him if I could do Thursdays and he agreed. I was the main DJ on Thursday nights from late '83 to '94 or so. When I picked up Thursdays, we were bringing in 400-500 people a night, which was actually pretty good at the time. But then Tut did something that was kind of interesting... he put in a new dance floor.

Karey Maurice Counts: I met Tut and we started talking, and I said, "Look, the floor is made of concrete, people can't really dance on this floor. You need to put down linoleum so that it's easier to dance on." I was the one who got him to put money out, because Tut wouldn't spend a penny on the building. Then I said, "Let me paint the walls." So I painted the front of the stage with these Keith Haring-esque kind of characters. After the stage was done, he allowed me to do the walls, and I painted these monstrous big feet... almost like a giant was walking up the walls or dancing up the walls. It actually did a lot for the visual aspect of the club, because it was pretty much naked. I did all of it in one night, the whole room, which was really amazing. Tut was watching me run from side to side, and he's like, "I didn't expect you to do the whole thing." I was like, well, it's too late now!

Carlos Santos: Tut actually put some money into the club. Meanwhile, a lot of the music that I had been playing for a while was now in heavy rotation on MTV—radio was picking up on it—and the next thing you know, we were having almost a thousand people in that club every

Thursday night. On some Thursdays, they had people lining up at the door and letting people in as others left because we were way past the occupancy limit.

John Morrison (Dance night regular): I knew City Gardens was a punk club, and I wasn't into punk, so I never had interest in going. I'd heard stories about fights and stuff, but then we went to dance night. I had listened to DJ Carlos on the radio and I had this huge fantasy about him, like he was this gorgeous Latino man. And I was like, "Ooooh, DJ Carlos is going to be there…" So I walked in, saw Carlos, and was like, [disappointed] "Oh." But we got to be really good friends, and we're still friends today.

Carlos Santos: I never really made much money as a Thursday night DJ, or as a DJ period. I had to buy my own records. Randy was a good guy. He made sure I was set up when he left, even though we had disagreements. Randy felt that I was the most obvious DJ to follow in his footsteps, with the music I was playing.

Doug Reinke: My experience with City Gardens was complex because I loved disco, I loved dance music, and I loved going out disco dancing. To be exposed to Nitzer Ebb and New Order, and this whole different realm of music was amazing. I used to be embarrassed that I liked disco. When I was in high school everyone was listening to Led Zeppelin and Lynyrd Skynyrd, and I had Donna Summer albums. In an interesting way, dance night gave me permission to still like dance music.

Rob Reid: I used to love what Carlos played. We heard songs on dance night and then went to the Princeton Record Exchange to buy it. That's how we found our music. Every Thursday I heard new music that I had to have. I still think about those days because they were probably the best times I ever had. I don't remember being a child. My childhood is a blank. But I remember City Gardens.

Randy Now: After a while, I went back to Tut and we decided to work together again, but Carlos stayed on as the Thursday DJ.

Rich O'Brien: I've discussed it with people who went there, and we agree that there was an actual City Gardens dance move. There was a kick-like move that everyone did. It was funny because you would see people at other clubs doing that move, and it was like, "Oh, they got that from City Gardens."

Rob Reid: I do believe I was the originator of that move. It began when Carlos was playing industrial music. I don't know how to describe it, but it was sort of a front kick-turn move. And you used your arms, because a lot of people didn't use their arms much back then. We started flailing our arms around. We were in great shape at that time because dancing was our form of exercise. To be honest with you, we drank on some nights, but it wasn't about going to the bar and drinking. It was about going there, dancing, and seeing everybody.

Ron Kernast: People who know me, and know how I dance, know to stay away from me. Stand clear! I have a scar on my hand from dancing. I hit Gal Gaiser's teeth as I was flinging my arms around.

Amy Yates Wuelfing: It was about four or five hours of vigorous dancing with short bathroom breaks. We weren't there to sit at the bar and get drunk... not that those shakers of red death didn't get to us some nights.

Doug Reinke: We would dance, sweat like pigs, and then go sit in a 7-11 parking lot, drink Big Gulps and eat tons of junk food, or go play Ms. Pac-Man at a diner until five in the morning.

Rob Reid: All of the elements were there: really cool people, great music, seeing different cultures, and seeing different fashions, and it made people more creative. I think a lot of careers were built out of the fun we had there. And how I treat other people was influenced by City Gardens. Everybody was accepted, and that's what I liked. Anybody could go there and everybody was treated exactly the same. There was no judgment in that place. And back in the early '80s, you couldn't go anywhere without being judged if you were different.

Carlos Santos: 90¢ Dance Night became massive, especially in the late '80s. Tut told me that if it wasn't for Thursday nights, the club would not have survived. The club couldn't make it on the bands coming in, because oftentimes people at shows didn't drink. And the bar is where the club made its money.

John Morrison: We called it the gay corner. If you were walking toward the stage, it was the right corner in the back, because that was where all the gay people hung out. But nobody cared. Everyone was kind of a reject anyway, including the straight people. It was like we found a home where we could just be ourselves and nobody cared. Even when the Trenton State College kids started coming, they were outnumbered so it wasn't a problem. I never had any incidents of homophobia or fights. We just had this attitude, like, *we own this place.*

Doug Reinke: I came out at the same time I started going to City Gardens, and I wasn't really comfortable going to the gay bars in New Hope. The crowd there was just very old-school gays who were like 15 to 20 years older than me and wanted to have you over for fussy dinner parties and then get in your pants. I knew I was gay, but I didn't want to be around these guys with mustaches and chest hair hanging out. I felt like that was a caricature of what being gay meant. Then, going to City Gardens on dance nights, there were gay people who were artists and funky and different and didn't all look alike. One had this style, and another had that style, and it was all so seamlessly mixed in with straight people, who were also creative. So it wasn't about being gay, really, because being gay was a secondary thing. That's how I always really felt about myself: I didn't want being gay to define who I am. I wanted to be able to experience what it meant to be gay, but on my own terms. I think that's really the only way I became truly comfortable coming out as gay, was because of City Gardens and dance night... that whole no-judgment environment and this sense of creativity that you could find on your own terms.

Rob Reid: I didn't go to gay clubs because I didn't go for the gay scene. I never have and still don't. I always went to—I wouldn't say straight clubs—but the unique clubs that played the best music and where fashion was cool. Gay clubs played gay music and I really wasn't into that. I liked more of the social thing, the camaraderie of City Gardens, and back then we kind of traveled as a pack. We all went to City Gardens, but then a whole subset of people would end up at Zadar another night, and yet a third group would go to Philadelphia. It was a society unto itself.

Bruce Markoff (City Gardens regular): There were definitely people at certain shows and not at others shows. And people who went to Dance

Night and not shows, just different cliques of people. But there was a lot of crossover, a lot of people who went to shows that maybe you wouldn't expect them to, and I think a lot of that had to do with City Gardens being a "these are my people" kind of thing. To risk being cliché, I felt that way from the get-go. I had gone to all these other places—dance nights and that kind of thing—and never felt comfortable until I was there.

Gal Gaiser: I deejayed at both City Gardens and Zadar, and about 80% of the music was the same, but at Zadar you could play poppier music. At Zadar, you could play Madonna, which you couldn't at City Gardens even though a lot of the same people at Zadar on Friday and were at City Gardens on Thursday. On Thursday they would hate Madonna, but on Friday they wanted to hear it. I could name names, if I had to.

Doug Reinke: We were all young and kind of floundering and finding ourselves, but in some strange way City Gardens added structure to our lives. If it was Thursday, we knew where we were going to be. It gave us stability during a scary time in our lives. It was like a home away from home and, for me, it opened my mind to different possibilities in life. I didn't want to follow this prescribed path, where I go to college and then get a house in the suburbs. I can be gay and live in the city and not necessarily have a traditional lifestyle. I tried to start a typical career working 9-5, and then I realized I didn't want that, I wanted an alternative life. I want to get up every day and do something I enjoy, and if I don't, I'm going to find a path with something different and better. I just want to live an honest life. I feel like that whole period of my life at City Gardens really gave me the strength and the vision to know that that is a real choice.

Carl Humenik (City Gardens security): My attitude has always been that I don't care what anyone else is, gay or straight, because people shouldn't care what I am. Nothing has changed my view on that. When I was working security, I did have to break up a few fights on dance nights, and it was usually the skinheads who were bothering someone. I remember vividly some guy with a shaved head came in one night, but he wasn't a skinhead, and he was gay. He had eyeliner on and all that, and the regular skinheads told him, "You can't dress like that if you have a shaved head!" and they started giving him shit. I walked over there, got in between them, and said, "Okay, what's the problem here?" They said, "He can't come in here dressed like that!" Blah blah blah. And I was like, "He can come here dressed any way he wants, and he can do anything he wants, and there's nothing you guys can do about it." They go, "Well, we don't like that kind of stuff here!" I said "Then you're free to leave. And I'm sure if you choose to stay the rest of the night, this is not going to be the last thing you see that offends you." I'm pretty sure the skinheads were there by mistake that night, like they came on a night that they didn't normally come, thinking they owned the place. That night, they found out they didn't.

Doug Reinke: It's an alternative lifestyle for me. It's so funny that that term has such a negative context, but for me, that's what I always aspired to after being exposed to City Gardens. Once I saw that, I never wanted anything less.

The biggest 90¢ Dance Night every year was Thanksgiving.

Carlos Santos: The thing about Thanksgiving night is that it brought out all of the old regulars who were in town and had eaten a ton of turkey and needed to burn it off. All of the new regulars would come out too, because this was their thing. The place was packed because it was several generations of City Gardens regulars all coming together on a single Thursday night—Thanksgiving. And some hardcore and punk kids who went to shows but didn't usually come on Thursdays would come just to get away from their families. Even when attendance for Thursdays in general started to drop off in '93 or so, it would still be mobbed on Thanksgiving.

Rich O'Brien: Thanksgiving was a perfect storm. Everybody would come home for Thanksgiving, and 90% of us had dysfunctional families or some bizarreness going on, which probably led us to City Gardens in the first place. So everyone would escape and go to City Gardens to hang with the other misfits. On Thanksgiving, after spending all day with your family by 8 o'clock, everyone was like, *I need a drink.* Most places were closed. City Gardens was one of the few places open.

In 1993, DJ Carlos left 90¢ Dance Night.

Carlos Santos: I had two reasons for leaving Thursday nights. One, I started losing interest in music. It was the early '90s, I was still into it, but not as much, and I couldn't afford the records. I was also married at that point, I had a kid, and things were changing. The club scene was changing too. People weren't coming out as much. Attendance started to drop because of Katmandu. Two, I think the audience for that type of music was dwindling. People were more interested in dancing to mainstream stuff. People wanted to dance to hip-hop and stuff like that, which I wasn't into.

Randy Now: After Carlos left Thursday nights, I went back and deejayed. I was doing an all-ages dance night on Friday night at City Gardens at the time, playing hip-hop and whatnot, so I just started doing both nights.

Carlos Santos: Katmandu started taking some of the people away, especially the college kids. Also, I think people were just not interested in going to clubs the way they had been in the '80s and the very beginning of the '90s. The whole scene was changing. We weren't the only people that noticed this. Other clubs were beginning to feel the hurt.

John Morrison: City Gardens approached me in the summer of '94 to create another dance night on Saturdays, and we called it Cyberflesh. The first one was a big success, and then Tut let us keep doing it. Everybody brought their own televisions from home, and we set it up to look cool. One person made this industrial kind of like sculpture with PVC pipes and constructed cages. I was in charge of doing promotional work, so I did all the cards and t-shirts, as well as being a DJ. It was a revolving cast of DJs.

I was taking a class on the Holocaust, and I learned that in the Nazi Constitution, paragraph 175, was the law that outlawed homosexuality. After the war, gay people were called "one-hundred-seventy-fivers" as a derogatory term. So my DJ name was DJ175. We did Cyberflesh for about a year.

In 1997 a new Trenton club, Katmandu, opened at Riverview Executive Plaza near the Waterfront Park in Mercer County, NJ. Located on the Delaware River, Katmandu was a large restaurant and bar, as well as a nightclub.

Karey Maurice Counts: I thought 90¢ Dance Night would last forever. But when Katmandu was erected, things changed. A lot of people said, "I'm not going to go there, I'm going to stay true to City Gardens." And what happened? People went right down there, down to the river, to Katmandu. What killed City Gardens was Katmandu and that dance night grew to a point where all the intimacy and the artistic expression was gone. You had homophobic people coming in, and that changed the dance floor.

Carlos Santos: As dance night got more popular, there were college kids who really weren't into the music showing up because it was a place to be seen. That was fine with me—a lot of the regulars hated them—but it paid the bills.

Gal Gaiser: We might call it 90¢ Dance Night, but a large number of people called it College Night.

Ron Kernast: We wanted to just dance, but there would be a bunch of people just standing there at the edge of the dance floor, drinking their beers, watching.

Gal Gaiser: I think those people maybe wanted to dance but were too self-conscious. To me, you look stupider just standing there drinking all night. They would dance if "How Soon Is Now" came on, or "Blue Monday." Those songs got everyone out.

Karey Maurice Counts: I'm talking about the people who were *spectators*, watching us on the dance floor until they made us uncomfortable. More people were hanging out and looking at the freaks rather than dancing. That's when it changed for me.

Randy Now: When Katmandu opened, they offered me a job booking bands, and they wanted to pay me $25,000 a year. I didn't take the job, and they never booked bands other than local stuff.

Jon Stewart: Did I have concerns for my safety while I was working [at City Gardens]? Of course! In the club... out of the club... around the club. I can remember those dashes to the car through the parking lot after work. Thank God I drove a piece of shit. It was hard to tell if my car ever got broken into there, because it's not like I locked it or it had anything in it. Not that that fence provided a great deal of protection. The parking lot was surrounded by half a chain-link fence. There'd be, like, two panels [of fence], and then a break, and then a couple more panels, then a break, then a hole, then another panel.

Gal Gaiser: I never felt scared there, but looking back on it now, I should have.

Karey Maurice Counts: Sure, there were a few car windows that got broken, but for a while the club kept growing. It got so big on Thursday nights that people who lived across the street, in the projects, would try to see if they could find a coin or two. The club had security, but it wasn't enough. There were always issues with the cops too. City Gardens was right on the dividing line between Trenton and Ewing, and the Trenton police did not want to deal with City Gardens. They would say it was Ewing's problem and Ewing said it was Trenton's problem.

Rich O'Brien: After 1994, when Randy stopped doing shows, that crowd stopped going to the club. They figured there was nothing going on. And a lot of people got older and didn't go out as much. Katmandu was nicer, newer, and had a better sound system, and they pulled a certain demographic away from City Gardens. In the bar business, if you have a happening night with 600 people, and 200 people leave and go elsewhere, the remaining 400 will think, *this isn't as cool as it used to be,* and they'll stop going too.

Ron Kernast: Tut put a pizza oven in and Wednesday was Pizza Night, and we'd order pizza with pickles. Rich [O'Brien] would play music and we'd hang out. At the end, especially on weeknights, it almost became like a local's bar. It slowly started to wind down.

Amy Yates Wuelfing: One the reasons dance night faded away was that people went on to live the lives they were meant to...because they were inspired by City Gardens and gained the confidence they needed to branch out. Some people moved to New York or Chicago to start new careers, and some people went back to school or started businesses. A few started families, although a lot of people stayed single and never had kids. Dance Night let people know that they didn't have to do what society expected them to do. Not many people from Dance Night are still friends with the people they went to high school with, but everybody's still friends with the people they went to Dance Night with.

Karey Maurice Counts: I didn't go to college. I went to disco.

City Gardens closed its doors for good in 1999. The next year, a new club opened in the old City Gardens building—Club XL. In 2001, Rich O'Brien arranged a "City Gardens Reunion" at Club XL.

Rich O'Brien: Toward the end of City Gardens, I had been doing some deejaying and dance nights, and I was the last person out the door on that final night. After it reopened as Club XL, the brothers who ran the club contacted me, since they knew I was involved with City Gardens. They told me, "We like your crowd and we're hoping that we can get a crowd like that in here." I knew their best bet was to do it over the Thanksgiving weekend, because so many people who had moved away come home, and Thanksgiving was always our biggest dance night. This was 2001, so we got the word out with email and word-of-mouth. The weird thing was that they didn't seem to have faith that our crowd would come out, so they tried to do an end-run around me. They got another DJ to play stuff too, which ended up being the only down part of the night.

Amy Yates Wuelfing: The old crowd was dying to see what they had done to the place, but it looked pretty much the same. The black and white checkerboard dance floor was still there. They moved the DJ booth, set up some white South Beach-like couches here and there, and hung some gauzy drapes, but overall it looked the same.

Rich O'Brien: I think they were expecting 75 people to show up, and we had about 550–600.

Postcard from the 2001 City Gardens Reunion at Club XL

Ron Kernast: Tut and Patti even came. Tut still owned the building, so I guess he just decided to come.

Amy Yates Wuelfing: The regulars who went to Club XL tolerated us that night, and a few of them even came out and danced. We literally drank the bar dry—they ran out of beer and had to go out to a liquor store to buy more. We also tipped the bartenders really well, and they were so pleased that, at the end of the night, they all stood up on the bar and applauded us. Overall, it was a really great night. It was just like old times.

Rich O'Brien: The first one at Thanksgiving went so well that we decided to do another one over Christmas break. We didn't get as many people for that one, probably about half. They wanted us to do the City Gardens stuff in the back part of the club though, and they would do the hip hop and house music up front. No one really liked it. We didn't like it, and the Club XL crowd didn't like it.

Amy Yates Wuelfing: The regulars that night were not happy about us being there and they made that clear. There were a few confrontations.

Rich O'Brien: It was almost like that scene in Animal House when the college kids walk into the club to see Otis Day and the Knights and everyone in the place stops and stares at them. Like, *who the hell is this guy with the purple mohawk?* And that was the last event we ever did.

Karey Maurice Counts: I went to Club XL once—just once. The dude that ran it, Derek, humiliated me because he knew I had a history at City Gardens. I did an art show there with [local graffiti artist] Leon Rainbow. We did a collaboration of paintings and a signing, and he stopped us from coming in the door at our own art show! He said, "Oh man, you're not dressed right." He made me wear one of his shirts to get in, and I looked like a clown. Now I remember this guy when he was a little kid, and he knew my history at City Gardens, and he was so rude and obnoxious. He made sure that I would not come back. It was a terrible club, because the music was corny, even though it was full of African Americans. I was used to a more diverse crowd. I won't even go in a place if it's all this or all that; it has to be diverse. I mean, that's the way I roll.

Joseph Kuzemka (Trenton Punk Rock Flea Market): There used to be a semi-pro basketball team in Trenton called the Trenton Shooting Stars, and I worked there as Creative Director. One night after a game, some of the game dancers with connections at Club XL invited me to go. Listen, it was not the place I should have been venturing into. I knew that a giant guy covered in tattoos, with a long goatee, probably wouldn't go over great, but I needed to get inside that building to see what it looked like.

The dancers had connections with the door guys. There was a line, not unlike what it was like at City Gardens, waiting to get inside the building, and we walked right past the line. Out of the 20 of us, probably half of us were white or clearly out of place. We didn't stay longer than 25 minutes, and the whole situation was sketchy. All eyes were definitely on us. I said to the people I was with, "We might want to get out of here. It just does not feel like this is a safe place." And I'm not that guy who thinks that way, but it really did not feel comfortable. We were getting ready to walk out and the guard says, "We're going to have to escort you to your cars." I said, "What the hell are you talking about? We've got to be escorted to our cars?" And he said, "A fight broke out outside because we let you guys in, and the people out there are really pissed off." I'm like, I never got beat up in all of my time going to City Gardens, getting into scuffles with skinheads in the middle of the pit. And now I'm going to get my ass kicked walking to my car at what was *formerly* City Gardens? Nothing happened, but it was surreal.

Club XL ran into trouble with local authorities after multiple robberies, shootings, and liquor-license violations. During an investigation, undercover officers witnessed "numerous sexual and lewd acts," and the owners were charged with using the club to promote prostitution. After a police raid on August 16, 2004, Club XL was shut down permanently.

   The building was vacant until early 2013, when it was purchased by Trenton-based businessman Lawrence Campbell. After Mr. Campbell renovates the badly damaged building, he intends to open it as a nightclub/restaurant called Exodus.

CHAPTER 8

1987–1988

1987

Top Ten Songs in 1987:
1. Walk Like an Egyptian, Bangles
2. Alone, Heart
3. Shake You Down, Gregory Abbott
4. I Wanna Dance With Somebody, Whitney Houston
5. Nothing's Gonna Stop Us Now, Starship
6. C'est la vie, Robbie Nevil
7. Here I Go Again, Whitesnake
8. The Way It Is, Bruce Hornsby and the Range
9. Shakedown, Bob Seger
10. Livin' on a Prayer, Bon Jovi

The all-ages/all-the-time atmosphere began to weigh on the older City Gardens regulars, who felt as through their space was being invaded by kids... and annoying kids at that. As the numbers of kids increased, the previous generation of City Gardens regulars began to drift away and find other venues.

"The Family" had been around since the early '80s, but it was approximately 1987 when they really began to make their mark. It's difficult to explain to an outsider exactly who (or what) The Family was. Many misconceptions surround them and their actions, from being mislabeled "white power" skins to being thought of as some kind of organized gang, which they weren't. The Family was simply a group of Trenton locals who came together because of City Gardens. Depending upon whom you ask, they were the best

thing about City Gardens or they were the worst thing about City Gardens. Regardless of which side of the argument you were on, this much is true: they were friends who looked out for one another, stuck by one another, and policed (rightly and wrongly) the crowds at City Gardens shows. They were skins, punks, metalheads, hardcore kids, and horror punks. They were black, white, and everything in between. They were a crew of friends who held court in the City Gardens' parking lot. Some of their antics were horrific; some are the stuff of legend. Every scene has a local crew, and these were the kids who represented Trenton.

Jonathan Levine: (City Gardens regular/art dealer): The Family kids were kids from Trenton, and Trenton kids were working-class kids who didn't have any money. They couldn't afford fucking Doc Martens. We couldn't afford that shit. We were walking around in fucking combat boots that we bought at the Army/Navy store or that we got from our dads from when they were in the Vietnam War or some shit.

Stephen Brown (City Gardens regular/Family member): Now, The Family was just us goofing around. It was a bunch of kids is all it was. And then once in a while we'd get drunk at a show and yell, "FAMILY," and that was it. We didn't really do anything. I mean, we beat a lot of people up, but that was about it. We had a lot of great fights in that place.

Nancy Leopardi (City Gardens regular): There was a time when [The Family] was a really positive thing and then, at some point, it turned ugly. It turned into beating people up. I don't know exactly what the turn was, but initially it was very much a tribal thing. They wanted to be the alpha males at City Gardens, and then it started to get ugly. It went from protecting each other from outsiders to being aggressive.

Johnny Thunders — January 10, 1987

Amy Yates Wuelfing: If you went to see Johnny Thunders, you were taking a risk. Would he show up? Would he be able to play? Would he berate the crowd? I saw him in Philly and it started off as a great show, but after about 20 minutes he yelled at the crowd, told us we were idiots, and walked offstage. The band kept playing, but after another 10 minutes people started yelling for Johnny. [Guitarist] Sylvain Sylvain went looking for Johnny, came back after a few minutes, and said, "Show's over."

However, the best was at Irving Plaza in New York. The band comes out and begins playing, the crowd is cheering, but no Johnny. More playing. Still no Johnny. Suddenly, Joey Ramone pushes Johnny Thunders out *in a wheelchair.* He was slumped over with his guitar in his lap, and they moved the mic down to his level. Figuring this has to be a comedy routine, everyone is laughing and clapping. It wasn't a routine. He obviously had no idea where he was or what he was doing, but Johnny did regain consciousness long enough to say, "Did I play?" and pass out again. After someone threw a beer that missed Johnny's head by inches, Sylvain Sylvain declared, "Show's over!" and wheeled him off stage.

Henry Hose (City Gardens regular): At City Gardens, even though he was strung out, he still managed to rally and play a great show. The only thing was he couldn't keep his tongue in his mouth. When he wasn't singing, his tongue hung out the side.

Stephen Brown: When Johnny Thunders played, he was on heroin and shit, and he couldn't play. They shut down everything on him because he couldn't play. He couldn't really do anything. He couldn't sing and he fell to the ground... just flopping around. The band got pissed and walked off the stage. It was supposed to be this big show. We were gonna see Johnny Thunders and it was a big deal. It was pathetic, a horrible show. But we got drunk anyway and beat up some people.

Controversy still surrounds the death of Johnny Thunders in New Orleans on April 23, 1991. He apparently died of drug-related causes, but it has been speculated that his death was the result of foul play. He was 38.

Peter Murphy—February 13, 1987

Jim Norton (stage manager/security): Peter Murphy, formerly of Bauhaus, played a few times, and there is one episode I remember clearly. The crew was supposed to be there at nine or ten in the morning for load-in, which was not uncommon for the bigger shows, especially for English bands, who tended to bring more production equipment, more lights, and so on. City Gardens was on that "alternative music" circuit… bands that would get played on [MTV's] *120 Minutes*, and these bands were typically much more popular in Europe than they were in the U.S. As a result, they were playing much larger places in other parts of the world and were used to a certain level of production. The next thing they know they're at City Gardens, this kind of weirdo, former Packard dealership in the middle of Nowhere, New Jersey.

Peter Murphy had played in New York the night before and—as often would happen with bands who had played in New York the night before—their nine or ten in the morning load-in would blow by with no sign of, or word from, the band. This was before cell phones. As the crew, we sat around for the whole afternoon waiting, and at three o'clock Peter Murphy's bus showed up. Not the equipment truck, mind you. That truck finally pulls up around four, and they proceed to load everything in and set up all the lighting. Typically, with a rock show, you do all your lighting stuff first. I don't know why, but that's how it is. They showed up five hours late and they then took five hours to do their lighting check, and the whole time I am there as the alleged stage manager trying to speed them up.

The lighting looked really amazing. He had great effects. There was one light that was a super-tight beam across the stage, and they had this one cue where he would hit a mark and all the lights in the club would go out except this one beam that shot across the stage, and it would illuminate just his face between his nose and his forehead. It was an awesome effect, but it took him an hour and a half just to get *that*. It was insane how much time it took to set up the lights. The doors were supposed to open at eight o'clock or so. It was cold out, snowing or raining, not good weather for people standing in line for three hours, and that is what happened to people who showed up early to get tickets. At nine o'clock, which was when the first band was supposed to go on, they finished their lighting check, and everyone was pretty much at the end of their rope.

Peter Murphy finally says, "Okay, lights are done… let's start the soundcheck." He was smack in the middle of the stage when I walked up and said, "No. There's no time." He said, "What?" and kind of harrumphs at me. "Well, we have to do a soundcheck." I said, "You can't. There's no time. We've got to get people in the door and get this band on stage and get the show going." And he said, "How do you expect us to put on a first-class show without a soundcheck?" I said, "Well, you could start by showing up on time." He didn't really like that. I continued, "But you didn't do that. You showed up at three in the afternoon without any equipment. Then you took five hours for a lighting check. If you're taking five hours for a lighting check, why am I supposed to think it's not going to take you another five hours to do a soundcheck?" And he said, "DO YOU KNOW WHO I AM?" I said, "I know who you are, but I don't give a shit who you are. Get the fuck off my stage so we can get this opening band in!" He said, "I should cancel the show," and I was like, "Okay, *you* go outside and tell everybody you cancelled the fucking show because you were up doing drugs up in New York and couldn't get your fucking ass out of bed to get here on time. If you can't do that—if you're too much of a coward to say that—then get the fuck off my stage so I can get this band on and we can start the show already."

He stepped up to me. I'm not a big guy, but I am *slightly* bigger than Peter Murphy. He might be taller, but I definitely remember *not* feeling threatened. He stepped up to me, and I looked at him, like, "Really?" Real quietly I said to him, "I've said it before, and I'll say it again, get the fuck off my stage BEFORE I FUCKING KILL YOU!" and I yelled the last part real loud. He stormed off in a huff and that was it. He did the show. He had another effect where they shot a beam to a specific point in the crowd. I don't know whether it was chance that it would land on a man or a woman, or if they just played the odds that it was always going to land on a woman, but they shot a beam to a spot on the top of the bleachers. At the time a very good friend of mine—a woman I had a huge crush on—stood in that exact spot. They shoot the beam to her, and all the lights go down, and it's just her and Peter Murphy lit up, and they're both sort of dancing together. That made her whole year. The next day when she was raving about how awesome it was, I had to explain to her what a fucking asshole he was. She was not happy with me.

Descendents/Gang Green/Dag Nasty/Half Life— March 8, 1987

Milo Aukerman (Descendents vocalist): We got pretty friendly with Dag Nasty. We did a whole tour together at one point, so they were close friends of ours. Whenever possible we tried to hang out, but we were traveling in different buses, and people place sleep at a high premium. You do the best you can to socialize, but also you're trying to survive in terms of getting sleep and getting to the clubs. With Dag Nasty, there's a bit of a "comrades in arms" thing, because they were going through all the same stuff we were. The bills were great. I would always try to check out the opening band. I like the shows where there are five bands on the bill, all of which are great bands. It reminds me of when we were getting started in L.A. You look at some of the fliers from that period and it's crazy. Black Flag, Minutemen, Saccharine Trust... the list goes on and on. Those were fun shows. It was almost like a festival there were so many bands.

D.O.A./Meatmen/fIREHOSE — March 14, 1987

Joey Shithead (D.O.A., vocalist): That was a great show. The Meatmen were playing before us. They came out and were wearing these furry outfits that would make them sweat profusely. The pants were cow skin or something, and Tesco Vee was all done up in all this fur and leather. He looked like the illegitimate, lost brother of Rick James.

Tesco Vee (Meatmen, vocalist): I remember those shows with D.O.A. being really great and really well attended. A lot of those '80s shows were.

Joey Shithead: It was the most bizarre-looking thing. He gets up there, and it was fucking hilarious because we had never seen them, but we had been hearing about them for a long time. Tesco gets up there and said, "All right people, Joey Shithead may *think* he's the most macho singer of all time, but I'm going to show you that I AM!"

Tesco Vee: Wow. I don't remember a lot of what I said onstage back in those days. I think it's because you're in the moment and you're kind of rolling with it. I was getting pretty stoned back then too, which is neither here nor there, but it does affect your memory a little bit.

Joey Shithead: The band had this whole thing with their album *Rock and Roll Juggernaut,* which we thought was the greatest title of all time. Tesco kept going all night, "So who's more macho: Me or Joe Shithead?"

He kept screaming at the crowd. They were such a great band and Tesco is nuts. They really destroyed it that night, and they were really fun to play with.

Tesco Vee: I think I was standing back by the bar while they were playing and the place was pretty packed that night. Good night, good band. D.O.A. were like a well-oiled machine. Every night they gave it their all. I had met them in 1981 or so at the club Doobie's in Lansing MI with the Necros and the Fix, and hardly anybody was there, but we didn't do anything with them until that show. It came together at City Gardens. And now Joey Shithead has his own bobblehead!

Joan Jett—March 15, 1987

Jim Norton (City Gardens security): I hadn't been working at City Gardens long. I was guarding the steps to Joan Jett's dressing room to make sure no one went up there. A couple came up to me and handed me a note. They asked if I would give it to Joan Jett, and I said I'd try. I opened up the note. It said, "Dear Joan, we are your number one fans in New Jersey. We love your music very much. Would you please play "Anarchy in the UK" for us tonight? Signed –Your Number One Fans in New Jersey: Anna and Cassie." Or something like that. Even though it was a guy and a girl, they signed it as two women. They actually had the nerve to ask her to play a Sex Pistols song, because apparently her catalogue wasn't deep enough for them. Maybe Joan did cover "Anarchy in the UK" once or twice, what the hell do I know? I went up and knocked on the dressing room door. A guy answers the door, the tour manager or something, and I went to hand the note to him and explained it was from some fans. He very graciously said, "Well, why don't you give it to her yourself?" I thought that was sort of odd. The whole day had been about protecting her from people and now, maybe twenty minutes before her show, I'm walking up and handing her a note? I said *okay* and took a few steps in. It wasn't super-crowded, but there were a good number of people there. I turned to somebody and said, "Uh, I'm sorry. Is Joan Jett around?" He motioned toward this couch that held four or five people. He said, "She's right over there on the couch."

I walked to the couch and sitting there are five Joan Jetts! There's Joan Jett on the left, a Joan Jett next to her, and a Joan Jett in the middle, a Joan Jett next to her, and a Joan Jett on the far right. They were identical, and the one in the middle had her arms around the two next to her. I scanned the couch and finally said, "I'm sorry... who's Joan Jett?" And the one in the middle, as though I were the one with the problem, says, "What do you think?" She said it nicely—she wasn't nasty about it all—but she was incredulous. I was thinking, *I see five Joan Jetts. It was not a crazy question.* I said, "This is a note from some fans," and she took it. I said, "Have a good show," and walked out.

I really liked the fact that there were five Joan Jetts and she was hanging with four women who looked exactly like her. There's something strange about that, but hey, whatever.

Bruce Markoff (City Gardens regular): This was right after the release of that terrible movie with Joan Jett and Michael J. Fox, *Light of Day*. She played, and after the show people were congregating at the bottom of the steps by the dressing room waiting for her to sign autographs. She was pretty big at that point. She came down with her little entourage, and a couple of people were shoving things at her to be signed. She was blowing them off, but it was one of those moments when somebody speaks and there's dead silence. At least that's how I remember it. This guy shouts above everybody else, "Hey Joan, do you think Michael J. Fox owns any Joan Jett records?" And she goes, "I don't know, why don't you come out to the bus and we'll talk about it?" She grabbed his hand, and the whole entourage blew everybody else off and went out the front door. I was kind of jealous and pissed off at the same time.

Cro-Mags/Mentors/Suburban Uprise/ Legitimate Reason—April 12, 1987

Some names have been changed, but not to protect the innocent.

Jamie Davis (City Gardens regular): I actually went to see the Mentors. El Duce was still playing drums. That was the best era of the Mentors, when he was still playing drums. He stopped playing drums after that and just sang.

Harley Flanagan (Cro-Mags, bassist): The gig that really stands out in my memory is when we played with, of all bands, the Mentors. That in itself is a ridiculous bill if you think about it: the *Age of Quarrel*-era Cro-Mags playing with the Mentors… Of course, El Duce was still alive, and that shit was ridiculous. I had met those guys once before back in '82, out in California.

Jamie Davis: The Mentors were hilarious. They had this other big fat guy—who was three times the size of the rest them—on stage wiping things with his ass and throwing them at people. He was wiping bumper stickers on his ass and throwing them. He was wiping sweat off his chest and flinging it at people, and he berated anybody close to the stage. Any girl who was up front really got it.

Jonathan LeVine (City Gardens regular): I heard a story about a friend of ours, Ivo, getting into some stuff with Harley at that show. Ivo was a gnarly dude, and I was sort of afraid of him back then. I heard that at this Cro-Mags show, their roadies caught Ivo in the bathroom and knocked his teeth out or something.

Karl "Hard Karl" Hedgepath (City Gardens regular): I know that Ivo had a confrontation in the bathroom at City Gardens. That haunted him for a long time. We went to DC once and a dude—I won't say his name—came running up to the van. He was looking in the van trying to find out if Ivo was there. He kept asking about somebody named Ivo, and we were all playing dumb, like, "I don't know who you're talking about…"

Dave Franklin (Vision, vocalist): My bass player, Ivo, was banned from City Gardens for life for fighting. He was one of the guys in The Family. He had a HUGE conflict with the Cro-Mags way before he was in Vision.

Harley Flanagan: One of our roadies and his younger brother got into some kind of an altercation during one of the opening bands. I don't know what the fuck happened. He got into some shit with one of the local tough guys of that era, of that scene. Every scene has the tough guys who gotta flex at every gig…

Jim Norton (stage manager/security): Ivo… good guy. I think all these years later it's okay to say it: He was a troublemaker. He was *that* guy. He was one of the few regulars who would take a swing at you, and he had a chip on his shoulder about getting thrown out for doing dumb stuff. He was the guy who would try to convince you that—whatever it was—whatever he was being accused of doing *this* week, he didn't do it.

Carl Humenik (City Gardens security): With Ivo, every time I would see him do something, he'd say, "I didn't do it. It wasn't me." And I'd be like, "I SAW YOU DO IT!"

Dave Franklin: At an earlier Cro-Mags show, there was a confrontation where The Family had beaten down a Cro-Mags roadie so severely that the next time the Cro-Mags came to town, they were looking for some kids to beat.

Harley Flanagan: Me and my roadies used to get into so many fucking fights…

Dave Franklin: Ivo was there early in the men's room, taking a leak, and he turns around and Harley and another dude were standing there, waiting for him. Harley had a baseball bat in his hand.

Harley Flanagan: Well, I guess he fucking flexed on my buddy and, I don't know what happened, but I walked into the bathroom and there was this dude crumpled up on the floor with blood running down his head. And my buddy Rich was standing over him, and his brother was standing next to him, and his brother had a baseball bat… When I walked in on that one, I was like, "Geez, I can't fucking go anywhere with you motherfuckers!"

Carl Humenik: With some people who came to shows, you couldn't believe a word they said. Ivo was one of them. That night, he came out of the bathroom, holding his tooth, with blood coming out of his mouth. He told me that Harley just beat the living shit out of him. I went into the men's room, but there was no one there. So, either Harley came out before him…but I don't understand why Harley would be in that bathroom unless he followed Ivo in. I only have what Ivo said to go by.

Harley Flanagan: Actually, from what I understand, he didn't even get to hit him with the baseball bat, because we all used to have—well, me and my roadie—we had these sack gloves. They've got eight ounces of powdered lead in the knuckles. So he just cracked him.

Dave Franklin: Harley actually handed the bat off to the other guy and punched Ivo in the face and knocked his front teeth out. The story got around that Harley beat Ivo with the bat, but he actually just punched him in the mouth.

Harley Flanagan: But I don't know exactly what happened; I just know the guy fucked with him on the dance floor, and he might have really laid him out, and there was some situation where all the guy's friends wanted to jump my roadie. Then I was out in the audience with a huge circle of people around me. I always carried this big tanto, which is like a Japanese knife. I kept it in my sleeve. I remember being in the middle of a circle of people and being like, "Yo, I will fuck people UP…" It was just one of these tense situations where you're surrounded by people and everybody is waiting. Like, is shit going to start any second? [It was like] I go to take a piss, and you're in here with a baseball bat, and some fucking guy is laying on the floor! I mean, Jesus Fucking Christ, can I take a piss in peace, man? I mean, what the fuck? What happened this time? What did you do? What did he say? What? Did he fucking bump into you? Was he fucking… Jesus Christ….

Anybody who used to go to Cro-Mags shows back then will tell you that it was always intense and we knew it. You could feel it. For weeks leading up to us coming to town, all my friends would tell me, "Yo man, when you guys had a gig coming up, for two or three weeks leading up to the show, everybody would be getting themselves amped up." So by the time we'd come to town, shit would fucking go off. There was always some kind of madness. It was a great time.

Jamie Davis: When the Cro-Mags came on, I was up at the front. They did the count-off and the fucking place blew up. I'd never seen so many bald heads fucking go off. To me, everyone was humungous. I just remember being smashed into the amps and thinking, "This is GREAT! This is the best band I've ever seen!" And that was without ever having heard them before! When you say that about a band, you *knew* you saw something incredible.

Harley Flanagan: The thing that stands out from that show for me is that was the last gig I ever played my Guild Starfire bass, the semi-hollow body that I played on the original demos. It stopped working at the end of our set. We came back to do some encores and it didn't work anymore. We couldn't figure out what happened, so I borrowed a bass. When I opened it up afterwards, [I realized] that I had sweated so much that the pickups were corroded. It died. It's sad [because] it was a beautiful bass, and it had an amazing sound. It was a fucking vintage, fucking beautiful instrument. That was the night that that bass died, and I had to buy a bass. It was the first time I ever got a new instrument.

Circle Jerks/Rollins Band — April 26, 1987

Henry Rollins: Those were the days when you played all the time, because if you didn't play, you didn't eat. The most significant date for me would be April 26, 1987, because that was the first ever Rollins Band show opening for the Circle Jerks. We recorded a live album at City Gardens for the Rollins Band, which came out in Japan as *Electro-Convulsive Therapy*.

Sim Cain (Gone/Rollins Band): [Black Flag's] Greg Ginn had a completely different aesthetic and take on life than anyone I've ever met. He's an incredible mind but... not a very good communicator. Henry Rollins had a very strong love and respect for Greg that I think Greg never understood. He saw conflict where there wasn't any. It was a tremendous misunderstanding. A lot of it hinged on recruiting the bass player of Black Flag after Kira left. Henry removed himself from the process because he thought it should be Greg's decision. Greg felt like Henry abandoned him when he had to slog through all the bass player auditions. And I don't think they ever had that conversation. Then Henry began his spoken-word thing, and the books, and he was dividing his interests. So, in the end, they had enough. When it ended, Henry was heartbroken. He was crushed.

Black Flag broke up, but Gone continued for another few months. By then we were burned out. We all went home again. In the meantime, Henry had made a record with [guitarist] Chris Haskett and a British rhythm section, and he was getting ready to tour for it. It was actually on [Black Flag roadie] Joe Cole's recommendation that Henry called Andrew and me, and we were available. That was how we joined Rollins Band. Some people think there was some sort of political aspect to it, but there wasn't.

Billy Kearns (City Gardens regular): At the time, [Circle Jerks singer] Keith Morris was my favorite. At this show, there was a big dude who was obviously dusted or on something. He was walking around literally knocking people out with punches to the head. Every time the bouncers threw the guy out, he would walk back in another door and continue hitting people. Because of this, my friends and I kept moving further and further back from the stage. At one point during Rollins' set, this homeless dude on crutches moved in front of me. He kept shaking his matted hair in my face in time to the music. I politely asked him to give me a break, and he told me to go fuck myself. I threatened to smack him around, thinking maybe then he'd stop. He again told me to fuck myself. My friends told me to leave him alone, as he was obviously homeless and crippled. So I called him an asshole and found another spot to watch the show. So imagine my surprise when the homeless dude ambled up on stage with the Circle Jerks and that unmistakable voice came out of him! I had wanted to smack my hero Keith Morris! Years later I told Keith that story, and he remembered the incident. I told him he was the reason I didn't join a punk band professionally. I figured that if they were the "Van Halen" of punk back then—and he looked like he couldn't afford a comb or a clean t shirt—then I certainly didn't stand a chance making any coin off punk.

Fishbone/ Adrenalin O.D.—May 1, 1987

Dave Scott (Adrenalin O.D., drummer): Fishbone was a legendary show for us because [Adrenalin O.D. guitarist] Bruce Wingate decided to go to Maxwell's in Hoboken to see Redd Kross instead. After waiting hours for him, we enlisted our friend Jim McMonagle from F.O.D. to wear an unplugged bass guitar and jump around the stage in an amazing show of air guitar fury. This was one of our funnier moments. People in the crowd had no idea he wasn't plugged in, nor did they know he wasn't a band member. At the end of the set I stood up on my drum stool for the big rock and roll ending, and accidentally fell into my drum set. It was a true *America's Funniest Videos* moment.

Bruce Wingate (Adrenalin O.D. guitarist): I didn't actually miss the show on purpose, but saying I did makes a better story, so that's the one I tell.

Suicidal Tendencies/McRad/Jersey Fresh—May 10, 1987

Jamie Davis (City Gardens regular): That was an amazing night. It was on Mother's Day, which was kind of funny. Suicidal did "I Saw Your Mommy and Your Mommy's Dead" as a "special" Mother's Day song.

Chuck Treece (McRad guitarist): I remember what went down at that show. It was crazy. It had nothing to do with us. I remember being there early, hanging out, and [Suicidal Tendencies singer] Mike Muir and the band pulled up in a tour bus. A real nice black tour bus.

Randy Now: Suicidal had a real tour bus. It wasn't a van and it wasn't a Winnebago. This was after I had tour-managed them, so I wasn't with them when they came in this bus. I was the first guy to think up renting Winnebagos from U-Haul for bands. Anthrax and a few other more successful bands rented them. They would beat the shit out of it, and a band would always go through two or three on a tour. U-Haul would come out and give you a fresh one when they broke down, which they inevitably would do. It was always something. The toilet would clog or the engine would burn out. Not surprisingly, after two or three years, U-Haul did away with their Winnebago rentals.

Tracy Parks-Pattik (City Gardens staff): Randy lived right around the corner from me, and one time this Winnebago is parked at his house. I wondered why he had a Winnebago, and it turns out it was Suicidal Tendencies. They came over to my house, and I remember a five-gallon jug of wine. Mikey Muir got me drunk as hell, and I was a young girl.

I was fucking 16! They went swimming in our pool while we were all really drunk. It was fucking Suicidal Tendencies in Bordentown, New Jersey—fucking suburbia! It was fun as shit.

Randy Now: I toured with Suicidal, and at a place in Florida we KNEW we got ripped off by the promoter. He made so much money, there were so many people there, but he refused to give us a bonus. Meanwhile, we took a crappy guarantee, because we knew so many people were going to show up that we'd get the bonus. But this promoter was horrible. We were the last ones to leave the club… even the promoter was gone. So we dumped all the raw sewage from the Winnebago out in the parking lot, right at the front door. That'll get you.

Tony Lee (City Gardens regular): Suicidal had gone real metal at that point. I couldn't get away from all this metal!

Dave Franklin (Vision): The Family trashed the bus that night. Suicidal showed up in a tour bus and The Family called them sell-outs. They trashed the entire bus. That kid Dave was involved, and afterwards Mike Muir went up to Randy and asked, "Who did this to our bus?" Randy said, "Some guys in The Family," and Mike asked, "How do I get to them?" Well, Mike got information on how to get to Dave's house. Dave was living with his dad at the time. There was a knock at the front door, and the Suicidal guys were standing there. They dragged him out and beat him down.

Randy Now: We heard it was this kid Dave who smashed the windows on the bus, and two of the bouncers knew where he lived. They went to his house, and either they kicked the shit out of him on the front porch or Mike broke windows at his house. Something like that. I don't know how that all went down.

John (City Gardens bouncer): This kid Dave had lived in California and had seen Suicidal play. The story I got was that he went up to Mike Muir after a show to get a signature and Mike blew him off. So, this kid moves back to Jersey and comes to the show, and by this point Suicidal are huge. They have a big fancy tour bus. After the show, this kid breaks out one whole side of windows on the bus.

Tony Lee: I don't think I backed Dave up on that whole thing. He had a beef with them for whatever reason. I think he took the whole "selling out" thing personal. But I could see the guys in the band being really pissed about [the bus]. These 15 and 16 year old kids were always causing trouble and breaking shit, and making it difficult for bands to come and play at City Gardens. It was punk, obviously, but it still had to be a huge headache for Randy.

Chuck Treece: I remember somebody threw a big-ass rock through their window, and it got really fucking heavy at the end of the show because of their bodyguards. I knew Mike Muir through the whole skating thing. His brother Jim Muir was an old Dog Town guy from back in the day. We had that whole thing: Suicidal, McRad, and members of Excel, and all those West Coast guys. I remember going to an Excel show out at a place called The Country Club in Reseda California, and it was like the whole nation of their people was out there. If you weren't in with their crew, the shit was just wild.

Tony Lee: Some people felt a sense of entitlement when it came to City Gardens, and Randy wasn't having any of that.

Randy Now: I've seen Mike Muir kick some ass in Miami, by himself. Two guys walked past us and called him a "wetback." He looked at me and said, "Let's get them" and— hell—I've never had a fight in my life, and I'm with the freaking strongest guy in the world. I walked on, but he turned around, and I watched him from a distance kick these two guys' asses. And then he invited them to the show!

Chuck Treece: I remember talking to Mike outside, and he was highly pissed off because he had to pay for all that damage, and their bodyguards went off and crushed a couple of dudes. They played a show, and then came out to find their bus completely destroyed. That would never go on today, unless someone had a specific beef with you or something. They weren't being rock stars. I mean, they were playing City Gardens! Minimal security, just a hall, a stage, and a PA, and they still kept it 'core. Most bands, if they get on a tour bus now, their ego is completely out of control.

That was like a $5,000 repair on a tour bus. After the show let out, it got fucking ugly. It got ugly quick, and it wasn't cool. I could only imagine the pressure that was on Mike Muir's head. He had to pay for that shit. It had to come out of his ass, so I think he was like, "I'm gonna take it out of somebody's ass…" Sometimes people just don't know who they're messing with… Mike is that way. There's no getting past it.

John (City Gardens bouncer): Another bouncer and I take Mike Muir out in a station wagon, driving through Trenton, looking for this kid's house. We can't find it, and Mike is just sitting in the back of the car, all quiet. No one's even talking. Since we can't find the place, we decide to pick up a prostitute. She's thinking what we want is not what we want. She's propositioning us, and the other bouncer is like, "Just shut up and tell us how to find this address. We'll pay." She directs us there—we give her $25 or whatever—and at the house we see two vans out in the front for some plumbing or electrical contractor. I guess it was his dad or uncle. I get into the driver's seat, Mike and the other bouncer get out, and all you hear are windows breaking. Can you imagine coming out to work in the morning and finding that? And they got back in the car and left.

Carl Humenik (City Gardens security): I've heard the story, and the other bouncers would have no reason to lie to me. They did damage the trucks parked in front of the house, but they didn't beat the crap out of anyone. I wouldn't blame them if they did, though.

Meatmen/Murphy's Law—June 5, 1987

Tesco Vee (Meatmen frontman): That was one of the better-attended ones that we did, and that was because Murphy's Law was huge on the East Coast. Randy was a Meatmen fan, and a promoter as a fan is a band's greatest ally. You get shows and put on great bills. I think we made Randy laugh. A lot of bands at that point were being real serious, and we never were. Murphy's Law were kindred spirits with the Meatmen, one of those "have a good time, fuck the world, have a beer, have a laugh" kind of bands. We really should have done a lot more with them. Their crowd was so loyal and knew all the words. It kind of makes me jealous when they're out there, and you see them launch into their set and you see the kids. They go nuts.

City Gardens regular Todd Waladkewics and his baby daughter,
Adriana, in the City Gardens parking lot circa 1987.

Mark "Repo" Pesetsky (City Gardens security): Anytime Murphy's Law came, it was crazy. They always brought a huge, huge crowd, and they were always violent. I'm working the floor, and there's this one kid who kept surfing the crowd, trying to jump on stage, I'm dragging him off, and he's hitting me in the face… kicking me. Finally I grab him, throw him out the back door, go out the door after him, and he takes off the hoodie and it's a girl. With huge jugs! I couldn't tell before that that it was a girl. She's yelling at me, "What the hell are you hitting a girl for?!" So she starts coming at me, and her boyfriend is coming at me. So I go back inside, the show ends, and I'm going to my car. I'm parked right in front of the door, and I'm standing there with my girlfriend and my friend John. Out of the corner of my eye, I see a lit cigarette coming at me, and it bounces off my head. I look up and see the boyfriend from earlier taking a swing at me. I duck it, and another security guy whacks the kid. He goes down and John starts kicking him like a soccer ball up against my car. Then the girl came after me again. It was nuts. But that was the Murphy's Law crowd.

Descendents/Rollins Band/M.I.A./
Cancerous Growth—June 21, 1987

Tim McMahon (Mouthpiece, vocalist): At some point, as I'm discovering different styles and genres of punk and hardcore, Tony [Rettman] tells me, "Hey, my brother Don is a DJ at City Gardens. Did you ever hear of City Gardens? It's this club in Trenton that all these punk bands play. Punk bands, metal bands, hardcore bands... I can always catch a ride with my brother and get in free." Don Rettman always got there hours before it opened with his records, and Tony would go in with him. Tony said, "If you ever want to come to a show, I'm sure you could get in with me and my brother." It took me a good solid year before I got up the balls to actually take him up on his offer.

Milo Aukerman (Descendents vocalist): I like Henry [Rollins] a lot, and I liked the first couple of records he put out. I really didn't hang too much with him. He kind of kept to himself, but he's fascinating to watch. I would study his onstage demeanor, not that I could ever pull it off, but just because it was so dramatic and you would feel him glaring out at people. It was all part of this... I don't know if it was an intimidation scheme or just the intensity of it. It was really impressive. I think that of all the Black Flag relationships, the one that is probably the warmest is between Henry and Bill [Stevenson, drummer]. There were never any sparks between Henry and Bill.

Tim McMahon: This was my first show. I remember Don had all these crates of records in the back of his station wagon. Randy met us at the door and was like, "What's going on guys? Come on in. Who's this guy?" He ushered us in and we went over to the DJ booth. Don got set up and we hung out, walked around a bit and checked things out. We didn't go too far. We hung around the DJ booth and waited for the doors to open.

Henry Rollins: That would be '87, when we put the Rollins Band together. The rhythm section, Andrew [Weiss] and Sim [Cain] were Trenton guys. Chris Haskett and I migrated to Trenton and lived on various members' floors. We would live on Sim's mother's floor, and then we were living on the bass player's floor, and sometimes the bass player's parent's floor, all in the Hopewell-Trenton area. And these people were very kind to us.

Tim McMahon: To me it was really shocking, really mind-blowing, when the doors opened and I started seeing the crowd pour into this place. All kinds of people that I had never seen before in my life. I felt like I was three feet tall. They were all giant, big, tattoo-covered, spiked, Mohawked, crazy-looking people. Torn-up jeans with bleach splatters, crazy-looking t-shirts with sleeves cut off, leather jackets... You had all these dirtbags and metalheads, just a little bit of everybody. It really wasn't just punks. It was all kinds of society's rejects. I stood there looking at these people, so intimidated and nervous, and wondering, "Do I belong here?" It was scary as shit. I felt like a riot could break out at any minute, and my little ass would be trampled or stabbed or shot.

Joe Z. (City Gardens soundman): I did sound at City Gardens on a regular basis, and I met Billy Tucker, Sim, and Andrew. I hooked up with Sim and Andrew in 1984 and we formed a band called Arrested Development, and we played City Gardens a few times. At that time, Henry Rollins was hanging around, and I introduced him to Sim and Andrew—and then he stole them to form the Rollins Band! I thought I was going to be in the Rollins Band too, but I got the flu and when I finally got better, I found out he got Chris [Haskett] to play guitar. There were no hard feelings, though. I let them rehearse at my house.

Henry Rollins: On and off, all the way up to '92, we would stay at Sim's mom's house and practice in Hopewell in the bass player's basement. That's where we wrote all the *End of Silence* songs. I became quite the Trenton local. I'd live there for months at a time to work on getting ready for a tour or getting ready for an album. I remember it was really fun to somehow feel like a local band. I really like that vibe, and I really liked my time in Trenton. Everyone was really cool to me. Some nights we would go down to City Gardens to see the shows, and they would always let me in for free, which was cool. We saw the Pixies, GWAR, Bad Brains... And I really enjoyed the Crystal Diner.

Sim Cain: Henry loved that place [Crystal Diner]. It's a Trenton landmark. He didn't have a driver's license, so I was chauffeuring him all around town.

Tim McMahon: I don't remember too much about Cancerous Growth playing, though I do remember Tony telling me later that they'd become a backing band for G.G. Allin. M.I.A. I really liked. They were sort of like a melodic, Social Distortion-sounding band. I bought one of their t-shirts. They were like a light in the dark for me. Even though I wasn't that familiar with them, I could tell they had a different vibe.

When Rollins went on, I was standing back by the DJ booth watching him, in awe that this was Henry Rollins. This was the singer from Black Flag. To me, Black Flag was as big as AC/DC. To be standing there, only forty feet away from him, was surreal. It was hard for me to grasp that you could be standing up in front of your favorite band and reach out and touch them. Rollins, as a performer... it was scary. He looks like a fucking lunatic. He's screaming... the way he's pacing around the stage and his body gestures and everything, and the stuff he was saying... I thought the guy could just jump off the stage and stab me or something! I remember thinking, "Wow, this guy is larger than life. This guy is a legitimate superstar." That show was really intimidating. Everything: from the crowd, to the venue, to the neighborhood.

Henry Rollins: It would be Chris and I living in Sim's mom's house, and we would try to be as unobtrusive as possible. We would find ways to disappear in the evening, to get out of her way, because she was so cool and hardworking. We would frequent the Crystal Diner. Typical diner fare, it has the nine-page menu. At two in the morning, you'd be like, "So, you guys really have eggplant parm? Right now?" and they'd be like, "Yeah." And they'd bring it out in seven minutes, and it was like, "Wow!" What's happening back in that kitchen? I have fond memories of that time. We wrote a lot of good songs in Trenton.

Sim Cain: Henry was crashing on my floor, basically. Our first rehearsals for the Rollins Band were in my basement in Trenton. We were working all the time, so it didn't really matter where we were actually living. We spent about a month rehearsing and getting the band together, and then we hit the road for the next ten years. There was a good stretch of time where we were touring so much, that I gave up the place I was living. When we weren't touring, Henry and Chris would stay at my mom's house, which was very funny. They were sleeping on the floor in the TV room, and I was so fed up with them that I was the one who didn't stay there. I would bring them home after rehearsal and go stay at a friend's house. I would leave them there with my mom and then jet. They made me crazy, but they got along well with my mom. She was team player. She actually sold merchandise for us at a couple shows, and she ran the merchandise booth at City Gardens a few times. Randy loved her. I mean *loved* her, but my mother can handle herself.

Tim McMahon: The Descendents headlined. It was the *All* tour. At the time they were one of my favorite bands. A little more on the poppy side, and they weren't crazy. They weren't violent. That was the band that I was really looking forward to seeing. They were incredible that night. I probably had five or ten dollars in my pocket and, instead of being smart and buying a Descendents shirt, I blew it on an M.I.A. shirt. I wasn't really "blowing" it, but still, I should have gotten a Descendents shirt. I was so blown away by them. They were great. Up until that point I had just listened to the tape, and to actually see them live in front of me, playing those songs… man. I went home and told my mom I got the shirt from Don or something. Little did she know what I had gone through to get that shirt.

Hoodoo Gurus — September 27, 1987

Randy Now: That was the most violent show in City Gardens' history. You would think it would be Fear or the Circle Jerks, but no. It was the Hoodoo Gurus.

Jim Norton (City Gardens security/stage manager): The biggest bouncer fight ever at City Gardens? People getting dragged out and beaten up by six bouncers? The biggest, most violent episode that I know of was *not* Murphy's Law, was *not* Agnostic Front, and it was *not* the Exploited. It was *not* at a Slayer show. The biggest, weirdest, bouncers-beating-people-up episode at City Gardens was the Hoodoo Gurus. Yes, the Hoodoo Gurus. In terms of a full-on brawl between security and patrons, the winner is Hoodoo Gurus. Like I have said, not everybody was cut from my same "why can't we all get along" community cloth. There were definitely people [working at City Gardens] who were antagonistic, and I didn't care for them. I didn't want to be closely associated with them. On a couple of occasions, I tried to get people fired for stuff that was obviously out of line. So the Hoodoo Gurus play, and there were these two guys who were 6'4", 6'5". Big dudes, probably bigger than most football players. They showed up and they had this general frat-guy look about them. They didn't look threatening. They didn't dress up or anything. They were probably just wearing rugby shirts and windbreakers.

The Hoodoo Gurus were… kind of a punk band… if you were not at all into punk. Good solid rock band, but not really punk. They started playing, and these two guys—in a crowd of people who wanted nothing to do with moshing or slamming—start swinging their arms around at everybody. And they are, by far, the biggest people in the club. So a couple of bouncers go in to calm them down, and these guys put up a fight. The bouncers, rather than backing off, decide that the move is punching these guys. You've got two or three bouncers fighting two or three guys twice their size in the middle of a crowd. Then more bouncers who were inclined toward that sort of behavior get involved as well, and the whole thing moves out the double doors. Normally the protocol for that sort of thing is to get the offender outside and then close the double doors, which have no handles on the outside. The offenders are on the outside of a brick building with no windows looking at two doors that don't have handles, and you're on the inside. Ha ha… joke's on them! They're out $24, and you go on with your merry life. That's what you're supposed to do.

Carl Humenik (City Gardens security): One bouncer went after the Marine-like dude and [bouncer] Repo went after the other guy. The Marine-dude and the bouncer start squaring up and they hit the ground. I jump in, and we start wrestling around, and the Marine rolls over onto his stomach. Me and the other bouncer are on top. I'm on the guy's head, I'm holding his neck, and I'm laying down putting all my weight on his head. The other bouncer is on his back. And the guy starts doing pushups, and COUNTING. He's going, "One … two …" and me and the other bouncer look at each other, like *fuck*. I'm going up and down with him, and I don't know what to do. I'm pounding him and he's still doing pushups. The other guy that Repo was fighting with left and got back inside. We go up to the front door to get a glass of water and calm down, because we were just so pumped up.

Jim Norton: What you're *not* supposed to do is follow them outside and close the doors. Now you're outside with two guys who are twice your size, who now realize they've been thrown out. They're out $24, and they're looking at the people who made it that way. I was not outside for this. However, all of the "bravado" that was displayed by the these bouncers afterwards—all of the bragging about how they really put it to those two assholes—did not take away from what their faces and arms and legs looked like. Whatever happened to those other two guys, those five or six bouncers got their asses kicked.

Carl Humenik: I'm there drinking my water and the guy comes running around the building. I'm standing outside trying to drink water, he comes running right up at me, and I threw the water in his face. The guy stops, and we just start punching him again. A different bouncer, Ronnie, gets a hold of him. The show ends, and Ronnie takes him to the men's room to hold him there until the police come. I go back there and look at him, and one of his friends is there trying to calm him down. And it hits me. I said, "Were you at [Philly punk club] Club Pizzazz last weekend?" And his friend goes, "Oh shit." It turns out that the Marine was the same Marine at a show at Pizzazz and he was causing trouble there! I worked security there, and we all got into a fight with him. We threw him down the steps at Pizzazz, and then he and bouncers were going at it in the street. The guy was just a troublemaker who came to shows and started fights.

Jim Norton: When those bouncers came in after the show, they looked like 50 miles of rough road. I think what *really* happened was that they got outside and got beat the fuck up. And they probably sat outside trying to figure out how they were gonna spin the story. The old "you shoulda seen the other guy" routine wouldn't have worked, because even if those two guys had been taken out on stretchers, they still won. Of all the ways it could have gone, in terms of possible violence at the club, it wasn't GWAR, it wasn't Agnostic Front. It wasn't any of that stuff. It was the fucking Hoodoo Gurus...

Red Hot Chili Peppers—November 8, 1987

Jack Irons (Red Hot Chili Peppers, drummer): I rejoined the band in '86. The Chilis were in need of another drummer, and I think [drummer] Cliff Martinez had reached the end of his rope. When I rejoined in '86, it was mostly touring. We played a lot of shows, the band had built a huge fan base and developed a circuit across the country, and we sort of hit it right away. Then we prepared to make *The Uplift MoFo Party Plan.* I remember one stint where we did 50 shows in 56 days in 50 different cities. It was pretty grueling, even if you pride yourself on being young and able to take it. I didn't take it very well. My history is pretty well documented at this point. I didn't take the stress very well, but we had a lot of fun. There were a lot of hard times, but a lot of good times. It's the camaraderie of being young and having been friends for so long that makes it. I always see the band as old friends, and there's definitely the traumatized times—the dark times—with drugs. But here we are now. It was a long time ago.

On June 25 1988, Red Hot Chili Peppers guitarist Hillel Slovak died of a heroin overdose, which prompted Jack Irons to leave the band.

Jack Irons: I stopped playing with the Chilis in '88 after Hillel passed away. I was headed for a big downward spiral anyway, so all that happened at the same time. I didn't know what was happening to me, and I was not in a good way. I remember I met with Flea and Anthony and said, "I can't do it anymore. I'm not well enough to do it." They went on to do great things.

One thing I feel strongly about is that every good, young musician should know it's a serious way of life. If I could give a virtual sniff of the different things that [touring musicians] go through, a lot of people would say, "I don't want that." You don't want to step into my body for ten minutes, let alone the amount of years I toured. I can't blame that on rock and roll. Rock and roll just exposed it for me. It was going to come one way or another.

D.O.A./Dag Nasty/No Means No/
American Standard—November 22, 1987

Dave Smalley (Dag Nasty vocalist): Look at that lineup! If I saw that lineup tomorrow, I'd go pay a hundred bucks to see it! That show was historic for one reason: I don't think that before that show you would have ever seen [Government Issue frontman] John Stabb and Dave Smalley put on dresses, come out on stage, and sing "Muskrat Love" by America. *[Ed.—It was actually Captain & Tennille.]* We changed the words to "Mohawk Love." Instead of the line, "Do the jitterbug down in muskrat land," it was, "Do the slam dance in muskrat land." It was a capella, and I'll never forget that moment… me and Stabb in dresses… Why did we do that? I have no fucking clue, but it was great. We were getting letters for months and months about it. It's almost a cliché to say how much I love Government Issue, because who doesn't love G.I.? But John Stabb was such a great friend. I love John a lot, as a person and a frontman. It was funny that night… we talked about it, we planned it, and we plotted it. It was so ridiculous. It was great! That show was magic for a bunch of reasons: the crowd, the energy, and the bands. Us putting on dresses and doing "Punk Rock Love." D.O.A. was at their peak at that point. They were really fucking good.

Ben Vaughn Combo—December 31, 1987

Ben Vaughn: New Year's Eve was all ages in the front and 21 and over in the back. So, you could only drink in the back room, but the bands were up front. This was a problem on New Year's Eve. We couldn't even have beers onstage. A bunch of people came in from Philly to see us on New Year's Eve, and when they realized they couldn't drink and watch us at the same time… Well, there was trouble. We had a lot of people who missed our show because it was New Year's Eve and they were getting drunk in the bar. I couldn't blame them! I said to Tut, "Can you put a speaker back there at least? Something?"

That was at the peak of our drawing power. We were doing really well. So many bands took themselves seriously, never smiled, never let their guard down. We were what we were. We didn't have an image. I just love rock n' roll. The Combo played enthusiastically every time.

Then the Combo broke up, and I continued to tour and make records under my name, which went well for a while. But around 1990 my label, Enigma Records, went out of business. Instead of looking for a new deal, I decided to see what else I could do in life. During that time I only played sporadically and put out two records, and I also produced a couple of records for Elektra. I went down to Nashville, but I was too weird for Nashville.

The whole time I was doing the Combo, I was working to raise a son. He turned 18 when I was 38 years old, and all of the sudden I started looking around. I realized I don't need to be here [in the Philadelphia area], I can be anywhere. What talent of mine would be something to pursue, and where would it be the best place? And I was always aware in film and TV shows when the music worked and when it didn't. I noted the different choices of music when certain themes showed up. I always thought I would be really good at that. In 1994 I met a music supervisor who told me that if I moved to L.A., she could probably get me work. I thought, *you know what? I'm gonna do it.* I threw my guitar, a boombox, and some clothes in my Rambler and drove cross country on New Year's Day 1995. Within three months I had [TV show] *Third Rock from the Sun.* I thought I would be working on some cool independent films that made no money, I assumed I would be broke, but *Third Rock* became a hit. Mainstream success is very strange for me. I never envisioned myself being accepted by the mainstream.

I still play out in dive bars, which is where I started. That suits me fine, because I like being closer to the people. If there's a gig where the bass player has to move because someone wants to use the bathroom, then I'm a happy man. Places with no stage, where you set up in the corner… I love that. It's great that it's also not connected to any upward movement within the industry. I'm not even sure if there is a record industry anymore.

1988

Top Ten Songs in 1988:

1. Faith, George Michael

2. Need You Tonight, INXS

3. Got My Mind Set On You, George Harrison

4. Never Gonna Give You Up, Rick Astley

5. Sweet Child O' Mine, Guns N' Roses

6. So Emotional, Whitney Houston

7. Heaven Is a Place On Earth, Belinda Carlisle

8. Could've Been, Tiffany

9. Hands to Heaven, Breathe

10. Roll With It, Steve Winwood

Exploited/The Uprise/Vision/Pagan Babies— January 22, 1988

Randy Now: I was the only person between Trenton and D.C. who would book the Exploited. I was the only one doing Oi! and those types of bands. The Exploited had a bad rep anyway, starting fights and trashing stages. You always heard that from other promoters.

Jamie Davis (City Gardens regular): I think Randy knew what the fuck he was doing. How could you not know there's going to be a riot when you put The Uprise with the Exploited? That's obvious right there. It's a given.

Mike Judge (Judge, vocals): One of the greatest performances I ever saw. Even though I never really liked the Exploited, I was blown away by how punk they were and the balls they had. A bunch of us drove down when they played at City Gardens.

Tony Rettman (City Gardens regular/author): My brother Don was the DJ at City Gardens, so I always got there early with him, usually about an hour or so before the doors opened. Whenever we got there, Randy always locked the doors behind us. Me and my friend were standing there in that little lobby by the door, and all of the sudden there was this banging. There were six guys outside yelling in real heavy accents, "We're the barmy army!" and we were like, "What the hell?" They were the Exploited's roadies. They had been locked out and kept yelling "barmy army." We couldn't understand them through the accents and had no idea what it meant.

Tim McMahon (Mouthpiece, vocals): Randy came up to me and Tony and said, "Exploited doesn't have a merch guy. Would you guys be able to sell their shirts for them?" We're little kids. Of course we wanted to! I remember looking at Tony like, *how the hell are we going to do this?* We did it. I don't know how we did it, but we pretended like this was something we had done before.

Dave Franklin (Vision, vocals): Randy Now called the house and asked, "Hey, I got a question. Would you guys like to play with the Exploited?" My bass player, Ivo, was banned from City Gardens for life for fighting. He was the lead guy in The Family.

Stephen Brown (member of The Family): Ivo! Ivo was tough as nails, man. He was fucking tough. He was in the parking lot one night when this real big, muscle-bound dude came out of the club like he's gonna whoop everybody's ass. We're drinking beer and hanging out, and he walks up and he grabs a beer from Ivo. Well, that's all she wrote. Ivo clocks him with one punch. Dude's laid out on the ground. And the guy starts crying because Ivo broke his nose! I was like, "Hey, those muscles ain't helping you out, man. You can't fight!" We took his beer from him, poured it on his head, and told him to get out of the parking lot. It was funny as hell. One punch.

Dave Franklin: I'm freaking out because I'm showing up to play our first show at City Gardens with somebody who is banned for life! I'm like, "How am I gonna' tell Randy that Ivo is my bass player? He's gonna freak." I get there and pull Randy aside, and I said, "Randy, I gotta talk to you. I have a little problem. The guy that plays bass, um, isn't really… um… welcome here." Randy was screaming in my face like he was my dad and I had just smashed the family china for no reason. He was spitting, screaming, cursing, pointing… I mean, literally, he was like, "You

The Uprise take the stage ahead of The Exploited.

fucking asshole, you're fucked! Fuck you! I don't have an opening band. You can't play here. There's no way you're playing here! Absolutcly not!" Screaming at the top of his lungs.

Randy Now: They did keep it a secret from me until the very last minute, and Dave is right. I did lose my fucking mind when I found out. I had to act that way to show that I was serious because it was my job. Ivo had to be good and not start any trouble to play that show.

Todd Linn (City Gardens security): I used to wear my Uprise shirt all the time. On the front was a big American Eagle emblem, and on the back it said, "Uprise Skinheads: Fun, Friends & Fights." I wore that shirt when I worked at City Gardens because, honest to God, I wanted everyone to know that I knew them. So if a whole bunch of shit was going to come down on me, people knew they were going to have to pay the price.

Dave Franklin: The guys in the Uprise and the Pagan Babies guys come right over and they're like, "What's the matter?" and Randy threw his hands up and walked away disgusted. I told them they were not going to let us play, and they said, "Well, if Vision's not gonna play, then the Uprise aren't playing." And the Pagan Babies guys were like, "Dude, if you guys aren't playing, we're not playing." My head was in my hands,

I was like, "Fuck, what am I gonna' do?" and the next thing you know [Exploited lead singer] Wattie and his manger come walking over. I could barely understand what he said, but he said something like, "What seems to be the problem?" I told him what happened and Wattie goes, "Did you come from far away?" and I go, "Not as far as you," and Wattie asks, "Well, how far?" I said, "About forty minutes down the road," and he says, "That's far enough. What's the name of the band?" I told him it was Vision and he goes, "If Vision doesn't play, the Exploited don't play." I was stunned. Randy threw his hands up and was like, "Okay, fine. You guys play and then Ivo walks off the stage and right out of the club the second you're done." I told him, "No problem. Whatever you want." So that's exactly what we did. We played our set, Ivo immediately left, and he was totally cool about it.

Randy Now: As far as Wattie saying he wouldn't play… I don't think that's true because I was his booking agent in New York back then. He wouldn't have pulled that on me. They were nice guys. I remember their manager at the time used to let Wattie babysit his kids! Wattie was a great guy. Of course, once they got on stage it was different story.

Mark Bless (City Gardens regular): Wattie was hanging out front and showing off his pierced cock to the ladies.

Eric Squadroni (Pagan Babies, guitarist): I was kind of confused about the whole skinhead scene. They would go in there and fuck with some of the bands if they didn't like them. I always thought it was just a bunch of fucking rich kids with that rich-kid mentality.

Ray Meister (City Gardens regular): I was a 15-year-old skater kid. Thinking back on it, my parents must have been out of their minds. They would drop me and my friends off in the middle of the 'hood any weekend there was a show, and The Exploited was definitely a show we wanted to see.

Alex Franklin (City Gardens regular): The Skins wanted to make it known that they did not appreciate the Exploited writing a song called "Fuck the U.S.A."

Bryan Kienlen (Bouncing Souls, bassist): It was an insane vibe that night. The skinheads had some issue with the Exploited because they were dissing the U.S.A. I think that's what it boiled down to, some patriotic thing.

Randy Now: It's weird, this whole "American" thing. When we opened the club, if I put "From England" on a Bauhaus flier, that made people come out to the show. But when I put the same thing on an Exploited flyer, people didn't come because of the whole "American" thing.

Bruce Boyd (Pagan Babies, drummer): We knew there was trouble coming because the Exploited have that song "Fuck the U.S.A." The skinheads back then—and I knew from all the punk shows I had seen from '83 on—were always very pro-American. They had all the American flag patches sewn on their green flight jackets. You knew that they were not going to be very nice to the Exploited.

Randy Now: They all loved The Clash song "I'm So Bored with the USA." What's the difference? It doesn't make any sense.

Mark Pingitore (Pagan Babies, bassist): We get in there and it's the Exploited. These guys are punk-rock rock stars. Our drum kit couldn't be on the riser with their drum kit, and we thought that was kind of funny because we were used to playing anywhere that would let us play. That was the first time we encountered that kind of attitude. It didn't hurt our feelings or anything. We didn't go out and hold a grudge against them. We were like, "Wow. So that's the reality of it."

Bruce Boyd: We're loading in that night, and there were some dudes from the Uprise crew hanging out. Everyone was excited about the show, but in the back of my mind I'm thinking, "There's gonna be fucking trouble."

Tony Rettman: The Uprise played right before the Exploited. The Exploited had set up their gear and left it on the stage, like, "You're just going to have to work around this." I think that added even more fuel to the fire.

Phil Stilton (City Gardens regular): The reason the whole thing started was because of the drums. The Exploited's drummer went up and kicked Rob's drums over when he saw them set up on their riser. A couple of months before, The Uprise had played at City Gardens, and they were kind of a punk band. They came back later re-invented as a skinhead band. I think the Exploited show might have been their first show as The Uprise. Rob had set his stuff up, and the Exploited's drummer came out and was setting up his gear. Rob was like, "Look man, we're just gonna use a small part of the riser, you can set up behind me and it'll be cool." The Exploited guy was having none of it. He was like, "I'm not setting up behind you." Then he kicks Rob's stuff right off the riser. They looked like they were ready to throw down right there. I think that was really the start of everything.

Alex Franklin: The Uprise always had a reputation as far as the people they brought with them. They were definitely a wild bunch.

Tim McMahon: The Uprise were definitely a skinhead band and it was kind of… questionable, as far as what they were into and what they were or weren't.

Ray Meister: The Uprise had nothing good to say about "The Limeys" coming to play in their country. Between songs they stopped for some quick hate speech against the Exploited, complaining about their drum set being so far forward on the stage and not on a riser because the Exploited's gear was set up behind them. By the time The Uprise stopped playing, there was a feeling of menace, which kept building until the Exploited hit the stage.

Alex Franklin: The Uprise played and the whole place went apeshit. All the skinheads went nuts. There were a lot of punks there that night, and there was a lot of tension between the skins and the punks. The Uprise did their thing and all the skinheads got worked up.

Carl Humenik: To this day, I still don't get it. Talking to Scott, Matt [Andrews], and Rob from the Uprise… a couple of them worked at City Gardens. I knew them all. I knew them before they were The Uprise.

When I first met them, they weren't like that. I think it was an act, I really do.

Karl "Hard Karl" Hedgepath: Then you had the thing with the flag. The Uprise had put an American flag out on the stage, and the Exploited tried to take it down.

Dave Franklin: The Uprise were great. Scott and Matt were full-blown skins. They knew there were going to be a lot of skinheads, so they came out wearing wigs! I saw Scott up on stage with this huge blonde afro and I was like, "What the hell is this guy doing?" And all they were doing was just making fun of everybody.

Tony Rettman: The Uprise set up a big American Flag on the stage, and that didn't help either. I think The Uprise guys put on big Afro wigs, too. They were being real sarcastic and said things like, "Oh, don't worry about the people from this country, we're fine. You guys can come over here and set your shit up. We'll work around it. It's fine."

Bruce Boyd: We had no trouble from the crowd. Vision had no trouble from the crowd. Everybody was moshing it up and loving it. Then I thought, "This is kind of weird to have the Exploited come out and headline this show." This was just not the scene for the first three bands and then the Exploited.

Tony Rettman: Then the Exploited came on. I just assumed that the skinheads would sort of like the Exploited. I mean, the skinheads wanted to be from England, the Exploited were from England… They all had that same meathead mentality.

Tim McMahon: When the Exploited went on, it was as if a storm had just come into the building. It seemed like the lights went out and it was just dark and creepy and scary. And I'm thinking, *what the hell's gonna' happen in here?*

Jamie Davis: From what I understand, the Exploited had this big security guard with them who was also [notorious "white power" band] Skrewdriver's security. He had a big Oi! shirt. The Exploited had big ties with Skrewdriver, from what I've heard.

Alex Franklin: When the Exploited came on, I was in the back, and all the skins were gathering at the back of the club. At one point somebody said, "All skinheads in the back." It was pretty organized. Their whole thing was to disrupt the show. As soon as the Exploited hit the stage the American flag came out. The Exploited were harassed from the get-go. They were giving the band the finger, "sieg-heiling" them, and flaunting the American flag in their face.

Bruce Boyd: As the Exploited played, you could see all these gobs of spit raining down on Wattie. You could literally see the gobs of spit being launched at him. You could see the skins in the crowd hocking loogies, just firing away, and they were landing everywhere. But the Exploited just kept on going.

Carl Humenik (City Gardens security): I was on stage with the Exploited, and it was a freakin' nightmare. I was covered in spit. I was trying to stop people from getting on stage, and one guy got up there and clubbed Wattie. Wattie just stood there like, "Okay, what do you got now?"

Mike Judge: The crowd seemed like they hated the band. They were spitting on Wattie.

Jamie Davis: The crowd wasn't fucking with the rest of the band. They didn't spit on any of them. Just Wattie.

Stephen Brown: The only reason we went after Wattie and the Exploited that night was because they got the skins all riled up. We had the American flags going and were having a great time, and the kick in the ass was that we were all American-ed up that night and The Exploited were like, "Fuck the U.S.A., fuck the U.S.A.!" So it kind of pissed everybody off.

Mike Judge: The skins all moved up to the front. They started by chanting, "U.S.A.! U.S.A.!" Then they all gave the finger. Then they started spitting on Wattie, but he never backed down or anything. He stood his ground. You could feel it in the air. Once all those skinheads began pushing their way up front, you just knew something was going to happen and that the Exploited were going to have a rough time of it.

Alex Franklin: The whole time they played Wattie was getting spit on. There was spit all over him. They were calling him a faggot, they were calling him a commie, and he was calling them wankers and spitting right back at them. Wattie had his Mohawk up and you could see one giant glob of spit got stuck in his Mohawk.

Jamie Davis: Wattie is the punkest motherfucker. He just kept playing. He had spit hanging from everywhere.

Mike Judge: I was like, "Damn, I don't know if I'll ever be a frontman who could pull that off."

Randy Now: Spitting started back in England… it was a way of showing appreciation. It didn't mean the same thing over there as over here. The Exploited were used to it, so it didn't really bother them.

Ray Meister: The typical [skinhead] "wall of death" was crashing again and again on the crowd.

Randy Now: The "wall of death" was when skinheads would link arms forming a giant steamroller. They would run full steam at the stage… and over anyone in the way.

Ray Meister: Any kids trying to start a mosh pit quickly had it squashed by skinheads, who seemed to outnumber everyone. They decided that no one was having any fun if they weren't going to take part in their bullshit. They tried to disrupt the show any way possible, pulling a few microphones out into the crowd. One roadie tried to stop this and ended up losing a tug-of-war that resulted in him being dragged into the crowd, roughed up, and thrown back onto the stage.

Bruce Boyd: I decided that was the time to go and meet some chicks or whatever. I mean, that's the reason I'm in a band in the first place: To get chicks.

Michael McManus (Pagan Babies, vocalist): From where I was standing, I saw that Wattie had an issue with some skinheads in the front. At one point somebody jumped on the stage and tried to swing at him.

Jamie Davis: Wattie hit some kid in the face. He tried to hit one of the skins that hit him, and he busted some other kid's face wide open with the microphone stand. Somebody from The Uprise jumped up to swing at Wattie and missed him. And Wattie kept right on playing. He played a whole entire set. It was awesome.

Randy Now: I went to the center of the pit, and I was 35 years old at the time and not a big guy. All these skinheads were huge, football-player types, and I went up to one I knew and said, "You can spit all you want, spit all night, but don't touch them!" And they didn't.

Ray Meister: Wattie's face and mohawk were completely disgusting, covered with spit, but he didn't stop. He played a full show, cursing them out between every song, which made me wonder if this was just a typical night for him. What a madhouse.

Stephen Brown: And Wattie's screaming, "The skins are me mates! The skins are me mates!" And we're like, "Fuck you!" We're spitting on them and shit. It was just us being us, that's all. When the shit went down, he probably thought it was all the skins against him, but it wasn't. He pissed us off because we were all American-ed up that night. Any other night, it probably wouldn't have mattered. We were doing chicken rides, we had the American flags flying… it was a great night.

Tony Rettman: And that was it. After that, it was chaos.

Michael McManus: Halfway through Exploited's set, I was out in the parking lot doing an interview with a fanzine. We were in the van bullshitting. The Exploited had a camper they traveled around in, which was odd anyway because most bands traveled in vans. It wasn't as big as a Winnebago, but it was pretty big. I don't think they were even done playing and the parking lot started filling up. I saw people swinging stuff at this camper. The guy who was interviewing me asked me, "What do you think of what is happening to the Exploited's van?" They blew out every window in that camper. They flattened every tire; they completely fucked that van up while we were sitting there.

Tony Rettman: I was outside interviewing the Pagan Babies in their van for *Jersey Beat* and it was like conducting an interview in Kuwait. There was noise everywhere, shit flying through the air. We saw through the window that people were throwing bottles. It was utter chaos.

Karl "Hard Karl" Hedgepath: I remember when they flipped over the U-Haul outside. It got really fucking ugly.

Randy Now: It only takes ten guys rocking an empty U-Haul trailer for couple minutes to tip over. It was empty because all the equipment was onstage! It was just a trailer, not the whole van.

Dave Franklin: They tipped their van over and chased them right out of Trenton. It was insane.

Mark Pingitore: I saw the aftermath of what went on outside the club. I walked out and saw the bus. It was really fucking funny. I saw the bus being rocked and went, "Wow." I had nothing else to say but, "Wow." I didn't expect it to go that far. I don't think anybody expected it to go that far. I stood back and watched, like, "What the fuck?" That was probably one of the craziest things I think I've ever seen.

Randy Now: They only tipped over the U-Haul trailer! It would have national news if they tipped over a whole van. That simply did not happen. Those kids are full of shit. And I don't remember any windows being smashed, maybe one or two got broken. That's it.

Eric Squadroni: I remember feeling so bad for the guys in the Exploited. Maybe I was wrong, maybe they were staying at some hotel down the road, maybe everything was good and they had a place to stay in the States. But, in my mind, these guys came all the way from England, they got this crappy fucking van and that's their home. Where the fuck are they going to go now? Of course I'm thinking: punk rock—they ain't getting paid. I imagine the Exploited didn't make a whole lot of money that night, probably not enough to put themselves up in a hotel. I just assumed they were fucked because of that. Fucked beyond any 17-year-old kid's understanding. Now we can look back on it, being older, and just imagine being on a road trip and then getting stuck in the middle of nowhere. I can't even imagine what it would be like if you're stuck in another country and all your passports and shit get trampled or ripped off.

Randy Now: The band really didn't care. It was good paying gig for them. And all those kids who came to the show and didn't like them and spit on them? They all bought t-shirts! The Exploited sold a shitload of merchandise. They would sell $2,000–3,000 worth of stuff a night. And the van? It couldn't have been anything that bad because they were able to drive it to the next gig. Maybe they had some duct tape over the windows. Maybe they called U-Haul and got a new van and trailer the next day, but they drove away in the van.

Tony Rettman: I got out of there before they kicked over the U-Haul and spray-painted all the racist graffiti on it. I wondered if they had to go to a U-Haul place to get another trailer or if they had to drive around with all kinds of white power graffiti painted on the side of the one that got trashed.

Ray Meister: At this point I realized my parents were probably in the parking lot and that I should get to them before they either thought I was part of this mob or in danger. Me and my friends piled into the car, and my mom asked me what was going on. I didn't want them to refuse to bring me to shows, so I told them the band was packing their gear into the van and people were just crowding around to see them. I don't think they bought it though.

Eric Squadroni: They busted up the trailer… who knows if one of those dudes busted inside and went through all their personal shit. It had to be a big hassle for them, a big pain in the ass, and for what? For some song? It was punk rock. They could sing about whatever the fuck they wanted!

Stephen Brown: A couple nights later one of the guys from The Uprise got stabbed in the parking lot. Some Philly guy stuck him right underneath his armpit as payback for some other shit that went down that night. So me and Sam Psycho found the guy, and we beat the hell out of him. We're tried to break his leg. We dragged him over to the curb and we jumped up and down on him, trying to get his leg to break, but it wouldn't break! He's all wobbly and stretchy, and we just couldn't get it to break. So we wound up peeing on him. That was the night Adams— this fat, pudgy guy who always had a Mohawk—stopped coming around because we were "too violent." See, when you're drunk all the time, it all kind of meshes together. There were a lot of great nights there, but all those crazy fights stand out. I miss those days. Now that I'm married with kids, I don't do shit anymore.

Eric Squadroni: That's the kind of shit that drove me away from punk rock and got me listening to jazz. It really was ugly to the point where it died. It fucking died, man. You couldn't fucking go see bands anymore because of that skinhead crap. It was such bullshit. Then all the bands were the same guys doing that shit, and the music sucked because it reflected that same kind of jock mentality. It got boring.

Carl Humenik: The funny thing is that I've read interviews with Wattie, and he said, "It was just another night for us. Whatever."

After it all happened, I was hanging out and people told me what happened. The Exploited's guitar player was right behind me and he said, "These are the only clothes I got for the rest of the tour." I gave him my hoodie. It was the only thing I had on me. They lost everything.

Mike Judge: Once I got into my own band and started going on tour and playing those small, little towns where people aren't so tolerant of you—especially if they think you come in with this big "New York attitude"—and the local tough guy wants to show up the singer of the New York band or whatever… Every time I had to go play in front a hostile crowd, I would always think of that show. I would always think of Wattie standing up to a whole crowd of people who were very vocal that they didn't like him. Just the balls that they had to stand out there and play through that. That's the performance I think of. It was impressive.

They Might Be Giants—January 23, 1988

This show was the day after the Exploited. The following is a partial transcript of an interview with They Might Be Giants from "The Daily Show with Jon Stewart" from 2001, where they discuss City Gardens.

John Flansburgh (They Might Be Giants): We pull up in our nice, brand-new Ford Econoline van, and we pull up to a loading area, in a place that looks like one giant loading area. And there is another van that looks like it has been flipped upside down and set on fire, and the fire was just recently extinguished.

Jon Stewart: Let me explain this. We used to have to run from the club to our cars, and we needed cover.

John Flansburgh: The PA was chained to the stage.

Jon Stewart: Someone actually tried to light a fire inside the club. Remember that band the Butthole Surfers?

Public Enemy/Schoolly D—January 29, 1988

Randy Now: Probably the worst riot we ever anticipated... that never happened. I booked Public Enemy for their first show after they had played Tennessee, where there had been a stampede and people were killed. It was the first time I had done a rap show, too. It was a little tense. I remember talking to either Chuck D. or Professor Griff on the phone about security. I said, "What do you want me to do for security? Do you want me to hire the Guardian Angels?" They said, "You're gonna need more than that," and I was like, "Ah, fuck!"

Bryan Bell (City Gardens regular): When we were rolling up to the show and walking across the parking lot to the door, some shitty old car full of scruffy white punks drove by, and one of them leaned out the window and yelled something like, "Y'all are gonna get fucked up!" That helped get the evening started with a suitable menacing edge, although the show hardly lived up to this potential.

Gregory Dicum (City Gardens regular): Public Enemy took the stage late, bitching and whining with some bullshit story of how Flavor Flav had been arrested. They did a thirty minute show and then packed it in.

Randy Now: They were terrible. Noise, feedback, skipping records... Chaos on stage! Chuck said, and I believe this was recorded, "We don't have Flav with us tonight, and we are not at full band level. We'll return in the future to do a free show for y'all. A black man's word is a black man's word." We never got the free show.

Bryan Bell (City Gardens regular): DJ Marc Coleman talked about how Terminator X kept totally fucking up... it was a total fiasco of a show. One of the few other white dudes at the show was wearing the same ridiculous/awesome red-white-and-black Run-DMC Adidas sweatshirt as me, just to add insult to injury.

Sinead O'Conner/MC Lyte—March 25, 1988

Gal Gaiser (City Gardens DJ): This was the most crowded I ever remember City Gardens. I literally could not get out of the DJ booth. It was only time I was ever told I had to play a certain type of music, because Sinead wanted all funk and rap played before her set. I remember her outside the building, and she was so slight, so little, leaning against the building with her arms folded, very quiet. She seemed introverted and shy and gave off a don't-get-near-me vibe, but then she got up on stage and roared.

Carl Humenik: I didn't even know who the hell she was. Her album had just come out. I saw a picture of her, and I was like, "What's this? Some skinhead girl singing 'Oi'!?" I was at the front door and heard knocking. I open the door and there she was. She was the most beautiful girl I'd ever seen in my life. I just stood there frozen. Her manager was like, "Can we get in please?" I was just like... She just smiled and walked past me. I had never heard her music, and then she gets up there and starts singing. She has the most beautiful voice in the world. I still listen to her all the time. There's not a song she sings that I don't like. I just fell in love with her as soon as I saw her.

Fachtna O'Ceallaigh (Sinead O'Conner's manager): I am not too sure that Sinead even remembers back that far. I was with her [at that show] as her manager, and I certainly remember being in Trenton. I am familiar with the name of the club, but not because Sinead played there, but because I was in Trenton on another occasion when I had made the acquaintance of MC Lyte, her brothers, and her manager/father. I had heard her first 12" single, "I Cram To Understand You, Sam" and flew to New York "find" her. I thought she would be great to do a rap remix of Sinead's song, "I Want Your Hands On Me." MC Lyte did it, and she

opened for Sinead at a number of shows. A couple of her dancers at that time were from Trenton. I remember going to some kind of open air, country fair type thing in Trenton, all African American, and MC Lyte performed.

Deirdre Humenik (City Gardens employee): Sinead ran around the outside of building, just ran around the building in a frantic way, running laps, working off I don't know what. Then she came into the back. I went to take her picture and she flipped out, and then she said, "I won't show up in the photo anyway."

Danzig/GWAR—April 9 1988

Randy Now: It was the first Danzig show ever. Glenn Danzig called me and said he wanted their first ever show to be in Jersey.

I knew it wasn't going to do good. I told him it wasn't going to do good, but he was expecting 1,000 people. He gave me all the help he could to make it work, but it just didn't. It was too far south of the whole Glenn Danzig/Lodi/North Jersey heavy metal/Misfits/WSOU zone. I had done Samhain a couple of times before, and that didn't do so well, either. I think Danzig ended up with 400 people, which isn't bad, but 400 people in a place that holds 1200…

Oderus Urungus (GWAR): That was Danzig's first show. We were surprised there was such a low turnout.

Tony Rettman (City Gardens regular/author): I knew what was in store before GWAR played. My brother had their first record and they looked crazy. Those guys were nuts, and you had no idea what they were going to do. You heard rumblings of what their shows were like, and I had an idea of what it was going to be like, but I had no idea what it was *really* going to be like. A lot of time and effort went into those shows.

Oderus Urungus: We never would have gone to City Gardens as fans. It was a horrible place! I'm not even sure how we started playing there. I'd heard about the venue from other bands and called Randy up.

Steven DiLodovico (author): One of the coolest punk-rock experiences I ever had was at that show.

Oderus Urungus: That was one of the only times GWAR opened for somebody, but people had heard about GWAR. We opened up for Danzig at City Gardens and at the Ritz in New York the very next night, but after that we didn't get a lot of calls to open for other bands. People heard that we were pouring shit all over the place and the shows were so fucking insane that nobody wanted to follow it. So, from the beginning, we got good crowds.

Randy Now: On the GWAR tour, the catch phrase was "pump and pay." We were in a gas station in Montana, and it was like ten degrees below zero. For GWAR's tours, they would go south in July and we'd all be sweating, and then we'd be in Canada and Montana in February. So, we're in Montana, where you have to pump your own gas, and it's three or four in the morning. This disembodied voice came over a loud speaker and said, "Pump and pay."

Oderus Urungus: Randy was one of the first huge supporters of GWAR, one of the first legitimate club owners that really backed us. I remember for the longest time when I was booking the band, Randy was my guy. He went out with us on the road, too. He wasn't a bad road manager, but I think he missed his postal route too much...

Randy Now: No one had ever heard of GWAR before. I had actually met them in DC years before when they were called Death Piggy, opening for the Meatmen. They were ready to break up right before I booked them to play Trenton.

Steven DiLodovico: The Misfits were my favorite hardcore band, but I was too young to have seen them. When I heard that Danzig had this new band, and they were playing their first show ever in Trenton, I had to go. I went with a dude named "The Moshing Fetus." He was the only person I knew who was willing to drive from Philly to Trenton. City Gardens, of course, had a huge reputation, and the stories we heard over in Philly were insane. No one I knew was willing to chance going there.

Ollie Grind (Crucial Youth): The only speeding ticket I ever got in my entire life was when I was driving to City Gardens to see Danzig. I'll never forget it: April 9, 1988. I went with my friend who was a total Misfits guy. He even had the "devilock" down to the middle of his forehead. I guess we got too excited listening to Misfits songs, and I was driving, like, 70 miles per hour and got pulled over. The cop said, "It smells like dirt in your car. Are you guys transporting drugs?" I said, "Uh, I don't even drink…" He was such a dick! No wonder everyone hates cops.

Eerie Von (Danzig/Samhain, bassist): When we did the first Danzig show, Samhain had been relatively popular, but not huge. In the beginning maybe 20 or 30 people would show up. Next time we came to town, maybe a few hundred would show up. But for that first Danzig show we had a tour manager, which was totally new for us. I made up these laminates, because we didn't have any, and we needed something. That was our first big gig, and all of the sudden we really thought we were going to be rock stars. The difference from Samhain to the first Danzig show… that was a big move. We were lucky enough to do it at City Gardens.

Tony Rettman: GWAR opened for Danzig and fucking completely blew him away. But it seemed that nobody else in attendance knew what was going to happen [during GWAR's set], and they really didn't like it. All the skinheads were mad because they got fake blood all over their Fred Perry polo shirts. They were doing the whole "wall of death," which I never understood. It was like that at every GWAR show: All the skinheads would get pissed off. I thought, "Don't you fucking get it? Are you really this fucking stupid? Your shit is going to get messed up. If you know this, why do you keep coming to these shows?"

Ollie Grind: We got there and I was so excited to see Danzig, and then GWAR comes on and I thought, "Who is this?" This crazy band comes out with costumes and blood, all this crazy shit, and it was so awesome. The other thing about GWAR was the hot chick on the stage. Dudes were trying to grab her, and she kicked them in the face!

Tony Rettman: At one point I was standing on that stairwell off to the side of the stage, and I had bought some new Nikes the day before. I got all this fake blood splattered on them, but I had already been planning on taking the sneakers back because they hurt my feet. I took them back and the lady opened the box, and there's blood splattered all over them. She probably thought I had killed somebody and was trying to get rid of the evidence.

Ollie Grind: I wonder how many people went to that show with Misfits and Samhain shirts and got blood on them because they didn't realize what was going on with GWAR?

Alex Franklin (City Gardens regular): I don't even remember GWAR playing. I was there because I wanted to see Danzig play Misfits songs. Everybody was amped up to hear Misfits songs. I don't think anybody gave a shit about his new songs.

Steven DiLodovico: I figured Danzig would just be a continuation of Samhain, and to an extent it was, but it was more heavy rock than punk. It kind of sounded like the later stuff from The Cult. The first record wasn't even out yet, so a lot of us didn't really know what they were going to sound like.

Eerie Von: Usually you don't want to go and play shows if you don't have a record out, because nobody knows [the songs]. I don't know why we got so big before we even had a record out. There could have been a bunch of publicity before that. It could have been that Glenn had a new band. A lot of it could have been The Misfits' legacy. That happened a lot, and it used to piss Glenn off. We were doing Danzig, but people kept asking about The Misfits. It was a few years after they broke up, and he was like, "Where were you when we needed you?" All these magazines started paying attention to Danzig, but all they wanted to ask Glenn about was The Misfits.

Alex Franklin: Here's the thing… You know Glenn Danzig portrays a particular kind of image. He's got one video where, in every other scene, he's flexing his muscles. He's got this whole way of putting up his arm up and flexing. He was not in shape. He was wearing his leather pants and he had a gut. He couldn't zipper his pants up, so his pants where unzipped and undone through the whole show.

Steven DiLodovico: Danzig got a hard time from the crowd. I had heard these legends about how Glenn was notorious for fighting with crowds. I kept waiting to see it go off, but nothing happened.

Oderus Urungus: I do remember the crowd actually chanting "GWAR" during his set at one point. I'm sure that didn't make him very happy.

Ollie Grind: Danzig opened with "Twist of Cain" that night, and they played a few old Misfits and Samhain songs, which we loved.

Alex Franklin: He was trying to play to the females in the crowd. The whole thing was so funny. He's trying to act cool and act like Elvis, and his fucking pants are undone! He has this gut, and he's wearing this tight shit, and looked ridiculous. And he never played any Misfits songs.

Steven DiLodovico: They played the hybrid version of "Twist of Cain" as well as "London Dungeon," which made the entire night for me. I didn't care what else they did. I had heard a Misfits song!

Eerie Von: One of the reasons we used to hang out after shows and sign autographs and take pictures was because if you didn't meet people, you wouldn't remember the gig. You go from one place to the next, and unless something happens, or unless there's some kind of event during the show or after the show, you don't even remember it. Especially after you start playing theaters and every one is kind of the same. You go from place to place to place, and you never really see anything. You just get up, play, and leave.

Steven DiLodovico: My whole existence was dependent upon meeting Glenn Danzig. I waited out in that little side alley, one of the scariest places I've ever been, and after hours of waiting he finally came out. He was very cool, and it was the only time I ever asked anyone for an autograph. He signed my bad Misfits bootlegs and told a few old school, punk rock, fight stories. I wore a standard punker biker leather jacket and underneath the crudely drawn Crimson Ghost I had painted on were the words, "Evil never dies..." Glenn saw this and signed my super-shredded rocker jeans: *"Evil is... GLENN DANZIG!"* Coolest fucking thing ever. Easily the best night of my life.

Eerie Von: We would stay in places for hours [talking to people]. We would go outside and hang around for hours. People would come around, and I would do my "act," talk, make people laugh, hang out, sign stuff... We all did it. Chuck [Biscuits, Danzig drummer] wasn't that big on it, because he didn't feel like a "rock star." I mean, he's been playing since he was 12, so he wasn't really that comfortable with all that. Sometimes he would just sit on the bus and we would pass things back to him to sign. Glenn still does it. He just has a little bit more security.

Bob Gorman (GWAR historian): I remember Bishop, our bass player, coming back with a lot of funny stories about Glenn. We had always idolized him. He mentioned how they were real rock stars and standoff-ish toward GWAR. He also said they didn't like the [stage prop] dicks or anything like that.

Oderus Urungus: We were in the dressing room after the show, and Danzig came in with his girlfriend and his little posse. They all kinda stood in a perfect line behind him. His girlfriend, for some reason, picked up one of the slave cocks and like held it up. She was like, "Look at this!" Suddenly, all this jizz dripped out of it! It went all over her, and she's screaming, "Eewww!" and dropped it. Danzig took one look at it, and turned his back on the room, and stormed out the door. A second later his whole posse did the same exact thing. I have never talked to Danzig since then.

ALL—April 10, 1988

Dave Smalley (ALL vocalist): One of the cool things about those days was the great bills. It's difficult to imagine how isolated punk rock was, even at that point in 1988. It was even more isolated in the early '80s. It was great. You would have guys like ALL, who definitely stood out. I certainly stood out, looking kind of freakish. Our hair was crazy. Then you'd have someone like HR, who definitely stood out. You had the Dough-boys, who all had dreadlocks. In fact, the Doughboys dreadlocked my hair on that tour. It hurt like hell to get those dreadlocks, I might add! It was a real joy to play with HR. At that point he still had a really good reputation. What I really remember about that show is the kids. Meeting the kids and realizing that this was such a special place. The people were cool, the energy was really cool, and it was unique. I remember being awed by how much graffiti and band stickers were in the dressing room. It was like CBGB's bathroom.

Mentors/UK Subs/Broken Bones—May 1, 1988

Amy Yates Wuelfing: The UK Subs were one of those bands that seemed to come through every six months. Charlie Harper, the leader singer, was easily 20–25 years older than everyone else. Behind his back, people would say, "You got to hand it to the old guy…" At this show, he was in his early 40s, which seemed ancient to the rest of us. Meanwhile, he still plays 150 shows a year. Punk rock keeps you young.

Rollins Band/Social Distortion/Red Kross— July 15, 1988

Randy Now: This line-up would have made sense to me at the time. Social Distortion were punk—or they used to be—and they were trying to reestablish themselves. But at the point, they were just an opening act.

Amy Yates Wuelfing: This show was at a weird in-between point for Social Distortion. The band had become a joke to most punks. They were over the hill. Their heyday was in 1984, and then the lead singer went to jail for drugs. When he got out, the band released the album *Prison Bound*, which was alt-country/cowpunk, and no one understood what they were doing. This was also before they signed to Epic Records and had the hits "Ball and Chain" and their cover of Johnny Cash's "Ring of Fire." They weren't attracting big crowds.

Randy Now: The kids in the crowd didn't know how to respond. You couldn't mosh or slam to their new music. They stood there looking at each other, waiting for Rollins to come on.

Agent Orange/Dag Nasty/Slammin' Watusis — July 17, 1988

Tim McMahon (Mouthpiece, vocals): Agent Orange and Dag Nasty were two of my all-time favorite bands. I was going to kill two birds with one stone. I got there thinking, "Okay, I'm going to walk right in with Tony and Don [Rettman]." I start to walk in and, for whatever reason, Randy says, "Hey, he can't come in." I was crushed. Maybe we didn't show up early enough, I don't remember. There was already a line, and I was like, "Oh, shit." I was scared to death because now I had to stand out front. Randy let me stand toward the front so I didn't have to go all the way to the end, which went all the way back toward the junkyard. I'm standing there and people are looking at me like, "Look at this little kid. Who the hell does this little jerk think he is?" I was looking down at the ground, kicking stones, looking at the wall.

A funny coincidence: I saw Chris Schuster there, who ended up playing with me in Mouthpiece many years later. He was a local skater kid who had a giant half-pipe in his yard. I looked at him and thought, "Oh, cool. I kind of know that dude. I've seen him skating around town before." I looked at him, and he looked at me, and he was like, "So?" He wasn't very inviting. Eventually the doors opened and I got in. Dag Nasty was on their *Field Day* tour, and I kept thinking how I had to get t-shirts for both bands. I got an Agent Orange shirt, and I wanted to get a Dag Nasty shirt and Dag Tags… those dog tags that had "Dag Nasty" on them. I tried to borrow money from Tony to buy one, but he was like, "No, those things are stupid."

Circle Jerks — July 24, 1988

Joseph Kuzemka (Trenton Punk Rock Flea Market): I won tickets to see Murphy's Law, The Mentors, and GWAR when I was 13 years old. I told my mother, "I won tickets on the radio to go see Murphy's Law, The Mentors, and GWAR!" She said, "I don't know who these bands are, play them for me." She forced me to play her The Mentors, which meant

I was never going to set foot in City Gardens ever in my life. I missed out on that opportunity, and then about six months later, a good friend of mine—who was my age—told me that his mother was going to let him see the Circle Jerks at City Gardens. I told him, "My mother said it's okay if I go see the Circle Jerks too, and your mother can drop us off." My mother did NOT know that I was going to City Gardens.

I made it a point to try to get there for every show from that point forward. I kept almost all of my punkcards that came in the mail, and I go through them probably once every six months just to remind myself of the amazing shows we saw back then. Where I lived in Trenton was not terribly bad, but then there was Calhoun Street, which was terribly bad. It was like going from one country to another.

ALL—July 30, 1988

Dave Smalley (ALL vocalist): I have a personal love affair with New Jersey, and I attribute that mostly to City Gardens. I always felt so welcome there by the kids, no matter what band I was in at the time. I met some really cool bands there and made some lasting friendships because of that place. I have roots in a lot of cities, but of the [places] that I haven't lived in, I'd have to say New Jersey is really special to me. A lot of that is due to City Gardens and the environment that it nurtured. I've played other clubs where they've treated us well, but when I see things like other clubs' security… [They were] some pretty tough cats. The guys at City Gardens were like my brothers. They understood ALL, and Randy made it clear that this whole thing is a joy—a movement and a special moment. It all trickled down from Randy. I would hang backstage and talk with him.

What's funny about City Gardens is that I met and saw plenty of parents at those shows. They weren't ostracized, and they weren't hiding. They might have been hanging out in the back like I would be if I took my kids to a show now. We were always happy to talk to them, and they were totally cool. We would have a nice little chat, and they would feel relieved about [having their kids at] the show.

GWAR/Murphy's Law/Mentors—August 28 1988

Bob Gorman (GWAR historian): I remember seeing GWAR before I was actually in GWAR. They played with the Mentors in Richmond, and it was a show that got booked at the last second. I think they kind of flew by the seat of their pants, and they would show up or maybe not show up. They didn't care. I remember Heathen Scum. He was such a great guitar player. I was always amazed at how actually good he was. Unfortunately I wasn't there for all the debauchery... the peeing on the school bus and all that.

Oderus Urungus (GWAR): [Mentors vocalist] El Duce used to have a guitar player—Sneaky Sperm Shooter—who he delighted in torturing. He would take this medicine ball he had and hock a big loogie on it, and then he would smack the guy's face with it. One day, when we were in this parking lot getting some sauce for El Duce, we saw him come out of the liquor store with liquor in his hand. He chugged half the bottle, then he whipped his dick out and peed all over the medicine ball, and then came back to the bus with it. We knew exactly what he wanted to do: he wanted to put his piss in Sneaky's face. We weren't going to let him do that. When he came running onto the bus with the medicine ball, we all jumped on him, knocked him down, and tried to get him off the bus. The medicine ball is floating up in the air while El Duce is trying to hold on to it and smack it in people's faces when, suddenly, Mike Bonner—who was one of our GWAR slaves—stuck his hand up in the air. Out of nowhere a switchblade appears. He stabs the fucking medicine ball and it exploded, and piss goes everywhere. I mean *everywhere*. Everyone was coated in a fine spray of El Duce's piss. When we finally all got back up, El Duce was completely unconscious, snoring away. He was the greatest.

I know how he really died: it was a stupid drunken accident. It's such a load of horseshit that people think that he had anything to do with Kurt Cobain's death or anything else. I got the true story... He was going back to his place from the fucking supermarket with his beer and was crossing the railroad tracks. He dropped his bottle of beer, stopped to get it, saw that he didn't have enough time to get out of the way of the train, *sieg heil*-ed the train, and then was disintegrated.

Bob Gorman: He was living out on the west coast for a short amount of time, too. I remember the first time we played the Hollywood Palladium, he was living in a cardboard box.

Oderus Urungus: Yeah, we pulled up and we were like, "Hmmm. Wonder where El Duce is?" We didn't have anywhere to stay, so we pulled in behind our friend's practice space on Hollywood Boulevard. We looked out the window of the bus at this big pile of cardboard boxes, and El Duce came crawling out of one.

Bob Gorman: It almost seemed like a gag, like a set up. We didn't believe it, but it was true… It was where he was staying. We were hanging out at the dressing room at the Palladium after the show, and it was right after we first blew up, so there were all these famous people there [Metallica's] James Hetfield and The Red Hot Chili Peppers, Ice T. And El Duce was back there screaming. Someone had put down a beer and there were cigarette butts in it, and El Duce was looking around for *anything* to drink. I was like, "No no no! Don't drink that one!" He looked at it, saw the cigarette butts, and was real casual. Like, "Ah, there's still plenty in here," and he chugged it down.

Oderus Urungus: He was the fucking greatest, man.

Bob Gorman: Playing with Murphy's Law was always fun, too.

Oderus Urungus: At this point they were putting us with some of the wilder bands, so it didn't really matter that we were getting shit all over the place. Murphy's Law are still really good friends of ours. Jimmy Gestapo is a good buddy. We see him every now and then in New York. He's more into running his tattoo parlor, but Murphy's Law is still playing shows. That show was the only time we ever had a problem there. There were tons of New York skinheads at that show, and they really didn't know what to make of GWAR. They were not really into us squirting shit on them. So at one point they all pulled back from the stage, formed the "wall of death," and charged. We were totally ready for them, and we fucking hosed them with a fucking barrage of spew! They all crashed into the stage and milled around in a confused blob while we hosed them blind. I think at that point, through osmosis, they realized this was actually fun, you know? We never had a problem with any punk or skinhead or gang element. Anyone who has a problem with GWAR realizes pretty quickly it's like getting angry about The Simpsons.

Danzig — September 17, 1988

Eerie Von (Danzig/Samhain, bassist): We had a real high drum riser and a big skull with the eyes cut out so we could put lights behind it. The thing was pretty big. It might have been a problem with the ceiling [at City Gardens]. Maybe we couldn't get Chuck up on the riser, and get the skull on there too. That happened a few times. Or maybe we couldn't even get the thing through the door. The horns used to come off the skull; they were separate pieces. But the whole thing was probably six feet tall or more, so sometimes we couldn't even get it through the door.

*In September 1988, Bon Jovi released the album **New Jersey** and wanted to play a free concert a club in New Jersey to celebrate. The band's management wanted that club to be City Gardens. However, the band could only do it on a Thursday, which would have meant canceling 90¢ Dance Night. City Gardens owner Frank refused and the show did not happen. **New Jersey** debuted at #8 on the Billboard Top 100 and spent four weeks at #1. It eventually sold 7 million copies in the United States.*

Rapeman — September 23, 1988

Amy Yates Wuelfing: I was writing for a magazine and had two interviews set up almost back-to-back. A friend and I were scheduled to talk to [Rapeman frontman] Steve Albini before the show, and a day or two later I was set to interview Marty Wilson Piper from The Church. I figured Marty would be fine, but I was concerned about Albini. He had a reputation of being a little snarky. In the end, Steve Albini was wonderful… a total gentleman and very respectful. Marty Wilson Piper was a completely pretentious asshole. You never can tell.

DEVO—November 11, 1988

Randy Now: The biggest bands are the easiest to work with, and Devo is a great example. This was a super sold-out show and they sold a lot of merchandise. [Devo frontman] Mark Mothersbaugh and I spoke about Ween, and he loved them. We also talked about Mark's side project with an instrumental surf band, The Wipe-outers.

Amy Yates Wuelfing: Before this show, they played a club in Philly. Before the doors opened, I went to a 7-11 down the block to get a drink and who is there, buying two hot dogs, but Mark Mothersbaugh, who I adored. I tried to think of something witty to say, but all I could come up with—playing off their whole de-evolution concept—was, "Wow, that's pretty de-vo!" He ignored me, and I don't blame him.

GWAR/GBH—November 19, 1988

Keene Hepburn (City Gardens soundman): The band came in and mounted these three giant heads with their mouths open to the ceiling, with hoses running from their mouths along the rafters. They attached the hoses to the old-fashioned looking fire extinguishers. I asked what was in them and they were like, "Oh. It's guar gum and carrageen, the stuff that makes ice cream sticky, and all kinds of other stuff." I asked when they were going to set it off, and they said, "We're just going to let it go in the middle of the set." During the show, they let it rip. They unleashed this nasty stuff on all the punks in the crowd. It came from the ceiling and rained down on everyone, and people couldn't figure out where it was coming from.

Joe Z. (City Gardens soundman): I was packing up the gear at the end of the show, and I told Oderus that Tut wasn't too happy about the band spraying the fake blood everywhere. He said, "Fuck 'em if they can't take a joke!"

Ministry—December 17, 1988

This is the last time Ministry would play City Gardens.

Al Jourgensen (Ministry): I knew we were getting big when the tour manager booked a separate room in the hotel just for our drugs. We had to go to that one room to shoot up. You couldn't do it in your own room [or you might] get arrested. That's when I knew I wasn't hitting on something good. This was a few years before "Jesus Built My Hotrod" with [Butthole Surfers frontman] Gibby Haynes. Gibby is the most astute, yet insane, person I have ever met in my life. He is absolutely astute and absolutely insane. He grew up with a famous TV clown for a dad, which would make anybody insane.

One time, me and my buddy Mike were at my house, and Gibby stole all my crack. Then he proceeded to smoke it all in front of us with my stolen pipe! Me and Mikey got pissed and beat the living crap out of Gibby. You know what he did? He got up, all bloody, and stole the rest of my crack. The guy is relentless. I love that guy. We're BFFs forever. You know what else? He did that to me twice.

Once he did so much crack he thought he was covered in spiders. He's freaking out and scratching himself to the point of blood. I take off his clothes and throw him in the shower, and he's in the shower, naked, washing the spiders off, or so he thinks. And what's in the shower? A black widow spider… a real one. He freaks out again, and I went got a gun and shot the spider. I blew up my shower stall for Gibby.

The first time I met him was at the first Lollapalooza. I got into a fist fight with Henry Rollins at that Lollapalooza. It was brutal. He called me a scumbag junkie, and I'm like, "What is your fucking malfunction? Live and let live." And then he started beating his chest like a gorilla and freaked out. We got into a fight, but people jumped in right away so I didn't get my ass kicked, because he would have kicked my ass. He had people holding him back, and he's yelling and screaming, and I'm just like, *whatever.*

So, later that night I'm at the studio and Gibby comes down. I had this song I didn't know what to do with vocally, so I said, "Why don't you take a crack at it?" I had met him a couple times before that. One time it was at a motel in Oklahoma, where we were doing mushrooms together, and I never laughed so hard in my life. That guy is the funniest motherfucker ever.

During the recording of "Jesus Built My Hotrod," Gibby was drunk off his ass, slurring all over the place, sitting on a stool. Then he's so drunk he can't even sit on the stool. He was literally falling… face planting on the floor. So we switched out the stool for a chair, and he can't even sing words. He starts singing gibberish. I spent the next two weeks editing it together to make a chorus and a verse out of it.

Randy Now: One time I called Al Jourgensen's house to talk to his wife Patty, who was his manager, to book him for a show. His little daughter answered the phone, crying. I said, "What's the matter?" She said, "Mommy's sleeping and won't wake up." I said, "Where is she?" She says, "She's on the floor sleeping, and she won't wake up." I asked if her daddy was there, and she says no. I had no idea what to do. This was before cell phones, the internet, Facebook. So I called the Chicago police department. I tried to explain what had just happened, but they just didn't get it. Plus I didn't have their address. I'm not sure what happened, if the police showed up or what. Patty didn't die, so I guess it turned out okay.

In 1986, former Regressive Aid guitarist William Tucker released a record under the name Swinging Pistons. The record got the attention of Al Jourgensen, who invited him to Chicago.

Sim Cain: Shortly thereafter, Billy [Tucker] moved to Chicago and things really took off for him. Billy contacted me about a year before he died, and the two of us went out. He wasn't drinking at the time, which was amazing. And he was telling me things like he was considering ideas like growing old gracefully. This shit was startling to me. First that he was telling me these things, and then a year later he took his own life. If people don't want to talk about Billy now, I think it's out of respect for him. He was capable of amazing sweetness. He was a rock star before he was famous. It was a lifestyle he embraced and an aesthetic he went for. He was a little Keith Richards, and a true music aficionado.

Amy Yates Wuelfing: I recall going into Princeton Record Exchange where Billy worked, and he had two records in his hand: Skinny Puppy and Swing Out Sister. He was equally excited about both of them. He wasn't snob about music. He loved it all.

Sim Cain: Billy even liked Ministry when they were doing that horrible Duran Duran type music. He chased down the musicians he really liked and ended up working with most of them. We all had a complete appreciation for music. We would take notes and catalog it all. We were like librarians with alcohol. There were a lot of amazingly creative people around at that time… a lot of artists and musicians. I thought all my friends were brilliant. I thought that someday people would be writing about us the way they did about the ex-pats in Paris. I was really lucky to have spent time in their presence.

On May 14, 1999 William Tucker took his own life. He was 38 years old.

Regressive Aid graphic novel The Anti-Chair!

BELOW: *The early days of City Gardens, with tables and chairs, before the checkered dance floor.*

D. Boon and Mike Watt of the Minutemen

Suicidal Tendencies, with frontman Mike Muir.

Henry Rollins and Greg Ginn of Black Flag.

Hüsker Dü yuk it up while reading Hard Times magazine.

*The photo that almost wasn't: Anton Corbijn's photo of
New Order taken at the county fair next door.*

The Descendents in front of their rolling death trap.

Samhain with the precursor to the Danzig skull.

Tesco Vee of the Meatmen.

DJ Gal and Ron Kearnest take the dance floor.

Art at City Gardens

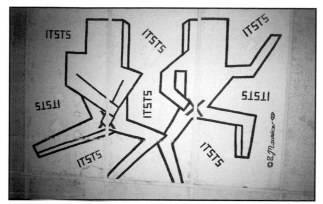

Keith Haring–like figures painted by Karey Maurice Counts.

Billy Idol says, "Dance!" (Artist Unknown)

T-Bone mural in the dressing room, circa 1986. (Artist Unknown)

Randy Now introduces Fugazi's Ian MacKaye to Spike Jones.

Ex-bartender Jon Stewart pays a visit to his old stomping grounds, with City Gardens owner Frank "Tut" Nalbone.

City Gardens regular "Old School" Alex Franklin
hangs out in the City Gardens parking lot.

The "Wall of Death" in full flight. A City Gardens pit was no joke.

"ALL SKINS TO THE FRONT!" The call went out as The Exploited took the stage. The band was met by some very pro-American skins who weren't too happy with the Exploited's song Fuck the U.S.A.

Skins Vs. Exploited frontman Wattie.

ABOVE: *City Garden's regular Paul Warfel kisses hallowed ground the last night the club was open.*

Mohawk Dave says farewell to City Gardens.

The last one out the door:
City Gardens DJ and Bouncer Rich O'Brien.

Chapter 9

1989–1990

The late 1980s ushered a new crowd into City Gardens. With all-ages shows happening every week, 'tweens and young teens began attending shows en masse, often being driven to the club by older friends, siblings, or even parents. Along with the teens came lawsuits. When a teen left a show with an injury from moshing, slamming, or stage diving, the parents seemingly went straight to a lawyer from the emergency room.

The "No Slam Dancing, No Stage Diving" era had begun.

1989

Top Ten Songs in 1989:

1. Look Away, Chicago

2. My Prerogative, Bobby Brown

3. Every Rose Has Its Thorn, Poison

4. Straight Up, Paula Abdul

5. Miss You Much, Janet Jackson

6. Cold Hearted, Paula Abdul

7. Wind Beneath My Wings, Bette Midler

8. Girl You Know It's True, Milli Vanilli

9. Baby, I Love Your Way / Freebird, Will To Power

10. Giving You the Best That I Got, Anita Baker

Carl Humenik (City Gardens security): This was an awkward time. Suddenly, you're telling punks that they can't have fun and do what they came to do. They would dance around and mock the rule, or they would purposely slam into someone and say, "Oh, I'm so sorry." And I would say, "Look guys, do what you want to do, but don't hurt anybody. That's all the owners care about." I would let people get away with stuff and have fun, but if I told them to stop, they would stop. I only got aggressive with people when it was warranted. I understood why they had to have the rule. Believe me. I got an earful as to why all the time.

One time [fellow bouncer] Rich O'Brien and I were working a show, and someone caught him in the face. He was wearing glasses and they got pushed into his forehead and cut him. We went to his house after the show, and his dad took a look at his head and wanted him to sue City Gardens.

Dawn Englehart (City Gardens regular): It's a badge of honor to say you went to City Gardens. I started going there when I was in ninth grade. I begged my parents to take me, and my dad would drive me and my friends and wait in the parking lot. Some of the other parents would take turns driving us, but they had no idea what we were up to in there. I was completely uninhibited. You were treated like a grown-up when you were there. There was no judgment on being young. I was out there slamming and moshing with everyone else.

My parents were just happy to know where I was. They knew I was obsessed with music. When I got older, I started sneaking to clubs in New York, like Limelight and Danceteria, and lying about where I went. At first, I would tell my parents where I was really going and they would forbid me to go, so I would say, "I'm sleeping over so-and-so's house," and then go to New York. My father would say, "I think you're lying to me." And I'd say, "Well, do you want to know the truth or do you want me to lie?" But all those experiences led me to my current career in music. My parents joke that they never should have sent me to college. They should have just let me go to clubs.

I never experienced any harassment there, only positive experiences. There was something magical about City Gardens I have never experienced elsewhere, and I've traveled on club tours all over the world. At City Gardens, I never felt out of place. I felt safe at City Gardens, even weighing 105 pounds and moshing with guys. I think spending my formative years hanging out at a grungy punk rock club has so much to do with where I am now. I see it in my approach to paying it forward. I'm mentoring a 13-year-old girl, and I take her to club shows and record shopping, and I teach her about the importance of rock clubs. I want her to know how to dive into the experience, and how those big stadium shows are fine, but the real essence of music is being in a hot, sweaty room with a couple hundred people who are entranced and totally into what's happening. I remember seeing Fugazi and their whole approach to making music for the people, and making sure it was accessible and affordable. That has always stuck with me.

Don Rettman (City Gardens regular/DJ): Sometimes I would drive around and pick up my little brother's school friends and take them to shows. I was like the hardcore soccer mom. I took him to see Black Flag when he was 13. I'm sure he got into trouble at school for getting [other kids] into that music. I know he took some flak for it, but eventually he got his clique going.

Circle Jerks/Deadspot—January 1, 1989

Greg Hetson (Circle Jerks, guitarist): Recently my daughter asked me if skinheads ever came to Circle Jerks shows. When I told her yes, she said, "Don't they know you're Jews?" I told her this story...

Stephen Ernest Saputelli (Deadspot, bassist): I remember how scared we were just driving through Trenton... that in itself was a rush. I had just joined the band, and we were opening for the Circle Jerks

Randy Now: We put the word out on the punkcards and fliers that no Doc Martens were allowed in the club. A cool person who wore Docs would understand and say, "I'll wear sneakers instead." I even had a slogan, "Wear your Chucks and save two bucks." That ban on Docs went on for a little while. It was stupid rule but it worked. It sent the message: no more fucking Nazi skinheads.

Tony Rettman (City Gardens regular): I don't know if all the skins had been partying all day or what, but they were ready for the Circle Jerks.

Steven DiLodovico (author): In '89 I was a total skin... except when I went to City Gardens. I always dressed down, mostly because you couldn't get in if you wore the skinhead "uniform," but also because the locals were pretty rough. I tried to be as invisible as possible in Trenton because it wasn't home turf. The day of the Circles Jerks show, I knew it was going to be rough. I had been to City Gardens enough times to know what the crowds were like, and the Circle Jerks were the kind of band that would inspire vociferous reaction from the crowd. I also knew the locals were going to give Deadspot a real hard time. Which they did.

Stephen Ernest Saputelli: We're up there, rocking out, and I didn't even notice I was getting spit on. Then I saw [Deadspot singer] Mike looking at me, and we were like, "What the hell is this?" I didn't know what to do, and it was funny because the other guys in the band were apologizing to me between songs, telling me to hang in there. What was I gonna' do? Jump off the stage and start kicking ass? I wasn't a tough guy or anything. We hung in there and did our thing. I didn't realize how scary it was going to get.

Stephen Brown (The Family): Randy kept saying, "No stage diving, no stage diving." And it was like, "Wait a minute. No stage diving? What's

gonna' happen? You just gonna' walk away you fucking wimp?" So we dove, you know?

Tony Rettman: I don't think Deadspot even got to finish their set. The regulars were knocking over their mic stands and acting like retards.

Stephen Ernest Saputelli: We got a really angry reaction from the crowd that night. I don't know what was up with the audience. They really hated us! I've seen opening bands get rough treatment before, but we had these like young skinhead kids hassling us the whole time. We probably could have beaten the crap out of them if we had to, but their back-up was really scary. The [older kids] didn't even bother coming to the front to mess with us, and it was more humiliating because we had these little kids abusing us while we were rocking out. I mean they were spitting on us, calling us "Baldspot." They were pretty fucking rough.

Steven DiLodovico: Man, they were fucking brutal. I actually liked Deadspot, and I felt so bad for them. At the same time, it was really fucking funny. "Baldspot" was cracking me up.

Nancy DeSimone (City Gardens regular): I usually hung out in the back because I didn't feel like getting my face kicked in. There was a lot going on that night and there were rumblings like, "Oh shit, something's going on."

Greg Hetson: There was a group of skinhead gentleman who decided to come to the show, take over the pit, dominate, and not let people near the stage. They were sieg-heiling and that kind of stuff, causing problems. They were fighting with the kids five-on-one, beating little kids up.

Randy Now: The "wall of death" was when skinheads would link arms forming a giant steamroller, and then they would run full steam at the stage… rolling over anyone who was in the way.

Alex Franklin (City Gardens regular): The wall of death… everybody did that. Murphy's Law wrote a song about it. It's just how it was. It was awesome.

Carl Humenik (City Gardens security): I, along with the other bouncers who worked there, would try to stop the wall of death from happening, but you just couldn't. You could try, but they were going to come at you no matter what.

Keith Morris (Circle Jerks vocalist): This wall of death is as stupid as it gets, and we've seen a lot of really ridiculous things because we are dealing with a ridiculous art form to begin with. City Gardens was the only place I had ever seen it. I've seen a lot of knucklehead dances. There's the one dance where they kick, and they punch, and it looks like a fucking spastic monkey or a gorilla with a fucking M-80 shoved up its ass.

Steven DiLodovico: The wall of death was something you knew was coming at just about every show. You knew to keep your head on a swivel because it was real spontaneous and could happen at any moment. You could really get fucked up if you weren't paying attention.

Keith Morris: The room at City Gardens has the floor that goes all the way back to the bar.

Alex Franklin: Kids were dancing and doing their thing. The thing is, Keith Morris is a West Coast guy. At West Coast punk shows, they still chase their tails. They still "circle pit" out there, even to this day. We stopped doing that in 1986. We were beyond it by then. We were all punks and skins and hardcore kids, and we moshed it up. The circle pit was for the old dudes.

Greg Hetson: At one point Keith told everybody to mellow out, and I guess they weren't having any of it.

Keith Morris: These skinheads— maybe 25 of them—decided they were going to show everybody who was in charge. It wasn't about the music and it wasn't about everybody having a good time, it was about them letting people know how tough they were and all of the crap that goes along with their scene.

Steven DiLodovico: It was easy to tell that it was going to be one of "those nights" when the locals were looking to really hurt some people. So I stayed clear of the pit.

Alex Franklin: I never took it as a malicious thing at all, like we were trying to hurt people. You did it to clear the pit out, and it was a good time.

Nancy DeSimone: Out of curiosity, I came out of the back and went up to the DJ booth to see what was going on. I could see this wall of dudes blocking off the entire floor just because they could, I guess.

Randy Now: Every skinhead was like Mr. America muscle head. They were all 6-foot-7. It was like the front line of the Philadelphia Eagles coming at you.

Keith Morris: They lined up at the back bar and locked arms. The Circle Jerks were performing, and I'm watching what's going on. All these kids were aware of what was going on around them; they weren't stupid statues. They noticed that something serious, something heavy, is ready to go down. Suddenly, I can see the floor in front of the stage, that black-and white-checkerboard floor. It was like the parting of the Red Sea. I'm wondering, "What the hell is going on? Why can I see the floor when, just a second ago, there was a mass of people covering it?"

I look to the back and see 15 or 20 skinheads, and they're locked arm-in-arm. It looked like a bullfight was about to happen. You have the bullfighter and the red cape, and the bull is huffing and puffing, and getting ready to charge. I look down to the floor and I see maybe 30 people in front of the stage. I put one and one together and get two. I realize that these guys mean harm, that they want to hurt people. And that's not what the Circle Jerks are about. That's not on the Circle Jerks' list of, "Things to let people do at our show today."

Steven DiLodovico: And it just kept coming… wave after wave of meaty, sweaty dudes running full speed at the stage.

Alex Franklin: Keith took it as if we were beating up on people, and we really weren't. It wasn't a malicious, let's-hurt-people kind of thing. That's how we danced and everybody knew that. As a "regular," you knew at some point that was going to happen. It was like having chicken fights. You weren't trying to hurt people, you were just having fun in the pit and being jackasses.

Steven DiLodovico: I was watching the band, and I couldn't believe how fucking great the Circle Jerks were. They ran through the classics, the newer shit sounded great, and the whole time you could tell that Keith was getting pissed.

Travis Nelson (Inspector 7, vocalist): [My friend] Roger wanted to fight Keith Morris. Granted, Keith Morris had two security guards with him. The Trenton skins were there, most notably my boy Roger, and he basically called Keith Morris out right on stage. Keith hopped off stage— little skinny Keith Morris—with his chest all puffed out. He rolled up to Roger like he was going to do something, but he also had two City Gardens' security guys with him, so… I don't think it would have been the same deal had they not been there with him.

Keith Morris: I saw them slowly charge towards the stage, and I jumped off the front of the stage and ran at them. It was me against 20 or 25 skinheads. I said, "You're not going to do that here. If you wanna do that, you can go out in the parking lot. All you guys can go out and play in the parking lot." People shook their heads like, "This guy's going to get killed. These guys are going to stomp him to death right here."

Jim Norton (City Gardens security/stage manager): I had a run-in with Keith Morris once before. It was during the first Circle Jerks show I worked at City Gardens. One of the regulars, Ivo, was fighting. I knew him well and had thrown him out many times before. I went to throw him out and Keith Morris, in his own, special way, was like, "We're not going to play! The bouncers are gorillas…" I was a fan of the band, but Keith kept going, "These guys are jocks and meatheads!" He went on this whole rant. "If you gorillas can't figure out how to clamp people down without hurting them, we're going to stop playing." I thought, "Me hurt him? This is Ivo! Are you kidding me?" When they finished that show I actually tried to get a word with him while he was walking back to the dressing room, and he was a complete knob. He told me to take my, "football player, cop mentality" somewhere else. I was like, "You're a dick." It really rubbed me the wrong way, and it colored the way I look at him. It definitely spoiled my "fandom." Even now, when I look at him, I think, *he's the dude who's always right*. I guess there's not a point where he can sit there and go, "Oh, it looked a little different from where I was. Maybe I was wrong."

Carl Humenik (bouncer): I worked many Circle Jerks shows before that. I personally never had a problem with Keith Morris. The whole band was pretty cool to me.

Keith Morris: You would think the bouncers would want to put a stop to all that. You don't want anyone getting hurt in your venue. Maybe I was going to be backed up by the bouncers. That's happened quite a bit, believe it or not. Fortunately for me, the bouncers had been paying attention to all of this. It seemed like they were wondering, "Okay, when do we get involved? Do we need to get involved? Do we just let these morons do whatever they're gonna do?" Obviously they'd seen it happen, because it was a regular occurrence at a lot of these shows. I had never seen it before.

Steven DiLodovico: There was also the usual contingent of white-power skins there that night, and they were all doing the usual bullshit… the sieg-heiling and all that.

Keith Morris: These skins formed an island in the slam pit and were sieg-heiling. We would play "Killing for Jesus" or "Making the Bomb" and they didn't understand the sarcasm and the humor behind those songs. They thought we really meant that stuff. They didn't understand that the make-up of the band is one-and-a-half Jews; at one point we were two-and-a-half Jews. I'm half-Jew, Greg Hetson is half-Jew, and Zander is, I believe, half-Jew, so it was like they just weren't smart enough to get the joke. We're here to have a good time. Yes, granted, we're singing songs with lyrical content that occasionally deals with some serious shit, but we're here to have a party. If you think you're going to get away with that, you're not. We will just stop playing.

Nancy DeSimone: They stopped playing at one point and tried to get everybody to stop, but they ignored the band and stood their ground. Keith started getting antagonistic and said something along the lines of, "Why don't you all do us a favor and smash your heads into the front of the stage." That got them all really pissed off. When I heard him say that, I was like, "Oh, fuck…"

Greg Hetson: Keith eventually invited them all to form a line and bend over, point their heads toward the stage, get a good running start, and smash their heads into the stage.

Randy Now: I got on the mic and said, "Hey, this isn't Geraldo Rivera. Let's play some music."

Alex Franklin: The next thing you know Keith Morris jumped off the damn stage! He jumped off the stage, and that's when everybody had a problem. Once you jump off that stage and you get into people's faces, and you're calling people out, it becomes a personal problem. When you are up on the stage, it's fine. We can have our moral differences. But he jumped down and was trying to get physical with other people. He was right in front of me and he started yelling at people, and calling them assholes and tough guys, and getting in their faces. He's only, like, five feet tall! The dudes he confronted were six-foot-tall meatheads, kill-you-for-ten-cents kind of people. They were rough dudes.

Greg Hetson: It was pretty gnarly. There were some big guys there.

Keith Morris: I was hoping, when it started to get ugly, that I was going to be backed up by some of the people who were just there to see the show. My ass was basically pulled out of the fire by the bouncers.

Carl Humenik: But as this wall was forming, Keith made it obvious that he wasn't going to let it happen. It was weird. He's a small guy, but he jumped down and took on this wall of skinheads. We were all like, "Oh shit!" It was our job as security [to step in], so all the bouncers came running from everywhere.

Alex Franklin: That's what people did at shows in the tri-state area. I don't think Keith got that.

Steven DiLodovico: Keith is not a big guy. I couldn't believe this little dude was confronting the biggest, scariest skinheads I had ever seen. I was amazed at the size of the balls he had on him.

Keith Morris: I'm in a confrontation with these skinheads, and I'm obviously going to get pummeled. The security guys, all of them, within seconds, were standing alongside me. There wasn't going to be a confrontation because the bouncers were pretty big guys. Even the biggest of the skinhead guys knew that something was going to happen. Maybe this was the time when the bouncers had finally had enough. Maybe they'd seen enough of the stupidity to say to themselves, "Here's this little guy getting in front of all of these scary skinheads..." I wasn't really thinking about the outcome. I was not going to allow them to do their wall of death, at whatever expense.

Steven DiLodovico: Amazingly, the skins never touched him. He was right up in their faces and they didn't do anything. Of course, he had a pretty decent amount of bouncers crowding around him.

Carl Humenik: I knew and could talk to most of the kids who did the wall of death. If I told them to stop, they would stop. But the skinheads, if you antagonize them, then no one can talk to them. We started by pushing the people we knew out of the way, and we knew they would just go away. But Keith wasn't going to stop. He was going to let them know what he thought, and I admire him for that. So we waited, and when Keith was done, it was over. He said his peace, actually stopped the wall of death from happening, and went back onstage.

Greg Hetson: The crowd all cheered and, the next thing you know, the crowd turned on the skinheads and security promptly threw them out of the club.

Stephen Brown: [Keith Morris] told a story about confronting skins trying to do a wall of death? It wasn't us. It sure as hell wasn't The Family. No way. We would have kicked his ass and broken his arms.

Russ Smith (City Gardens regular): I do remember getting caught up in the wall of death a few times. If you were careful you just stayed out of their way they would eventually tire out. It was great because it opened up the area in front of the stage and I could get closer. The stage divers were a pain sometimes, but a good trick was to take their shoe off and throw it in the crowd. They couldn't see who took their shoe, and it would take them a good two or three songs to find it. You couldn't get high tops off, so you just had to grab it and untie the laces.

Alex Franklin: It was going to get ugly, but Big Ed and a few of the other bouncers got in the middle of it and diffused any problems.

Keith Morris: I'm not pro or con when it comes to bouncers, because I've seen bouncers do some amazingly fucked-up shit. But, at the same time, it's either them or the police, and on many occasions there are people in the crowd who try to pull off some ridiculous stunt that has no business being attempted in the first place, and they wonder why they're being thrown out. Why they're handcuffed and being taken off to jail. But the Nazis knocked out a couple more kids, and that's when the bouncers went to the island and started punching. There shouldn't be any violence at these shows. We're singing about violence, we live in a violent world. All we are is just a mirror of society. But this was one time when it was warranted. This was one time when I didn't say anything, when they had the biggest kid and were dragging him out face-down, and he was kicking and trying to punch. You don't punch a bouncer... are you kidding? You don't walk up to Mike Tyson and spit in his face. You're gonna get killed! You lose! If you're stupid enough to do that, then you deserve whatever kind of stupid treatment they dole out. If you've got 50 bouncers, there will be at least a dozen that are level-headed and aren't there just to fight.

Jim Norton: After hearing Keith talk about how appreciative he was of the City Gardens bouncers helping him, maybe the part where I said, "He never thought it looked different from where I was," was completely wrong. Maybe I need to turn that back on myself. Maybe both of us are right. Maybe it was a conditional thing. One man's goon is another man's… whatever. I would appreciate it if the parts where I sort of hedge and describe how it looked from my side were placed before the nice things Keith said about the bouncers backing him up. Maybe I was the douche. A little self-realization—a little personal growth—never hurt anyone…

Nancy DeSimone: The show is over and the security guys were all circling around the band and to make sure nobody was going backstage. They weren't letting anybody get near the band.

Stephen Ernest Saputelli: By the end of the night, our guitar player Paul was like, "Those guys [in the audience] want to kick our asses. Let's get out of here!" Randy told us that we couldn't leave because all the skins were out in the parking lot waiting to fucking kill us! The staff came back, and they told us we couldn't walk out and get in our van. We gave the keys to the sound guy, who got our van and drove it around back, and we scurried off. I never had to run for my life before. It was cool, though, in spite of everything. I really dug being on that stage.

Keith Morris: When we get through playing, we would [usually] hang out. The guys would want to drink a few beers, dry off, collect our thoughts, try to get laid… all of that fun stuff. But then the owner of the club says, "You guys can't leave right now because there's a parking lot full of skinheads." And I'm thinking, "There was a room full of skinheads twenty minutes ago. What's the big deal?" But the more I thought about it, the more I realized that it was going to be ten guys versus fifty guys. It was going to turn into this big, ugly, brutal thing out in the parking lot. It's not like I was afraid or anything, it's just the way the owner explained it. He said, "If you want, you can take a look outside."

Keith Morris: The only way you could look outside was by opening the front door, and I saw four cars, with five or six guys in each car, driving around in circles in the parking lot. I'm like, "Okay, what are they trying to prove? What are they doing here? Why don't they just go home?" Well, they wanted to beat up and kill the lead singer of the Circle Jerks. I thought about it and cracked up! I'm not going anywhere.

Randy Now: They had to stay in the club for a while after the show. There were skinheads outside who wanted to kill them.

Carl Humenik: That wasn't just the Circle Jerks shows. That situation happened a number of times. Anytime there was a problem on the floor, they would go outside and wait for the guy they had a problem with to come out. If I have a problem with someone, I tell them. I don't go out and get a bunch of my friends and circle the parking lot waiting for them. It's an instance of someone trying to show off and be a man but never actually doing anything.

Nancy DeSimone: For what seemed like a really long time we couldn't leave. The guards were outside saying that a bunch of people were waiting out in the parking lot. We were sitting inside like, "What the fuck?" We couldn't leave!

Greg Hetson: We just hung out playing ping pong and pinball.

Nancy DeSimone: I was terrified because I had never had any sort of run-ins with skinheads before, and everyone was taking the whole situation pretty seriously. Well, Keith was all, "Fuck them!" but everyone else sat there drinking beer and was thinking, "You know… we didn't sign up for this."

Keith Morris: They're out there driving around in circles waiting for us to come out, and the really ridiculous thing is that if they really wanted to fuck with us, they could have slashed all the tires on the van, on the trailer, smashed out all the windows. But apparently they weren't even smart enough to do that.

Nancy DeSimone: Eventually, when the coast was clear, we barreled into our cars and went to Denny's or something, and then we went to the Red Roof Inn. All City Gardens bands stayed there, but none of the skinheads even thought to come to the Red Roof.

Greg Hetson: I guess eventually their parents came to pick their little boys up and take them home.

Keith Morris: When we left, nothing happened. We got in the van and drove away. They were long gone. We hung out with the staff and Randy, and we went upstairs and played pinball. You get really good at pinball when you're on tour.

Steven DiLodovico: In a weird kind of epilogue, my friend Brian and I were riding back to Philly after the show. We were driving down I-95 and we notice this small pickup truck with a ton of gear in the back. We pull up alongside, and it's the guys from Deadspot. We had known those guys for a while. Brian had had them on his radio show a few times, and we would see them at all these Philly gigs. They are making the waving motion, like "come on, follow us!" So we did. We ended up following them back to some trashy apartment complex in Delaware County. We go upstairs, and there's a small party happening. We knew no one there except for the guys in the band, but everyone was cool to us. We were in some back room drinking and laughing about the show when someone came in and made an announcement that one of their oldest friends had just committed suicide. You can imagine how weird and uncomfortable it was, especially for me and Brian. Everyone's crying and in shock, and me and Brian tiptoed out, trying to be as unobtrusive as possible. What a strange, strange night.

Jane's Addiction/Dog Of Mystery—February 26, 1989

Jim Norton (Dog of Mystery): Did you ask me if I was in the opening band at this show? The band that Randy said was the worst band to ever play City Gardens? Yes, the name of the band was Dog of Mystery, and they later morphed into Monster Magnet.

Steven DiLodovico (author): I kind of got dragged to Jane's Addiction. Back then I hung out a lot at a college radio station at Widener University, and we would always get on the guest list for City Gardens shows. We would go see just about anything that came through there. Jane's Addiction was not at all what I was into at the time, but I went anyway, because it was a show.

Jim Norton: The reason Jane's Addiction even played City Gardens was because of a band from Philly called Exccutive Slacks who were friends with Jane's Addiction. They had been around for years, and they called Randy and said, "If we can get Jane's Addiction to play City Gardens, can we open for them?" Randy was like, "Absolutely." He had been try-ing to get Jane's Addiction [for a while]. The Slacks somehow convinced Jane's Addiction that they should play City Gardens and that Execu-tive Slacks were going to open. They booked the show and it sold out weeks in advance, but two days before the gig, Executive Slacks broke up. Randy had to rush to find an opening band, and for whatever stupid reason, no band could play that fucking show. Nobody. You name a band, he called them. No one could do it.

Steven DiLodovico: I don't even remember any opening bands. I was probably outside getting high.

Jim Norton: I was talking to Randy the night before the show from the pizza place where I worked. I said, "Well, there is this one band… it's this band I'm in that I never told you about." Which should have been red flag number one. I lived at Randy's house, we were good friends, and I never told him about this band I was in? I said, "It's kind of what you might call heavy college metal." Grunge hadn't been invented yet. It was kind of like TAD or an [record label] Amphetamine Reptile band. He didn't know what any off that stuff was. He asked me the name of the band and I told him "Dog of Mystery." *Dog: singular. D-O-G.* He instantly added an 's.' He said, "You can get Dogs of Mystery to play? Then Dogs of Mystery are playing. Great." He has never gotten it right since then. He still brings it up from time to time… "Dogs of Mystery… oh my God, you guys were terrible." As soon as we finished, I knew Randy hated it. He had this look on his face. First thing I said, as soon as he got close enough, was, "Randy! The guys loved playing here! We wanna know if we can play Reggae Sunsplash." He said, "Buddy… that was rough." The sound guy came up and said, "I love it! It's the return of knuckle-dragging drug rock!" And that sort of stuck.

Carl Humenik: That's another show where I hated the crowd because they were like, "I know more about music than you do." And it was packed with weirdos. This guy comes up to me says, "Don't look at me like that." I'm like, "What are you talking about?" He goes, "You're looking at me with your left eye." I go, "What the hell does that mean?" He says, "The left eye means you're aggressive." I said, "Well, I'm about to be aggressive if you don't get away from me."

Jim Norton: We were in the "dressing room" that was above the stage, and I poured a bucket of water over [Jane's Addiction guitarist] Dave Navarro's head. A pitcher of ice water right over him. Why? Because they were standing right beneath that window, waiting to go on stage, and we heard one of them say, "Did you hear that fucking opening band? They were terrible. That's the worst fucking shit I've ever seen!" So I dumped water on his head.

Nancy Leopardi (City Gardens regular): Jane's Addiction was a real big band for me. That was a really great show. That tour I traveled around and saw them in Philly, the Cat Club, and The World. I was so obsessed with them because they really crossed that boundary between punk and metal and pop and art rock, and it was just so creative and artistic and emotional. They were one of the bands that really stand out for me. I had a lot of musical phases: I had my English Punk phase where I only wanted to see GBH and the Exploited and Broken Bones and that stuff. And then I kind of had a goth thing where all I wanted to see was Peter Murphy and Love and Rockets, but Jane's Addiction crossed all those lines.

Tony Lee: I saw Jane's Addiction [that night], and it was intense. It was really good. Perry un-zipped himself. He had a black latex thing he was wearing, and he pulled out his dick and was flapping it all around. It was funny because when I had found out about Jane's Addiction, I was really not into the whole hardcore thing anymore. Hardcore and metal had crossed over so much that they were almost indistinguishable.

Nancy Leopardi: Jane's Addiction were such a great mix of everything. Perry Farrell was an original performer. He brought the best of Mick Jagger and Iggy and Bowie and all the great frontmen in history. He was such an amazing, amazing performer. I was always surprised at every show by what he would bring to it. They were one of the bands that compelled me to go see them anywhere and everywhere. I would take pictures of them everywhere.

Steven DiLodovico: I was fucking blown away. I was into really heavy stuff at the time, and, to me, Jane's Addiction were wimpy little art-rockers from L.A. They came on, and the thing I remember most clearly was the rhythm section of [bassist Eric] Avery and [drummer Stephen] Perkins. They drove that whole sound. Intense doesn't even begin to describe it. The whole band was at their peak. They had yet to release the *Ritual De Lo Habitual* album, but they still played some songs off of it, including the 10 minute epic "Three Days." I left that show a huge fan. Who knew they would become so big?

Nancy Leopardi: The funny thing is, now that I live in L.A., I see Dave Navarro all the time at the high-end celebrity gym here. It is so funny to be on the treadmill behind him! I know he has a lot of contact with porn stars, but I haven't really asked him about his porno career. I've seen him go through his bad phases with drugs, and then when he's clean and healthy you see him every day at the same time at the gym, on the same treadmill. I couldn't have imagined it back then, and I am sure he couldn't have imagined it either! I couldn't imagine myself at a gym, let alone Dave Navarro.

Paul Stanley/Warrant — March 10, 1989

Fred Zara (filmmaker/City Gardens regular): We had a thing that if we couldn't pay to get into City Gardens, there was a door by the back alleyway that we would sneak in. The security guards would be out there, but every once in a while you would see your opportunity and go for it. I did it once, but a lot of our friends got in to City Gardens [that way] all the time. So me and my brother Joe were at the Paul Stanley show, and I don't even know why. My band P.O.W. was supposed to play that coming Sunday night, and it was going to be a big show. We had all kinds of people coming and were excited about it. So, me and Joe were inside the club, and [bandmates] Sam and Chris, and a bunch of other people, were out in the parking lot. Sam tried to sneak in that back door and Randy caught him! Randy found me and Joe and he said, "Your boy just tried to sneak in the back door. You guys aren't playing here Sunday night!" and he walked away.

Joe was trying to chase Randy down inside the club, begging him, "Randy, come on! We got all these people coming and it's two days away! You know Sam, he's just fucking around." And Randy said, "No. Fuck you guys." Joe was freaking out and starts yelling, and he charged at Randy! Randy had already walked away, and the security guards all grabbed Joe and were trying to throw him out the door. I jumped on the security guys like, "Get the fuck off my brother!" and it was a big fucking melee. They threw us all out and that was it, we were done. Our second show at City Gardens never happened. You could see the show printed on the punkcard. We were supposed to play but it never happened.

Randy Now: What nobody sees: I paid Paul Stanley from Kiss with Warrant opening—and Paul refused to let us advertise Warrant in the ads—a guarantee of, let's say $10,000, yet only 400 people came to the show. I lost five grand. Nobody said, "Here Randy, I'll knock a few thousand off your loss tonight…"

Dark Angel — March 26, 1989 (Easter Sunday)

Randy Now: The one big fat guy in Dark Angel says, "Where's our food?" I said, "I cut the food out because no one is going to come today. It's Easter Sunday. I didn't want to do this show in the first place." And he goes, "We're not going play!" and I'm like, "Fine!" I got my briefcase, closed it up, and said, "Let's go home. I didn't want to be here today, I'm doing this show as a favor to your agent. You were stuck for a date to play for Easter Sunday. I don't like you or your band." They backed down and played the show with no food, and I probably broke even. I didn't take a cut of their merchandise concession. I remember a lot of fat New Jersey chicks in black spandex. I told the agent, "For that show, I should have charged people by the pound to get in."

Jamie Davis (City Gardens regular): I remember Gene Hoaglin from Dark Angel hanging out outside. He was just a kid, then, too. He must have been 18. And he was still humungous! They were not much older than us. They were all drinking Jolt sodas! Those metal bands, they did tours like punk bands back then… get in the van and play places like City Gardens.

Vision/Underdog—May 21, 1989

Dave Franklin (Vision, vocalist): There were a lot of fights at that show. That was the night I knocked out an A.C. [Atlantic City] Skin during Underdog's set. You know that side door that led to the front parking lot where they threw everybody out when someone tried to stage dive? We had kind of a small pit over there, and this kid Billy, who used to roadie for us, was dancing while Underdog was playing. He was going nuts. There was an A.C. Skin there trying to start fights. He obviously knew who I was because we had just played. He came swinging, and I shoved him from behind. He went around the pit one more time and came back, and he was coming after me. You know, doing his little "skinhead skip," and he threw a punch. I ducked, got up, and punched him in the face, and the bouncer grabbed him and threw him right out that side door. It was a crazy show.

Richie Birkenhead (Underdog, vocalist): I actually got into it one night because Chuck Treece was in Underdog, and we had a beef with some white-power kids who actually ended up backing down. I knew that City Gardens had a reputation, but there were so many venues with a lot of violence. City Gardens never seemed any less or any more violent than any other big venues that would have multiple hardcore bands play. The white-power thing was really unfortunate, but it seems we encountered it in a lot of places. The [incident] started with a racial slur directed at Chuck. I remember it only in the broadest terms. I think when we tried to confront those people and call out whoever it was, they wanted no part of actually fighting. I think those kinds of kids were more interested in finding some skinny kid who's at his first show and having five of their friends beat him up at once. If someone was willing to stand there, one on one, and pound their faces in, they'd find all kinds of excuses not to fight.

Chuck Treece (Underdog/McRad): It was crazy back then. There was almost a fight at every show. But the thing I always remember about City Gardens was the fun. It was always fun getting that many random, crazy people together. We used to be at shows with people who carried knives or guns, and there were no fucking cops anywhere. All those times we went there and made it out without getting hurt? That's crazy! There is way more security at shows now, and people get hurt even worse.

Peter Tabbot (Vision, guitar): This was during a terrific time for hardcore punk music in New Jersey and for our band. We had played City Gardens a couple times, including our first show with The Exploited, and a show opening for The Ramones. Underdog were pretty big at the time, especially in New Jersey and New York. Into the late '80s, there was a small contingent of skins at City Gardens and South Jersey in general who were white-power or who identified with that group, and it was confusing to me how such a small number of idiots could, in a way, intimidate or dictate what was to go down—or not go down—at any given show. Especially when they would be outnumbered 10 or 20 to 1 on the average night.

When the second wave of the New York hardcore scene and the whole second wave of straight edge blew up in the late '80s, I think those guys finally faded away, and you wouldn't see much of them at City Gardens or most places. I do remember that [Vision vocalist] Dave was more than happy to give it back to any one of those guys. He didn't invite trouble, per se, but I think he was more than happy to show a few lunkheads that they were insignificant, both in number and influence, and that no one was going to be made to feel threatened at one of our shows.

At this show, our roadie and best friend, Billy was hanging with us in front of the stage off toward the side. We all were friends with Underdog and loved their music, so we were dancing and singing along. Billy was going off and enjoying Underdog, and one of those moron white-power skins, who had been violent in the pit and looking for trouble, barreled into Billy for absolutely no reason other than to provoke a fight. The next time that kid came around, you could just see him looking in our direction, and he was completely going to hurt someone, probably Billy. I remember Dave got caught in a pretty aggressive shove with the guy and then dropped him with one punch. We were there as fans and also as a band, and that place was kind of sacred to us. It was home in many ways. So some asshole doesn't come into the house that we revere and share with our friends and cause trouble. Dave believed that and would stand up to anyone at all who compromised the safety of his friends or the place we called home.

Fights and violence were always a part of the punk rock scene and at places like City Gardens, and we weren't naïve enough to think those things wouldn't happen…the violence is part of what made the scene so cool, enticing, and taboo when I was a teenager. But again, someone like Dave wasn't going to let a few idiots, with no agenda but to cause trouble for the sake of trouble, ruin a positive, fun place. It was around this time that the small presence of white-power skins seemed to dissolve at City Gardens.

Public Image Limited (canceled)—July 23, 1989

Randy Now: This was the last date on the tour and they just wanted to go home. They probably didn't have a great tour, and they canceled at the last minute. Public Image's food rider was over $1,200, and I had to go out and buy all this really weird stuff… Jamaican beer and stuff like that. So I have everything and then they cancelled the show. A lot of British bands were like that. I remember one time Bow Wow Wow wasn't going to play, so I said I'll give you $300 more, and then they were like, "Okay we'll do it." The Happy Mondays … same thing.

24-7 Spyz/Vision/Killing Time/Shades Apart— July 30, 1989

Dave Franklin (Vision, vocalist): In '89 we had booked our *In the Blink of an Eye* tour. Johnny Stiff from New York City, who used to do all the punk and hardcore tours, was booking everybody. Our tour, Insted, Underdog… everybody's tours were falling apart. Back then there was no internet and there were no cell phones. He booked everything in all these different venues and got in way over his head, and tours just collapsed all over the place. He booked the *In the Blink of an Eye* tour, so we made all of our "Tour '89" shirts and stuff. We printed twelve dozen of them for the entire tour. A week before the tour was supposed to start, we played City Gardens. We set up the merchandise. The line came in the door, and went right to the Vision t-shirts. We sold every shirt we had. We could have sold more. 144 shirts, gone. Then the show went off and it was absolute, total chaos. The 24-7 Spyz guys, who we had never met before, were up on the side of the stage when we played. They were like "HOLY SHIT, THESE GUYS ARE AWESOME!!!" Even the Killing Time guys were like, "That's it, man, you guys got it. You've got 900 kids here going nuts."

Today, if you are a band that is touring and bringing 900 kids to a venue…you're a huge band. You're doing it, You're making a living off it. Back then it was impossible because City Gardens was the only place that big that did those kinds of shows. The old Ritz was too big. You had to be the Bad Brains or the Cro-Mags to sell out those shows.

Pete Tabbot (Vision, guitarist): We had just committed to our first full-length tour, supporting our first album, which was to last most of the summer. We had a terrific buzz going and were psyched to tour the entire country, and we had made plans accordingly. We also invested all the money we could scramble into a summer's worth of merchandise for the tour. Johnny Stiff, who was booking the tour, resigned, so we were left with just two shows. We played City Gardens around the time we had planned on leaving for our tour, and we completely sold out of merchandise. It was kind of mind-boggling, actually, and it took a bit of the sting out of not only losing our first national tour, but also spending any money we had to promote the tour.

We had a great show, but what I probably remember most was how absolutely sick 24-7 Spyz were live. The Spyz guys were completely off the hook, hanging from the rafters and slaying the club. What great performers and musicians. Our set was similarly chaotic, and Killing Time was amazing, too. All in all, this one amazing City Gardens show was somehow enough to console four 19 and 20 year old kids who had put their entire summer, school, and jobs on hold to tour, only to have it fall apart. But good shows at City Gardens had that effect and potential. If you played or attended an epic show there, and I was lucky enough to do both numerous times, you tended to forget that the outside world existed, at least for a while.

Bad Brains/Leeway—August 6th

Rob Vitale (Black Train Jack): Leeway had played CBGB and the next show was at City Gardens. [Leeway's] Eddie came out with this sign that said, "Trenton or Bust." And then the Bad Brains come on and out comes [Bad Brains frontman] HR with the same sign: Trenton or Bust.

Steven DiLodovico (author): Hottest show ever. EVER. To this day people still talk about how goddamn hot that show was.

Jamie Davis (City Gardens regular): Bad Brains only played about five songs because the power kept going out. It was so hot in there that the power would blow out. Leeway was amazing. The best part about Leeway was that the bouncers were all outside and everyone realized it, and everyone was stagediving like crazy through the whole Leeway set. There were so many people outside trying to get in, so that's where all the bouncers were. Everyone was going nuts. Leeway blew them away, anyway. The Bad Brains came on late, played, like, two songs, said it was too hot, and stopped.

Social Distortion/Chain Of Strength/Insight/ Sobering Consequences/Up Front—August 27, 1989

Jeff Terranova (Up Front): We did not have any interaction with [Social Distortion] because they weren't very friendly. They soundchecked for two hours, and they were assholes the whole time. We were a little bummed out by it, because a lot of the first-generation hardcore and punk-rock guys we met were really cool and down to earth. I'm not saying that they were our idols and we were worshipping them, but they paved the way for us. And to see them up on stage, dressed rock-n-roll, and doing this two-hour soundcheck, bitching and whining about everything and being snappy and rude to the crew. It was like, "Wow these guys are jerks"

Big Audio Dynamite—September 22, 1989

Randy Now: That was the biggest guarantee I ever had for a band, but it worked out. But right after the show, I was standing at the front door as the crowd was leaving, and out of the blue, a guy comes up a starts strangling me. Really choking me. The security guys had to pull him off. I never saw him before or after.

Joe Strummer—November 10, 1989

Bruce Markoff (City Gardens regular): That first solo record that Joe Strummer did was just okay. And that's coming from a fan. And I think people were still a little pissed off at the way the whole end of the Clash went down, with Joe getting rid of [Clash guitarist] Mick Jones.

Carl Humenik: I had never been one to be star-struck, but Joe Strummer is my idol. My dog is named after him—Rudy Can't Fail Strummer. I loved the Clash the first time I heard them, so it was like, *this is my night.* Joe Strummer was a nice guy, but I couldn't talk. There was not one person in my life—ever—that I couldn't talk to besides him and Sinead O'Connor. But he was so nice, and after a while he was like, "Okay..." and walked away. I thought, "I blew it, I can't believe I just blew it." But it was an amazing show, and he played a lot of Clash stuff, so I was in my zone. That night was my night, and no one else mattered in the world.

Randy Now: This show was not well attended. I was surprised. I thought it would do a lot better.

George Clinton—November 26th

Maurice Karey Counts (City Gardens regular): Of all the musicians I met there over the years, there was only one who hurt my feelings, and that was George Clinton. I brought a George Clinton poster, and I got most the band to sign it. As George walked by me I said, "George, can you sign my poster?" And he went, "Nah man." I said, "Everybody else signed it, even Maceo Parker signed it." He looked at me and walked away. I couldn't believe I got dissed by George Clinton.

7 Seconds/Token Entry/76% Uncertain— December 3, 1989

Carl Humenik: Kevin Seconds is a dickhead. People argue with me over that one, but I stand by it. I've had one interaction with him and he was a douchebag. I liked their music until that point, and then, just like I won't listen to the Dead Kennedys because Jello is an ass, I won't listen to 7 Seconds. This show was packed, and when the band came in, their manager pulled out his laminate and said to me, "If someone doesn't have one of these, they don't get in [on the guest list]. *No matter what.*" I said *okay.* It was plain: no credentials, they're not getting in. So this girl comes up to me and says, "I'm on the guest list." I said, "We don't have a guest list tonight, you have to have a laminate." She says, "I'm Kevin Seconds' girlfriend." I said, "Then where's your laminate?" She said she didn't have one, so I told her she couldn't come in. She goes off and starts yelling at me, and I said, "Show me your laminate and you can go in," and she's like no, no, no. Just then, Kevin's coming in, and she starts telling him what happened, and he starts yelling at me! I said, "Kevin, do you have your laminate?" He said *yeah.* And I said, "She doesn't!" He's yelling at me, "She's my girlfriend," on and on. Yelling at me for like five minutes, and I just said, "Did your manager not tell me a half hour ago, if they don't have a laminate, they can't get in?" He's like, "But this is my girlfriend!" And I'm like, "I don't care!" Total dickhead.

GWAR—December 31, 1989

Carl Humenik: I want to tell you this, and people don't realize it when they're out in the crowd at a GWAR show. When the spray comes out and hits them, it lands on them like rain. But it's a power washer. If I was up on stage and got in front of it, it would give me bruises. I had to make sure I was out of the way of the spray, but I was still getting soaked. I always wore clothes I knew I was never going to wear again, because I would have to throw away whatever it was. I mean, people can't like the music. There's no way you can like that music. If I had better ear protection back then, I would have had it on.

1990

Top Ten Songs in 1990:

1. Hold On, Wilson Phillips

2. It Must Have Been Love, Roxette

3. Nothing Compares 2 U, Sinead O'Connor

4. Poison, Bell Biv Devoe

5. Vogue, Madonna

6. Vision of Love, Mariah Carey

7. Another Day In Paradise, Phil Collins

8. Hold On, En Vogue

9. Cradle of Love, Billy Idol

10. Blaze of Glory, Jon Bon Jovi

Bouncing Souls—January 19, 1990

Randy Now: The Bouncing Souls were rough, but they had a different sound to them. And as they got better and more popular, they would move up in the bill. They used to come to a lot of shows, too, and they were poor. They lived the punk-rock lifestyle when they started. They lived in a flophouse in a really scary section of New Brunswick [New Jersey]. In fact, they always had people coming and going, and it is because of them that New Brunswick passed a law about how many people who are not related to each other can live in one house.

Greg Attonito (Bouncing Souls): When we formed the band, it was our dream to play City Gardens, like "Guys, we could play here….." That was the whole goal. It was like a temple to us. Being in high school and going to City Gardens, seeing live music, opened my mind to new things. Now we have the internet and it's different: you can go right to iTunes and experience all this music.

Randy Now: I was tour managing Bad Religion and sitting with [Bad Religion guitarist] Brett Gurewitz, who owned Epitaph Records, and he asked me what New Jersey band he should sign. I told him Bouncing Souls.

Bryan Kienlen (Bouncing Souls): City Gardens made me feel like I was okay. You didn't feel like as much of an alien, like we did in high school. It was really empowering.

Greg Attonito: You went there and the people were dressed weird, and it was okay. Everyone was cool with it. It's a different world now.

Bryan Kienlen: People were so much more imaginative back then because you had to come up with this stuff yourself, you couldn't buy it. And there were so many different kinds of bands. You would go one weekend and see the Circle Jerks, and then the next weekend it would be a ska show or a reggae show. All the members of the Bouncing Souls went to those shows together, so it really helped to form us as a band. It was a ritual, going to shows. It would start at your house, you would drive to the club, see the show, and hope your car was still there when you got out. And then you'd stop at a pizza place or 7-11.

Greg Attonito: So many amazing bands and so many genres… so many scenes. It was a real scene of people going to experience music of all kinds. I really miss that, and you don't see it now. Everyone is scene-oriented and music-style oriented, as opposed to it just being music. City Gardens totally affected me and my whole mentality.

Judge/Outburst A.K.A "The Video Shoot." — March 11, 1990

Jamie Davis (City Gardens regular): Did Uppercut play that show, too?

Mike Judge (Judge, vocals): We wrote the song "Where It Went" without that fast part in the middle that bridges everything to the very slow ending. We thought we wrote the coolest hardcore skanking song. Then we came up with the very slow ending; the *do you feel what I feel* part. We needed to get it in that song, but it sounded too shoe-horned. We had that mid-tempo part from a song that was on the *Chung King* record. Since that record and its songs were scrapped, we decided to try it and it sounded like it belonged there. When it was finally written and finalized, we were pretty sure we wrote a perfect song that you could skank to, from beginning to end, with a short breather 3/4 of the way through.

The video was going to be a live setting, so [City Gardens] was an obvious choice.

Randy Now: I didn't even know they were planning on shooting a video. It was just a regular show for us. We didn't promote it as a video shoot, but I guess everyone knew by word of mouth.

Todd Linn (City Gardens security): They must've played "Where It Went" about 27 times before the doors ever opened, because they were shooting all the close-ups. All the kids were waiting in line outside, and they would look through the side door when it opened to see all the shit going on and the cameras and stuff. They're saying, "Oh my God, we're going to be on TV! We're going to be on MTV!" Fellow bouncer Carl [Humenik] and I heard these kids talk, so we said, "Oh yeah, yeah, definitely. *Headbangers Ball* is here, man. Riki Rachtman's here. He's here, and you're going to be on MTV. There's no doubt."

Mike Judge: The guy who shot the video, Eric Seefranz, was from my town, and we went to high school together. We hung out a lot and shot a lot of pool together. He was going to college for video editing, and he was like, "I could do the video cheap if you give me a chance." I talked to the rest of the band, and they were like, "Cool, let's do it." Honestly, I don't remember who came up with the idea of doing it at City Gardens, but once it was brought up we were into it.

Sam Siegler (Judge, drummer): That day stands out in my mind. We were there all day. We filmed during soundcheck and we filmed while people were there. I think it was largely because City Gardens felt like a big room, and we were going for that look in the video. We wanted a bigger stage and a bigger vibe. There was more room to shoot, and I had a good rapport with Randy. He would let us do it, and it wasn't like he was going to charge us a lot of money to shoot. We were playing there anyway, so it just sort of made sense and the feeling was right. CBGB was kind of political, as far as getting in and shooting a video.

Mike Judge: The club itself, to us… it made us look bigger than we actually were. It was a big stage, a big room, and the sound was awesome. The sound inside the club was as good as any New York club. I guess the

only thing that scared us was worrying if we were going to get enough people there to make it look cool. I didn't know what kind of pull we were actually going to have in New Jersey since we were the New York Crew band, you know?

Pat Baker (Semibeings): That was an incredible night. They played a normal set. When it was time for them to record the video, the place went completely insane! I believe at one point the entire club was up on stage. Then the power went out. I remember this weird silence where all you heard was the drums and people singing. People were flying everywhere... bodies kept falling on your head. It was nuts.

Mike Judge: It was my first experience being videoed and lip-syncing to tracks and stuff, and I was like; "Oh my God, I feel ridiculous." I was almost wishing there was nobody there at that point! They kept telling me, "You gotta make it look like you're playing." And I'm like, "Ah, man... it feels like I'm listening to the radio, though." I spent a lot of time as a little kid wanting to be in a band. I used to be in my bedroom listening to David Bowie records and playing air guitar and thinking,

"I'm in a band." Now, suddenly, I *am* in a band and they're telling me it's time to play air guitar again. They kept telling me things like, "Okay, now look mean!"

Todd Linn: That night was fucking bedlam, because everyone wanted to be on the video. No one was sure what it was, but they were like, "Goddamn it, I'm getting on stage and I'm going to get on this videotape!"

Jeremy Weiss (City Gardens regular): Everybody went berserk because they wanted to be in that damn video.

Vince Spina (Harvcore Records): That one was bananas. Everyone was there because they knew Judge was filming, so it made it even crazier.

Carl Humenik (City Gardens security): I was on stage for that. It was me and Jim Norton. And I can tell you, me and Norton earned our $40 that night. If you watch the video, you see us occasionally, because it switches back and forth between when they filmed before the show, and then they filmed live. When they played live, Norton and me were trying to keep people off stage. But if I was holding one person back, someone was climbing over him, and then someone would try to climb over that person. I was like, "What should we do?" People were using my back to dive off onto the crowd. And you know what? I didn't care. I was having as much fun as they were, because that was why I was there. Because the music made people live, and if I'm sitting there listening to Fear and someone doesn't like Fear, if they tell me not to enjoy it, I'm going to be like, fuck you. So I'm not going to sit there and tell them not to like Judge, because obviously they love 'em! Go ahead. It's not going to kill me if someone uses me as a launching pad. Just please try to use my back softly.

Mike Judge: There's actually a picture—a snapshot I have—and I remember it because it's when they told me to stare at the crowd and "Do that face you do when you're playing live!" But, meanwhile, I can't even see the crowd because there's a guy with a camera right in my face. I'm supposed to look all angry and shit while I am staring into the lens of a camera. It was so ridiculous! Not to mention we had played the song at least four or five times.

Vince Spina: I remember it was me, my brother, and my friend Darren. We were all in Edgewise at the time, and during the video shoot they were definitely more liberal with allowing crazy stage antics if you were diving. So, me, my brother, and Darren all jump up on the stage at the same time and do, like, three dives in a row. I don't think we ever made it into the video.

Mike Judge: I really didn't have to work too hard to pump up the crowd, even though we were like, "Okay, we're going to do this song *again.* Try and go off *again…*" It was our first video, and it was my buddy Eric's first video. Everybody was like, "This might be our first and only shot at this," so I guess everybody just did their part. And it was great.

Jeremy Weiss: I remember sitting up watching *Headbangers Ball* the one time it was going to be shown. We waited until three in the morning! Right before they ended the show they played the video, and I think every kid in that fucking show was looking for himself!

Todd Linn: If you watch the video, I don't think you see one kid in the damned thing.

Mike Judge: Most of my City Gardens memories revolve around that day because it was such a pivotal point. I never got to do another video. And I still love that video. So many of my friends are in it. If you look real close, one of my best friends is standing behind one of the amps.

Voivod/Soundgarden/Faith No More—March 16, 1990

Alex Franklin (City Gardens regular): Faith No More and Soundgarden. I'm not a real big fan of either of those bands, but let me tell you about that night and the show they put on. It was incredible. It was so packed at that show that I couldn't even get to the bathroom!

I don't know what happened. I don't know if Faith No More had a problem with their road crew, but we got picked to help load and unload their equipment. City Gardens was a huge club and most of the bands that played would come in on a small bus or with a small trailer. They had a ton of gear. To load that kind of equipment out of a huge 18-wheel trailer was really cool because they had all these huge lighting rigs and ridiculous audio equipment. These guys had multiple stacks. We had a ritual: The doors at City Gardens would open at 6 or 7, but we would get there at 2 or 3 in the afternoon and hang out. If it was spring or summer, there would be a keg of beer in the parking lot, people would have their boom boxes out, and you'd be listening to punk or hardcore, drinking and hanging out and waiting for the show to start. Everybody did that. This show was different. It wasn't a punk or hardcore show. It was before either of those bands got really huge, but it was right on the cusp of those guys blowing up.

Todd Linn (City Gardens security): There was a bouncer at City Gardens named Big Ed and [City Gardens owners] Patti and Tut had a Doberman… at least one, if not two, at all times. Before the shows, Big Ed—being a 6'10" black man with a security hat on—would take a Doberman, go through that back parking lot before the gigs, and fucking take kids' weed or beer. He'd confiscate stuff.

If you're a kid in the parking lot smoking pot, and this large man with a Doberman comes up to you, and says, "Give it up," a kid would give it up. He would literally end up with fucking stockpile of weed and beer. He'd throw the beer in the back of my pickup truck, and then he'd keep the weed! It was hilarious! He'd say, "Look how much weed I got tonight!"

Alex Franklin: We met all the guys in Faith No More. They treated us like the road crew. They were really nice to us. They shared their food with us and everything. They played a killer fucking show. The crowd was different. There were punk and hardcore kids of course, but overall it was a different crowd. It was a great experience. [Soundgarden's] Chris Cornell jumped up and was swinging from the ceiling. I'm sure Randy had a heart attack over that one.

Scott Foster (1124 Records): Chris Cornell climbed up into the rafters and was hanging upside down. He was crawling around up there and the bouncers were chasing him and trying to grab him by his hair, but they couldn't get him down.

Nancy Leopardi (City Gardens regular): At one point, Soundgarden were having technical problems, so there was a delay before they could play. Chris Cornell came out and sang *Freebird* a capella. Up until that point I didn't believe that any of the rock stars that I liked could actually sing! But he sang it so beautifully. I remember him climbing up into the lighting rig, up in the rafters. He was climbing around and swinging around like a circus performer up there. That was an amazing show.

Chain of Strength/Vision/Killing Time — March 25, 1990

Carl Porcaro (Killing Time, guitar): I knew of City Gardens mostly from hearing the older punk bands like Black Flag talk about it in interviews. I had never been there until we started playing shows. I knew it as one of the long-standing, legendary punk clubs.

Dave Franklin (Vision, vocals): I remember this show because we were real close with Killing Time. For at least two years, I spent every weekend in New York City at [Killing Time member] Anthony's house. Me, him, and Arthur from Gorilla Biscuits would go out on the town. At that particular show, there was a big deal between some of Sick of It All's road crew and the Chain of Strength kids. I don't remember [the details]. I just remember there was some kind of beef.

Carl Porcaro: I remember there was a beef going on at the time. It was typical hardcore shit. If I remember correctly, the story goes something like: Sick of It All, or maybe one of the other New York hardcore bands, was out in California, and one of the guys in Chain of Strength and one of the guys on tour with Sick of It All got into a little thing with one of the guys out in California.

Jim Norton (City Gardens stage manager): When Chain of Strength played City Gardens, they were absolutely, without a doubt, the most concerned with the way they looked of any band I've ever come across. Especially for a hardcore band. I'm talking about, "Dude, it's a pair of vans and some skateboard shorts and a Vision Streetwear shirt. Why are you deciding *which* Vision Streetwear shirt is most…'rad'? Just fucking pick one!" They were doing their hair just right; they had their tips all bleached out with just the right shade of dark underneath… They took *forever.*

Carl Porcaro: So we were going to play with Chain of Strength, first in New York. And the hardcore scene being how it was, we decided we weren't going to like these guys, even before we had met them, because they had shit with one of our buddies. They were coming all the way from California, one of their first gigs on the east coast, and we made them play last. Most of the crowd left before they went on.

Jim Norton: It was an early hardcore show, and Chain of Strength were supposed to be on the stage at 9… 9:15 at the latest. City Gardens had a hard curfew of ten o'clock on Sundays. The opening bands get on stage on time, and get off stage on time. It was a point of pride for me. If a band was late getting on stage, they were only late by, like, three minutes. It wasn't this thing where they'd drag it on and on or any of that nonsense. They got on in time, but more importantly, they got *off* on time.

Dave Franklin: Killing Time wanted us to headline, but Chain of Strength wanted to go on between Killing Time and Vision, and we were like, "No way." So we had them go on last, and more than half the place had already left. That was a great show, though. Any time Killing Time and Vision played together was a good time.

Jeremy Weiss (City Gardens regular): The rules of the game back then were: if you're from the furthest point away, you have to headline. I remember how scared they were. They thought everyone would leave because they were on the east coast and all these huge, epic east coast bands played before them.

Jim Norton: The previous band gets off by 8:45, 8:50. All of Chain of Strength's stuff is up on stage, but the band is nowhere to be found. Nine o'clock comes and goes, so at five after nine I go to the dressing room and said, "Hey guys… time to go on stage." And they're literally huddled around a mirror, meticulously combing their hair. I kept telling them it was time and they kept saying, "Yeah, yeah, we'll be right there." I tell them about the ten o'clock curfew again. "Yeah, whatever. We'll be right down." Ten after nine… nothing. Now people are starting to get pissed off. So I go back up. They finally came down at twenty minutes to ten. It was almost an hour between bands! I'm pointing at my watch going, "Five minutes! Five minutes!" This guy on stage left shoots me this look like, "Yeah, right dude. Whatever. We're Chain of Strength, bro..."

Carl Porcaro: I think that could have possibly been Uppercut's last show, too. At least until they got back together in 2006. I remember [Uppercut's] Steve Murphy diving out of that little window in the backstage area onto the stage for their set.

Jim Norton: So Chain of Strength do one song. They finish the song and I shoot them the sign, "One more. Only time for one more song and that's it." They played that song, whatever it was. Then the singer starts with, "This next song is called..." I looked down at the set of [electrical] breakers off the stage, and I shut off the power and turned on the fluorescent lights. Before they could even get to clicking off the song, I pulled the plug. It hit them, instantly: "Oh, we look like assholes." The crowd had just sat through an hour-long set change for a fucking hardcore band at a club where the audience is used to a fifteen-minute set change. The crowd knows that *something's* up.

It's one thing to be watching a band and be like, "I'm supposed to be home by 10:30. I'm not going to make it, but the rock is right in front of me, man! The hardcore is right in front of me! I'm in the pit now!" It's another thing to be standing around listening to Don Rettman spin records. You're like, "This is beat. This isn't hardcore. What's going on? Let's get a burrito..." It fits in nicely with the idea that they're sitting upstairs making sure that their hair pointed up perfectly, like a Gotti son. And remember: City Gardens had a pretty open stage. The crowd had to have seen me on the side going, "Five minutes, five minutes."

They decide that they are going to play the song with no amps, just drums and vocals. Then the PA is shut off. It's just them, with their perfect hair, onstage with drums under fluorescent lights. They were so pissed off. Yep, I'm the guy who pulled the plug on Chain of Strength and made them look like idiots under fluorescent lights with no guitars and no vocals. And frosted hair. They looked *great*...

Toasters/Scram/Bim Skala Bim—March 30, 1990

Alex Franklin (City Gardens regular): There was a really strong ska scene at City Gardens. If you go to ska shows now, it sucks. Back in that heyday when the Toasters would play all the time, there was nothing like it. There were so many people who were in to it.

Token Entry/Bigger Thomas/Bouncing Souls— April 29, 1990

Rob Vitale (Black Train Jack): The first time I ever went to City Gardens was as a roadie for Token Entry. City Gardens was the big spot in Jersey. There were a lot of little places to play, but City Gardens was the one that was huge. It was a special place because it was a big club with a big stage, and they had gigantic touring bands play with these little local openers. And those little local openers eventually became big touring bands. You'd pull up to this crazy looking warehouse space. It was pitch black, and you never want to park down around the back because you knew your car was going to get broken into. It was scary. You always thought you were going to get stuck down there. You'd be running out of the club to check on your car.

Marc Wasserman (Bigger Thomas): That was another interesting bill. We had asked Randy, "Please consider us for non-ska shows." He came up with one of the most diverse shows for us that we could have imagined. I think, at that point, Bouncing Souls were still kind of new. Token Entry was great. It's amazing to look back now, so many years later, and see how popular and what a great band and what a great career they've had. Back then I remember thinking, "These guys are really interesting." It was almost a perfect bill: You had the ska band open up, and then you move into Bouncing Souls, who were kind of doing what we were doing but in a harder, funkier kind of way, and then you bring on the hardcore band!

It was also a perfect bill for a City Gardens show in a lot of ways. We didn't care who we played with; we just loved being there and hanging out. We got to play a show and see all of our friends, and that's what it was all about. I couldn't think of anything else I really wanted to do. Small crowds didn't bother me. Some of the best shows we played at City Gardens were for small crowds, and I have wonderful memories of them, regardless.

Tim Chunks (Token Entry vocalist): I remember the first time we played with the Bouncing Souls. We had the dressing room upstairs, and [Bouncing Souls] Bryan, Greg, and Pete and everybody came in, and we were hanging out before the show. Everybody was getting along and then the Souls went out on stage. I remember watching them and thinking, "Oh, my God, they're horrendous. Holy crap, they are so bad." I couldn't believe how bad they were. It's funny thinking back on how bad they were at that show, because a few years later they're my best friends and we're all living together and having a great time. They had become much, much better after a year's worth of shows. They turned into one of the best bands I ever knew.

Alex Franklin: The thing about Randy... he would book shows that would cross musical boundaries. He would have a band like Bim Skala Bim play with The Bouncing Souls, who were like a punk-slash-funk band. He would always try to mix it up by having punk bands play with hardcore bands, and maybe he'd throw a ska band on the bill or a metal band... I don't remember ever seeing that anywhere else.

Social Distortion/Gang Green — May 18, 1990

Randy Now: Every time Social Distortion came back to town, they sold a few more tickets, but they never broke 1,000 like the Circle Jerks or 7 Seconds. I had become pretty good friends with [Social D. lead singer] Mike Ness, and I always made sure that they got a good hotel. They were always very picky about sound and would soundcheck for hours. And once they had everything set up, you couldn't move it. Not a mic, not a knob on the mixing board, not a guitar stand, nothing. They would mark on the stage where all the mic stands went.

For this show, I went to the hotel to pick the band up, and Mike says to me, "Sorry, we can't play. Our road manager says that the sound isn't good enough for us." Just like that, day of show, they cancel. We sold over 500 tickets, and they refused to play. Social Distortion came back six months later and played with Screaming Trees, and by then they had a different road manager who had no problem with the sound.

Gang Green played, but I didn't like dealing with them because they were a bunch of drunks. I had seen them in Toronto at the club El Mocambo and their agent had just signed them. He knew I was going and he asked me to report back on how the show went, and they started a riot that night. Their lead singer, Chris Doherty, was always drunk and a pain in the ass to work with. Not difficult, just drunk. But I had to tell everyone that Social D wasn't going to play and that I'd give them part of their money back, but Gang Green was still on!

Bigger Thomas/Toasters—June 15, 1990

Marc Wasserman (Bigger Thomas): That was probably the Toasters—if you want to use the athletic metaphor—at the height of their career. Like Michael Jordan playing the best game of his life. That show was probably when the Toasters were playing the best shows of their lives. Whenever we had a chance to play with them, it was a special occasion for us because they brought people to that club. I saw them back in New York in the early '80s when they first got started, so I knew who they were. They are one of the greatest American ska bands that ever existed, and I know for a fact that [Toaster's frontman] Bucket really appreciated City Gardens because it wasn't far from New York, but it was still a separate crowd. They cultivated that whole scene down there by playing City Gardens. Bucket also had his own label back then, Moon Records, and he could count on Randy to book a lot of his bands. I don't know what I can say except that they were the best.

Bad Religion/ALL/Vision/Shades Apart—June 29, 1990

Dave Franklin (Vision, vocals): Shades Apart opened up, then we went on, then ALL, and then Bad Religion. The night before Shades Apart opened for Bad Religion at the [punk club] Anthrax in Connecticut. I went up with the Shades Apart guys to see Bad Religion, and there were maybe 150 people there, 200 tops. I was hanging out talking to [Bad

Religion's] Brett Gurewitz and Greg Hetson, and they were both like, "Man, I thought we were a little bit bigger on the East Coast." And I was like, "This is kind of a weird place." I mean, it was a great place to play—totally cool people—but was hit-or-miss. I said, "Tomorrow night in Trenton, at City Gardens, the show is going to be off the charts."

When the next night came and we pulled into City Gardens, there was already a line around the building. Then the Bad Religion guys pulled up in their van. The first thing Brett said to me was, "You weren't kidding!" The place was already sold out.

Peter Tabbot (Vision, guitar): This was another amazing City Gardens show. Bad Religion are/were…well…BAD RELIGION. One of my favorite bands, and we were all so psyched to share a stage with them in Trenton. They had pretty much come back from the dead just a couple of years before with the release of *Suffer* and *No Control*. This may have been their *Against the Grain* tour, and they had totally reestablished themselves as the smartest, best punk-rock band around. ALL just had a release or two out at the time, I think, and they were still kind of riding the coattails of The Descendents popularity while generating their own fan base with their kind of prog-punk melodic style. But they were definitely a good draw on their own.

With us and Shades Apart, even though we were local bands, we both had a significant following. The show was packed. I would never, ever throw my band into a conversation about the great shows you would catch routinely at City Gardens, but objectively, it was a pretty good bill in 1990. It was typical of what Randy would do: four bands, each of whom has a significant audience psyched to see them for $7 or $8. Randy would put that together every single weekend, for seemingly years on end. You'd get two, three, or even four national touring acts on the same bill, and then the next night you'd get another fantastic show. Maybe it would be hardcore/metal one night, and then punk/indie the next night, but always amazing shows for just a few bucks.

What I remember most about shows like this Bad Religion show at City Gardens [is that] you knew a fair number of the people. And you often went to whatever shows were happening on the weekend, even if it wasn't a band or style that you closely identified with. A place where you knew the bouncers and the bartenders. I would imagine that this happened, to a lesser degree, at places like CBGB or The Ritz in New York, but those places didn't have that same feeling. As large as City Gardens was, and as many people as you'd see there for bigger shows, it always felt like someone was having a great show in your backyard. That is, if your backyard happened to be the bowels of Trenton. This show is a really good example of Randy pairing great national acts with some pretty decent local bands.

Scott Reynolds (ALL, vocals): I remember the stage smelled like puke all the time. We'd come in and load in and every time we'd be like, "God, it smells like puke up here!" I mean it was really, *really* strong. It was really gross, and you could smell it while you were playing. It was part of the charm, I guess.

Dave Franklin: That was a great show. I recall I was in back bar and the Shades Apart had just finished. The crew was setting up Vision's equipment, and [Shades Apart bassist] Kevin was there with his brother and a bunch of other people I knew. I wasn't *in* the conversation, but I was probably three or four people away from the conversation, and I could hear Kevin saying, "Wait 'til Vision goes on, this place is gonna' go CRAZY!" And sure enough, we went on and the place just went absolutely crazy. *Blink of an Eye* was out, and we were already like the house band. Everybody knew our songs and went nuts! Bad Religion and ALL were amazed by the crowd.

Scott Reynolds: That was always one of my favorite places to play. We had big shows there.

Jeremy Weiss (City Gardens regular): The show was sold out. This is a true story: I was a very resourceful kid. I knew how [clubs] worked because I'd started booking shows, and I knew back then that bouncers would just as soon check IDs at the local bars as they would at City Gardens. I also knew they were susceptible to bribes. So I walked around the back, I knocked on the door, and this towering individual popped his head out and said, "What?" I said, "I'll give you $100 to let us in." He didn't say one word, nodded, put his hand out. I gave him $100 and me and four of my friends jetted right into the show while 275 other people stood out front, bummed out. We got into that show and were completely blown away. It was so packed that it was raining inside the club.

Scott Foster (1124 Records): I caught just about every ALL show that came through there. They were one of my favorites. That night we were waiting in line outside, and I saw some guys playing catch with a baseball. One of the guys missed it and the ball rolled over to me, so I picked it up, and, when I went to give it back to him, I realized it was [ALL's] Karl [Alvarez] and Scott [Reynolds] playing catch. Karl said, "You wanna take over for a second?" and he gave me his glove. I played catch with Scott Reynolds for ten minutes while Karl did something else.

Shelter/Quicksand/Inside Out—July 1, 1990

Walter Schriefels (Quicksand/Gorilla Biscuits): City Gardens was really cool because it had the feeling of being really big while still keeping a kind of intimate atmosphere. It was a bigger venue than the places we played in New York, and that was exciting. I heard there were a lot of Nazi skins there, but that was never the case at our shows. It was a fun place to play and a great audience for hardcore bands. As far as the stage, the room itself, for hardcore standards it was really big. The shows were always packed with kids from Jersey, Philadelphia, New York, and such. It was interesting to go down there and find there was this other world of people who were totally into what was going on.

Nine Inch Nails—June 13, 1990

Alex Franklin (City Gardens regular): This show was so sold out that there were well over a thousand people. More than 1,200 people. They had this kind of roll-cage going across the front of the stage. There were girls in skimpy leather outfits climbing up and down this cage. Everything was backlit with these bright floodlights that were blue and orange and red, so you couldn't really see any details. They were just silhouettes.

D.R.I.—August 12, 1990

Randy Now: This kid sent me a letter giving me a hard time about $10 ticket prices and how I was "getting rich" off the kids. I told him, "You come out next Sunday for D.R.I., and I'll show where it all goes." So, the kid shows up—he was maybe 16—and I put him to work. He came around 12 noon, I treated him like a crew member, fed him, and, at the end of the night, I took him in the back to pay the bands, the crew, security, the whole thing. He left, and I never heard from or saw him again. I said, "Now do you see what really goes on?" He got a lesson in economics that day.

D.O.A.—August 19, 1990

Joey Shithead (D.O.A. vocals): In August of 1990 we were scheduled to headline. I think we were supposed to play with Elvis Hitler and the Gaye Bikers on Acid, but I don't think we ever played that show. We pretty much broke up on that tour. There's a good chance we might have cancelled that show. We had about eight or nine days left on the tour, and we probably went, "Ah, this sucks," and quit. That *never* happened with D.O.A. That's probably the only time we ever did it. It was really hot and the tour wasn't very good. It was kind of a, *what the hell are we doing?* thing. We drove home, just two or three of us, all the way across the country from the east coast.

Soundgarden—August 20, 1990

Deidre Humenik: That was the night I quit. Randy drove me to it by embarrassing me in front of a bunch of people. I didn't really go back for shows even. It was that bad.

Iggy Pop—November 2, 1990

Steven DiLodovico: I went to this show to see a legend. I wasn't expecting much. Let's be honest, this was Iggy in 1990. He had that hit single,

"Candy," with B-52's singer Kate Pierson. So my whole reason for going was pretty much just to be able to say I saw Iggy at some point in my life. It was one of the loudest shows I've ever seen. I'm a guy who has seen Motörhead several times and once saw Manowar, who, at one time, held the world record for decibels! Iggy was intense, and you could see hints of the utter madman he had been in the '70s. He didn't cut himself or anything, but he rocked. Hard.

Social Distortion/Screaming Trees— November 3, 1990

Steven DiLodovico: I was happy that Social Distortion played a few of the old songs from their "glory days" but, overall, I was kind of disappointed with the new stuff. [Singer] Mike Ness still wore the "sympathetic" eyeliner but was dressed up in some kind of 1940s hipster look. He wore the wife beater, suspenders, khaki Chinos, and a fedora. I was right up against the stage, and I'm pretty sure he hit me with a loogie.

Murphy's Law/Supertouch—November 11, 1990

Jeff "Stress" Davis (Suburban Hoodz): One incident I remember clearly was when the security guy, Big Ed, chucked a skinhead out of the show for whatever reason, and [Murphy's Law frontman] Jimmy Gestapo held up the show for, like, 45 minutes and went outside with the dude. He hung out and drank beer with the kid until they let that kid back in. That was really cool.

Mark "Repo" Pesetsky (City Gardens security): At Murphy's Law show, you could look at the audience and tell that they were thinking, "Should I do it? Should I not?" These people were New Yorkers… therefore, not too bright.

Jim Norton (City Gardens stage manager): I'm on stage, and Murphy's Law is on stage, and Jimmy Gestapo is saying to a crowd of 600 people, "Hey, fuck the bouncers! These guys are fucking dicks, fuck them! There are 600 of you and fucking 10 of them. Do the math." And I was like,

"Yeah, I get it." I didn't have a problem with him saying it, because it didn't seem like he was trying to incite a riot. What he really seemed to be saying was, "Pay no attention [to the bouncers]." Looking back, all these years later, you can't get upset about it. But I told Randy that the next time he booked Murphy's Law, I wasn't working.

Agnostic Front/Sick of It All/Bouncing Souls— November 24, 1990

Roger Miret (Agnostic Front, vocalist): One of my favorite memories from City Gardens was a show we did with Sick of It All. The kids, the vibe… everything was great.

Joseph Kuzemka (Trenton Punk Rock Flea Market): This was my first hardcore show and I was terrified. I was absolutely, positively terrified. I'd been to punk shows before, but that was my first full-blown New York hardcore show. We walked inside, and I was looking at skinheads and guys with liberty spikes, and I'd only seen that stuff on record covers for the most part. The Circle Jerks is one thing… everyone's jumping up and down, they're pogoing, they're circle pitting… a completely different kind of show than a New York hardcore show. I stood on the bleachers the entire night because I was terrified to go down on the floor, and then I finally got the balls to go down when Agnostic Front played "Cruci-fied." Something in me said, "I gotta do it." So I went down and I got socked right in the face. I caught someone's hand and it whacked me right in the forehead. I fell down, and thought, *what the fuck did I just do?* I got up, went back into the pit, and it was a love affair ever since. I think a lot of people feel that way.

For me, I was an outsider. I was the kid in Catholic school who wore a Slayer shirt on dress-down day. My *South of Heaven* shirt always went over really well. I didn't have the friends that most kids my age did, because I was the weird kid. I was the giant kid who was weird and listened to heavy metal and punk rock, and I found something there that changed my life. I mean City Gardens literally changed my life. It introduced me to straight edge around the age of 15, and that literally

changed the path of my life. I could've gone down a really different path than what I've chosen, and I attribute a lot of that to City Gardens.

It inspired me to start two different fanzines, run a record label, all of those things that I consider to be a really important part of my history. I didn't go there as long as a lot of other people, but it was an important place, and it changed me. I can only assume it changed a lot of other people, if it had that kind of effect on me.

Being there gave me confidence, because at that point, I realized there were other people like me, and they're not on record covers or in a magazine. It made me realize there were other people who believed the same things that I did and who liked the heavy music, and that meant the world to me. I interviewed [Agnostic Front guitarist] Vinnie Stigma in front of City Gardens, which was unbelievably surreal. It was my first brush with meeting someone [of that stature in the scene]. I went in with the idea of interviewing Roger Miret. I couldn't find Roger, so I went up to Vinnie and I said, "I do a 'zine." I was nervous as hell, and I'm sure I was stuttering and stammering. I said, "Can I interview you?" He said, "Yeah, man, let's go outside." We talked for probably 45 minutes, and it was really amazing. At the end of the interview, he said that if he ever dies, I could cut off all of his skin and make a lampshade out of him. I said, "Okay, I'll hold you to that!" He's not dead yet, so I don't have a lampshade.

GWAR/Tesco Vee's Hate Police—December 16, 1990

Bob Gorman (GWAR Historian): I remember seeing the bill and saying, "Wow we're playing with Tesco?" Yeah, Randy would book anyone together as long as it was a strong bill.

Oderus Urungus (GWAR): We didn't really know Tesco until we played with him. He was pretty shocked and appalled at what he saw [when he looked at us]. We were doing horrible stuff. We actually used two tour busses on that tour, and Tesco's Hate Police got half of one of the tour busses. It's funny, because Tesco and I became pretty good friends after that. It turned out that he lived in the same neighborhood as my mom. When my mom passed away, he ended up buying my fence. He came over, we dug up my mom's old fence, and he hauled it off to his house. So somewhere out there, he's got my fence.

Tesco Vee: Oh yeah, I did do that. He was having a big estate sale, and he had all his childhood toys, which he didn't want to sell. It was him and his brother's toys, which was pretty wild. They had everything for sale.

Bob Gorman: The thing about Tesco is that he's really a kitten, you know? A lot of that anti-women stuff is really overblown. He's totally devoted to his wife.

Oderus Urungus: It wasn't really the stuff we were doing on stage that shocked him, it was more the off-stage behavior. When he came into the back lounge [on the bus] and found us discovering what crack was, it freaked him out pretty bad. Our old guitar player used to be a complete fiend. This weird Rasta dude came on the bus with us, along with his weird girlfriend, and he broke out this super elaborate crack-smoking device. We were all like, "Whoa! What's that, man?" Then the door opens up and there's Tesco. Oh my God, it was horrible! Also, we were playing music by that band The Frogs, and he couldn't handle that. All those songs about having sex with little boys and stuff... We were back there listening to The Frogs and smoking crack. Poor Tesco. He couldn't handle it.

Tesco Vee: The look on my face must have been like a little, naïve kid from the Midwest meeting his first prostitute. Wonderful. I must have blocked that out. Jesus.

Bob Gorman: Tesco was up front with his jug of Metamucil. He'd also have a tub of pistachios, and he had to have Yoo-hoo and Skor bars. By the end of the tour I loved pistachios, Yoo-hoo, and Skor bars. I still don't need the Metamucil, though. I think the time we played with The Hate Police was the first time we really hung out with him.

Tesco Vee: That was a great tour rider. I don't even remember the Metamucil. I must have really been into proper evacuation, I guess. I can't imagine. I probably dragged it from home and was gulping it down. Constipation on the road can be killer with all the shit food that you eat.

Oderus Urungus: We were good buddies with [all-female band] the Lunachicks for a really long time and still sort of keep in touch with them. They were our little New York rock goddesses, and we were these weird little barbarian dudes from Virginia. I think we had sex with all of them on various occasions. I was madly in love with [Lunachicks member] Squid for a long time, but Jimmy Gestapo was her on again/off again boyfriend, so there was a weird thing going on there.

Tesco Vee: We were the perfect opening act for GWAR. Those shows were great. We got exposed to a lot more people by playing with them.

Sim Cain (Rollins Band): GWAR asked Jello Biafra to come onstage with them, and Jello was like, "Okay, I'm going to come up and give my speech about Nicaragua, and then you can do your thing." The GWAR guys all looked at each other and said, "Into the meat grinder," because they had this huge meat grinder onstage. So, during the show, they're like, "Ladies and gentlemen, Jello Biafra!" Jello comes out, gets one word out, and they pick him up and throw him into the meat grinder! All the way down, Jello is yelling, "You assholes!" He was really pissed off.

Leeway—December 30, 1990

Travis Nelson (Inspecter 7, vocals): That's when Joe Rowan got stabbed.

Steven DiLodovico: The only thing I remember about this show was the huge fucking skinhead riot outside. Some Nazis showed up, but not enough. I have never seen anything so violent in my life.

Travis Nelson: I used to talk to Joe a lot in the parking lot of City Gardens. We used to hang out. Joe was who he was. The Trenton skins knew him. Everybody kind of knew him through connections in our lives. He would talk to me because I was cool with the Trenton skins. Joe was a pretty prominent white-power skinhead at the time. He was the singer of Nordic Thunder, which was a white-power band. He didn't hide it back then.

Probably about a week before that incident, I had debate with him. I said, "Hey, you got all this stuff on your jacket—all these swastikas and other assorted symbols—and yet, here you are with me, chilling out in the parking lot, drinking a beer... Not only am I not white, I am your worst nightmare. I'm mixed. I'm everything you supposedly stand against." He gave me the, "Oh, well you're different... You're cool," response. And I said, "Well, by saying that, you're taking me on an individual basis... you're kind of flushing your philosophy down the toilet, don't you think?" We debated for another 20 minutes. Glaring contradictions kept coming up in what he was saying, but... a lot of times, with that whole white-power thing, I don't think the people even believe it. I think, for a lot of them, it was just something they were looking to belong to. A lot of them were intelligent enough to see the glaring contradictions, and yet they were still involved. I said to Joe, "You see what's been going on around here. Be careful." I didn't mean it as a threat. I meant it as a warning.

Jamie Davis (City Gardens regular): That's [the show] where the Nazis got it pretty bad. It started as two guys doing a fair fight outside the back door where the alley is.

Travis Nelson: Joe and another guy fought. They got into it one-on-one in the parking lot. And it was a good fight! The security guards didn't even break it up. It was a good five- or ten- minute fight, they were rubbing each other's faces in the pavement! All the people that wanted to fuck the Nazis up were standing around in a circle, watching.

Jamie Davis: People were like, "Fuck this!" and everyone jumped in. All hell broke loose. The Nazis ran for their car, and then the whole place— hundreds of people—started throwing things at their car... and there was plenty of stuff to throw in that parking lot. All the windows were broken. Some people got stabbed.

Travis Nelson: Everyone was there. DMS was there, Tri-State was there, Hate Squad was there. Everyone was there.

Steven DiLodovico: Out in the parking lot, it was chaos. I saw one anti-white-power dude beating a Nazi with what looked like a piece of garden hose. The Nazi was kind of slumped on his knees, and the dude kept smacking him in the face.

Travis Nelson: Suddenly, there was a loud, open-handed slap being dealt [to one of the Nazis] that literally lifted this kid off of his seat. Two of them made a break for it, trying to get back to the building.

Jamie Davis: Eventually the Nazis made it to their car and tried to drive out. It was a white Honda, if I remember correctly.

Travis Nelson: The driver hunkered down while his car was dismantled by this fucking crowd. When it was over, his car looked like it had rolled down a hill 20 times. He tried to get out of there, but you heard all the tires deflate as people were puncturing his tires with knives and shit.

As racist accusations fly, tw

By PETER ASELTINE
Staff Writer

TRENTON — Two young men escaped serious injury when they were stabbed by members of an angry mob last night outside a city rock club after concert-goers leaving the club accused the victims of shouting racial slurs and being "Nazi skinheads," according to witnesses.

The victims and their attackers were all white, witnesses said. The victims, who denied making any racial remarks or being skinheads, in turn accused their attackers of being skinheads.

Joseph Rowan 18, of Newtown, Pa., was stabbed in the neck with a broken bottle, and Patrick Barkley, 20, also of Newtown, was stabbed in the lower back, upper chest and elbow with a knife, police said.

The attack occurred outside City Gardens on Calhoun Street shortly before 11 p.m., police said.

The victims were getting into a car with another youth when members of a crowd gathered outside the club accused the victims of making racist remarks and called the three youths Nazis, according to Jim Demarest, 18 of Point Pleasant. Demarest and his friends, Andrew Aronowicz, 16, and James Lauer, 16,

Jamie Davis: The crowd absolutely destroyed the car… every bit of glass was smashed, all four tires were slashed. In their panic, they were gunning the engine and the rims kept spinning on the gravel and shooting up sparks.

Travis Nelson: When all was said and done, everyone walked away after they got bored of pummeling this guy in his car. The guy gets out and starts walking around his car, and he's like, "Holy shit, holy shit," looking at his car. And—like he needed any more aggravation after what had just happened—my friend E-Rail rolls up to him and is like, "COME ON, MOTHERFUCKER!" The driver dropped to his knees and started begging for mercy. He's like, "Please, I got kids! I'm not white power. I was just with them…" E-Rail said, "Yeah, you're not white power. You're just a white pussy." He walked off and left him. I don't remember cops coming, either, at least not for a while. They didn't come during the fight, and it was a pretty good, long one-on-one fight. I do know a couple of them went to the hospital, though.

Steven DiLodovico: All the tires were slashed. It made this god-awful noise when they tried to put the car in reverse; it almost exploded. Somebody threw a big hunk of cinderblock or something through the windshield. The tires were completely gone, and they were trying to get out on the rims.

men hurt in Trenton melee

'They threw a trash can at the car.'

— Jim Demarest

—oth of Point Pleasant, drove the wounded victims to a gas station at Calhoun Street and Pennington Avenue after the attack to call for help, police said.

A large group of youths surrounded the victim's car, slashing the tires and smashing out the windows as the victims attempted to drive away, Demarest said.

"They threw a trash can at the car," Demarest said. "They kicked out the windows and threw bottles through the windows. The guys in the car had it floored, but the tires were all flat and smoke just poured out."

One man was hit in the back of the head with a bottle. Demarest said.

The third youth in the car, who identified himself only as Paul, said the victims were stabbed through the open windows and did not realize they were cut until they were driven away from the scene. They were treated at Helene Fuld Medical Center.

Travis Nelson: The next day, in the newspaper, it was the funniest fucking thing. The reporters were so confused. To them—to the media—"skinhead" automatically meant "Nazi." They were so baffled. It was like, "So…some skinheads got stabbed by a bunch of guys who said they were skinheads…" They didn't get it. To them, all skinheads were racists. The article said something like, "The real skinheads… (they saw the Nazis as being 'real' skinheads) were stabbed by a bunch of guys 'dressed' as skinheads." It was ridiculous. I remember cracking up at their total confusion and the fact that it wound up in the newspaper.

From the Trenton Times *article dated January 1, 1991:*

> *Detective Sgt. Robert Tedder said the victims, Joseph Rowan and Patrick Barkley, both of Newtown, told police their alleged assailants were "skinheads." But, said Tedder, the term may merely have described their appearance, not an affiliation with the racist group of that name.*
>
> *Witnesses said both the victims, who denied making racist remarks, and their attackers were white.*

Typically, skinheads have shaved or nearly shaved heads, wear billowing fatigue pants tucked in black military jump boots and favor tattoos, Schroeder said. Authentic skinheads are blatantly racist in their violence, he said. "They're basically a group of young men who believe in white supremacy." said Schroeder, noting they are usually associated with such groups as the Neo-Nazis, the Ku Klux Klan and the Aryan Nation.

But, Schroeder said, the only skinhead group known in New Jersey was based near the Shore.

Victims claim assault by skinheads

By HANK WALTHER
Staff Writer

TRENTON — Police are investigating the Sunday night assault on two Pennsylvania men who alleged their attackers were skinheads, officials said.

Detective Sgt. Robert Tedder said the victims, Joseph Rowan and Patrick Barkley, both of Newtown, told with the racist group of that name.

"Police believe that there are no organized skinhead groups operating in this immediate area," said John Schroeder, city police information officer.

Further interviews with the victims are planned, Tedder said.

Rowan, 18, and Barkley, 20, were leaving City Gardens night club on Calhoun Street when they exchanged shouted accusations and ra- stab wounds and their car was extensively damaged, police said.

The victims escaped in a car driven by friends, witnesses said Sunday.

Witnesses said both the victims, who denied making racist remarks, and their attackers were white.

Barkley was in stable condition last night at Helene Fuld Medical Center, where Rowan had been treated and released following the

Typically, skinheads have shaved or nearly shaved heads, wear billowing fatigue pants tucked into black military jump boots and favor tattoos, Schroeder said.

Authentic skinheads are blatantly racist in their violence, he said.

"They're basically a group of young men who believe in white supremacy," said Schroeder, noting they are usually associated with such groups as the Neo-Nazis, the Ku

PART FOUR

THIS IS THE END, MY FRIEND, THE END

CHAPTER 10

1991–1992

1991

Top Ten Songs in 1991:

1. (Everything I Do) I Do It for You, Bryan Adams

2. I Wanna Sex You Up, Color Me Badd

3. Gonna Make You Sweat, C+C Music Factory

4. Rush, Rush, Paula Abdul

5. One More Try, Timmy T

6. Unbelievable, EMF

7. More Than Words, Extreme

8. I Like the Way (The Kissing Game), Hi-Five

9. The First Time, Surface

10. Baby, Baby, Amy Grant

A lot of older City Gardens regulars stopped going to shows. Many felt the vibe of the club had changed. Attendance began to decline.

Ron Kearnest (City Gardens regular): With real punks, you would go in the pit and get crazy, but if someone was on the floor, you would pick them up. But then you started getting all these idiots coming in like, "Let's beat people up and get into fights." They weren't real punks. It was more about getting hurt and hurting other people. It was the beginning of the end.

Deirdre Humenik (City Gardens employee): Things started to get violent. I had to search the girls when they came into shows to make sure they didn't have weapons. We would have to take away their hair spray way to keep it from being used as a flame thrower. But some of them would put razor blades in their pockets, so that when I stuck my hand in to check for contraband, my hands would get cut up. That was the mentality.

Jeff Feuerzeig (TV producer): At a certain point the shows started getting scary. I'm a Jewish record geek, not a skinhead. I enjoy hardcore, but I'm not there to get my ass kicked. There were fights happening, people getting thrown out, and you think to yourself, *what the hell am I doing here?*

Chuck Treece (McRad/Underdog/Bad Brains): I watched the scene change, and City Gardens changed with it. Most clubs couldn't do that. Once their scene ended so did the club. But I watched as the crowds went from older, pissed-off drunk dudes to younger kids who were more into dancing and the intensity of the shows.

Travis Nelson (Inspector 7, vocalist): Things started changing in 1989. I feel like, in 1989, people finally got sick of the white-power bullshit. That's when all the fights began happening. It seemed like there was constant warring between '89 and '92. You were always checking for the white-power guys. People were more militant about it. You'd even have straight-edge kids fighting along S.H.A.R.P. skins… everyone got sick of the bullshit.

Rollins Band/Tesco Vee's Hate Police — January 13 1991

Tesco Vee (Meatmen vocalist): In '83, for my magazine *Touch and Go*, I had [artist] Pushead do the back cover with a really nice drawing of Henry Rollins. Henry was sitting cross-legged with the long hair and the beard, looking kind of like an old shaman with the incense burning and everything. We were simply making fun of Henry that he had long hair and turned into kind of a hippie dude. Well, anyway, he got really mad. He called me and yelled at me. He called Pushead and yelled at him. Now, this was 1983, okay? Cut to eight years later, and it's 1991. I had run into Rollins maybe one time before 1991, maybe around four or five years after the *Touch and Go* incident happened. He was cool toward me, standoffish, but he wasn't openly hostile. Randy had to talk me into doing this show. He said, "Come on, Tesco. This will be a good bill. You've got to do this." I had my brother-in-law with me at this show, and he had never seen us play. I dragged his ass up to City Gardens from Virginia. So we walk in the club and even though it's day time, it was pitch black inside. We were standing in the darkness trying to get our bearings, and my drummer walks up and says, "Dude, I forgot my cymbals."

If you know anything about this stuff, you know that drummers will loan you their kit, guitarists will loan you their heads and their cabinets, but cymbals… cymbals are like NO WAY. I'm like, "Oh, shit, you idiot!" and I said, "Well, we'll have to talk to Rollins' drummer, and you had better hope he lets you use his." And from out of the darkness, over by the bleachers, comes Henry. He's wearing black, cut-off shorts, and he's clutching a pool ball. I extended my hand and said, "Henry! Long time, huh?" He did not extend his hand. He said, "You want to borrow cymbals? You talk to *me*. And the answer is probably 'no.'" And he kept on walking.

I just stood there. I'm sure my face was the color of a tomato. I was totally like, "Shit, I guess he's still mad." We didn't talk the whole night. I'm sure he wasn't in the audience while we were playing. It was a big crowd, because it was Rollins, and we were laying an egg. I mean there was absolutely no connection. The crowd was not into us at all. I might have had a handful—maybe 30 to 40 fans—who had come to see me, but it was just one of those nights where you want it to be over with. I was making cracks on stage like, "Oh Henry. I still love you and want to have your baby." That was probably making it worse.

Afterwards, I said something to Randy, who rolled his eyes, like, "Sorry, dude. Whatever. Shit happens." It was a horrible pairing. A Rollins crowd is not a Tesco Vee crowd. It was one of the great failings in punk rock history. And, of course, my brother-in-law was there, and I wanted to say, "It's not usually like this! The fans usually like what we're doing!" Oh, it was terrible. Might be one of the worst shows I've ever played. But Henry was cool enough to write a forward for the *Touch and Go* book, so I guess it worked out okay.

Nine Inch Nails/Die Warsau— January 20, 1991

Deirdre Humenik: Trent was so stinking shy that if he needed something, he would ask me to go ask someone for him. He didn't want to talk to anyone. Nice as pie, but timid.

Randy Now: By this show, [Nine Inch Nails] was too big to be playing City Gardens, but Trent remembered that I tour managed GWAR and wanted to play a show for me. The place was packed, and the band set a new record for the amount of merchandise sold.

From a live review in B-Side magazine by Sandra A. Garcia: It fascinated me how many women fought, shoved, and clawed their way to the front of the stage in Trenton. There were some beefy guys near the front during Die Warsau, but once Nine Inch Nails took the stage suddenly there were all women in front screaming along to the songs. Not singing, but bellowing with pumping fists. Tribal warfare indeed. You could see how they were getting all their aggressions into the open. The guys were still the idiots launching themselves off the stage; I'd like to think that women know better than to stage dive... Continuing in his gentle tradition, Trent abused his own band members, sending his guitarist into the audience. In Trenton, he pushed his guitarist so hard he almost went flying backstage.

Fugazi—March 19, 1991

Pat Baker (The Semibeings): I remember Fugazi would only charge $5.00 at the door, which was great, and when the band played, they had two super-bright spotlights right up on the stage. You always knew that with Fugazi you were in for an amazing, memorable time.

Ian MacKaye (Fugazi): I have a really distinct memory of the atmosphere of the shows. The… I'm trying to think of the right word… the smell of it. Not that it was a bad smell.

I have a pretty acute memory usually. I always remember if something out of the ordinary happened, but the thing I remember most about City Gardens was Randy Now and hanging out with him. We stayed at his house in New Hope. City Gardens is very interesting from my point of view. In the later '80s, this hardcore thing really started to take form. And it was not entirely but largely informed by what was happening in New York. The New York hardcore scene and that era of hardcore, which was more of a metal-tinged hardcore… like Samhain and those kinds of bands.

City Gardens was not a venue that I really took much interest in or knew much about, because it was similar to Fenders out in Los Angeles. It was a playground for the hardcore madness. Shows at Fenders were notorious for kids beating the crap out of each other. I never played Fenders, ever. Quite pointedly never played it. I kind of felt the same way [about City Gardens], but then, at some point, I talked to Randy. He was a really nice guy, so I thought, "Well, we'll give it a shot." But our crowds were getting so big that we needed a room large enough for that many people and that was also safe… not a dangerous room.

Alex Franklin (City Gardens regular): There's this thing at shows now called "headwalking." You can pretty much tell what it is by the name. It happens at a lot of "posi" shows these days. Instead of diving, they just run off the stage and see how far they can get walking on people's heads and hands. Well, ["Kung Fu"] Lou [DeCarolis, a City Gardens regular] would do that. When Fugazi played it was always packed. First, they only charged $5 and second, they always drew a lot of people anyway. I was in the back watching them, and I see Lou standing. He's walking as if he were walking across a stream of slippery rocks on people's heads. He's like ten feet in the air walking on these people's fucking heads and shoulders trying to make it across the crowd. And what happens? Ian MacKaye [yells], "You! Motherfucker! Stop fucking doing that!" Man, Ian MacKaye... he did not like that at all.

Tony Rettman (City Gardens regular): I had a friend, Dave, who was the first one of us to get out of the "straight edge" thing and start smoking weed. Fugazi were coming to City Gardens, and he was into it. "Fugazi are coming to City Gardens? FUCK THAT! I'm wearing a Champion hoodie, I'm X-ing up... I'M MOSHING!!!" I was like, "Okay Dave, whatever you say." I was standing by the front door and I saw him walking in with gigantic X's on his hands, a red Champion hoodie that he probably hadn't worn in years, camo shorts... the whole deal. Fugazi played, he started moshing, and Ian yelled at him. Dave was loaded! He gave Ian the finger all night.

Ben Vaughn (Ben Vaughn Combo): The first time I saw Ween, they opened for Fugazi. The audience booed them and threw shit at them the whole time. And WEEN's set got better and better. They really fed off of the negative energy.

Jello Biafra (Spoken Word) — April 24, 1991

Alex Franklin (City Gardens regular): When they started the spoken word thing... that was unheard of. Jello or Rollins would do these spoken word shows every couple of months. People didn't understand the concept. Jello Biafra did one, and I remember he did this whole catchphrase of "smoke more pot" all night.

Jello Biafra: I've always liked Randy, I've always gotten along well with him, but I kind of wish he hadn't shaved off that great big moustache he had at a time when punk people were not supposed to have moustaches. He had a moustache, the hat, and the shorts halfway down his ass, and I told people, "Hey, if you get to City Gardens, look for the dude who looks like a catfish. That's the one you need to know." They always figured out who he was quickly, and I mean that with the greatest affection. But

like any underground place, you never knew what might happen or what might go wrong. I mean, the first time we were there in '81, I don't know where everybody else was, but I was putting some dry clothes on in the backstage bathroom when a guy began pounding on the door, saying he had a knife and that he wanted to stab me and kill me. He did that over and over and over again. Luckily the door was locked, and he never tried to break it down. So, no knife in me and that was the end of that, but you never knew.

De La Soul/Bigger Thomas — May 4, 1991

Marc Wasserman (Bigger Thomas): That bill was crazy. I give Randy a lot of credit; he was very experimental. He would try things that other clubs would never have considered, like putting bands together you wouldn't think go together. Sometimes it worked. It didn't always work, but I like to think that all the times he gave us a chance to do something out of the ordinary, it worked. We would say to him, "Don't always put us on a ska bill." We really wanted to break out and expand our audience. To play in front of a hip-hop crowd, opening for De La Soul, was kind of crazy. They didn't really know what to make of us. There were a lot of people with crossed arms and funny looks on their faces. Remember, hip-hop shows back in the day used to be a DJ, a couple of turntables, records without the vocals, and then the rappers up front with their mics. The crowd didn't expect to see a full band with instruments open up the show! I remember seeing a couple of people bobbing their heads and moving, but a lot of people were looking at us like, "When are these people going to get off?" It was the first time we had to really work hard, and it was almost like, "What do we have to do to get you people to react? Light ourselves on fire?" We'd finish a song and there'd be silence. We came off thinking we sucked!

We were also kind of excited to meet De La Soul, but I also didn't realize until then how rap shows worked. Randy had to pay for a limo to pick them up in New York and drive them down to City Gardens. They didn't arrive until five minutes before they went on. They walked in, they did about a thirty-five minute set while the limo waited for them, and then they ran right off the stage, jumped in the limo and drove back to New York! It was surprising, too, because they got a lot of money... like seven or eight grand, and it wasn't a long set.

Vision/Insted/Mouthpiece/Eye For An Eye—
May 5, 1991

Pat Baker (Mouthpiece/The Semibeings): This was my first time on that stage and it is something I'll never forget. To be able to play at the place I idolized was incredible. I think I was 16 years old, and that was odd in itself.

Tim McMahon (Mouthpiece, vocals): We had played with Insted in Reading at the Unisound, and somehow we got on the bill at City Gardens. Randy reached out and asked us if we wanted to open the show. We were floored. It all came full circle. You start thinking about the very first time you did a stage dive there, whether it was legal or not. You start thinking about all this stuff like, *holy shit. I'm going to play City Gardens.* I had only been going to shows there like three or four years, but it seemed like an eternity. 1987 shows seemed completely different from 1990 shows. Totally different crowd, totally different feeling… it could have been a whole different club. Those early shows I went to seemed so dark and heavy and punk. [Later], the scene looked different. You went from punk rockers to kids who were clean-cut looking. By 1990, it seemed my whole high school knew about City Gardens. Kids who weren't into punk or hardcore were going to shows at City Gardens because it was close and because it was the place to go.

Jeff "Stress" Davis (Suburban Hoodz): I got jumped, and I got sucker-punched. My buddy, Jay Kilroy, was on the corner side, near the bath-rooms, and I was walking toward him. Someone tapped me on the shoulder, but when I turned around, no one was there. I kept walking. Someone shoved me from behind, and when I turned around he fucking decked me. BLAM! He split my lip open. I was so dazed, but I put my hands up to go at it. The security guard came out of nowhere and com-pletely fucked this dude up. It ended up being someone from Vision's squad who jumped me. They said I went up to two of his girl pals and said, "What's up?" and punched them in the face. I said, "What are you talking about?" That never happened! It was crazy. They stitched my lip up with no anesthesia, and the douchebag doctor shaved the left half of my mustache off and left the right side on! I think he did it on purpose.

Dave Franklin (Vision, vocals): Insted was out here on tour, and the only way that Randy would let them play was if Vision played with them. This is another funny one. After our bass player Ivo—who had been banned for life from City Gardens—was allowed back into the venue to play and see shows, there was a Circle Jerks show. There was a big pit in the front and a smaller pit in the back, by the bar. The place was packed. Some dude was at the edge of the second pit acting like a retard, running into people and not really dancing or anything. He ran into Ivo, who pushed him away, no problem. He runs into Ivo a second time, and Ivo again pushes him away. Third time he comes around, and Ivo drops him. I watched Ivo nail the dude. He was out cold, nose broken, the whole deal. Sure enough, Ivo was banned again.

By that time we had turned Vision into a five-piece. We added an extra guitar player, and, because of that incident, Vin had to play bass. Ivo couldn't play this show, but we already had it booked. We played as a four-piece that night.

Tim McMahon: I remember thinking, *my God, this is it! We have reached our goal and this is the greatest thing ever! I'm up here and the giant City Gardens stage is ALL MINE!* I had watched so many bands play on that stage, and I'd be thinking to myself while I'm watching, *dude, why isn't that singer jumping off of that drum riser?* Now *I'm* the guy up there, and I'm going go off. In your mind, you kind of invent what the perfect show is going to be: the band is going crazy, the crowd is singing along, diving, and going crazy. You've seen videos of it happening and you want to see it happen while you're there. I'm up on that stage and I'm thinking *I'm just going to go fucking nuts. I'm gonna jump around every chance I get. I'm gonna run all over the place. I'm gonna dive off into the crowd... Oh, and I guess I'm gonna sing a little bit, too...* There were no drugs that could make me feel any higher than I was going to feel on that day, on that stage, playing this place where I saw my first shows and where I saw so many great bands.

Dave Franklin: That one really stands out in my mind. I pulled up in the parking lot and saw Lou and Pete Koller from Sick of It All. I was really good friends with those guys, but I didn't know they were coming to the show. They came all the way from Queens and I asked them what they were doing. I thought they came because Insted was in town. They didn't even know those guys. They had actually come to see us!

Tim McMahon: I think we had a pretty good show. At the end of the set, our drummer kicked his kit over. We knocked over the guitars, threw them down, and let them feedback. My thing was, at the end of the shows, I would always dive into the crowd. The guitars are ringing, the drums are knocked over, and I'm gonna do a flip into the crowd. The one security guy, Judd, was standing there yelling, "Man, you fucking guys are never playing here again!" I remember hearing that as I'm up on top of the crowd, and I'm just like, "Fuck yeah! We just did it! We just played City Gardens!" That's how we ended our set. The crowd put me down on the floor and I just walked up, went back up to the dressing room, and that was it.

Dave Franklin: So when we played, the place went so crazy that Lou and Pete were up on the stage to keep people from smashing up the gear. By that time, Randy had given in and was letting people get on stage. In fact—and I don't remember if it was this particular show or not— but at one show we cut our set short for some reason, and everybody was like "You gotta finish!" We hadn't played "Falling Apart" yet, and the place was going nuts, chanting for us and everything. So we start playing it and everybody piles on the stage. Randy was so pissed he came up on stage and pulled the cords out of our amplifiers. He unplugged everybody so it was just the drummer playing the song. It didn't matter, everybody in the crowd sang along until the song was done! We pissed Randy off many times.

ALL/Dickies—July 21, 1991

Scott Reynolds (ALL, vocals): I went upstairs to that little band room that overlooked the stage and saw Leonard from the Dickies up there. He had just gotten off stage and was lying on his back on the floor. He had just thrown up, and rolls his head over and says, "You're gonna die." It was so fucking hot that I went behind the amps and vomited twice during our set. Some girl down front was getting smashed against the front of the stage. There was no barrier in that place, which was great, but you'd have these bodies pushing against the stage all the time… hundreds of them. This girl was on her feet but she had passed out, and I could see her chin was about to catch the stage as she was falling. I thought she was going to die. I pointed to the biggest guys around her that I could find and said, "Make a space, make a space!" so she could get some air. They put their hands on the stage and shoved back about four or five feet, making a little bit of a crack to give her some room. Me and Buckface, our roadie, lifted her up by her armpits onto the stage, set her on a chair in the corner, and threw some water in her face, and she came back to life. It was pretty cool. Nobody meant to squish her… it was just one of those things that happens at shows.

Nirvana—September 27, 1991

Tracy Parks-Pattik (City Gardens employee): I worked there so I saw everybody. I was at that Nirvana show. I was like, "Look, it's Dave [Grohl] from Scream!" I remember thinking how good they were.

Carl Humenik (City Gardens security): When they played, I thought to myself, "These guys are going to be huge someday." Two weeks later, they were!

Benefit for Jim Rollhauser, with MC Henry Rollins—October 2, 1991

Rich O'Brien: This was a benefit for Jim Rollhauser, who was a local guy that got cancer. He was probably the one of the first people we all knew who got sick like that and one of my closest friends to die from a protracted illness. He didn't have insurance. None of us did back then. I remember going down to visit him when he was in the hospital right before he died, and he was delusional. He was talking about driving his car around the city and whatnot. It was so sad.

Randy Now: He was one of the first people to have a video camera, because they were really expensive, and he taped a lot of shows. He offered to tape the shows for the bands and the club. Henry Rollins was in town and he offered to MC the show, and GWAR donated a huge old helmet they had. [GWAR's] Beefcake was really mad that it didn't go for more money.

Mighty Mighty Bosstones—November 2, 1991

Carl Humenik (City Gardens security): Most bands liked having me up on stage, because I would let people get away with stuff and enjoy the show. For this show, I was on the left hand side of the stage between two monitors. [Bosstones lead singer] Dicky Barrett liked to get up close to the crowd and sing. A lot of bands would do that, but they'd put their hand on me as they got close to the edge of the stage. About halfway through this show I'm doing my job—holding people off stage—and he starts to get perturbed with me. Between songs he said to me, "You've got to calm down," and I was like, "I'm just pushing people back." I'm doing my job and he starts putting his hand on me, he's squeezing my shoulder really hard, trying to stop me from pushing people. If he saw someone coming toward me, he'd lean down and try to stop me from keeping them off the stage. He started elbowing me as he's singing, and then at one point, he knocked me from behind with his foot. That's when I stood up, turned around, and was getting ready to deck him. I was like, "Let's go." He stopped and stood back, and I said, "Okay?" I turned around, got back in my position, when someone from the crowd comes up on stage. This guy had been doing it all night. I grabbed him and walked him down the steps, off the stage, and I start taking him through the crowd to the outside door. Dicky jumped on me from behind—he still has the microphone in his hand—and starts strangling me. I have no idea it's him. One of the other bouncers got him off me, and Dicky started yelling stuff like, "You've got to calm down. There's more of us than there are of you!" It's me and the other bouncer standing there against the crowd, and he's attacking me for doing my job, [which is] keeping people off the stage. And he was instigating, because he still had the microphone. Otherwise he would have just been talking to me.

I told [City Gardens owner] Frank, "You have to end this show! The guy just attacked me." They let the show go on and, after it was over, Dicky and two other band members come walking up to me. He does this fake apology type thing. He's got his chest pumped out, and he's like, "I just want to apologize…" He put his hand out, and I looked at him and said, "Fuck you." He gets ready to throw a punch, but another bouncer steps forward and ends it. From that point on, they wouldn't let me work Bosstones shows because they knew I wanted to kill the guy. Years later, my son wanted to go see them, and I was like, "No fucking way."

Gorilla Biscuits/NOFX/ Resurrection—
November 10, 1991

Randy Now: I remember this show because this is when it became clear to me I was getting burnt out. Booking the bands had turned into a job for me, and it wasn't fun anymore. I was working the door for Gorilla Biscuits and NOFX and a lady came running in. She was saying stuff like, "I want to talk to the head of security—where is he? I need to make sure my children are going to be safe. Who is the security chief?" I said, "Ma'am, don't leave your children here if you're worried about their safety. I'm not a babysitter. I'll buy back your tickets and sell them to someone else." And that's exactly what I did. I looked at Fat Mike from NOFX and said, "I hate this job."

GWAR—December 31, 1991

Bob Gorman (GWAR historian): Ween was supposed to open, and we threw a Destroy All Monsters show together. That was kind of embarrassing. If we don't have a show specifically built, we'll do a Destroy All Monsters show. If we write it correctly and actually practice once or twice, they turn out pretty good. We have a bunch of costumes we don't use anymore, so we just work out some choreography and write half-assed story.

Oderus Urungus (GWAR, vocalist): Destroy All Monsters is a name for a particular variety of GWAR show that has got about a 10% success rate, especially when you get people who do not know how to wear the costumes up there.

Some of our guys were editing one of our big movies that got nominated for a Grammy, so we didn't have our whole crew. We had fill-ins who got drunk and ended up stumbling around in monster costumes. It was really embarrassing. Like, "Oh yeah, we'll just get our friends together, it'll be no problem." Well, they all got wasted and it was like, "This is the only night I'll ever be in GWAR, so I'm gonna get fucked up!"

Bob Gorman: We were kind of banking on the fact that Ween was going to open up for us, because they were starting to get bigger and bigger at that point. They decided to play their friend's party instead and totally dissed us. At the end of the show there was a big climax where all these drunk guys in monster costumes kind of collided, then we did the encore, and the lights came up. I remember a couple of kids standing up front as we were cleaning the stage, and the kids were like, "That's it?" I was like, "Oh, man..."

Oderus Urungus: That's where that term "the walk of shame" began for us, because the dressing room was all the way back, at the other end of the club. After the show was over they turned all the lights on, and we had to walk all the way back through the crowd. We just had this feeling that we'd done a really bad show and that people were mad at us. It was horrible. We got dissed by Ween! It was crushing news. The turnout was really light, and we were like, "Oh, don't worry. People will come because Ween is playing." And then we got the news that they weren't. We were just like, "Oh, my god..."

1992

Top Ten Songs in 1992:

1. End of the Road, Boyz II Men

2. Baby Got Back, Sir Mix-a-Lot

3. Jump, Kris Kross

4. Save the Best for Last, Vanessa Williams

5. Baby-Baby-Baby, TLC

6. Tears In Heaven, Eric Clapton

7. My Lovin (You're Never Gonna Get It), En Vogue

8. Under the Bridge, Red Hot Chili Peppers

9. All 4 Love, Color Me Badd

10. Just Another Day, Jon Secada

Shelter/Bouncing Souls—January 5, 1992

Greg Attonito (Bouncing Souls, vocals): I had a big ponytail and cut it off onstage. It was a pretty dramatic move [Laughs]. I wanted to cut my hair and I figured, we got a show coming up, might as well make an event out of it. I always tried to bring some event to the show. Some girl caught the ponytail and had it for a long time, and then she tried to sell it on eBay. I saw that and I was like, "I don't even want to know about this…"

Carl Humenik (City Gardens security): When bands like that came around, when they knew there was going to be a lot of stage diving and they knew there was going to be a lot of people up onstage, they would ask Randy to put a cool punk-rock type person onstage. That was me. Usually, after the first time a band played, they would ask for me. Bands like Shelter, Youth of Today, Fear, Ian MacKaye from Fugazi would say, "That cool guy that was up there last time, can we have him?" because I wasn't a dick. If you were being a dick, you got pushed off, but I wasn't a dick about it, and they liked that. They also liked the fact that I enjoyed the music, and if I knew the song I would sing along.

Shelter used to ask for me, and I would hang out with them after the shows. I used to make fun of them after the shows, because I would get kicked eight or nine times [by a band member] during the show. I'd say, "How can you get up there, preach peace and love and all that, and then start the music and kick the shit out of everybody that comes up?" And they're like, "We're not aiming at people, we're just dancing. If they get in our way, they get in our way." I said, "But you're peace and love, you should know that's going to happen." They would say, "We feel the music." I was like, "All right, that's cool."

Ice-T's Body Count—February 26, 1992

Randy Now: Ice-T was taking a lot of flack at the time because of the song "Cop Killer." I had him on the *Power* tour and no one was there, but he remembered that, and he became friends with Rollins. A lady wrote to me that her son was dying of AIDS that he got from a blood transfusion, and his dying wish was to meet Ice-T. I called his manager and arranged for him to meet this kid. I called the Trenton Times newspaper and they put it on the front page. It relieved the tension in Trenton, at least when he played the show.

There were a lot of times we had to call the police to come to City Gardens. The back parking lot was Ewing Township, and the front was Trenton. Neither of them wanted to come to the place. Straight up, the cops used to sit in their cars and drink beer. You could pay them off with six packs of beer! Obviously not all of them, but there were some. Either way, they never wanted to come when we called because it was such a pain in the ass. They would always ask which parking lot the trouble was in before they came, to see if they could get out of it. They told us they would not help us if there was trouble at the Body Count show because of "Cop Killer." It was a wild, wild night. So many people got hurt. Not because of fighting or riots… it was just a rough show. We just crossed our fingers and waited for it to be over.

Fugazi—April 14, 1992

Ian MacKaye (Fugazi): Trenton and City Gardens are in our movie *Instrument*. All the stuff— like the kids [standing] in the line—a lot of that is City Gardens. If you go back and look at it again, I think toward the end there's this incredibly fogged-out footage where everything has halos around it because of the steam. It's black and white and there's soundtrack, but no audio… that's City Gardens.

Also, there's a scene where we are backstage, and I think [Fugazi guitarist] Guy Picciotto is wearing this crazy outfit he made of an apron and a gourmet [chef's] hat made out of newspaper. There's a quick shot of Randy in all that. We played with Shudder To Think. There were 950 people there, and we made $1600. We paid each of the bands ourselves, out of our end.

Rollins Band — August 22 & 23, 1992

Steven DiLodovico: I went to both shows. Rollins had just gotten a new bass player, Melvin Gibbs. Rollins comes out at the first show and says something to the effect of, "Since we got a new bass player, and he didn't want to be in a cover band, we are only going to do one old song, and after that it's all new material." They launched into "Hard" and killed it. Everything else sucked. Both nights. The best part was riding home the first night. I had gone with my friend Tim, who we called Knobhead. He had brought this girl with him, and she blew him on the way back to Philly. I rode in the backseat while he drove home. While she had her head in his lap, he kept high-fiving me.

Shudder To Think/Jawbox — August 30, 1992

Craig Wedren (Shudder To Think, vocalist): It was the *Get Your Goat* tour. City Gardens was one of our favorite places to play. There were a few places outside of DC that were the first footholds of really memorable shows with hardcore fans, and Trenton was one of those places. I remember in the earlier days of Shudder To Think, we would get so psyched to play at City Gardens. It was essentially a weird, hollowed-out, giant brick of a club in the middle of a parking lot in the middle of nowhere. Whenever we had a show there, we would get unreasonably, indescribably excited because we knew it was just gonna be *on*. The audience was going to be with us, and there was going to be a special and unique communal vibration, for lack of a better word.

For some reason I remember that parking lot and the actual structure of the club. I remember the stage and that it had a killer sound system. It was a little bit raw. It was very Jersey... but not in a cheesy "rock club" kind of way. It was entirely what the bands and the audience would make of it.

Bad Brains — December 26, 1992

Ralph Michal (City Gardens regular): A friend of mine had been stage-diving, and on one pass he landed on his head so bad he thought he had broken his neck. He recovered, but then he realized he had to go to the bathroom. Like *really had to go*. Like, *number two* had to go. He went to the men's room, which was just a toilet... no stall around it or anything. There were skinheads in there, even a couple of girls. People were smoking and doing all kinds of stuff. And there was no toilet paper, and it was 105 degrees. So he just did what he had to do, got dressed, went to the bar to get some napkins, went back to the bathroom, and "dropped trou" to clean up. In front of everyone. He wasn't going to miss the Bad Brains. That's punk rock.

Live/The Semibeings — December 30, 1992

Joseph Baker (The Semibeings): City Gardens was already legendary to us by that point. I didn't believe we'd ever be able to get a gig there. We had made a demo and sent it to Randy, and he loved it. He booked us to open for Live sight unseen, which I thought was crazy! This was right before Live really broke, right after their first album. They had that first hit going, and you knew they were ready to blow up. It was probably when they were recording their second album, the one that became huge.

We got there and Live were doing their soundcheck. For the most part, they seemed like nice enough guys, but they were a bit full of themselves. They had an attitude, which was unlike a lot of the bands that we played with. Bands like Jawbox or Shudder To Think... those guys were down-to-earth and cool. Most of the bands we played with had that real DIY ethic, and there was a real sense of camaraderie. Live just seemed like a bunch of frat-boys who lucked out and scored a hit without really having to struggle. They had a bit of cockiness to them. Not that they weren't nice.

Pat Baker (The Semibeings): During our soundcheck that night, about an hour before the doors opened on what would be our first time playing there, our drummer broke his snare drum head and didn't have a replacement. That's a pretty important part of the drum kit. I believe he asked the drummer in Live if he could borrow his snare drum. I guess, realistically, it made sense that the guy refused. Our drummer had to go to a music store thirty minutes away. At the same time, if they had been a little more down-to-earth, maybe they would have been able to sympathize with somebody in that situation.

Joe Baker: During their soundcheck, they were wearing their regular clothes. Then, when we went on and they went to their backstage room, they changed into their "grunge gear." They put on ski hats and flannel. This, of course, was right after grunge exploded. We were like, "Look at these poseurs!"

Pat Baker: I had forgotten about that! What can you say about that? It was possible that two months before they started to blow up, they could have been totally different people, who knows? They were just starting to get famous and they had that kind of attitude. They definitely didn't treat us like their peers or anything.

Joe Baker: They were one of *those* bands. I was never a fan of theirs to begin with and never really became a fan. They are technically good musicians, and they probably deserved all the success they had, but from our end they just seemed like poseurs. Especially compared to all the other groups we played with.

CHAPTER 11

1993–1994

1993

Top Ten Songs in 1993:

1. I Will Always Love You, Whitney Houston
2. Whoomp! (There It Is), Tag Team
3. (I Can't Help) Falling In Love With You, UB40
4. That's the Way Love Goes, Janet Jackson
5. Freak Me, Silk
6. Weak, SWV
7. If I Ever Fall In Love, Shai
8. Dreamlover, Mariah Carey
9. Rump Shaker, Wreckx-N-Effect
10. Informer, Snow

The melee outside the Leeway show in December 1992 signaled an end to the reign of the white-power skinheads at City Gardens, but the violence continued. Promoter Randy Now and club owners Frank and Patti tired of the grind. The price of event insurance for each show was astronomical thanks to all the lawsuits. Randy recalls that every time a notice came from the Post Office that a certified letter was waiting—and probably another lawsuit—Frank would shake from being so nervous. This sucked all the fun out of putting on shows and as a result, events began to taper off.

Green Day/Shades Apart/Headstrong—
January 17, 1993

Jim Testa (*Jersey Beat* publisher): City Gardens was quite a distance from me, so I didn't get down there that often. I probably became aware of the place in the early '90s. The most distinct show I remember was Green Day. They played there twice: the last show of their last tour when they were on Lookout Records and at the beginning of the *Dookie* tour, after they were on [record label] Reprise. The reason I remember so distinctly is because I interviewed [Green Day bassist] Mike Dirnt right at the time they were putting *Dookie* together. It wasn't out yet, and everyone in the punk scene was still talking about how Green Day had signed to a major label. No one knew, least of all Warner Bros [the parent company of Reprise], that they were going to sell eight million records. They were already selling 50,000 or 60,000 on Lookout, so everyone was guessing 100,000 or maybe 200,000.

I interviewed Mike Dirnt, who I knew because he had recorded with Screeching Weasel… through that connection, and because I knew the people at Lookout. Once *Dookie* started selling 8 bazillion records, the band reflexively shut down. They stopped doing interviews unless you were *Rolling Stone* or MTV, because everybody in the world was trying to interview them. I already had this interview with Mike in the can, and it wound up getting re-printed in two national magazines. I was in the right place at the right time.

Jamie Davis (City Gardens regular): By this time, in '93, people were just… it was a different crowd. Me and Kyle, *(Ed. - who's black, which does have something to do with the story)* were driving up there, and we see the people lined up. This is how you could tell it was a different crowd. Any other time we would line up and wrap around the building or to that back parking lot. This was the only show most of these people had been to, so the line went straight back, out into the street. They didn't even know how to line up! We drive up, me and Kyle, and we're blasting Skrewdriver and sieg-heiling people as we went past… as a joke. We cleared the line. We just drove right through it. There were girls and thirty-year-old emo kids diving to get out of the way, looking back at this black guy sieg-heiling.

Timmy Chunks (Token Entry/Headstrong, vocals): Headstrong actually opened that show. At the time I was singing for them. I was also working at City Gardens, and Randy asked if we wanted to open for Green Day. At that point I had only heard the name of the band. I had never heard them. When you're in a band and someone asks you if you want to play a show, you play it. It doesn't matter who it is. So I told Randy, yeah, we definitely wanted to play it. We showed up, we went on and did our show. The place was packed. Afterwards, Mike Dirnt comes up and says, "Hey, great show guys!" and gives me a shirt. I thought it was really cool, and I said, "Thanks!"

Randy Now: Billy Joe said into the mic, "We've never played for so many people before!" He told me this was their first show ever with monitors! [Green Day drummer] Tre Cool kissed me on the cheek after they sold, like, $3000 in t-shirts. Up until then they did $400–$500 tops, and that was probably back home in California. These were five-dollar t-shirts!

Timmy Chunks: They go on stage, the place is packed, and my jaw dropped. I was like, "How come I haven't heard these guys?!" I could not believe how amazing they were. I had no idea.

Alex Franklin (City Gardens regular): [City Gardens regular] Kung Fu Lou got into a whole thing with Green Day. Green Day played and we were a bunch of goons. We were hardcore kids and we wanted to go nuts. We were there to have a good time and watch some bands play, but we were also rowdy dudes. Towards the front of the club Lou was dancing. The people at the show really didn't understand the way we danced. They thought we were assholes. Looking back on it, we probably were. It might not have been appropriate, but it is what it is. Everybody was dancing and doing their thing, and then a fight breaks out towards the front. You know how we were: if someone hits us, we're going to hit them back. So that breaks out and Billie Joe stops playing. He points at Lou and says, "You! You! That's bullshit! What you're doing is fucked up!" All the hardcore kids took offense to it. It was just one of those misunderstandings; fights happen at shows. What do you expect? It turned into a yelling match between members of the crowd and Billie Joe. There were threats abounding that Billie Joe was going to get beat up. Nothing ever came of it.

Randy Now: And then the band appropriately, or inappropriately, trashed the dressing room. That's when I knew they were going to be big, after they trashed the dressing room. The shit heads!

Mike Dirnt (Green Day, bassist): The night we sold out City Gardens, and we realized we could sell out a place that held over a thousand people. When we went back home to Berkeley, we seriously sat down and started talking about *where do we go from here?*

Jim Testa: That show woke them up to the fact that they weren't this little band that played [San Francisco club] Gilman Street anymore. That's why that always stood out in my memory.

Ned's Atomic Dustbin — January 20, 1993

Timmy Chunks (Token Entry, vocals/City Gardens stage manager): That was a really cool show. They were fucking great. That was the first time I ever ate lasagna. I hadn't had anything to eat for two days. I had no real job. I was only working at City Gardens once every other week or something. They had lasagna. I guess it was in their rider or something, and I was so hungry I snuck some of it.

Fear — January 24, 1993

Travis Nelson (Inspector 7, vocals): I guess it was around '92 or so when the Nazis stopped coming around. Except for what I like to call their "last stand" show, when they came to see Fear.

Rich O'Brien: That was the most violent show I can remember. Fear would always bring a large amount of skinheads to their shows. All these Atlantic City skinheads showed up. They called themselves the AC Skins, but they were from all over. I swear there were at least 100 people fighting at that show. And so we, the bouncers, fought too. When I was searching people at the door, I confiscated more weapons than at any other show. Brass knuckles, knives, a lot of spikes, box cutters, people with rolls of quarters in their pockets that they said they were going to pay the cover [entry fee] with.

Travis Nelson: We hadn't seen the AC Skins in a year or two. They stopped coming because every time they would come, they'd get fucked up. So, Fear is playing, and it's me, Jamie Davis, Kyle, and a bunch of Philly guys. Some of the newer skins in Trenton were there, and some of the newer punks. The Nazis must have networked and coordinated, because everyone was there. All the AC Skins and a whole lot of eastern Pennsylvania skins… they came out in force. I'm looking around, and there were plenty of guys who, if shit went down, would fight. But they had numbers. It was mostly a bunch of punk kids, but still… there were a lot of [skinheads].

Jamie Davis (City Gardens regular): The Nazis did fuck with Kyle, who is black. Then a bunch of people got into a fight with them.

Tony Rettman (author/City Gardens regular): I thought that whole white-power skinhead thing had faded away by the '90s, and it was replaced by this thugish urban-wannabe vibe of hardcore. That had come in with the baggy pants and the kickboxing moves. When all those AC guys walked in, I was like, "Skinheads? Do they still make those?" It was like guys walking in with fucking powdered wigs on or something. They showed up and started sieg-heiling, and I thought "Has anyone told these guys that this whole thing is over? Do they live in a time capsule in Atlantic City?" I was mesmerized.

Travis Nelson: I know Randy was nervous. He was saying stuff like, "I wonder if I give them their money back if they would leave?" And I'm like, "Um, I doubt it!"

Rich O'Brien: There was black kid named Lester at the show. There were also about 75 to 100 skinheads, and some of them started picking on Lester, who was skinny and never hurt anybody. Real thin. The skinheads jumped Lester in the pit, and all the regulars turned on the AC Skins. The regulars weren't going to put up with this crap… someone from outside picking on one of them. All the regulars knew the security guys, and they would help us out. They usually had our backs and we had theirs. A couple times I got sucker punched at a show, and some of the regular patrons jumped in and beat the crap out the guy who punched me.

Travis Nelson: Everything was generally cool at first. When me and Kyle were in the pit we would feel "sneaks," these little sucker punches to our backs and shit. I think it was after the set when it finally broke out. I don't even know how it started. I remember thinking, "Oh wow, we got through the show and nothing happened. And there's a fucking army of Nazis here." That's when all hell broke loose. I mean it *broke loose*.

Rich O'Brien: It was almost like a gang war. It was unequivocally the biggest fight at the club. It was outside skinheads on one side, and the regulars and security on the other. There were chairs flying, there were tables flying, and the band's playing. Everyone who was there—everyone—was rolling around fighting. It was nasty. The police wouldn't come, so we didn't even bother to call.

Travis Nelson: Everyone seemed to be fighting everyone. I mean, there were motherfuckers there who weren't skinheads. They were straight-up white supremacists. Usually the Nazis were heavily outnumbered, but for some reason, this night, there was a shitload of them. The bouncers were throwing out people who were fighting, but then they realized there was still a shitload of Nazis inside. They weren't going to be able to control this fucking situation by themselves.

Rich O'Brien: There was easily 100 people fighting, and it took a while to break it up. The band stopped playing, and Fear was up on stage watching the action.

Jamie Davis: We actually got thrown out, but then they let us back in. That was the only time the bouncers at City Gardens had ever said, "We want you back in there because we don't know what to do!"

Tony Rettman: I watched an explosion of bodies come tumbling out that side door, people fighting and punching. There was one kid—I guess he was trying to look cool—he picked up one of those plastic chairs that were sitting around. They were like those old plastic chairs you had in your high school cafeteria. He picked it up like he was going to hurl it or something, but he brought it outside instead. I thought to myself, "He's probably going to sit down in that chair and watch the fight."

Rich O'Brien: The lights went up, and we pushed out the AC Skins that were fighting. Once they got thrown out, they didn't have the numbers to be a force anymore, so they just left on their own. Then Fear just finished their set.

Henry Rollins/Don Bajema (spoken word)— February 17, 1993

Steven DiLodovico (author/City Gardens regular): This was easily one of my favorite nights at City Gardens. I rode to Trenton with a friend of mine. By this time I had seen Rollins do his spoken word several times over and was a big fan. There was a HUGE turnout, especially for a spoken word gig. Rollins was at the height of his popularity by then, so a lot of kids came to check him out. Then this Don Bajema guy comes out. I wasn't really paying attention, until he starts to read excerpts from his book *Boy in the Air* which Rollins had released on his 2.13.61 Publications. He started reading this piece entitled, "Blacktop," and it fucking blew me away. It was really powerful. Everything Bajema read or wrote sucked me in, and as I learned more about his life, I was more drawn in. This guy was the real deal, and a fantastic writer. To this day he is still one of my favorite authors.

Don Bajema (author): Henry was never anything but a gentleman. Always eager to learn… curious, deeply appreciative, and a great talent. A very shamanistic type of man.

The show was in the winter, and it was really, really cold. Henry and I had dinner at a diner down the road, at a place I believe he always ate when he was there. When we got to City Gardens, it was dark and rainy, and there was a line of shivering kids—to me, kids. Most of them were my oldest daughter's age at the time—a long line of these hipsters lined against a concrete bunker off the highway. I remarked to Henry about it, and he said, "They're tough as hell out here." As usual for Henry, we got there very early. We had quite awhile before we were to go on, and the hall was empty. As the minutes turned to an hour, I asked the guy at the venue if we could let them in a little early. And they did. Everyone in winter gear, home-invasion hats, and boots, and they were such great people. Really warm and friendly. But Henry also said, "If they start fighting, break out Don. It gets wild in here."

When I told Henry they should open the doors early, he smiled and said, "This is the toughest audience in the world. They're fine, but confine them too long they'll go crazy." I could see that from the squint in their eyes and the take-no-shit-or-prisoners looks on their faces, but beneath it, they were the nicest, coolest kids. I've thought about that show many times.

Steven DiLodovico: After Bajema read, everyone was waiting for Rollins. The place filled up fast, and soon we were all squashed in, like it was a hardcore show or something. Rollins came out, and he was real low-key. He invited a bunch of us to sit up on the stage next to him so we could make some room for everyone else. Before the words were even out of his mouth, I was scrambling up the stage. I sat less than two feet from him. I had worn a Morrissey shirt, and he ragged on me all night.

Quicksand/Black Train Jack—February 27, 1993

Rob Vitale (Black Train Jack, vocalist): I still have the hat that I stole from a security guard at that show. It's one of those reflective hats that says "Security" on it. I stole it right off the guy's head. I have a chair from the place that I stole too. It was this chair that was always backstage, and one night—I don't even know why—we decided to steal it. In the backstage area, all the couches were dug out. They had big holes and springs sticking out, and everybody had tagged up the wall. It was like being backstage at CBGB except it was in Jersey. I don't know why we stole the chair, because afterwards I had no place to sit. But, being the dicks that we were, we stole it. Somehow it ended up in our practice space, and to this day I still have it in storage with some of our equipment.

I always loved playing there. We came back from Europe, and one of our first shows was at City Gardens. It was sold out. We were like, "Holy shit, all these kids are here to see *us!*" I think that was the show where [bassist] Brian kicked me out into the crowd, that fucker. I was bent over singing, and he snuck up behind and kicked me right into the audience.

Breakdown/Confusion/Hard Response/Kurbjaw— March 21 1993

Jeff Perlin (Breakdown, vocals): At the time, well, even now, we didn't do riders. But back then everything was on a good faith. Everybody in the hardcore scene kind of knows each other, and you try not to rip each other off. We never really had too many problems with that. We played, and there were a lot of people there. The guy who booked the show was somebody we knew. Since it was a long time ago, it's water under the bridge and I don't want to bring up any dirty laundry, but it was kind of disappointing.

Travis Nelson (Inspector 7, vocals): Randy Now decided to give Alex Franklin and myself a chance to dabble in the wonderful world of show promotion. He had us put together the lineup, book the bands, and everything. As you can see, the lineup was amazing, at least in my humble opinion. Powermove was booked, but they cancelled. They were replaced by Kurbjaw, Lou DiCarolis' band at the time.

Jeff Perlin: We were supposed to get paid something like $250, but at the end of the show, the guy was like, "Yeah, I can't really give you any money. We didn't really make any money tonight." This wasn't anyone connected with City Gardens. It was somebody else. Basically, it was somebody we knew from another band who had booked the show. He was giving us the excuses, "There weren't enough people here, we didn't make enough money, etc." Now, there were plenty of people there. So we were like, "Nah, you gotta pay us. No matter what, you made the agreement with us, and you have to pay us." We had a couple of band practices, and gas and tolls, that's $250 right there. It's like beer money, you know?

Tony Triano (Hard Response, vocals): There was a beef about money that night. The turn-out was lousy, and Jeff wanted his guarantee. It did get out of hand, as it did back then. Cops, parking lot antics, shit like that… I had fun though. We didn't get paid either, but who cares? It was punk rock, ya know…

Travis Nelson: Nonetheless, the result was a very light turnout. Randy was getting surrounded, harassed, and threatened by Breakdown. I remember Jeff Perlin saying, "Give us our money, you fuckin' nerd!" There was a "miscommunication" over their guarantee, and their drummer, Joe Farley, was escorted out by the Trenton police.

Jeff Perlin: So it started getting heated, and some of the bouncers got called over. Next thing I know there's a circle of bouncers around us. We started saying, "This is BS, and we want to get paid." Next thing you know, the cops are there. We tell them, "Yeah, we just played a show, we're supposed to get paid, and the guy's refusing to pay us." The cop said, "Do you have a contract?" And, of course, we didn't. He said, "Well then, you're screwed."

Our drummer, Joe Farley—who was the [nicest] guy—he lifts one finger up, sort of to say, "Wait one second here," and [moments later], the dude was hog-tied on the floor. Like BANG! Hog-tied. They lifted him up, pulled him out the door, and put him in the police van. We're still inside and the cops are explaining, "Well, if you don't have a contract you can't get paid." There was nothing we could do about it.

I had this weird feeling, so I went out to where they had taken Joe. I go up to the van, and these two cops look at me and walk away. Joe's like, "Dude, you just saved me. Those guys were going to beat the crap out of me!" We had to bail him out of jail. That was our fun, exciting experience in Trenton. I don't think Randy was involved in any of this. It was just the dude who booked the show. It was a really good show… the kids went off, they knew all the songs, and everybody had a great time. It just sucked that it ended up like that. But that's part of playing in a band… you're going to go through experiences like that.

Travis Nelson: So yeah… that was our first and last production at City Gardens.

Fugazi—August 17 & 18, 1993

Ian MacKaye (Fugazi): The next time we came, we did two nights: August 17th and 18th, 1993. We had 1000 people both nights, and we made $1000 a night. We made less because I think we paid each of the bands out of our end. I think we paid them $400 each.

In the early days of Fugazi, we were able to play in unorthodox rooms or venues. We did weird little gigs. We weren't playing in "rock clubs," but the crowds started becoming so substantial that the band felt a responsibility to make sure, if we were drawing that many people, we had a room that not only safe for the people but also safe for the show. It doesn't do any good to book a show that will be shut down by the police. You can do a show with a hundred people or two hundred people under the radar. But when you get into the thousands, it's difficult. The police start saying, "Hey, what's going on? Ok, show's over."

That happened to us a number of times early on, and we thought, "You know what? From now on we've got to do rooms that are not going to get shut down." New Jersey was somewhat notorious for... head-knocking. The kids were pretty radical or just angry. They were the people who wanted to see Fugazi, and they're our people, so we decided, "We're going to give this a shot." The shows were intense and always, always super-hot. We always made them turn the air conditioning off. That's just our way. You've got to sweat. Those shows were high-compression gigs... if you were in there, you were working with us.

I never had any beef with the business aspect. It was always straight-up, and Randy was a good dude. He was a mailman. I also remember he introduced me to Spike Jones. Not the director, the [comedian] from the '40's and '50s... We were in Randy's apartment, and he said, "You've got to check out Spike Jones." We're like, "What?" He put [a video] on, and we spent all night watching it. He sent me—and I still have it— a VHS tape of *The Spike Jones Show*.

Rollins Band—October 5, 1993

Henry Rollins: October 5th, 1993 was the last time we played there. We were testing new material right before we were ready to record.

Toward the end [of Randy's time at City Gardens], it was always Randy vs. Tut. Tut didn't want bands in there. All the staffers, without exception, were cool to me, so I never had any problems. I remember Randy was struggling to keep himself in that place, and it was always a money thing. Tut really liked those Thursday [dance] nights. They played records and the place was packed, and the bar rocked. When we were in town, [Rollins Band members] Andrew and Sim would go there, because all their friends would be there. I don't know if I ever went for those things. I doubt it. I'd probably be furiously writing, and too angry and self-involved, to hang out like that. I probably missed out on a lot of fun.

[The crowds] were never violent to me. In fact, they were always appreciative. Black Flag, the spoken words shows, or the Rollins Band. I never had a bad night where the band bombed or I bombed alone onstage. The people were always receptive. With Black Flag, we played there so often we were almost locals, and with Rollins Band, people knew we were a Trenton-based band. So, we were an international touring act that made their home in Trenton, and people were quite into that, I think. People would see me around town and be like, "What are you doing here?" and I'd say I was living down by the river. I'd take that little train out to Princeton, and we'd all go the Princeton Record Exchange, we'd eat at the Crystal Diner, and go to shows at City Gardens.

Randy was always really good to us. He booked the first Rollins Band tour. He was always extremely straight ahead and helped us a lot.

I never heard anything bad about [City Gardens]. I know local bands had a problem with Randy and the politics of being the opening band for the headlining act. That was local political subterfuge. There was always someone griping. City Gardens was the place where everybody played, and I never heard any stories like *fuck City Gardens*. Everybody played there, and if those walls could talk... Iggy, the Ramones, everybody...

ALL/Sloppy Seconds/Sleeper—October 24, 1993
(Milo fills in for ailing Chad Price)

Milo Aukerman (Descendents, vocalist): This show I have more memories of than anything else. I probably have more memory of it because it was a one-off thing. It wasn't part of a tour where you're brain dead or where you're barely waking up in time to jump on stage.

This show was exciting because I had given up music for several years, and [drummer] Bill Stevenson called me out of the blue. He told me that [ALL's lead singer] Chad was sick, and how would I feel about [filling in] for one show. I liked the whole spur-of-the-moment quality of it... the novelty of it. I had left the band behind and was trying to do science, and science kind of sucked at that point. I needed the diversion, even if it was just an hour-long diversion. It seemed whacky enough to be fun, and it was fun to come back to City Gardens. It was like, "Ahh, back in my element." Driving up to the club, I thought, "Yeah, here we are in the seedy part of town. Exactly where you'd expect a punk-rock club to be." It felt so comfortable.

Amy Yates Wuelfing: I was set up to interview ALL that day, and, because Milo was in and out so fast, I didn't get to speak to him. I was so excited about it being a Descendents reunion, and I said to [ALL's bassist] Karl Alvarez, "This is a really big deal." This was before the internet and cell phones, so you couldn't call people and tell them what was happening. You were either there or you weren't.

Carl Humenik (City Gardens security): I walked in, and another security guys says, "Milo's coming." I thought he meant Milo was coming to watch the show. But he said, "No, Milo's going to sing," and I was like, "AAAAHHHH!!!" So I got on the pay phone and called a whole bunch of my friends. I spent $10 calling people.

Jamie Davis: This was back when they still had pay phones. I was calling everyone in Philly and telling them, "You better get down here!" Nobody was around!

Jeremy Weiss (City Gardens regular): I was going to school at the University of Pittsburgh. I was great friends with the guys in Serpico, who were called Sleeper back then. They were playing one night at City Gardens with ALL. From City Gardens, it's a four-hour drive to Pittsburgh, and it's a Sunday night. I wasn't going to go to the show. My friend John calls me and says, "You're not going back to school tonight." And I said, "John, I love your band. You know damn well I want to be there, and I really like ALL, but I got to go back to school." He said, "No, you're not. You're butt is coming down to City Gardens. Tonight." I said, "I'm not," and all he said was, "If you don't come to City Gardens tonight, you will *never* forgive yourself." Nothing else—no further information. I took it on faith. I told my parents I was going back to college, but I drove down to City Gardens.

After the show, I drove back to school and I got to Pitt at 7:30 in the morning, but not before seeing a band that swore up and down that they would never reunite. Now, that seems like a silly notion, because they subsequently have years later.

Jamie Davis (City Gardens regular): The only reason I went to that show was because on Sundays I would go to see my grandmother in Levittown, PA. I was thinking, "Ah, I'll drive over to City Gardens and see if anyone is outside." I would do that on any random day. So I go over there and talked to one of the bouncers, who was like, "You are going to want to go to this show." And I'm like, "Eh, I don't like ALL. I'm really not a fan." And he said, "No, they got Milo. The other dude's sick and Milo's doing a reunion." And I'm like, "What?!" And then I found out Sloppy Seconds was playing, too. They weren't even on the bill. No one ever mentions that that they played. They might have played without even being announced.

Jeremy Weiss: The thing was, when I got to the show [ALL's singer] Chad was in the parking lot. I saw him, and I didn't understand what my friend was telling me. He had been sworn to absolute secrecy. He was good friends with Bill Stevenson, and they made him swear up and down that he wouldn't tell. They thought if it got out, even for a day, that it would kill ALL's momentum, and everyone would be wondering if Milo was coming back to sing for the band for good. So they really wanted to sneak it in, just one time, and it was only because Chad Price had a very severe throat infection and could hardly talk.

Milo Aukerman: Bill booked me a quick flight and I got there, and the big question was, what songs do we do? Do we do Descendents songs or do we do ALL songs? I wanted to do some ALL songs, just because I knew that the band would probably prefer ALL songs. We ended up doing 60/40, like 60% Descendents, 40% ALL. That was fine, except that some of those ALL songs I had to learn on the fly. When they picked me up at the airport, I requested lyrics from some of the other guys in the band, and I tried to memorize them as best as I could. [It turns out] I remembered the ALL songs but forgot the lyrics to a Descendents song. Those receded further into my memory. ALL had been playing for six or seven years, and they were my favorite band, so I knew their lyrics better than my own.

I remember attempting to sing [the ALL song] "Shreen" and totally failing. A very majestic sort of failure, where I had no hope of hitting the right notes and then realizing why Chad was their singer and not me... because he could do it justice and I couldn't.

I'm not sure when the buzz started, but there was some buzz. Like, "Oh, isn't that Milo? What's he doing here?" By the time I got on stage, a lot of people had figured it out and started saying my name. I thought, "How do they know"? We think we're pulling the wool over the crowd's eyes, but they're totally on to it. I said something like, "Needless to say, this is not the normal ALL lineup, and we're doing something a little different tonight."

Jeremy Weiss: My best friend Andy and I go right up to the stage, and it's packed. We're standing there, dead center, right at the stage like nerds, waiting for 20 minutes for ALL to come out. Out of nowhere, Milo Aukerman walks on stage.

Milo Aukerman: In some respect, it helped reignite my desire to keep doing it, and, of course, a few years later we made a record. If Bill hadn't called me—I can't say for certain—but if he hadn't called me and set this show up, we might not have gotten back together again in '96. Each of these little events reminds me how much fun it is, how much getting up on stage can be a blast, and I think that event reignited something that kept the ball rolling for further music in '96 and 2002.

I'm sure Bill didn't know how much I was hating science. We were sporadically in touch at that time. Whenever ALL played [nearby], I was there, and I used those opportunities to catch up. I'm not sure whether his motivation was, "Oh, we need a singer. Let's get Milo," or whether he was thinking, "Maybe this is a way of getting Milo back in the fold a little bit." I'm guessing it was the former. Whether he knew it or not, Bill was reigniting my need to rock. The band has had its ups and downs, and I've left and I've come back, but it's always been predicated on the need to rock and that night, obviously, I felt pretty good being back on stage.

Scott Foster (1124 Records): There was a rumor that Milo was going to be there and Dave Smalley, who was in the opening band Down By Law, was going to sing a few songs, but he didn't sing anything with them. One of the coolest parts of that show was, when they finished their set, they all switched instruments. Bill got on guitar, and Steven got on the drums, and they did about four Black Flag songs. It was fucking awesome!

Jamie Davis: You could see all these new kids who didn't even know the Descendents. They actually wanted to see ALL! I was like, "Are you nuts? What the hell do you care about ALL songs when the Descendents are playing?" These people were only into ALL because they didn't know the Descendents.

Amy Yates Wuelfing: Everyone felt privileged to be witnessing this. But Karl Alvarez was very laid back about it, and he said—and this is a direct quote—"What you have to understand is, back when we were the Descendents, not that many people were into us. People thought we were sexist, people thought that [the album] *All* was noisy, chaotic heavy metal. People were yelling, 'You suck!' back when we were touring as the Descendents." People forget that these bands that are legendary now weren't that popular at the time and had to put up with a lot of adversity.

Milo Aukerman: At this show, I was almost 31 years old. The early songs were initially about other people, and then they start becoming about us, you know? Like, "I Don't Want To Grow Up." It's one of those things where, when you're 20 you can say that with a straight face, and then when you're 50 you go, "Well, I still don't want to grow up. However, I have."

Jeremy Weiss: After they finished everyone was going so berserk, and then they switched instruments and played Black Flag's "Nervous Breakdown." It was absolutely incredible. It was easily one of my favorite nights.

Milo Aukerman: We still do those songs live. For me, one of the main reasons I keep doing music is to try to stay young, to keep that youthful energy, so when I'm singing a song like "When I Get Old," it's a bit of denial. I'm old, right? The song is a theme for my life in terms of denying the aging process. Physically, our bodies are falling apart... my body is falling apart... but if we are in denial about the other part of it, then maybe you can still have some fun. Maybe you can still pretend like you're not one foot in the grave. People think about denial as being a bad thing; but I think, in this case, denial is a good thing. You're saying, "No, I refuse to get old!"

What we do now is, rather than tour, we book shows and fly in. We may fly in and play one or two or three shows in a row, but we're never actually on tour. The notion of a tour bus, a tour van, doesn't even enter into the equation. If I'm playing someplace local where we can drive, then [my kids] will come. We played Jones Beach opening for Sublime and drove up with the kids to make weekend of it. I like to have the kids come because they like to get on stage with me. We have the "All-O-Gistics" song with the Ten Commandments thing, and they participate in that. They read the commandments off the sign, and it gets a good response because they mess it up in funny ways. Like my daughter, instead of saying, "Thou shalt not partake of decaf," she said, "Thou shalt not partake of death." When she came out with that one, everyone doubled over laughing. And then we thought about it and realized, *no, that's a good one.* Thou shalt not partake of death! We need to stay alive! She gave us a new commandment.

There are some lyrics, in the light of [today], that might make you say, "Okay, that was written by me when I was 17. Do I still feel that way?" I've tried to modify some lyrics. A song like "Loser," which I didn't actually write... I look at the lyrics now and say, "I need to change some of these," and I have. But I'm waiting for that point when [my kids] have questions about [certain song lyrics]. Then I gotta deal with it as best I can. It's tough because I'm trying to transport myself back into my teenage years. I enjoyed those years. But those years were perhaps not politically correct. You look in the rearview mirror, and you have to place these lyrics in the context of the time. The only time it gets dicey is when we're still playing live. Then I have to transport myself back a 17-year-old guy, because if I were to think about it too much, it's a little weird. A song like "Pervert" or whatever… it's fun to play. It's a barn-burner punk-rock song, and so we do it, but the lyrics … Well, it's not sexist, but it's got some crudity to it. So you just have to say, "Well, I'm okay with being crude."

Killing Time/Vision/Dandelion—December 12 1993

Carl Porcaro: (Killing Time, guitarist): Randy tried to charge us once for people stagediving at a show. There was a time when—and I know this happens everywhere and we understand this—it seemed like every show you played the promoters were going crazy about stopping the kids from stagediving. I am sure it coincided with some tragedy. We all remember kids who got badly hurt, or in some cases died, from stage-diving. Randy, as a result of something that had happened there, initiated this rule where the bands would get charged money for each stage dive… it's fucking hilarious. I wonder if he'll even remember that shit happened.

Randy Now: That never happened. The most logical thing I could think of was maybe a band invited people up to jump off after we had said DON'T, and I took money away from them. You know, this whole stage diving thing is like, "Hey, can I come over you house and jump up and down on your furniture? Can I jump up and down on the hood of your car? Can I break something that's yours?" We let kids stage dive for years at dozens— if not hundreds— of shows until, as the saying goes, someone got their eye poked out. That's what started happening: Kids were getting seriously hurt, and we were getting sued by parents, over and over. It got so bad that when a certified notice came in the mail, those yellow notices that you have to sign—I think they are pink now—we were afraid to open it.

Carl Porcaro: With Killing Time, we never made a huge deal about money in the early days. We were about playing as many shows as possible anywhere we could. But there was this one gig at City Gardens, this gig with Dandelion in December of '93, where we were getting a reasonably good amount of money, and we were really psyched. And then [Randy] had this rule about stagediving. So immediately, from the first song, someone is diving and this bouncer, the guy from Crucial Youth [Jim Norton], is doing the tally! He's actually counting stage divers one by one!

Randy Now: The story about getting Jim Norton to count stage divers… that's ridiculous.

Jim Norton (City Gardens bouncer/stage manager): If that show was in December '93, then it definitely was not me. In '93 I was on tour throughout all of December. I came home from Montreal on the night of the 23rd. I was home for Christmas Eve and Christmas Day. I had to get glasses on the 26th, and I flew out on the 27th. It was not me.

Carl Porcaro: Norton's counting the number of dives so Randy could charge us for them later! It was a great show, too. Everything was cool. Afterwards we go back to get paid by Randy, and he fucking tells us that we're not getting paid, that we used up all our money on stage dives! Dude, it was hysterical! It would have been a decent payday for a hardcore band in the early '90s.

Dave Franklin (Vision, vocals): I remember the [stagediver fine] policy. There was a time when Vision was guaranteed $700, which for us was a lot of money, and I think we ended up with $100 because there were six stage dives. And it was all by people who came with us, all the crew guys! Maybe even a couple by me. I don't know if I got docked for stagediving or not! The policy had been going on for a while. The cool thing about City Gardens was there was never a barricade. You were pressed right up against the stage, and all you had to do was pull yourself up. If it was a crowd-participation thing, [club management] didn't give you a hard time. But if it was the guys in the band diving into the crowd, or your crew members, or some of your friends, then you got waffled $100 per dive.

Carl Porcaro: The band would get charged. I don't remember the exact amount with Randy, but, yeah, he was trying to charge us per stage dive! So we start playing and, of course, fucking immediately, like the first song, somebody's on stage and they do a stage dive. City Gardens was the real deal for stagediving, too. It was a really high stage. You'd get some serious air, you know?

Jim Norton: That sounds very Randy. Right there, for better and worse, that is *very* Randy. I think he realized, as he was saying things to these bands like, "I'm going to charge you $100 per dive" that there was no way he was going to be able to make it stick. If he did actually try to make it stick, they would probably have set his car on fire. At the very least someone was going to mysteriously disappear from the parking lot, and word's going to get around real fast. There are definitely promoters who do things like that, but that was not Randy's style.

Roger Miret (Agnostic Front, vocals): I do remember that "no stagediving" rule. I think Randy might have tried to charge us, too. Agnostic Front shows were always nuts, and Randy would always get on our case about our guys diving. The shows were *always* nuts… plenty of punching people, kicking people… one of things I was notorious for was swinging the mic and hitting people in the head. I used to jump off stage and walk on top of the crowd. That was another one of my things. I was always a maniac up on that stage. We never paid it, though. I mean, it's a hardcore show.

Dave Franklin: The bands only got wacked with the penalty if they were the ones diving. If the people diving were in the crowd, and not part of your crew or part of the band and got up there and did it on their own, you weren't responsible for it because you had no control over it. There was one night where the show was so great and the crowd was so pumped that we didn't care about losing the money. Nobody in the band even gave a shit. As a matter of fact, I think that three or four of our stage dives were from the band members. Everybody except the drummer, and we got docked $500. I guess I thought that this was common knowledge. A lot of it, too, wasn't until the later days of City Gardens, like the '92, '93, '94 era, when all the lawsuits started happening. I guess the way they thought they could control it was by docking everybody's pay. Most of the bands didn't give a shit, because when you were in the heat of the moment and it was off the chain, everybody was like, "Let's GO, man!"

Jim Norton: While I was definitely not involved with the $100 per band-member fee, I could see [why Randy might implement the policy]. But, again, he booked the show. There's going to be 400 people there paying ten bucks a head, he still looked at that and said, "Okay."

Randy Now: My Saturn turned into an ambulance for taking kids over to the hospital, which luckily was two blocks away. It was getting to be every show that someone was hurt bad. You know these bands, maybe they are talking about one or two shows they played or attended, but hey, I was at EVERY SHOW, EVERY WEEK, and I'm telling you, kids were breaking bones. One guy laid on the floor paralyzed until an ambulance and EMTs came and literally scooped him up. A few times I would say I was going to cut a bands pay, but I usually gave them what they were originally told, it was sometimes said to just keep them in order during their time there. I remember more times giving bands bonuses, and I mean BIG bonuses. I loved Shelter, and, as a quasi-1960s era Hare Krishna fan, I gave Ray [Cappo] and John a few hundred dollars extra. I would tell them to give it to the temple. We always shared when the night was a home run at the door.

Carl Porcaro: Anthony [Comunale, vocalist for Killing Time] was not having it. He went fucking crazy back there! It was just me, Randy, and Anthony. At one point Anthony was up on the guy's desk screaming about how we were not going to get charged and we were going to get every cent of our money! And you know what? We got paid! We walked out of there with everything we were supposed to get. I think in the face of such a tremendous argument, Randy realized he was being ridiculous. I'm sure he got away with charging some band somewhere along the lines. I guess we caught him on a particularly bad week and he was trying to do something about it.

Anthony Comunale (Killing Time, vocalist): I don't know what Randy is saying, because he definitely tried to charge us. He said our roadies were stage diving, which was true. Randy didn't want to pay us, so I was jumping on his desk, giving examples of stage dives, and he thought I was nuts. Eventually we settled it and everything was fine. City Gardens also had those silly "no flight jackets or Doc Martens" rules. It was just fashion. Give me a break.

Marc Wasserman (Bigger Thomas, bassist): Randy instituted the infamous "No Doc Martens" policy, which pissed a lot of skinheads off. Looking back on it, it was actually a really clever way to deal with that. You know, you could wear anything but Doc Martens, and even a lot of the S.H.A.R.P skinheads were pissed off. That was one of those things where Randy was forced to come up with a creative way to deal with a problem that, potentially, could have shut the club down, because there was a lot of violence.

Anthony Comunale: But, I guess Randy had a point. My cousin Mike is paralyzed from someone stagediving on him. Randy was just being cautious, and I respect that. Overall, his heart was in the right place.

1994

Top Ten Songs in 1994:

1. The Sign, Ace Of Base

2. I Swear, All-4-One

3. I'll Make Love to You, Boyz II Men

4. The Power of Love, Celine Dion

5. Hero, Mariah Carey

6. Stay (I Missed You), Lisa Loeb and Nine Stories

7. Breathe Again, Toni Braxton

8. All for Love, Bryan Adams, Rod Stewart, and Sting

9. All That She Wants, Ace Of Base

10. Don't Turn Around, Ace Of Base

As the difficulties from putting on shows worsened, Randy Now lost the drive he once had, and his passion waned. 1994 was the last year he booked the club.

Bad Religion—January 22 & 23, 1994

Carl Porcaro (Killing Time, guitarist): That [show] was a bummer in some respects. We were all Bad Religion fans from back in the early half of the '80s, but those guys were talking shit about us! I guess someone had put it in their heads that we were a Nazi band. You would think these guys had been around a long time and wouldn't have to engage in that kind of shit, but they did. They might have even said something to Randy about not wanting to play with us because we were a Nazi band, which was fucking ridiculous.

Dave Franklin (Vision): Yeah, that was true. Where it came from, I have no idea. All I know is I heard it from [Killing Time's] Anthony the minute I got to the show. I was like, "Where the hell did that come from?" Anthony was a HUGE Bad Religion fan, and we both used to love that band way before Killing Time played with them. Anthony was so upset. You know how these things are in the hardcore scene, though... Bad Religion may have never even said that. It could have been someone from the road crew, or it could have been nobody at all.

Arthur Smilios (Gorilla Biscuits, bassist): Where would they get that idea? Why would they ever say that? Look at any of Killing Time's songs....They were a miserable bunch of lyrics, but they were all personal, never political. They were the most apolitical band out there. To call someone a Nazi in our scene is probably the most hateful, damaging thing you could do, especially back in those days. It's absurd. There are certain accusations that you just don't level at people unless you are absolutely sure. It's like calling someone a rapist. Unless you know for a fact, you really shouldn't put that word on someone.

Anthony Comunale (Killing Time, vocalist): That Nazi thing was another story. The rumor was started by Bad Religion after we played with them at City Gardens, because people were putting fliers on cars in the parking lot. We were playing in Philly, and a lot of our friends said people weren't coming to the show because we were supposedly a Nazi band. Killing Time was never a political band, so I didn't know where it came from. People said Bad Religion had said it at their show the week before. I called their booking agent, Stormy, and told her to straighten them out and that it was bullshit. Our lyrics have always been personal, not political. Since then I can't even listen to one of my favorite hardcore bands because of childish rumors. They should have minded their own business if they didn't know the facts.

Green Day—March 18, 1994

Jim Testa (*Jersey Beat*): As a "thank you," they went back and played City Gardens again and sold it out a second time, though they could have played a much bigger place. That first show, the one before *Dookie* came out, was the only show they had ever played in New Jersey or New York before they signed to Reprise. Even with all the touring they did, they never came to New Jersey.

Rich O'Brien: This show was videotaped and eventually wound up on YouTube. Whenever I see it I crack up, because I was working the stage and look like a giant next to Billy Joe Armstrong.

I saw a fight break out by the door. I jumped down, and it was two guys with no shirts on, all sweaty. It was like trying to wrestle two greased pigs out the door. The one kid was bald, so the only thing I could grab to throw him out was his ears. I felt people being jostled around, so I looked back, and Billy Joe was standing next to me, trying to intervene to keep the guys from being thrown out. I grabbed him and gently directed him back to the stage.

Afghan Whigs—April 8, 1994

On April 8, 1994, it was announced that Kurt Cobain was discovered in the greenhouse above his garage, dead of a self-inflicted gunshot.

Greg Dulli (Afghan Whigs, vocals): I only ever played City Gardens once. That was a really weird day. I had actually heard the news already [regarding Cobain]. We played the Academy the night before and found out what happened after the show. I was interviewed by [MTV personality] Matt Pinfield right after. That night at City Gardens, I didn't know what to expect, but people needed a place to go to be with other people who felt the same way.

Kurt was a young man who had achieved iconic status in a way that few people do. I knew him peripherally, but the times I met him, he was a sweet guy. The Whigs were outsiders, and we were the first band from outside the northwest to be signed to [Seattle-based record label] Sub Pop. We were the Rosa Parks of Sub Pop, and Kurt was very welcoming and friendly. I had heard [Nirvana's album] *Bleach* and loved it… you could tell he was a songwriter right away.

Watching the events unfold from afar, I was like, *oh my god*. It was in the tabloids and everything. That night I felt I had to oversee the proceedings and shepherd the feelings of everyone. It was a heavy night, and there was no getting around it. I'm sure John Lennon's contemporaries had a similar experience. That's the only thing I can compare it to.

Steven DiLodovico: I had a weird thing with the Whigs. They were not a band I should have liked, and, except for that one album, *Gentlemen*, I really don't. But that album hit me at the right time, and I wanted to see them live. None of my friends would go with me. In fact, if I had told them I was going, I would have been ridiculed. But I thought, *fuck it*, and I drove the hour to Trenton by myself. I don't remember who opened that night, and I don't remember being consciously aware of Cobain's suicide.

I don't remember Dulli even mentioning it. What I do remember is this: the Afghan Whigs were incredible. They were really fucking loud. They ran through most of the *Gentlemen* LP. They also took a couple of shots at Philadelphia. I remember Greg saying, "You know why we don't play Philadelphia?" and he commenced singing, in a contemptuous, derisively mocking voice, the hook from that *Motown Philly* song by Boys II Men. I guess he took exception to them declaring Philadelphia as "the new Motown."

Bigger Thomas/Voodoo Glow Skulls/Inspecter 7— April 9, 1994

Travis Nelson (Inspecter 7, vocals): Randy always had this joke that me and Alex Franklin should start a ska band together. We always laughed it off. Fast forward to 1994, and I wind up joining a ska band. I was living in New Brunswick. It started in 1992, they were called Agent 86. In '93 they changed their name to The Crash Bars, and by '94 they were called Inspecter 7. I was always their drunken fan who would go see them at the Melody Bar or the Brighton Bar [in New Brunswick, NJ] or wherever they played. One day, Inspecter 7 gets booked at City Gardens. We were the new band opening up. To me, it was a trip. "Wow, I'm on the stage at City Gardens. How weird." I was accustomed to being [in the audience] all these years. It was hilarious.

We even had a fight break out that night. During Bigger Thomas's set, the trumpet player for Voodoo Glow Skulls kept jumping on the stage and stage diving. Now, Bigger Thomas isn't really a 'hard' band, by any means. They're kind of happy, funky ska. But this dude is flying into the audience, and everyone was getting pissed off. On one of the jumps he nailed this girl in the head with his knee, and all these newer Trenton skins jumped him. They were fucking him up. I actually went to help him… I didn't know the dude for nothing, but he was getting fucked up and had had enough. Me and one of the bouncers start pulling people off him. He's getting his ass kicked, so he's all pumped up with adrenaline and clocks me in the head. I guess he didn't know who was attacking and who was helping. I look at the security guy like, "This motherfucker…" and the security guy looks the other way. I start fucking this guy up and, of course, all the Trenton skins jump on him again. He ended up getting thrown out, which sometimes unfortunately happened at City Gardens… you get your ass kicked, and then you get thrown out.

Life of Agony/Sheer Terror—April 10, 1994

Travis Nelson: The very next night it was Sheer Terror, who I really wanted to see because they're one of my favorite bands of all time, and Life of Agony, who my friends all loved but I never cared for. Life of Agony were big then, and everybody was there: New York, New Brunswick, Trenton, Philly. I was dancing for Life of Agony, so that's my fault for dancing to a band I didn't like. I'm in mid-air, spin-kicking-who-knows-what-the-fuck, and I get yanked back from behind really, really hard. All I see is this maroon sleeve under my leg and then feel this jerking, and my head smashes on the floor. My fucking head was split open. I stood up, and my first reaction was to start fighting someone. But then I was like, "You know what? It's a head injury. Maybe I should, uh, make sure that my brain's not fucking floating out of my skull before I go and fight someone." I was getting older and wiser, I guess. I was maturing.

Sure enough, I put my hand to the back of my head, and it's covered in blood. I look for the only maroon sweatshirt I can see, and there's this big, college jock, rocker-looking dude, and I made sure to remember him. I went to the back to assess my wound and decide if I should go fight this guy or if I should go to the hospital. Randy looks at it and says, "Oh yeah, you're going to need stitches." But he was cool about it.

I guess because of my past, Tut got a couple of bouncers to walk me out. My friend was going to take me to the hospital, and Tut was like, "Walk him out. Don't let him go after this dude," which was fucking bullshit. God knows he had nine million lawsuits, so I guess I understand. I broke off from the bouncers to get my coat, and everybody comes running up to me because they wanted to know what happened. They heard I got hit with a bottle, that I got stabbed in the head, all kinds of crazy shit. They asked me, "Who was it? Who was it?" I said, "That guy right over there, in the maroon shirt. *That guy.*"

I figured they were going to get him in the parking lot afterwards, which was fine with me. I didn't give a fuck. I was the one who had to go get my fucking head stapled up. I couldn't do anything anyway because the bouncers were all watching me. So I get my jacket, they walk me out, and I am waiting by my friend Kelly's car to go. That's when I hear the music stop, like a needle scratching across a record. I see the lights go, and I hear, "No! Stop the violence! Stop the violence!" I was like, "Oh shit! What's going on?" There was total chaos in there for a good five minutes. Then, busting out the front-side door come the dudes! It was the dude in maroon, his girl, and their friends. They're running out screaming. The girls are screaming, the guys' shirts are gone, they're all bloody and fucked up, and I'm like, "Oh shit! They did it right in there!" I start laughing. Tut comes storming out the front door, and he's like, "WHERE IS TRAVIS?" I'm like, "What?" Tut's screaming at me, "You caused a problem in there!" I said, "I caused the problem in there? By getting my fucking head split open?"

I go to the hospital and get 14 staples in my head, and the next day Alex [Franklin] calls me and says, "Dude, you're banned." I said, "Yeah, I figured that." Later I talked to Randy and he said, "You're barred." I said, "Yeah I know, I know, I know…" Apparently they had surveillance cameras. Tut watched the footage, and he saw me point out the guy. He thought he was going to get sued.

Not surprisingly, the Tri-State Crew set it off. The dude who actually [caused the head injury] was apologetic, but his friend got lippy. Apparently the guy was in mid-sentence and somebody went off on him. Then they swarmed. All the bouncers ran over and tried to get the Tri-State guys off of them. They start running for the door, and, BOOM, there's Hate Squad. So then Hate Squad starts beating on them. The same four or five bouncers run over, and now they're trying to get Hate Squad off of them! As soon as they get them off, there's the New York City guys. Everywhere they tried to run there were different crews fucking them up. It took them forever to get outside. Every time they took a step there was someone else fucking them up! They were just getting beat all around the club. I basically got banned for inciting a riot.

I found it ironic that, with all the acts of violence I carried out inside those walls over the years—after all the horrible acts of violence I committed in there—I get banned the night I didn't fucking lay a hand on anyone! I didn't touch anyone that night. I got my head split open!

I don't know how, but Inspector 7 wound up getting booked there later that year opening for Dancehall Crashers. I knew I wasn't allowed in the club, but I wasn't sure if that was as a patron or as a performer, too. I figured, "Eh… let's just show up and see what happens." But Randy's like, "You're barred, man. Tut's not going to let you in." We were making jokes about getting a wireless mic so I could do the show from the parking lot. I ended up hanging out in the parking lot, listening to my band play.

Shelter/Sick Of It All/Snapcase—July 10, 1994

Tim McMahon (Mouthpiece, vocalist): As far as I can remember, that was the last big show that everybody was excited about.

Ralph Michal (City Gardens regular): The week before, I had seen Youth of Today at a secret show in New York. Youth of Today had broken up and formed Shelter. I was in New York seeing Shelter, and I spoke to [Shelter/Youth of Today leader] Ray Cappo. He told me that the other members of Youth of Today were going to join him onstage at the end of the Shelter set and play some old Youth of Today songs. I was really excited.

Tim McMahon: The rumor was going around that at the end of Shelter's set, Walter [Schriefels, Youth of Today] was going to come out and do a Youth of Today set. Well, it wasn't a rumor to me, because I knew those guys.

Ralph Michal: Some friends were going to New York to see the Cro-Mags, and I told them not to. I said to come to City Gardens to see Shelter, because it will be another Youth of Today reunion. And, at the end set, just as Ray said, Walter from Quicksand and Gorilla Biscuits, with Tim Brooks from Bold on drums, came out and played.

Tim McMahon: They played about five songs and the place just erupted. At this point, in 1994, you were pretty much allowed to stage dive. It added a whole new element to the show. It was almost like stepping into a time machine. We were so stoked. It all happened so quickly.

Ralph Michal: They started with "Flame Still Burns," and the place erupted into chaos. I made it through three songs, and then, while they

were playing "Make a Change," I don't know what hit me—someone's fist, a boot to the face, whatever—I tripped over someone who was already on the ground and I could feel blood rushing down my face. I found my hat and started making my way toward the bar. As I remember it, the crowd parted like the Red Sea, I guess because no one wanted to come near me. At the bar, they gave me napkins and ice, and I watched the rest of the show from the back. I didn't want to leave because this was my one shot to see Youth of Today. Even though it was a horrible experience, it was a great experience. I'd do it all again.

Tim McMahon: Youth of Today opened with "Flame Still Burns," and it has that opening line where Ray screams, "We're back!" When Sick of It All came on, I remember [Sick of It All leader singer] Lou screaming, "We never left!" It was funny. That was my last really good memory of City Gardens.

Offspring/Rancid—July 30, 1994
(Or, "The Night Madonna Almost Came to City Gardens")

Jim Norton: (City Gardens security/stage manager): I'm telling you this story about the Roseland ballroom for a reason. Around September or October of 1994, I was tour managing Rancid while they opened for

The Offspring. The Offspring had blown up already, they had sold four million records in the US. Green Day had blown up already, and record labels were looking for the next Green Day or the next Offspring. The big money was on Rancid.

Rancid were friends with Sick of It All. They were lining up a tour with Sick of It All opening for Rancid. Offspring's tour manager was completely incompetent. He was not qualified to manage that tour. He had never toured the U.S. and, if he had, he had certainly never done it as a tour manager. He was essentially a guy who had driven the bus a few times in Europe, and they liked him. Sick of It All was huge in Europe at the time, playing 5,000- to 8,000-capacity shows in small hockey arenas. This guy really wanted to get close to and friendly with Sick of It All, because he wanted to convince them that they should hire him to tour manage them in Europe.

The night before they played City Gardens, Rancid and Offspring played at Roseland Ballroom in New York. Roseland has a very tight downstairs, where the dressing room is. They'd been fined by fire marshals before, so they really, really wanted to keep people out of the hallways and have as few people downstairs as possible. I'd seen them go bananas keeping people out of there. For three weeks, right from the beginning of the tour, I had been telling Rancid that New York was going to be tough and it was going to suck. I said I was going to call in advance and have them set up a V.I.P. area, which they often did at the Roseland, behind the stage. The whole point was: don't have Sick of It All and their 77 friends downstairs. It cannot happen that way.

I roll up to the gig with Rancid, and there is The Offspring's tour manager handing out all-access passes to Sick of It All by the handful—like 30 or 40 at a time—and they all say "Rancid" on them. They are Offspring tour passes, and he writes "Rancid" and checks "all access." So he has, effectively, just dropped this whole problem in my lap.

Rancid goes on stage, and the entire side and back is lined with Sick of It All, their friends, their crew, their crew's cousins… everybody was there. No exaggeration, it had to be like 40 people on and around the stage. I knew that there was going to be a hassle. Rancid finishes and leaves the stage. The roadie and the T-shirt guy and I are all moving the gear, and I turn around to see that it's a ghost town. There's nobody on stage and nobody in that V.I.P. area that I had had set up, so I know there's only one place they can be: downstairs. I know that somebody, somewhere, is going bananas because there are 50 people in that tiny hallway. I go down and hear the manager of Rancid saying, "And this is Matt Freeman. He's the bass player..." Now, Matt Freeman is a take-no-guff, chain-smoking guy whose dad was an Oakland cop during the riots, and he has taken on a bit of that world-weariness himself. He's not one to suffer fools gladly. Then I hear Matt Freeman say, "It's very nice to meet you," and something to the effect of "I'm a fan of your music." I'm thinking, "That doesn't sound like the Matt Freeman I've been working for." I pop down to the lower level and look toward the dressing rooms, and I see all these New York tough guys standing against the walls with their hands at their sides, staring at the floor like 7th grade boys at their first dance. Something doesn't fit.

By this time I'm mad because these people were clogging the hallway and they had passes with Rancid's name on it. The people who ran the club were looking at me like, "Well, what are you going to do about this? This is not cool." The Offspring's manager says to me, very calmly, "And this is Jim Norton, our tour manager." He's saying this to someone standing in a doorway immediately to my right. I turn, not really paying much attention, and say; "Hey, how ya doing?" kind of brusquely. I'm pissed. My attention is focused immediately back to the hallway, and I say, "All right everybody, you can't hang out in this hallway. I'm really sorry. I set up a V.I.P. area upstairs, but you got all-access passes like they were birthday invitations, so I guess you're my problem now. At least get into the dressing rooms. Just get the hell out of the hallway." And for whatever reason, it worked. All the New York tough guys I was terrified of slunk back into the room.

Matt Freeman walks in, sits down, and says, "Kind of crazy, right?" and I say, "Yeah." And then, after a moment, I say, "Was that Madonna I just blew off?" and he said, "Yeah." I said, "That was pretty fucking cool." And Matt said, "It was really cool, actually." We had a good laugh. All I remember is a short blonde woman whose dress made me think, *that dress is way too nice for this gig*.

The next day Rancid was playing at City Gardens, opening for The Offspring. During soundcheck, Matt Freeman is back to his old, loveable self, and I see him come walking out of the office shaking his head, probably smoking a cigarette. I said, "What's up?" and he doesn't want to talk about it. I call Rancid's manager, and I hear that Madonna wants to come to City Gardens and see Rancid tonight. She wanted to sign them to Maverick Records.

Over the next hour or two, I have conversations with Madonna's management office. It turns out that the tall, grey guy I ignored, along with Madonna, was her manger, Freddy DeMann. He was also the manager of Michael Jackson during the *Thriller* period, among other pop luminaries. I call the woman at Maverick thinking, *why the hell do I have to talk to you at all? You're a record company.* She was obviously concerned [about Madonna]. I said, "Are you worried something's going to happen to Madonna at some dive of a punk rock club in Trenton New Jersey?" She said, "Yeah, kind of." I said, "Okay, let me ask you this… How is she getting down here?" The woman tells me that Armand, her driver, is driving her down from New York. I told her to get Armand to page me when he reached a certain point and that I would call him back. I told her, "Armand is going to pull up to the back corner of the building where there will be six or seven security people waiting. I will be outside. [*Ed. – Jim Norton goes on to recite detailed and meticulously planned security process to get Madonna into the building safely and without anyone noticing*]. When the show ends, we will reverse the process [to get her out]."

The woman at Maverick Records was exceedingly relieved to hear this. I had already, within moments of hearing the news that Madonna was going to be there, had a security protocol in line. She did not know that Madonna was going to get the same security treatment as Joey Ramone! Because at City Gardens, there is no one bigger than Joey Ramone. Whether it's Joey Ramone or Madonna or the Pope, there's only so much we can do for you.

The Maverick woman says, "I am so glad you're the person we're dealing with. Freddy told me that I didn't have to worry with you because you are a seasoned veteran and a true professional." This is from Freddy DeMann! The guy I didn't speak to, walked past, and totally blew off. For all he knows, I went into that room and shot heroin into my neck! From one incident of being pissed off at the Offspring's tour manager and blowing off Madonna, because I didn't know she was Madonna, I am now entrusted with Madonna's personal safety at City Gardens, of all places.

They were relieved because they thought they were going to be dealing with some kid... well, I was 25 years old, so basically I *was* some kid. I just happened to be the kid who stuck his arm into Joey Ramone's gelatinous stomach. So now I call up the management company, ready to do the whole dance again, except now I feel a whole better about it because I've just impressed some record company lackey.

Madonna couldn't make it. She was filming either *Dick Tracy* or *Evita* at the time. I can't remember which one it was. She had a wardrobe appointment that night. Like everybody from New York, Madonna thought Trenton was five minutes through the tunnel because it's Jersey, and Jersey is small. When she found out it was not going to be running down there for an hour and running back, she realized she would have to cancel the entire wardrobe session for that night. To cancel and reschedule it was going to cost her $50,000. She was not coming, but she was going to send her main A&R guy, Guy Oseary. Guy Oseary looks a hell of a lot better on the guest list than "Madonna plus one."

If forty Sick of It All people had shown up in New York, then at least sixty of them came to Trenton. Since it was City Gardens, I didn't give a shit. I said, "We're sharing that dressing room. Keep in mind that, when you give a pass that says "all access," it includes the dressing rooms. Go take a look at that dressing room and you decide how many Sick of It All people you want in there." Apparently, that number was 60, because that's how many he handed out. I don't give a shit. It's his fucking problem, not mine.

Rancid played, and there were about fifty people on stage. City Gardens' stage was not that sturdy; it was kind of bouncy with fifty people on it. In fact, it was pretty bouncy with 12 people on it. People were doing their "Yo dance" over in the corner, shaking their fists and making it look like an Onyx video, and the amps were rocking back and forth in a dangerous way. At one point, [Rancid guitarist] Lars' amp lost its head. That was fun. But there was nothing to do about it because they were all bros of the band. They had all-access passes, and they're scaring the shit out of me. There are sixty of them!

Afterwards, I leave the stage area and go to the dressing room. It is packed... with wall-to-wall stupid. There is not a combined IQ of 150 in that room. Walking through, I see Offspring, who have sold four million records and are playing small clubs at $10 ticket when they could be charging $25, pinned against the back wall. They were pushed back to the far wall in their own dressing room, with nobody to fend for them, because their own tour manager was busy kissing ass to Sick of It All. I asked if they wanted me to clear the room out. They said, "Nah, it's not a big deal." I said, "Well, it's kind of a big deal to me." These Offspring guys are totally cool. They are not "rock stars" at all. They were being way cooler to Rancid than they needed to be. So I try to clear the room. The first people I go to are the four members of Sick of It All, because they're in a band. I said to them, "I don't mean to be a douchebag, but The Offspring have to go on in twenty minutes and this place is packed. Would you do me a favor and take it downstairs? You can come right back up once Offspring hits the stage." They were very agreeable, giving the "Yo" wave to the Offspring as they went out the door, like, "Have a good show."

Then the next job was going after all the girlfriends. I tried to be nice. I said "please" and "can you do me a favor" and all that kind of stuff. Finally, I get them to go. Then the random hangers-on… the guys who are like, "I drove so-and-so's girlfriend here." I'd say, "That's fantastic, but both so-and-so and his girlfriend have gone downstairs. Therefore…" And they would respond with, "But I have an all-access pass." "I know you have an all-access pass. We went through this before." I repeat the same thing about forty times. Eventually I'm get most of them to leave.

Then I got down to the real problems, and there were quite a few of those. One guy in particular, who was not dealt a good hand [in life], flat-out could not comprehend what I was saying. He was not being tough or mean. He was simply confused. "I know you're with Sick of It All, but Sick of It All has gone. Please, go downstairs, I'm clearing everybody out. Everybody. The only people who are going to be left in this dressing room are people who perform music on stage or who are going to perform music on stage. Even *I'm* even going to leave. I promise you. And when the Offspring goes on stage, you can come right back up." He says, "I'm with Sick of It All, though…" I felt bad, but, eventually I started to lose my cool.

Then there were the last two idiots in the room, sitting in the corner watching the whole thing. I walked over and said, "What the fuck, guys? You just saw me go through that whole thing with that guy. Get the fuck out." They're like, "You don't have to be an asshole about it…" Yeah, you just watched me kick fifty people out of here, and *I'm* the fucking asshole.

Now the only people left are The Offspring, who are sitting at one end of the dressing room, and Rancid, who are sitting at the long folding table. Their manager is sitting next to them, and one final idiot. He was wearing a black army jacket and big Timberland boots with a goatee, walking that line of *am I hip hop or hardcore or both?* I roll up on this dude and say, "What the fuck is wrong with you? Why are you still fucking sitting here?" And he's like, "But…" and I said, "But nothing!" I go fucking bananas. I'm screaming in his face. He holds his hands up like, *whoa, whoa,* and impressed with myself because that's the second time in two days the scared shitless, chubby kid from Jersey has totally yelled down some bad-ass New York tough guy. He gets up and walks out the door. Then I turned to Jeff Goldman [Rancid's manager] and said, "I'm a man of my word. You and I are going to be the last two people out of here. When we walk out of here, the only people left will be the people who play music on stage tonight."

I turn back to Rancid and say, "Guys, I'm sorry it had to go that way," and I say to The Offspring, "Thank you very much for sharing your dressing room with us. Thank you very much for being so nice on tour. You guys are awesome." Downstairs, in the little hallway between the front showroom and the back bar, I see Jeff Goldman talking to the guy I just yelled and screamed at, and in whose face I pointed my finger, and who I called all kinds of names. Jeff looks at me and says, "Jim, this Guy Oseary from Maverick Records." Of course, my jaw dropped, and I asked him why he didn't tell me that in the first place. Guy said, "I tried, but you wouldn't let me!" I was so fucking embarrassed, but he was like, "No, it was totally cool, brother! Totally cool. You got the job done. I've never seen someone go off like that. That was fucking awesome!" We ended up being friendly after that.

And that's the story of the night Madonna *almost* came to City Gardens.

Into Another/Shift/Hogan's Heroes—August 10 1994

On the following pages is a typical band rider for a City Gardens show.

LEAVE HOME BOOKING

contract # 6091

# of musicians: 4

P.O Box 749   SLC, UT 84110
Phone: 801-521-3753   Fax: 801-521-8200

On this 10 day of August , 19 94 , (name) INTO ANOTHER (hereinafter referred to as "Artist") and (name) Randy Ellis (hereinafter referred to as "Purchaser"), contract and agree to the following:

1. **Engagement:** (Venue/Phone) City Gardens - 609-695-2482

   (Address) 1701 Calhoun St. - Trenton, NJ

   (Ticket price) $8 adv. / $10 day of show (Capacity) 950

   (Gross potential) $9,500.00 TAX: X0% 6%

2. **Artist Name:** INTO ANOTHER

   (Support Acts) Shift, Hogan's Heroes

3.) **Date of Engagement:** Sunday, September 11, 1994   ALL AGES SHOW!!!

4.) **Type of Engagement:** concert   **Set length:** 60 minutes

5.) **Load in:** 4:00 pm   **Soundcheck:** 4:30 pm   **Doors open:** 6:30 pm

6.) **Show starts:** 6:50 pm   **Artist on stage:** 8:45 pm   **MERCHANDISE RATE:** 83%X 15%

7.) **Billing Position:** headline

8.) **Full Compensation Agreed Upon:** (For above named Artist only!!!)

   Wage agreed upon (terms and amount): $1200.00 guaranteed plus 70% gross door receipts after $4933.50 fixed promoter expenses.

NOTICE: Amount shown above for fixed promoter expenses is a maximum and must be verified by receipts and proper documentation. Purchaser agrees to deliver receipts and documentation to Artist, or Artist's representative upon request. Artist has full right to have a representative present in the box office at all times. Representative shall have access to the box office records of the Purchaser relating to the gross receipts of this engagement only. Full payment as outlined above will be paid in U.S. funds (cash) by Purchaser no later than immediately following Artist's performance to: Richard Birkenhead (Artist's spokesperson).

9.) a.) A deposit of _____ shall be paid by Purchaser in the form of a certified check or money order to Artist's agent _____ due on or before:_____ .

   b.) The balance of _____ shall be paid by the Purchaser to Artist or Artist's representative in cash no later than_____. When deposit is required, bonuses or percentages will be paid to above named person immediately following Artist's performance.

10.) **Cancellation:** Purchaser agrees to pay a cancellation fee of 50% (fifty percent) of the agreed compensation to Artist in the event that this engagement is canceled by Purchaser for reasons other than riot, epidemic, strike, an act of God, or other legitimate reasons beyond Purchaser control.

11.) **Taxes:** Purchaser shall pay and hold Artist exempt from any and all taxes, fees, dues related to or based upon this performance.

11.) Indemnification:

A.) Purchaser agrees to indemnify Artist, contractors, employees and agents against and from any costs (including attorneys fees and court costs), claims, expenses, liabilities, damages, losses or judgments arising out of, or in connection with, any type of claim, action or demand made by any person or third party, if any are sustained as an indirect or direct consequence of engagement.

B.) Purchaser also agrees to indemnify Artist, contractors, agents and employees against and from any and all loss, damage and/or destruction occurring to its and or its contractors, employees, agents, Artist's instruments and equipment at place of performance.

12.) The validity, construction and effect of this contract and any attached rider(s) shall be construed, governed and interpreted pursuant to the laws of the state of Utah.

13.) All riders attached hereto are hereby made part of this contract.

14.) Signed contracts, rider and deposit when requested must be received no later than 8-19-94 or Artist or representative has the right to void this contract. In addition, the Artist of representative thereof will be entitled to examine all receipts from the night of performance upon request. The additional copy of this signed contract and its attached rider(s) (including any approved changes) must be sent at the same time to:

Leave Home Booking: P.O. Box 749 Salt Lake City, UT 84110

In witness thereof, the parties hereto have set their names in mutual agreement to the above terms, sealing the day and year of agreement first above written.

*If there are any problems in meeting any of these conditions, please contact Stormy Shepherd at: 801-521-3753 or fax 801-521-8200.

Agreed and accepted:

Purchaser	Artist (or Artist Rep.)
Signature	Signature
Street address	Street address
City/state/zip	City/state/zip

CONTRACT RIDER FOR: ___INTO ANOTHER___

This rider attached to and made a part of contract # 6091 ____ dated 8-10-94 between ___INTO ANOTHER___ (herein after referred to as 'Artist') and Randy Ellis ____ (herein after referred to as 'Purchaser').

1.) BILLING: (In all types of advertising)
Artist shall receive 100% headline billing in any and all types of paid or publicity advertisements. Purchaser is expected to advertise performance of Artist at least two weeks prior to engagement through media (radio, print, or television) and/or flyers or posters at Purchaser's sole expense. Artist shall be listed as headliner on all signs, marquees, and recorded messages and calenders. If the Artist is to appear in support of another performer, Artist shall receive 75% guest billing.

2.) SECURITY:
Purchaser hereby agrees to supply qualified, adequate security who are sober and able-bodied for this type of performance. If stage-diving does occur, it is security's responsibility to keep "divers" away from the Artist and Artist's equipment. Security must protect the Artist from this occurrence in a rational, responsible and respectable manner. If fighting does occur, Artist will not tolerate security using unnecessary physical force on any audience member. Please have the problem removed immediately without abusive treatment. Abusive treatment, brutality, violent behavior or any type of mishandling on the part of said security or staff for any reason whatsoever is out of line, and thereby gives the Artist the right to either relieve that person from any further duties for the remainder of this engagement, and or exit the stage and receive full payment. If Purchaser or Artist anticipate crowd problems, it is advisable to hold a meeting with security and Artist before doors open to go over security procedures for the engagement.

3.) MERCHANDISE:
Artist must be supplied with adequate space within the venue (preferably near the entrance) for sales of merchandise including one 6 foot table, a chair and two clip-on lights near an electrical outlet. Artist and Artist's employees shall sell merchandise at Artist's price and not be subjected to other Artist's prices performing at the same engagement. Merchandise prices will not be subject to any venue restrictions on prices. Purchaser will not take any percentage of Artist's merchandise sales or prohibit them from selling merchandise inside of venue. Proper documentation must be sent to Artist's agent upon confirmation of date if percentage is being taken. We would ask that Purchaser and said staff refrain from asking Artist for free merchandise as we cannot afford to give out free merchandise every night. We would appreciate your honoring this part of the rider as often times the money made off of merchandise sales is food and gas money for the Artist.

4.) CROWD CONTROL:
Although it is not always possible to foresee crowd behavior, we would very much appreciate Purchaser and employees not admitting any person outwardly displaying racist attitudes or beliefs.

5.) PERFORMANCE:
Artist retains one hundred (100) percent of their performance. Artist retains sole control over performance, production and presentation of performance for the entirety of this engagement. Every aspect of engagement is subject to Artist's approval. Any forms of sponsorship or endorsement must be approved by Artist's representative before confirmation of performance.

6.) COMPLIMENTARY TICKETS:
Purchaser agrees to provide Artist with twenty-five (25) complimentary tickets. Any unused portion of Artist's complimentary tickets may be issued for sale at the door on the night of the engagement upon Artist's approval.. If Artist's pay is measured in part by gross door receipts, percentages, or overages, Artist has the right to limit Purchaser's complimentary tickets to a maximum of fifty (50). This includes, but is not limited to: press, radio giveaways and personalities, Purchaser, staff, employees, VIP's, agents, etc... Artist's representative shall have the right to be present in the box office at all times. Purchaser must be able to document all expenses, tickets sold and given out at Artist's representatives request.

7.) RECORDING, PHOTOGRAPHING, ETC...
No portion of this performance shall be recorded, reproduced or transmitted from the place of performance, in any manner or by any means whatsoever without the specific written approval of the Artist or representative. All unauthorized recording devices shall be confiscated by the Purchaser and held until the completion of performance. Absolutely NO video or audio recorders will be admitted!!

8.) TICKET PRICE:
The agreed ticket price will not be changed. Purchaser will not raise or lower ticket price from what has been agreed upon. Ticket price will not be based upon age. Ticket price will be sold for the same amount to all persons regardless of age. In the event Purchaser raises the price without the agent's approval, the Artist reserves the right to refrain from performing until the difference is refunded in cash to all ticket holders of the higher priced ticket immediately.

9.) LIGHTING:
Purchaser agrees to provide a stage lighting system at his or her sole expense. Purple and green lights/gels must be included.

10.) SUPPORT ACTS:
The Artist must have approval of any support acts. In the event that any support act engaged by the Purchaser uses any large or obstructive equipment, the equipment should be removed from the stage area in preparation for the Artist's performance. If the above named Artist is headlining, there should be no more than two opening bands unless approved by Artist's representative.

11.) DRESSING ROOM:
Purchaser agrees to provide a clean, well-lit, air conditioned or heated room for the Artist and crew members to be kept private. Room should lock, or have security provided the entire time that the Artist will be at the venue. Dressing room needs to have at least one mirror (full length preferred), and two armless folding chairs in addition to other seating. Each Artist and crew member will be allowed to enter and exit the venue at any time during the engagement.
Upon Artist's arrival dressing room should have ready: herbal tea and coffee, non-dairy creamer or soy milk (plain or vanilla), and assorted fruit juices (not from concentrate).

12.) SOUND REQUIREMENTS:
Purchaser will provide a professional twenty-four (24) channel house mixing board, two (2) compression units and a minimum of four (4) delay reverb units.

CHANNEL	MICROPHONE LISTING (TYPE)
KICK DRUM	EV RV-20
SNARE	SHURE SM-57
HI HAT	SHURE SM-81
RACK TOM 1	SENNHEISER 421
RACK TOM 2	SENNHEISER 421
RACK TOM 3	SENNHEISER 421
FLOOR TOM	SENNHEISER 421
OVERHEAD LEFT	SHURE SM-81
OVERHEAD RIGHT	SHURE SM-81
BASS (DI)	DI
BASS (MIC)	SENNHEISER 421
GUITAR (STAGE LEFT)	SHURE SM-57
GUITAR (STAGE RIGHT)	SHURE SM-57
VOCAL (CENTER STAGE)	SHURE SM-58

13.) MONITOR REQUIREMENTS:
Purchaser will provide a monitor system with four (4) separate mixes and a qualified engineer to be available at ALL times. Monitor system needs to include a professional soundboard that provides a 16x24 mix, four (4) floor wedges, each with at least two (2) 15" speakers and one (1) horn and adequate equalizers for each mix.

14.) LOADERS:
At time of load-in and out, Purchaser will provide two (2) able-bodied loaders to assist Artist with their equipment.

15.) PARKING:
Purchaser will reserve and notify Artist of two (2) well-lit, secure parking spaces for Artist's van/bus. If there is a charge for parking, Purchaser will provide Artist with validations or pass, or pay parking charges.

16.) HOSPITALITY:
Purchaser agrees to provide at his or her sole expense, the following for the Artist and crew members in the dressing room at time of arrival.
- Seven (7) bottles of quality bottled water chilled
- Seven (7) hot VEGAN meals (no meat or dairy products) unless otherwise requested.
- Fresh whole organic fruit (not cut up, canned or frozen) ex. bananas, apples, pears, oranges, grapes, melons, etc..
- Fresh whole organic vegetables (not cut up, canned or frozen) ex. tomatoes, carrots, celery, broccoli, cauliflower
- Natural almond or peanut butter (10-12 oz.)
- Two (2) loaves of dairy-free bread
- One (1) case Budweiser beer

*As far as utensils and dishes Artist prefers glass and silverware. If paper products are necessary please use:
- utensils for seven (7)
- Eleven (11) recycled paper cups (no styrofoam)
- Eleven (11) recycled paper plates (no styrofoam)
- Twenty (20) recycled napkins

* If meals cannot be provided at venue, there is a $6.00 buy out per person for seven (7) people and directions to a restaurant upon Artist's description immediately following soundcheck.

17.) SOUNDCHECK:
Purchaser agrees to ensure that Artist will have full sound and lighting checks at least one hour prior to admission of audience. A sixty (60) minute soundcheck is required. Access to venue at this time will be strictly limited to the Artist, the Artist crew members, Artist guests, Purchaser, support acts, and the venue's staff.

18.) CONTRACT RIDER FULFILLMENT:
All terms of this rider are specifically accepted by the Purchaser unless they are waived by the Artist. Such waivers shall be effective only if initiated by both a representative of the Artist and Purchaser. Where any of the above requirements cannot be met, Purchaser agrees to inform Artist's representative for approval.

Agree and accepted:
Purchaser_____ Artist (or Artist's Rep.) _____
Date_____ Date_____

Rancid/Bouncing Souls—September 25, 1994

Bryan Kienlen (Bouncing Souls): [Bouncing Souls singer] Greg [Attonito] and I did an arm-in-arm stage dive during a Rancid show. That didn't work out very well. I hit the floor pretty hard.

Randy Now: Whenever you tour with a band, there's always a catch phrase that starts at the beginning of a tour. I used to take a lot of bands to the Crystal Diner, which was not far from the club. One time I took Rancid there with the guys from Sick of It All. On the menu they had a kiddies section with different cartoon characters, like the Flintstones. They had Snoopy, but they misspelled it Snoppy. I picked up on it and Lars [*Frederiksen, Rancid*] loved it. They began using it as a verb, an adjective, in place of people's names. Like, "Hey Snoppy. Hand me that!" Everything was Snoppy.

With Bad Religion, I once picked them up at the Newark Airport, and all they had was a $100 bill to pay the porters. They wanted me to cover the tip, but all I had was a $20 to pay these porters for transporting all their equipment—drums and cymbals and all this other crap. Those porters were NOT happy, and one guy put his fist in my face and said, "I'll bust your shit!" Bad Religion got behind me and the police came, and all the porters got behind the bust-your-shit guy. That was the running joke for the rest of the tour: "I'll bust your shit."

WEEN—December 2, 1994
(The last show Randy Now booked at City Gardens)

Jamie Davis: Me and Alex [Franklin] were hanging out. We were like, "Eh, it's the last night; we should go." We had pretty much spent our whole lives there. We were hanging out, talking to the bouncers and shit, and Randy was like, "Yeah, just go in." We didn't think of it as an "end of an era" kind of thing.

Ben Vaughn: Ween sent me a tape and said, "We want to make a country record." I listened to it, called them back, and said, "What country?" And they're like, "You don't hear it?" I said the only thing to do with this is to go to Nashville and hire all the A-list session players who played on

Loretta Lynn, Conway Twitty, and Dolly Parton records....the guys who are ready to retire from the union and start collecting their pensions. We got the Jordanaires, who used to play with Elvis. They were like, "We love it; let's do it." We cut the whole record in three days.

I thought it would go over better if I presented them as a brother act. I called each Jordanaire individually and said, "Okay, the Ween Brothers are coming in." I told them there were going to be some blue lyrics here and there and asked if they were okay with that. Only two guys said no. One guy said, "I'm a Deacon at my church, and I'm not gonna play on this record. But when you come down to Nashville, I'd like to sit down and have a talk with these boys and try to straighten their asses out."

Pig Robbins, one of the most recorded piano players in history of country music, is blind. When they brought him into the sessions, he was like, "Where's these Ween brothers?" And we're like, "Right here." Pig Robbins goes, "We got some country motherfuckers here, eh?" And then we were off to the races. By the end of it, the drummer took Mickey fishing with him. That album became *12 Golden Country Greats*.

With that last Ween show, the Randy Now era of City Gardens was over. Various legal troubles contributed to the end of Randy's partnership with Tut and City Gardens. As with the beginning of the club, no one knew at the time it was the end.

Many factors contributed to the demise of City Gardens, both as a venue and as a way of life. Things were changing... the "digital age" was about to take on a new meaning as more people gained access to the internet. It wasn't long before any music fan with an internet connection could steal his or her favorite artists' music. At the same time, with more and better video technology becoming readily available (and with its quality reaching new heights) the need to go out to a venue and see a band perform was diminished. You could watch most groups' performances online. Hell, if you are in a band, you can practically book and promote an entire tour from your cell phone.

The decline of record stores and venues, coupled with corporate music entities capitalizing on youth-oriented trends, severely fractured a scene that once prided itself on its insular nature and anti-corporate stance. The late '90s saw the co-opting of anything that might have once been considered "alternative" and turned the average music-hungry connoisseur into a demographic target.

Once-hallowed grounds that had hosted music's most important moments disappeared into myth. Many venues were forced to change the way they did business. Others closed for good. By 2013, Ian MacKaye was selling Minor Threat t-shirts in Urban Outfitters and Greg Ginn was suing every person who ever said the words "Black Flag."

"Punk" t-shirts were readily available at every shopping mall with a Hot Topic.

Jello Biafra (Dead Kennedys): It's harder to tour underground today in a way, though there are many more promoters and venues. Lots of cool bands and music labels, but the guarantees from the promoters, numerically, are about the same as they were when I was in Dead Kennedys. Meanwhile, everything else has skyrocketed. Not just gasoline and accommodations, and your rent back home, but the ticket prices have multiplied by ten in many cases, but the bands ain't seeing that money. A lot of times the promoters aren't either… it's the insurance companies. All it takes is one cutie with a rich lawyer daddy to fall in the pit, and they sue, and then it's either no more shows or they have to buy a lot of insurance and charge the public accordingly.

Randy Now: We never made a decision to stop forever. We just decided to take a break from it for a couple reasons. We had a couple years of bad weather during the winter, which made it tough. Tut was getting hit with all the lawsuits and would shake everyday going to the mailbox. I felt like, "Fuck this. I'm tired of it." It had become a job, and it wasn't fun. Going back to the '80s and '90s, nobody would book these bands. They came to me over and over again. I'd get them when nobody wanted them, and then we'd build them up, and they stayed with me right until we closed down. Nowadays, I get a lot of people saying things like, "That's was really good what you did back then, even if we bitched about the ticket prices. But, looking back, it was a great deal."

It was a big PA, a big room, big insurance. I had to feed the bands and pay for security and advertising. When a band comes, you've got to advertise all over the East Coast, and there were no computers. The insurance was a killer. I had to buy individual policies for every show just for myself, let alone for the club. And they were $750. I had to guarantee 30 shows a year to get it down to $350 per event. In the 1980s and early '90s, $350 for a show for insurance… There were a thousand people there at times, but (more often) there were only 100 people. It was like a dollar or two dollars per person. It went up to $650 for a Bad Brains show. I almost told the insurance company that they were a folk band. If I had told them the Bad Brains were punk, it would have cost a thousand dollars.

The owner's old man came up with an idea of having the pit roped off, and you could only go in if you paid an extra $8. The skinheads would have loved that, and they would have paid it! It would have taken care of the insurance. But I also had to guarantee 30 shows a year at $350. It was almost a $12,000 policy, and it got used quite a few times.

Another problem was shows in Philly at VFW halls [featuring] eight bands for five dollars. We were competing with that. It was tough, balancing all that while being cool with the kids and the bands. We tried to pay the bands as well as we could. We didn't have alcohol sales, and when we finally had the chance to sell alcohol, everyone was under 21. The bar would make $27, and the bartenders would make $3 in tips.

Dave Franklin (Vision): I cannot overstate enough how important City Gardens was. In a world of non-rock stars, that place that made you feel like a rock star.

Chuck Treece (McRad): It's lacking right now. We don't have a City Gardens. That club, that scene, is irreplaceable. To imagine what kind of aggression that was in that building on a weekly basis is fucking crazy. It's a part of our youth.

Craig Wedren (Shudder To Think): Where is the City Gardens of now? Where does it exist and what's it like? You think of the way that club looked, of the bands that played there, and of Randy and the kind of energy that was in the place, good and bad… where is that now? It was a specific convergence of time, place, and creativity. I know that was happening to a greater or lesser degree all over the country and the world at the time, but it was tough to put your finger on it and appreciate fully, except in hindsight.

Tim McMahon (Mouthpiece): There were always rumors about City Gardens closing toward the end. By the later days, in the mid-'90s, there were tons of shows going on everywhere, all the time. We had this attitude like, "Oh well. If it closes, it closes." We took it for granted.

That's what I keep thinking back on. We said, "It's City Gardens. It'll always be there." And then one day, boom… it wasn't there anymore. Nothing ever took its place. We thought other places would fill the void and it wouldn't matter, but it did. It really did.

Going to City Gardens… it felt like our place. Everywhere you turned there were people you knew. There was nothing like it. I look back now and regret that I took it for granted.

Dave Smalley (D.Y.S./Dag Nasty/ALL/Down By Law): [The scene] didn't exist in a vacuum. It existed because of the spirit and the purpose and the goals that made punk rock what it was. It wasn't just a quick moment in time that we all enjoyed and then went off to become accountants who forgot what we were. We didn't check our values at the door. It wasn't just entertainment. It was a way of life.

Mike Watt (Minutemen/fIREHOSE/The Stooges): Safe to go crazy… I try to keep that from being an old idea, and I still put it out there when I play. The big challenge is to be creative, but maybe that challenge should never be solved. Maybe it should always be difficult. "What can I think of? What can I do?" It's timeless. Trotsky was talking about this idea, "permanent revelation," and he used the metaphor of the penknife. He said, "The art is not in the penknife; the art is in what is to be carved." So maybe that's the way a scene is: it can only go so far, and then the humans have to get involved. A scene is only the instrument.

Epilogue

Nikki Nailbomb (Trenton-based musician): My parents owned City Gardens, so I grew up there. We always had a Doberman pinscher, I remember it was me and the Doberman at the club. They would take me there, turn on the lights, and let me run around. I ran around the bar, behind the bar. My mom worked her butt off getting everything ready. If I drop the name City Gardens around town, especially to people who are older, they warm up to me right away. I don't have bad intentions, so I don't feel bad doing it.

Wade Wilson (Trenton-based rapper): I can't say there weren't music scenes in other places where I've lived, but I guess the music scene here is why I call Trenton home. When I started learning about City Gardens—don't ask me why—but I felt something kindred. Once people told me about it, I looked up almost everything about City Gardens online. I started educating myself and learning more and more about what had happened there before I became a part of [the Trenton] scene. I was so intrigued by it.

Nikki Nailbomb: I remember being at the club when I was four, and my dad was fixing all these holes in the walls. He was frustrated, and he said to me, "Do you know what punks are?!" And I'm like, "No." He points at the hole in the wall he was fixing and goes, "You see this?! Punks kick holes in the wall!" That was my impression of punks when I was a kid.

Wade Wilson: These legendary bands that were influences on me played City Gardens. I usually wouldn't even say this out loud, because I feel like it sounds pretentious, but in my head and heart, I feel like, "Dude, we have a legacy of that! We're part of that." Those things gave us a foundation to stand on.

Nikki Nailbomb: When I was about 12-years-old, I was at City Gardens and saw a girl come out of the bathroom with red high heels. She walked past me, got onstage, grabbed a guitar, and started playing. It was the all-girl band The Friggs, and that's when I thought, "Maybe I can do that too." My dad played Chopin and I studied cello for nine years, so I always liked classical music, but I also love punk. I played cello in high school, and some stoner kids were like, "You play cello? Play bass in our band!"

Randy Now: During the early part of the 2000s, I was dealing with [the medical condition] vertigo. It was completely debilitating, and I couldn't do anything. I couldn't function. In 2005, I had surgery to fix it. It worked, but I lost hearing in my left ear as a result.

Once I started feeling better in January 2006, the first thing I did was hold a dance night to get all the old City Gardens people back together. I thought 30 people would show up, but we ended up with about 250. That went well, so I did more dance nights.

Steve Tozzi (director of City Gardens documentary *Riot On The Dancefloor*): I think the overarching thing with Randy is that he's an entertainer. Maybe he couldn't be the musician or be in the band, but he likes to entertain a crowd. On top of that, he really loves music. Even today, with his store Mancave, he's finding new bands to promote that get popular a year or two years later. He just likes to be around music any way that he can.

Joseph Kuzemka (Trenton Punk Rock Flea Market): I hate to say it's like the wild, wild west in Trenton, but to some degree it is. Especially for someone who wants to come in, do something positive in the community, and make a name for themselves. It's not that difficult to get something off the ground here.

Lawrence Campbell (current owner of 1701 Calhoun Street): I'm Jamaican and moved to New York around 35 years ago. I went to a private school in New York, and then we moved to Trenton. In Trenton, I went to Embry Riddle Aeronautical University and then into the military after that. Following ten years in the Marine Corps, I started a construction firm. This building [1701 Calhoun Street] always interested me. [Former owner] Frank would say, "It's for sale." But it was almost $300,000, and I was like, "No, I can't afford that." The price dropped and dropped, and then people started breaking into the building. I told Frank about that, and he was disturbed about it. After that, he was really trying to push for a sale.

Steve Tozzi: There's a nice groundswell of activity in Trenton, like Art All Night, and the Trenton Punk Rock Flea Market. The culture is here. It's the attitude that people can make something happen. I just did the Trenton Ride, where you ride through the town during summer. The same people who organize that are the people you see at the Trenton Punk Rock Flea Market or at Art All Night. It's a small collective, which reminds me of what City Gardens was: certain people making things happen that other people would show up to see. It's nice, but, without the city getting behind them in a bigger way, I don't know how far they can go.

Right now, you have to have the stomach for going into Trenton. I know people who just say, "I'm not going there. Period. It's a dump." It's kind of like City Gardens: you had to have a stomach to drive there, to park there, to get inside, and to get out. Doing nothing in the city is the worst thing you can do. Go in and experience what is safe enough to experience. Not everybody wants to try, and I think that's a shame.

Nikki Nailbomb: I moved to Trenton two or three years ago. I didn't want to come here at first, since I heard it wasn't the greatest area, and it took me awhile to get my bearings. I went through cars and motorcycles, but now I ride my bike everywhere. It's a small town. There's not a whole lot going for it, so it's easy to change and improve.

Lawrence Campbell: Trenton right now is sort of a broken city, but we're coming back, and hopefully, with my help, we can rebuild Trenton. The city didn't want just anyone to open up this place. Apparently a bunch of people have gone to the city to acquire this property, but they didn't have a plan for the city; they had a plan for themselves, which was to make money. No civic duty or responsibility.

Joseph Kuzemka: I always want to make sure that if I'm doing an event, that on some level it is going to give back. To have a food drive, raise money, that type of thing. I cringe at the thought of someone not being able to enjoy a Thanksgiving dinner, especially a local family who might be struggling through hard times. It messes with me a bit, and I hate the fact that it could happen, so we're going to try to do another food drive. Hopefully we can raise even more food and help more local families in need.

Lawrence Campbell: A building this big brings along with it a lot of responsibility. They just refurbished the park next door for several million dollars, and they refurbished the Ewing Indoor Flea Market [formerly the Fine Fair], and this place is stuck in the middle. They aren't looking for more alcohol, gunshots, and killings. They're looking for an upscale establishment, and they're looking for something community-service related. I brought those things to the table. I told the city that I wanted to do community service a couple of times a year for high school students. My plan is to get the Marine Corps, the Army, the Navy, and the Air Force here several times a year. In addition to the police departments from surrounding areas, I will bring in professionals from Capital Health System—doctors and nurses—and university professors and deans from the local and colleges and universities to come and talk to some of these kids who are about to graduate from local schools. They can let them know that after they are done with high school, they don't have to be here killing, shooting, raping, getting people pregnant or getting pregnant, or being up to no good. Be a professional. Do something worthwhile with your damn life. Then come back and be a good steward to your neighborhoods, your area, and uplift the community. That was one of my points when I spoke to the city council concerning opening up this place, and they liked the idea.

Wade Wilson: When I saw that the City Gardens building was for sale, I actually put on Facebook, "Yo, who wants to go in and buy old City Gardens? Let's get it done!" People were like, "That's the best idea in a minute!" If there's ways we can harness that energy… I feel like you can somehow.

Nikki Nailbomb: The main club in Trenton now is the Mill Hill. It's a classic place. It's kind of looks like [the TV show] *Cheers* upstairs, and in the basement we have punk-rock shows. We also have friends who do underground house parties with bands.

Joseph Kuzemka: I'm a flea marketer by nature, and my wife and I enjoy going to local flea markets and looking at vintage items and antiques. One day I decided it would be cool to have a punk rock flea market in Trenton, since I love the one in Philly. I didn't know if it would work in the city as it is now, because a lot of people don't want to venture into it. The headlines suggest that it's a dangerous place. I talked to some friends and asked, "If I did something like this, would you attend? Do you think your friends would attend?" I was out at a bar called Trenton Social, and everybody was pushing me to do it. The next morning I woke up at 6 a.m. and immediately jumped on my computer. I designed the logo, the web site, and I launched a Facebook page. Within a matter of a week it sold out.

At the first Punk Rock Flea Market, we had 2,000 people. We set up a Facebook [promotion], and a week before the event, legendary NYC hardcore guy Ratbones, the original singer of War Zone, posted on the event page: "I'm going down to this. Does anyone else want to go?" I said, "I've done it. Ratbones is coming to the Trenton Punk Rock Flea Market. Shit." We had [a huge crowd] and raised money for Superstorm Sandy relief.

The second one drew 3,000 people, and we collected over 500 cans of food for the Ministries of Mercer County food banks. We had four bands play, and it was an amazing day. I rely heavily on social media to promote the events, but I also pound the pavement. I drive all over the state, dropping off fliers at record stores and coffee shops. I like to keep it old-school, which helps me stay grounded and remember my roots.

Wade Wilson: I think a bunch of people would come out to shows and events, but it's like [Trenton] is at that weird tipping point. You gotta' get enough people so that other people will feel left out if they're not [included].

Randy Now: After I did the dance night, I got a job at a record store and was deejaying outside just for fun, and I played a Sally Starr record. The owner of the store said, "I know who that is!" Sally was local, so we found her and did an in-store with her. It was one of her last appearances before she died. She was supposed to come in for two hours and get $400, but we had close to 1000 people waiting in line. She said she wasn't going to leave until she said hello and gave an autograph to everyone, and she did. She took time with everyone, and she was 86! By the time she left, her arm hurt from writing her name over and over.

My favorite part was that she fell asleep and snored when I was driving her home. When we got to her house, she said, "Can you do me a favor? Take my boots off for me?" I had to take the cowgirl, go-go boots off an 86-year-old woman! I loved it though. That day made me think, *let's get a band or two in here.* The store wasn't doing great, so we brought in Chuck Treese and others to do free shows and bring people in.

Joseph Kuzemka: I run another event in Trenton called Art All Night, which started in 2007. The building is a 50,000-square-foot former Roebling factory that used to make the wire for the Brooklyn Bridge, the Golden Gate Bridge, and other original suspension bridges. There is a lot of history in that building, and the history of Trenton has always appealed to me. A friend of mine said, "I work for an arts organization, and I've got this idea. It sounds crazy, but I want to do it, and I need your help." The whole theory behind the event is that you invite artists to submit one piece of artwork to be put on display for a 24-hour period. I thought it was a good cause, but I didn't think that it would work in any way, shape, or form. I didn't think the city would support it. I didn't think people would come into the city to support it, either, but I gave it a shot. That first year we had about 1,700 people and 300 pieces of art.

It was completely grass roots, with little marketing. The second year we had 5,000 people and 400 pieces of artwork. Fast-forward to 2013, when we had 30,000 attendees. That not only the most successful but also the most rewarding event I've ever run.

I made friends with a young man named Robbie, who I think is nine years old [as of this writing]. He submits a piece of artwork every year. At the end of the event—we're there for 24 hours and it's exhausting— I'm dead on my feet. Robbie tugged on my shorts, and I knelt down. He said, "Thank you," and I said, "For what?" He said, "Thank you for doing this, because I love showing my art here." It was a moment I'll never forget.

That instilled even more passion to continue running events in the city of Trenton, because it's important in a downtrodden area to show people that there are positive things. You don't have to damage properties and you don't have to hurt other people. You can do good things. As long as there are people who embrace [community improvement], it grows.

Randy Now: The turning point was when I got Pete Best and Peter Tork to come. I came up with the headline, "A Beatle and a Monkey come to Bordentown." It took off from there.

I like seeing people happy and entertained. It's a real high when I can get a big show. Everything else is the job… the promoting, the fliers, the set-up, and so on. The best part is getting a call from an agent telling me a show is confirmed.

Joseph Kuzemka: The City of Trenton is in a state of flux. It's not in a good place right now. I think the city has started to realize how important the event is and the economic impact we have on other businesses when we draw 30,000 people. The fact that we can bring that many people into town, in spite of all of the bad things going on, [has led the city] to become supportive. I think they're starting to understand that positive events and bringing people into the city are a way to change the city.

Wade Wilson: When I started getting into punk rock, somebody here in Trenton introduced me to Bad Brains. I thought, "Dude, this is it." What's crazy is that I didn't even know they were black. As I went into high school, my mom and my grandmother were pushing me to conform, because I was out of the norm already. As I got more into music and started coming to Trenton again, I was all about my skateboard and listening to the Beastie Boys. I've been rapping since I was nine, but nobody took me seriously until I got to Trenton.

Dave Hart (Trenton historian): Trenton today? When you ask anyone inside or even outside the city, the first word that comes to their mind is crime, and that's a real sin. The hope for Trenton, honestly, is the Hispanic community. They can bring in people who are industrious, people who want to work, people who enjoy family values and community, and can create this sense of unity that is needed for a community. Important to that is knowing the history of the place. I want people who live in Trenton to be able to say, "Yes, these are my roots, this is my city, and I'm proud of it." And when you do that, you create a community.

* * *

Randy Now owns a memorabilia store, Mancave, in Bordentown, New Jersey and continues to book shows.
(Information available at mancavenj.com.)

Steve Tozzi will release the City Gardens documentary "Riot On the Dance Floor" *in 2014. (Information at citygardensfilm.com)*

Lawrence Campbell is renovating the building at 1701 Calhoun Street and plans to open it in mid-2014 as Exodus Entertainment.

Joseph Kuzemka organizes Trenton Punk Rock Flea Market and Art All Night.
(Information at trentonpunkrockfleamarket.com and artworkstrenton.org/artallnight)

Nikki Nailbomb and Wade Wilson continue to perform at Trenton clubs.

Source Notes

All quotes are from original interviews done with the authors or film director Steve Tozzi, except for the following material quoted from other sources:

Part One: Welcome To Trenton, New Jersey

Chapter 1: No America Without Trenton: All original interviews
Chapter 2: It begins …: *Peter Buck:* From Tony Fletcher, *R.E.M. Perfect Circle* (New York, Omnibus Press, 2013.)
Chapter 3: 1983–1984: All original interviews

Part Two: Things Take Off

Chapter 4: Radio, Raconteurs and Records Stores - All original interviews
Chapter 5: 1985–1986: *Mike Diamond:* From the liner notes of *Beastie Boys Anthology: The Sounds of Science* (Audio CD, New York, Capitol Records, 1999)
Chapter 6: The Ramones: *Monte A. Melnick:* Some material from Monte A. Melnick, *On the Road with The Ramones* (New York, Bobcat Books, 2003).
Johnny Ramone, Clem Burke, and *George Tabb:* From Monte A. Melnick, *On the Road with The Ramones.*

Part Three: Come As You Are

Chapter 7: Every Thursday… It's 90 Cent Dance Night: All original interviews
Chapter 8: 1987–1988: All original interviews
Chapter 9: 1989–1990: All original interviews

Part Four: This Is The End, My Friend, The End

Chapter 10: 1991–1992: All original interviews
Chapter 11: 1993–1994: *Mike Dirnt:* From Jersey Beat magazine

Photo Credits

Page 6: Dee Dee Ramone photo courtesy of Michael McLaughlin.

Page 7: Ramones photo courtesy of Greg Sapnar.

    Henry Rollins photo courtesy of Ken Salerno

Page 8: All photos courtesy of Ken Salerno.

Page 9: All photos courtesy of Ken Salerno.

Page 10: All photos courtesy of Ken Salerno.

Page 11: All photos courtesy of Ken Salerno.

Page 12: Descendents reunion photos courtesy of Ken Hinchey.

COLOR PHOTO SECTION:

Page 1: Regressive Aid graphic novel cover art courtesy of artist Matt Howarth. (www.matthowarth.com)

    City Gardens photo courtesy of Ron Gregorio.

Page 2: All photos courtesy of Ron Gregorio.

Page 3: All photos courtesy of Ron Gregorio.

Page 4: New Order photo courtesy of Anton Corbijn. (www.corbijn.co.uk)

Page 5: All photos courtesy of Ron Gregorio.

Page 6: Meatmen photo courtesy of Ron Gregorio.

    DJ Gal & Ron photo courtesy of Bruce Markoff.

Page 7: All photos courtesy of Lisa Zachmann, except T-Bone mural which is courtesy of Ron Gregorio.

Page 8: Randy Now and Ian MacKaye—photographer unknown.

    Jon Stewart photo courtesy of Rich O'Brien.

Page 9: Alex Franklin photo courtesy of Travis Nelson.

    Pit photo courtesy of Ken Salerno.

Page 10: All photos courtesy of Ken Salerno.

Page 11: All photos courtesy of Lisa Zachmann.

Page 12: Rich O'Brien photo courtesy of Ed Jollimore.

To Our Kickstarter Badasses

Below is a list of people without whom this book would never have happened. Each person on this list is responsible for donating to a fund that was run through Kickstarter. [If you are unfamiliar, Kickstarter is a website designed to help independent projects get funded through grassroots fundraising. Money comes directly from those interested in seeing a project come to fruition]

For us, Kickstarter was a godsend. After meeting with indifference and rejection from traditional publishing routes, the concept of going directly to the people who truly believed in this project seemed like the best option. Even more important to us was retaining the ability to control every aspect of this book. Plenty of times we were told the subject matter was too niche, the audience too narrow, and the book would not appeal to people outside New Jersey. We were "advised" that several changes were required to make the book more attractive to a wider audience. At one point, we were even told to change the title—a title that had been decided upon by Amy at the project's outset, some 15 years ago. We were told we needed "bigger, sexier" names in the book. (We're still not sure what that meant. *What? Henry Rollins isn't sexy enough for you?!*)

We were told that the individual stories of "no-name fans" (read: the people who faithfully attended City Gardens' shows and dance nights) would not be interesting to outside readers. By using Kickstarter, we were able to laugh off these ridiculous "suggestions" and carry on in the way we saw fit.

Kickstarter, and other crowd-funding websites, certainly have their critics, and even we cringed at the "digital panhandling" required to be successful in this type of endeavor. But, in the end, we feel we made the right decision.

We've always worked under the unspoken premise that this book is for YOU; for those whose lives were touched, in some way, by City Gardens and the music played there. These are your stories; this is your book. We are obligated only to each other to make sure this history is preserved, whether it interests anyone outside of the particular sphere of City Gardens' influence or not. I think the most telling aspect of how the money was raised for the production of *No Slam Dancing, No Stage Div-*

ing, No Spikes is the fact that over 350 people contributed to the project, and no donation topped $500. There is no singular "big-time backer" holding the purse strings and telling us how to do things. This book was produced by a collective, a community who wanted to see this project done, and—because of their generosity and faith—we were able to do it.

To the 363 people who donated, there are no superlatives strong enough to describe our gratitude.

Thank you.

— Steven and Amy

This book is for:

Jennifer Rivers-Flasko...

Aaron Elliot Ross and Richard O'Brien...

Pete Helfrich, Russ Smith, Joe Kauffman, and Robert Mars...

Vanessa Varian...

Aaron J. Scolnick, Brendan Perry, Bushwick Country Club, Mr. Carey and Linda Gates, Chris Newman, Cole, Dale Battaglia, Debra Flamm von Ohlen, Douglas Bogar, Doug Jurczak, Eric Wayne Norlander, Jennifer Michenfelder, Karen Schisler Palmer, Nick Myers, Mike Z, Nancy (Big) DeSimone, Penny Parks, Peter Gerhardt, Ricky Schiel, Bob Conrad, Rob Florig, Scott Sommers, Rich Gracey, Fulton, and Berry and Beanie...

Donna DiLodovico and Michael Keogh...

Andy Schwartz, Anne LaBate, Brian McCullough - Dr. Death WDNR, Brian Oakes, Carl Duhnoski, Carl Humenik - *Bouncer Extraordinaire*, Cathy Vocke, Many thanks to Donal and Tin Angel, C. David Kieser, Elysia J. Mancini Duerr, Esq., Eric Bergman, Fran Taylor: Tri-State Crew Forever, Frank S. Dardzinski, Franny Bennett, Harry Wilson, Chris Farmer of Strange One Records, Jason "Hate Squad" Dermer, Jason Kenton, Jennifer Grega, Jenny and Jimmy O'Neill, and John Zygmunt...

Jonathan LeVine Gallery, Joseph Kuzemka and the Trenton Punk Rock Flea Market, Judy Weinberg, Katie Storck, Kurt Sermas, Kyle Anderson, Lisa Zachmann, Mark A. Adams, Matt Brown, Matt Fry, Max Tritremmel, Megan McCamy Drobes, Mike Barry from Brick, Michael

"Mookie" Delin, Michelle E. Borek, Nicole McPherson, Paul Oeser, Paula Risell and Eileen White, Rockin' Richie Lustre, Bob Klasky, Russ Ceccola, Scott Aivazian, Susan Leiper, Todd Schwartz, Troy DeAngelis, Valerie-Anne Lutz, South Jersey Taper, Walter Duke Henkels, Severin Wuelfing, and Tedward Jacobs…

Alan Vieiro, Barbara Adams, Joe Z., Julie Snow, Kara Vives, Keene Hepburn, Lynn and Scott Yates, and Todd Linn…

Frank Burge UK, Jamie Bakum, and Simone Stewart…

"Oldschool" Alex Franklin, Alexis Wilson-Castaldi, Alfred Vitale, Alison Zorn-Szpyhulsky, Amanda Elizabeth Rivella, Anita Marie Murano-Sweetman, Anonymous, Anthony Annoyance, Atomic Age, Beth Scullin, Betty Callahan, Brett Beach, Brian BONES Jones, Carl Gunhouse, Carolyn Giordano, Donald & Catherine Wygal, Charlene Howard, Cheryl Tapper, Chris Hewitt, Colin Helb & Carolyn Reinhardt, David Lorenz, David Wilson, Dave Wright, Kyle and Jenn O'Donnell, Dawn Englehart, Derek Roseman, Bighead Brown, Diane Cooper, Mary Nichols (DJ Fusion/FuseBox Radio Broadcast), Don Kanicki, and Doug Wolff…

Gregory Dicum, Hal Stern, Heath Row, Heidi Gonzalez, Holly Duthie, Howard Wuelfing, Ian A. Zimmerman, Jack Guida, Jason Friedman, Jason Lewandowski, Jason G. Miller, Jay Zaun, Jeff Barthold, Jeff Jotz, Jen Hilbert, Jennifer Barons, Jessica Vadino, Jim Houser, Navy Jim Nargiso, The Right Reverend Gentleman Jim Norton - *Master of All He Surveys*, and Jordan D. Haar…

Joe Borthwick, Joe Knotts, John Cooper, John Morrison, Johnny Caps, Johnny Trevisani, Joseph Pattisall, Kelly Candelori, Ken Katkin, Ken Lamb, Kenny Kolanko, Kevin Plant, Kim Martin, Kirby Bell, Liam and Nuala Donovan, Linda Kayser, Lisa Kruger, Liz Sapnar Gambino, Loren Hunt, and Luke Stemmerman….

Mai Reitmeyer, Mark Pingitore - Pagan Babies, Matt Riga, Meirav Devash, Mischelle Marte, Pamela Biasi Zielinski, Paul Hilcoff, Raymond Meister, Renée LoBue, Richard Kaczynski, Robert Bowes, and Ryan McCarroll…

Sally Jacob, Sam Zimmerman, Sanders Keel, Savneet K. Chattha, Scott Dietrich, Scott Kenney, Sean Thorne, Sharon D. Levis, Stacey Tighelaar Bowie, Steve Petras, Susie DiVietro, Ted Dougherty, Tim Zatzariny Jr., Vicki Marshall, and Wendy Destremps Mecke…

Jennifer Kraska, Joan Arkuszewski , and Mark and Erica DiLodovico...

Aaron Cromie, Adam David, Chris Albee, Andrew Vesty, Art Zawodny, Beau Phillips, Bob Ritger, Brian "BREM" Hagen, Carolyn Matthews Craft, Carey Heck, Charlotte Doyle, D Morrissey, Damien Glonek, Dan Sagherian, Daniel Tinsman, Christine and Darren Young, David Shoemaker, Dawn Zoe, Dona Warner, Bridget Rutkowski, Edgar C. Wilburn III, Eric Fusco, Fran Chismar, and Frank Straker...

G. Jason Head, James Curtis, Janice L. Heinold, Janice Marie, Jason S. Hunt, Jeanette D, Jeff Downing, Jeff DeYoung, Jennifer (LaBrozzi) McLaren, Jennifer Sirko Chmura, Jim Scheers, and John S. O'Brien Jr....

Karen (Boyer) Pumphrey, Ken Capelli, Kimmie Kurowski Murray, Leon B. Hojegian, Lisa Stansbury, Lissy Sablenik, Marc Wasserman, Daniel Tinsman, Mark Gibbons, Mark Van Doren, Mary Marciante, Mary Tokash Juarez, Matt Ruzicka, Mike Minton, and Miranda and Todd Brewer...   `

Paul and Laura Alig, Paul Lewis, Pete Jager, Ray Gonzalez, Renee Rogers, Rick Bergacs, Rob Schorr, Ruin, Skwardog aka Mark Skwara, Shamus, Stephanie and Mike Neuhaus, Steve "Ango" Angelini, Tom Ciocco, and Tony Lee...

Allison Walker Rabbitt, Amber Hipps-Lakatosh, Ed Hall, Kerry Kristine, Kris Bedell, and Lisa Albaladejo...

M. Parker, Mike Dagney, and Anita Lobotomy...

Alex O'Brien, Andrew Hollister, Daniel Houseworth for his brother Kenny Houseworth, Gail B. Gaiser (DJ Gal), Gregg Delso, Jared Kennedy, Jason Weber, Kathy Phlogiston, Melissa Bogda Brown, Meshell Kimbel, Paul Westenberger "Westy", Bob McDevitt, Tim Welsh, Tom Lear, Vincent Stanley, Bill Drummer, and Joseph Brown...

David Blumenthal, Steve T. Lezan, and Willard J. Hoppe...

Adam Luce, Andy Purple, Anne Baker, Ben Danaher, Badass Beth S., Brandon Spodek, Cynthia Schilke, Dave Gaughan, David Hoffman, Debbie Kaplan, Domenick J. Marmorato, Eric L. Lutz, Eric Lindberger, Eric Quigley, Erica Schaeffer, The Dark Lord of the Abyss...

Gerard aka Dorian Malisheski, Greta Tate, James H. Carter II, Jason Mckown, Jason Paul, For Christopher Shields for letting me come along, Jeff Feuerzeig, Jennifah Chard, Jen Eagen-McCloskey, Dan and Jennifer Hankinson, Joe Stanley, John L. Kolb, John Herguth, John Mariakis,

John P. Begley, Jon Young, Jon "Ribeye" Kleiman, Kate Manion, Ace Bear Space Bear…

Lou De Lauro, Luke Myers, Lungfish, Lydia E. Bruneo, Positive Craze's Mark X and Eileen McCloskey, Martin Ganteföhr, Matthew Brown, Michael Lehane, Mike Zacek, Mike Haber, Michael Vito, Nathan James Konda Esquire, Patty Weber, Pat Higgins, Patrick Baker, Renetta Sitoy, Ryan Skagen, Shilough Hopwood, Stephen Sincoskie, Steve Jackson- External 732 Fanzine, Steve Larger, Sue Lappan-Meyers, Thomas and Sebastian Meyers, and Suzanne Wilson…

The Brooklyn Quarterly, Tim Konek, Timothy Arnold, Tom LaVolpe, Tony Chiaverini, and Vince and Anne Harvcore…

It's official. You are badasses. And your name is in a book to prove it…